POPULAR-MUSIC CULTURE IN AMERICA

PRINCE DOROUGH
MISSISSIPPI UNIVERSITY FOR WOMEN

ARDSLEY HOUSE PUBLISHERS, INC.
NEW YORK

Address orders and editorial
correspondence to:
Ardsley House, Publishers, Inc.
320 Central Park West
New York, NY 10025

ISBN: 1-880157-04-7

Printed in the United States of America

10 9 8 7 6 5 4 3 2

Contents

Preface

Historical research falls into two basic categories, causal-comparative studies, and descriptive studies. This text belongs in the latter category. A concerted effort has been put forth to place the events reported upon into a clear, logical, and comprehensive framework and to avoid any appearance of discovering cause and assigning effect.

In texts of this nature, the materials and facts included for study are the products of two basic considerations: the preconceptions of the author and the historical record as seen and reported upon by a majority of authoritative sources. This text is no exception. Because of these considerations, many events and subjects seen within their immediate context and time frame as important have been excluded. Such exclusions are not meant to indicate that these events and subjects have no importance. On the contrary, they are a vital part of the history of American popular music. However, this text is intended to serve the classroom and the reader as an overview, not as an in-depth study. As such, I felt it important to confine the subjects, events, and areas covered to those acknowledged by a majority of sources to be of consequence in the continuing development of American popular music.

In the past, popular-music texts of any nature have given the rock-and-roll era small consideration in relation to the other areas of American popular music. This apparent disregard has often led to the generalization that either little material exists on the rock era or that the material is not worthy of any in-depth treatment. In fact, there is a plethora of materials on rock music, and in my view, it is highly relevant to the study of popular music in America. Because of its significance and the current relevance of rock to worldwide youth culture, the chapters on rock contain a relatively high level of detail. This is not meant to belittle the music that appeared prior to the rock era. Without everything that came before, there would be no rock-and-roll. However, in this present culture, rock is the dominant force in popular music, and, as such, deserves at least as much consideration as any form of pop music that preceded it.

In present-day society, the term *popular music* connotes transiency, a quality of here today, gone tomorrow. This characteristic does not render popular music useless, nor does it in any way defame the genre. It is this very characteristic that gives popular music its value as a mirror and repository of American common culture. Tastes change over brief periods. Tastes in automobiles change with the annual introduction of the newest in personal transportation. Tastes in clothing change with the seasons. Certain foods become the vogue because of sudden, inexplicable surges in popularity. Each generation of youth develops its own slang. All of these changes occur not because of a loss of value, but because of the nature of man. Popular music is a mere reflection of that nature. Perhaps the most frustrating pursuit in life is the never-ending attempt to appeal to man's transiency. No one knows why tastes change.

So it is in popular music. All the popularity charts worldwide for the past one hundred years have served merely as tracking devices. They cannot explain such phenomena as Elvis or the Beatles or Buddy Holly or Kiss or punk or rap or any of the countless changes in taste that dictate the rises and falls in popularity. Many theories have been set forth. None have provided satisfactory explanations. All this points to a single fact. In most instances, there are no logical reasons for shifts in popularity in music or in any other consumer-oriented product. Thus, in a descriptive text of this nature, it becomes all the more imperative simply to record such changes in a clear and logical fashion. To attempt to do more would prove both futile and beyond the scope of this work.

The additional readings and suggested recordings are meant to be used simply as classroom enhancement materials. There is a noticeable lack of theoretical material included. This exclusion was made deliberately. In addition to serving as a pop-music survey for music majors, this text may also be used in a course designed to satisfy a fine-arts requirement for those not majoring in music. Many texts used in the past for nonmusic majors have included theoretical materials which confused and at times dismayed nonmajors. Many of the sources cited in this text do, in fact, contain a considerable amount of music theory concerning such areas as ragtime and jazz. Unfortunately, there are few texts available on the theory of post-1955 popular music.

This text must not be construed as a definitive work. For the past two hundred years, American popular music has remained in a state of constant growth and change. This aspect alone would prevent it from becoming static enough to write about definitively. Even as the book arrives in the marketplace and in the hands of instructors and students, its potential contents will have increased significantly. This text is merely a quick look at a phenomenon which is in a state of perpetual mutation. As the sum of American popular music changes and grows, so must texts of this nature.

Acknowledgments

Within this little space I must attempt to express my gratitude to all those who have contributed to the completion of this book, an impossible task at best. To Dr. Charles Leonhard: I thank you for your belief in me, for your patience with me, and for your kind guidance as a reader. To Dr. John Bingham: your friendship over the past ten years has served to anchor me in my search for the Grail, and your wise counsel has served me well when I have come at least close to the castle. For these and countless other things shared, I thank you.

I owe an unpayable debt to those of my colleagues who played much-needed devil's advocates during the early stages of this book; Pam and Chris Gordon, Dr. Richard Montalto, Dr. John Bell, and others too numerous to mention. I thank you for your ideas and your honest comments, though I am certain that at times I appeared less than grateful for them. I am indebted to Mississippi University for Women for supporting the early stages of research with encouragement and with a well-timed research grant.

For the past nine months, the staff of the Galva Public Library, Galva, Illinois, has responded to my every request with immense good cheer and expedience. To the head librarian, Ann Larson, and the staff librarians, Shearon Armel, Melody Heck, and Rebecca Duytschaver, I extend my heartfelt gratitude. Ladies, without your constant help, this project would not have been possible.

Finally, I must attempt to thank the one person without whose help and understanding this project would have been a miserable failure—my wife. Dina, only we will ever know the price we have paid to complete this book. Had it not been for your unfailing faith in the book and my ability, I surely could not have reached this point. Words are never adequate vehicles for deep-felt human emotion. But I must at least try to say thank you.

Chapter 1
Foundations

In his book, *The Great American Popular Singers,* Henry Pleasants remarked that to many, describing the performance of American popular musicians as art appears to be a contradiction in terms. The most probable reason is that countless numbers of the best of American popular musicians have for generations made what they do appear too easy to be real art. They have served as shining examples of the adage, "Art is that which disguises art."

Most who are familiar with classical music in any form are also familiar with its inherent difficulties. Audiences gauge a classical artist's greatness by the ease with which he or she surmounts these difficulties. Because of this very familiarity, audiences all too often take for granted the ability and artistry required to negotiate these difficulties. As a rule, such audiences view with a jaundiced eye those perceived to have less ability and/or training. In their view, "popular" musicians cannot possibly possess the talent, the tools, or the music with which to fashion genuine art.

This is not to disparage classical musicians. "They work in a musical idiom, essentially European, whose criteria and conventions nowadays are in certain respects incompatible with the objectives of American popular song."[1]

---

[1]Pleasants, Henry. *The Great American Popular Singers.* (New York: Simon and Schuster, 1974), p. 1.

On the other hand, popular musicians do things, "primarily in matters of phrasing, shading, rhythm, enunciation, [articulation], accentuation and even vocal [and tonal] production, that lie beyond the capabilities and predilections of most classical [musicians]."[2] This, then, becomes an issue of musical idiom, rather than of superiority or inferiority.

Pleasants was convinced that the modern American pop artist is usually closer in concept and practice to the original objectives and standards of European performance than the classically trained musician. In Pleasant's view, the pop artist demonstrates superior enunciation or articulation. He applies richer, more imaginative, and more varied embellishments. He displays a greater rhythmic perception, particularly in the use of rubato. And he is stylistically more secure in almost every respect.

Most classical musicians are well-educated. Many hold university degrees. They read music, count time, and read well at sight. Many pop artists do not even graduate from high school. Many have no formal training in music and cannot read music at all. Pleasants believed pop artists possess an innate and unique creativity. He believed that the absence of formal musical schooling was offset by the development of performance skills in a real environment before a paying public. This, more than any other factor, contributed to their innovative powers. Pleasants concluded, "They learned from one another, from the instrumentalists and composer-arrangers with whom they have worked, and from the public. Who else, come to think of it, could have taught them?"[3]

Tudor England

Henry VIII, the second English Tudor King, was married to Catherine of Aragon for twenty years. During that time, Catherine gave birth to six children, all female. Of these, only Mary survived beyond childhood. Frustrated because he had no male heir, Henry petitioned Pope Clement VII for an annulment of the marriage. When the Pope refused, Henry repudiated the Pope's spiritual authority, and in 1534, set himself up as head of the English, or Anglican, Church. In 1517, Martin Luther had nailed his ninety-nine theses to a church door in Wittenburg, Germany, and launched the Protestant Reformation. By the time Henry declared himself spiritual leader of the Anglican Church, Lutheran Protestantism had found its way into England. By 1547, the influence of the two churches, Anglican and Lutheran, had converted most of England to a Protestant nation.

---

[2]Pleasants, p. 1.
[3]Pleasants, p. 3.

HENRY VIII AND HIS COUNCIL (FROM HALL'S CHRONICLE, 1548).

Mary I, daughter of Henry VIII, ascended the throne in 1553. A devout Catholic, she set about restoring Roman Catholicism as the dominant form of worship in England. In her zeal, she executed many who had converted to the newly formed Anglican Church and to Lutheran Protestantism, and gained for herself the unenviable title, "Bloody Mary." Despite her efforts, the Anglican Church became permanently ensconced as the official Church of England.

Elizabeth I, the last of the Tudors, replaced her sister on the throne in 1558. Elizabeth was more interested in politics than in religion. During her reign, a group of radical Protestants evolved within the Anglican Church who believed the Church still resembled the Roman Catholic Church too closely. They advocated purification of Anglicanism. Critics called them "Puritans." At first, this title was unsavory to the group. Eventually, it became a badge of honor. Though the Puritans disagreed with the practices of the Church, they remained professed Anglicans, and worked for change. However, when James I succeeded Elizabeth in 1603, the Puritans became increasingly alarmed. James was a Scot of the Stuart royal family, and the Stuarts had supported Mary in her attempts to restore Catholicism 50 years earlier.

The Pilgrims

In 1606, certain members of the church at Scrooby, Nottinghamshire, became convinced that the Anglican Church was irreparably corrupt, and separated themselves from it. In seventeenth-century England, these Separatists had few choices concerning the practice of their faith. They could either go underground or go into exile. They chose the latter. In 1608, a group of about 125 of these people migrated to Holland.

The Separatist Pilgrims who settled in Amsterdam were led by the Reverend Henry Ainsworth. In 1612, Ainsworth collected, translated, and published a psalter, or psalm book, for his congregation. Doubtless, it was this psalter, or at least materials from it, that followed the Dutch Pilgrims when they crossed the Atlantic to the New World.

The New England colonists were fiercely devout, and obviously considered the singing of psalms to be an integral part of life. A member of one of the groups that set sail for the New World from Delftshaven, Holland, in 1620, told about spending the night in Leyden at the house of the group's pastor. There they refreshed themselves by singing psalms, "making joyful melody in our hearts as well as with the voice, there being many of our congregation very expert in music; and indeed it was the sweetest melody that ever mine ears heard."[4] Obviously, there were many who came to the shores of the New World quite literate in music. In years to come, this was to change dramatically.

Ainsworth's psalter continued to be used by the Plymouth Pilgrims, and also by settlers at Ipswich and Salem, until 1692, though the Puritans rejected the Ainsworth tunes. They thought the tunes were too difficult. In 1692, the Ainsworth psalter was replaced by the Bay Psalm Book. This psalter was produced by the Massachusetts Bay Colony, which had been using the Sternhold and Hopkins psalm book. Famous as the first real book to be published in the British colonies, the Bay Psalm Book was first printed in 1640, and until 1692, was used in conjunction with both the Ainsworth and the Sternhold and Hopkins psalters. Its title was actually an abbreviation of *The Whole Booke of Psalmes Faithfully Translated Into English Metre.* It proved enormously popular,

---

[4]Hitchcock, H. Wiley. *Music in the United States. A Historical Introduction.* (Englewood Cliffs, New Jersey: Prentice-Hall, Inc., 1974), p. 3.

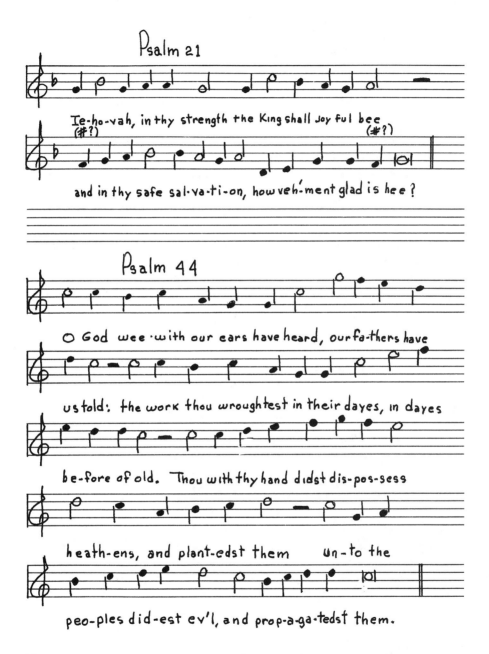

Psalm 21

Ie-ho-vah, in thy strength the King shall Joy ful bee
(#?)   (#?)

and in thy safe sal-va-ti-on, how veh-'ment glad is hee?

Psalm 44

O God wee-with our ears have heard, our fa-thers have

us told: the work thou wroughtest in their dayes, in dayes

be-fore of old. Thou with thy hand didst dis-pos-sess

heath-ens, and plant-edst them   un-to the

peo-ples did-est ev'l, and prop-a-ga-tedst them.

THESE TWO EXAMPLES WERE TAKEN FROM THE AINSWORTH PSALTER, DATED 1612.

and was published in nine editions in the seventeenth century alone. No music was included in early editions, but an "Admonition to the Reader" advised that all the psalms could be sung to several familiar tunes in various meters.

All, or at least most, of the early colonists could sing those familiar melodies from memory. However, as the first generation of settlers grew old and passed away, so did many of the hymn tunes they had brought with them. As succeeding generations of colonists moved farther and farther away from those first settlers, more and more of the hymn tunes carried on by oral tradition became significantly altered, or slipped entirely from memory. People began making up their own melodies. On any given Sunday, within one congregational body, five or six melodies might be sung at the same time to the same set of words. And most of those melodies might bear little or no resemblance to one another! By about 1717 or 1718, Puritan ministers were raising horrified outcries against the pitiful singing in their churches. One such minister was a certain Thomas Walter. In 1721, Reverend Walter complained that all the sacred melodies brought to the New World by the early settlers were being twisted into "an Horrid Medly of confused and disorderly Noises..."[5] Walter accurately identified the problem. He pointed out the lack of any kind of standard to which congregations could appeal.

Singing Schools

In an effort to alleviate this painful situation, the Reverend Thomas Symmes suggested, in his now famous 1720 sermon, "The Reasonableness of Regular Singing," that singing schools be established to promote better psalm singing. He pointed out that people who wished to acquire some proficiency in singing could, without difficulty or disadvantage, get someone skilled in the art of singing to meet with them several times during the week to instruct them.

Reverend Symmes probably did not realize the significance of the venture he was suggesting. He was merely attempting to improve congregational singing within his own flock. However, the concept blossomed almost overnight throughout the colonies into a full-fledged institution.

As early as 1722, Boston had its first church-based school established specifically for the purpose of teaching the rudiments of music reading and promoting better singing within the church. On March 5 of that year, the *New England Courant* published a short, but significant, article. The article reported that a lecture had been given during the preceding week at the New Brick

---

[5]Hitchcock, p. 5.

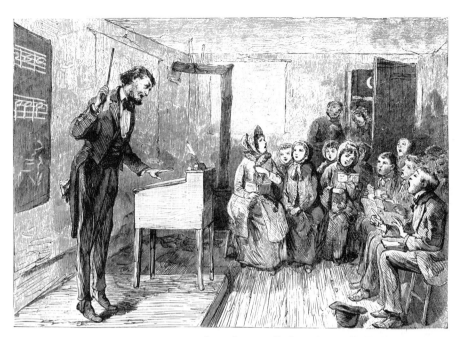

A SINGING SCHOOL.

Church in Boston by the Society for Promoting Regular Singing. Research indicates that this society was probably the first of its kind in America to meet on a regular basis for the express purpose of promoting better congregational singing. The same Reverend Thomas Walter, who had complained in 1721 about the poor singing of his congregation, preached a sermon entitled, "The Sweet Psalmist of Israel." More importantly, perhaps, "The Singing was perform'd in Three Parts (according to rule) by about ninety Persons skill'd in that Science, to the great Satisfaction of a Numerous Assembly there Present."[6] The insert, "according to rule," lends credence to the theory that those who sang "in three parts," had been rehearsed in some kind of uniform fashion, in an effort to improve their performance. It also supports the belief that these people were singing by note rather than by rote, a skill they had acquired in some kind of formal instructive setting.

The Puritan ministers were apparently gaining ground in their efforts to improve the singing of their respective congregations. The idea of singing schools quickly spread across the colonies until the singing school became an integral part of colonial life. Two things are significant about the establishing

---

[6]Chase, Gilbert. *America's Music.* (New York: McGraw-Hill Book Company, 1966), p. 27.

of these musical-training organizations: First, singing schools represent the beginning of formal music education in the United States; second, they contain the seeds for the socialization of music, and the beginning of a popular-music tradition. Wiley Hitchcock observed,

> From that time on, the singing school, convened to learn, practice, and demonstrate the skill of reading music at sight, became an important institution in the colonies, social as well as musical. Although originally begun in an attempt to improve church music, and although their music was for the most part religious, the singing schools were as much secular institutions as sacred, as much social outlets as pious assemblies. One student at Yale, for example, wrote to a friend with characteristic undergraduate querulousness: 'At present I have no inclination for anything, for I am almost sick of the World & were it not for the Hopes of going to the singing-meeting tonight & indulging myself a little in some of the carnal Delights of the Flesh, such as kissing, squeezing &c. &c. I should willingly leave it now.' In a society that recognized no split between religion and everyday life, the singing school was a popular meeting ground for both.[7]

During the eighteenth century, the singing school flourished. It was an institution for city dwellers as well as for country folk. So much time separates us now from the singing school's heyday that it is often difficult, if not impossible, to get an accurate account of exactly what a singing school was. Gilbert Chase discovered two important and picturesque fragments of singing-school history, both of which serve as delightful insights into what must have been a fascinating setting.

The first is a notice that appeared in the *Pennsylvania Gazette* of 1760, advising that a singing school, which had been meeting recently above a Mr. Williams' school, would again begin meeting on Monday evening, the third of November, at the same place and time. As usual, the "Art of Psalmody" would be taught "in the best manner," on Monday and Friday evenings from six to eight o'clock. Interestingly, the article also advised, "…if any Number of Ladies and Gentlemen incline to make up an exclusive set, to Sing on two other Nights, they may be gratified by making Application in time."[8]

The second fragment is an actual description of a singing school, given by the Reverend E. Wentworth around 1880. Reverend Wentworth refers to a time when he attended his first singing school as a boy. Though lengthy, the account bears quoting almost in full because of the curious and wistful details it contains.

> Time, sixty years ago; place, south-eastern Connecticut; locality, a suburban school-house; personelle, the choir of a Congregational church, and two dozen young aspirants, thirsting for musical knowledge; teacher, a peripatetic Faw-sol-law-sol, who

---

[7]Hitchcock, pp. 7-8.
[8]Chase, p. 184.

went from town to town during the winter months, holding two schools a week in each place; wages, two dollars a night and board for himself and horse, distributed from house to house among his patrons, according to hospitality or ability; instrument, none but pitch-pipe or tuning-fork; qualifications of teacher, a knowledge of plain psalmody, ability to lead an old style "set piece" or anthem, a light, sweet, tenor voice, and a winning manner... For beginners, the first ordeal was trial of voice. The master made the circuit for the room, and sounded a note or two for each separate neophyte to imitate. The youth who failed to "sound the notes" was banished to the back bench to play listener, and go home with the girls when school was out. The book put into our hands was Thomas Hastings' *Musica Sacra*, published in Utica in 1819, in shape like a modern hymnal. There were four pages of elements and two hundred tunes, half of them written in three parts, wanting the alto or confounding it with the tenor. The elements were given out as a lesson to be memorized, studied by question and answer for a couple of evenings or so, and then we were supposed to be initiated into all the mysteries of staff, signature, clef, flats, sharps, and naturals, notes, rests, scales, and above all ability to find the place of the "mi." Only four notes were in use — faw, sol, law, mi, and the scale ran faw, sol, law, faw, sol, law, mi, faw. The table for the "mi" had to be recited as glibly as the catechism, and was about as intelligible as some of its theology;—

The natural place for mi is B;
If B be flat, the mi is in E;
If B and E, the mi is in A and C;
If F be sharp, the mi is in G;
If F and C, the mi is in C and C.

The Continental scale, do, re, mi, had not yet been imported. The key-note was called the "pitch," and preliminary to singing, even in church, was taking the key from the leader, and sounding the "pitch" of the respective parts, bass, tenor, and treble, in the notes of the common chord. A few simple elements mastered, or supposed to be, the school plunged at once into the heart of the book, and began to psalmodize in the second week of the brief term... The rest of the winter's work comprehended "Barby," "St. Ann's," "St. Martin's," "Colchester," "Portugal," "Tallis," "Winchester," "Shirland," "Silver Street," "Easter Hymn," "Amsterdam," and many others now forgotten. The favorite fugues (i.e. fuging tunes) of the preceding century had passed out of fashion, and the leading church airs of this were not yet. A few anthems of the simpler sort we tackled, such as "Denmark," "Dying Christian," and "Lord of All Power and Might"... That, reader, was sixty years ago. Germany and Italy have since been transported to America, and musically, we live in a new earth and a new heaven. Yet the simple strains of those days were as perfectly adapted to those who made them as Wagner, Liszt, Mendelssohn, and Chopin are to us today![9]

During this time in our history, almost every member of our early society participated in the making of music. Those who could, played the few instruments that existed in those early settlements. Understandably, there was little or no musical culture as we know it today. Musical cultivation, such as there

---

[9]Chase, Gilbert. *America's Music*, revised second edition. (New York: McGraw-Hill Book Company, 1966), pp. 184–196. Used by permission of McGraw-Hill.

was, was common to all. The singing school became the musical instructor of everyone. Edward Bailey Birge, in his book, *History of Public School Music in the United States,* said the singing school provided the only culture that existed during those early days. The ability to sing and read music was the product of this home-spun institution. According to Birge, this singing-school culture was a genuine community product that functioned in homes and in social and religious settings as well.

Singing schools were vital to the development of American popular music for several reasons: They encouraged whole communities to participate in the making of music, they became centers for social gatherings in which music played a crucial role, and they provided a setting in which sacred music was used for secular entertainment.

English Music Publishing

Long before there was any established tradition of popular music in the New World, John Playford, a London businessman, had established himself as England's first full-service music publisher. He was born to a Norwich bookseller in 1623. During his mid-teens he was apprenticed to a bookseller in London, then a city of 350,000. He completed his apprenticeship before 1648, and during that same year, his name appeared in the register of the Stationer's Guild.

As Russell Sanjek observed, the book trade was full of peril and risk during this time in London's history. After the execution of Charles Stuart in 1649, Parliament enacted severe martial laws to purge the press and publishers for what it considered seditious publications against the English government. Nine months after the enactment of these martial laws, Parliament issued the Printing and Licensing Act of 1649. This act carried with it severe punishments for any infraction, and not just for Londoners. A wandering balladeer, with a collection of new songs he had been singing to some townspeople, was seized one Sunday after prayers, and locked in an "ugly hole under a bridge, where by extreme dampness and closeness of the place, he was suffocated within a few hours later."[10]

This new law prompted the issuing of a warrant for the arrest of John Playford and two other printers. The three had published a pamphlet whose topic was Charles' trial, last speech, and execution. Apparently Playford was forgiven for these crimes against the crown because he had also printed and

---

[10]Sanjek, Russel. *American Popular Music and Its Business,* Vol. 1. (New York: Oxford University Press, 1988), p. 149.

sold commonwealth documents and pamphlets. However, his name did not appear for almost a year in the guild register.

Playford issued his first collection of popular music on November 7, 1649. The publication was called *The Dancing Master,* or *Plain and Easy Rules for the Dancing of Country Dances.* It contained the tunes to each dance and 104 ballads. This publication went through eighteen editions in all, and by 1728, had grown to 900 tunes in three thick volumes. After the significant success of this publication, Playford abandoned most other kinds of material, and pursued with vigor the almost exclusive publication of popular music.

In 1681, Playford retired, wealthy and highly respected. He made his fortune publishing popular music. He left the business to his son, Henry, and though Henry was not to be the giant his father was, the popular-music-publishing business in England was nonetheless firmly established. The practices, rules, and regulations of the English popular-music-publishing firms served as models for similar publishing houses established in early America. Several of the early American publishers, such as Benjamin Carr and his father, Joseph, immigrated to America from England, bringing with them their knowledge of English popular-music publishing. This fledgling business became the cornerstone of the most crucial element in the modern American popular-music industry.

Music Publishing in Early America

Before the mid-1770s, what little music sold in the United States could be found only in bookshops and stationers. Composers were responsible for publishing their own works, usually backed by subscribers. Psalm books and church music were distributed by those who printed them, but the composers or compilers bore the publication costs. Before 1786, with one exception, there were no music shops or music publishers in the New World. This exception was in Philadelphia.

In 1760, Philadelphia was the largest city in the colonies. From 1750 on, the musical life of the city advanced rapidly. It was only natural, then, that the first music shop of record in America should be opened there. Michael Hillegas officially embarked in the music business late in 1759 at his home on Second Street, where he kept an extensive assortment of instruments, music, and music paper. There is no record of Hillegas having published any music. However, as advertised in the January 5, 1764 *Pennsylvania Gazette,* his stock of music was amazing. He discontinued his business sometime after 1765, and eventually became the first treasurer of the United States.

From 1791 to 1798 or 1799, Thomas Dobson was a printer and bookseller at 41 North Second Street. Records indicate he was the first printer in

Philadelphia to publish music. As was to become common practice, he did so with composer and/or compiler bearing publication risks and costs. In August, 1787, he printed a *Select Collection of the most favorite Scot's Tunes* for compiler and arranger, Alexander Reinagle. In 1789, Dobson printed a *Collection of Favorite Songs* for himself. So far as is known, Dobson also printed the first publication by an American-born composer, the book of *Seven Songs for the Harpsichord or Forte Piano* by Francis Hopkinson. This neat little book of eleven engraved pages containing eight songs was advertised in the November 29, 1788, *Federal Gazette,* as "This day published and to be sold by Thomas Dobson, at the Stone House in Second Street, between Chestnut and Market Streets."

Dobson was both a stationer and book printer. The first Philadelphia company to publish music exclusively was the firm of Moller & Capron. This firm had a piano store and music school at 163 North Third Street. In the March, 1793 *Federal Gazette,* Moller & Capron advertised for subscribers to a series of monthly six-page numbers that would contain all that was new in both instrumental and vocal music. At least three such numbers were issued. However, Moller & Capron was short-lived, and credit for establishing music publishing in Philadelphia must be given to Benjamin Carr.

Carr was an English singer, pianist, organist, conductor, and composer. He arrived in Philadelphia in 1793 at the age of twenty-four. Until his death on May 24, 1831, he continued to participate actively in the musical life of his city. He opened his Musical Magazine Repository in 1793, where he sold music and instruments of all types. In 1798, Carr issued the original edition of *Hail Columbia,* and in 1799, he advertised his publication of Haydn's *Canzonets,* the first American edition, and a song by Mozart, whose name at that time was virtually unknown outside Salsburg and Vienna. About 1800, Carr abandoned the publishing business to devote his full energies to editing the *Musical Journal,* a weekly publication founded by his father.

For a short period, John Aitken, a music engraver, operated a music store on South Third Street. He published music in limited amounts. George Blake arrived in the New World from England in 1793. He taught flute and clarinet, and later published music. From 1794 to 1803, Robert Shaw, a ballad singer, oboist, bassoonist, and composer, operated a Philadelphia music store. He also tried his hand at music publishing.

In November, 1794, George Willig opened his *Musical Magazine* in the same building that had housed Moller & Capron. Though he published very popular vocal selections, he appears to have given more attention to instrumental music than his rivals. Willig continued selling and publishing music in Philadelphia until Lee & Walker absorbed his business in 1865. In 1875, Lee & Walker's catalog and stock were purchased by Oliver Ditson & Co. of Boston. This purchase links Ditson to the beginnings of music publishing in Philadelphia.

Benjamin Carr is rightfully credited with being one of the foremost pioneer music publishers in Philadelphia. However, similar credit must be given to his father, Joseph. Joseph had been a music publisher in London. He and Benjamin's brother, Thomas, followed Benjamin to America in 1794, and opened a branch of Benjamin's store in Baltimore in August of that year. The August 6 *Maryland Journal* advised, "J. Carr, Music Importer, lately from London, Respectfully informs the public that he has opened a Store entirely in the Musical line, and has for sale, Finger and barrel organs, double and single key'd harpsichords; piano fortes and common guitars." His two most famous publications historically were Francis' Hopkinson's *Ode from Ossian's Poems* and the first edition of *The Star Spangled Banner,* adapted and arranged by Thomas.

From the evidence, it is obvious there was a struggling, but growing, music-publishing industry in late eighteenth-century America. The pioneers of this industry naturally reproduced the music that was currently in demand. English songs dominated the popular scene, many of them taken from the London ballad-operas of Arne, Attwood, Dibbin, Hook, Kelly, Linley, Reeve, Shield, Storace, and others. These early publishers established one of the cornerstones necessary to the support of today's popular-music industry.

Little of the music, popular or otherwise, published in eighteenth-century America has survived. In his book, *Music in the United States: A Historical Introduction,* H.W. Hitchcock noted that there is very little hard evidence of the existence of secular, or popular, music in colonial America, at least until the mid-eighteenth century and even later. But, as Hitchcock says, it is impossible to believe that, even given the extensive use of sacred music in secular settings, our early American colonists did not enjoy secular songs and dances along with hymnody and psalmody. In fact, there is ample evidence that they did.

Popular Music in the Colonies

We have an abundance of Anglo-Scottish-Irish "folk songs" that came to the New World with our original settlers. Hitchcock said these were the popular music of the day, a living music of everyday use by all. During the American colonial period, very little of this music was written, partly because it was from an age-old tradition whereby popular music was transmitted orally, and partly because the press in early America was almost entirely under the control of the clergy, who obviously had no interest in propagating or memorializing secular music. Nonetheless, there is strong evidence of a very lively underground popular-music culture that existed in the American colonies.

About 100 of the 300-odd traditional British ballads, the Child Ballads, so-called after Francis James Child (1825–1896), their collector and commentator, have been traced (and are still sung) in this country more than in living British tradition. The colonists were selective. Older songs on themes irrelevant to the colonial experience (e.g., courtly or chivalric) tended to be dropped. Many that were preserved have to do with sexual rivalry as seen through feminine eyes (*Barbara Ellen, The Gypsie Laddie, Little Musgrove, Jimmie Randall*) or relate directly to the New World experience (*Captain Kidd, The Golden Vanity*). The colonists, of course, altered the details of many British songs to fit the American context and developing character. One example is a song from southern England (known also in Ireland), *My Jolly Red Herring* or *The Red Herring Song*, which was transformed into a tale of Yankee resourcefulness and thrift (with a comic note) as *The Sow Took the Measles*. Another is *The Foggy Dew*, of which the original explicit sexuality ("I rolled my love all over the foggy dew") was tempered by Puritan sensibility ("The only thing I did that was wrong/Was to keep her from the foggy dew").[11]

In addition to the Child Ballads and other songs brought to the New World and preserved through oral tradition, the colonists had copies of various British publications containing popular and traditional songs and tunes: *Pammelia: Musick's Miscellanie, Deuteromelia: or the Second Part of Musick's Melodie* (which includes the first published version of *Three Blind Mice*), *Melismata, Musicall Phansies, The English Dancing Master, Wit and Mirth: or Pills to Purge Melancholy, The Musical Miscellany,* and *The Compleat Country Dancing Master.*

Against the background of this British ballad tradition, Americans created their own popular ballads. The earliest that can be dated with certainty is *Springfield Mountain,* a re-creation in song of the death by snakebite on August 7, 1761, of Timothy Myrick of Springfield Mountain (now Wilbraham), Massachusetts.

Early American Concerts

By the 1730s, the colonists had begun attending public concerts of vocal and instrumental music. The first of these that we know about with any certainty was announced December 16, 1731 in the Boston Weekly News Letter as a forthcoming "Concert of Music on sundry Instruments at Mr. Pelham's great Room... Tickets to be delivered at the place of performance at Five shillings each. The concert to begin exactly at Six o'clock..." In 1735, Charleston, South Carolinians went to see *Flora,* or *Hob in the Well,* and *The*

---

[11]Hitchcock, p. 29.

ON THURSDAY EVENING, OCTOBER 12th,
Will be performed at the Court House,
BY THE
THEATRICAL SOCIETY
IN THIS TOWN,
The Celebrated Tragedy of
DOUGLAS;
To which will be added,
The Celebrated Comedy of
LOVE-A-LA-MODE,
And the Mufical entertainment of the
PADLOCK.
☞ No Admittance behind the Scenes.
Wafhington Sept. 29, 1796.

AN ANNOUNCEMENT OF A THEATRICAL PERFORMANCE,
FROM *THE MIRROR,* WASHINGTON, KENTUCKY,
SEPTEMBER 30, 1797.

Devil to Pay in 1736. The 1735 performance of *Hob in the Well* marks the first documented performance of an opera in America. Both these delightful little "operas" were actually a form of English ballad opera, modeled after John Gay and Christopher Pepusch's *The Beggar's Opera,* heard by English audiences, and performed in New York in 1750 and 1751. When the Kean and Murray Company opened the new theater in Upper Marlborough, Maryland, in 1752, with *Beggar's Opera,* an orchestra was used for the first time in an American opera performance.

In the eighteenth century, the American operatic centers were the cities from New York south, though the 1750 antitheater blue law of Boston had put an effective check on establishing ballad opera there. Two major American opera companies were renowned by century's end; the Old American, William Hallam's London troupe, which began its American career in Williamsburg, Virginia in 1752, and its archrival, the New Company, founded in Philadelphia in 1792 by Thomas Wignell, English actor and singer, and Alexander Reinagle. New Company played in the celebrated New Theatre on Chestnut Street, an uncommonly attractive hall with a stage 36 feet wide, 71 feet deep, and seating about two thousand. Nine hundred of the seats were located in two tiers of boxes, above which hung a large gallery.

It seems abundantly clear, then, that before 1800, there was a strong tradition of secular or popular music in colonial America. Though sacred music still maintained its dominant status as the music most in use, the records reflect quite a lively underground of popular-music culture. At first, that culture employed the folk and popular music imported from England and the continent. Then, with the appearance of *Springfield Mountain,* the early settlers began their own tradition of folk music and ballads. As the eighteenth century drew to a close, greater and greater separation between actual sacred and secular music could be discerned. More and more, secular music became the music routinely employed in social and concert settings. Popular music was beginning to establish itself.

Additional Readings

Birge, Edward Bailey. *History of Public School Music in the United States.* New York: Oliver Ditson Company, 1928.

Chase Gilbert. *America's Music.* Rev. 2nd ed. New York: McGraw Hill, 1966.

Fisher, William Arms. *One Hundred and Fifty Years of Music Publishing in the United States.* Boston: Oliver Ditson Company, Inc., 1933.

Hitchcock, H. Wiley. *Music in the United States: A Historical Introduction.* 2nd. ed. Englewood Cliffs, N.J.: Prentice-Hall, 1974.

Howard, John Tasker. *Our American Music.* 5th ed. New York: Thomas Y. Crowell Company, 1939.

Sanjek, Russell. *American Popular Music and Its Business.* Vol. 1. The Beginning to 1790. New York: Oxford University Press, 1988

Sonneck, Oscar George Theodore. *A Bibliography of Early Secular American Music* (18th Century), revised and enlarged by William Trent Upton. Washington: The Library of Congress, Music Division, 1945.

van der Merwe, Peter. *Origins of the Popular Style.* New York: Oxford University Press, 1989.

Selected Recordings

From the *Ainsworth Psalter,* collected and published by Henry Ainsworth, Amsterdam, 1612. Psalm 21. Hayden HSL-2068, Psalm 34. Hayden HSL-2068

Belcher, Supply. *An Anthem of Praise.* Musical Heritage Society 4077

———. *Heroism.* Musical Heritage Society 4077

Billings, William. *An Anthem for Christmas.* Musical Heritage Society 1126

———. *Chester.* Capitol-(S)W-1688

———. *David's Lamentation.* Columbia ML-5386

———. *Easter Anthem.* Folkways FA-2377

———. *Judea (A Virgin Unspotted).* Advent 5018

Morgan, Justin. *Judgement Anthem.* Vox SVBX-5350

Peter, Johann Friedrich. *It Is a Precious Thing.* Columbia ML-5427

Read, Daniel. *Down Steers the Bass.* Vox SVBX-5350

Swann, Timothy. *China.* Vox SVBX-5350

Chapter 2
American Pop
Grows

Paul Henry Lang on popular music in the United States: "The history of popular music from the death in obscurity of Stephen Foster to the widely lamented passing of Oscar Hammerstein II is a tale of creative aspiration and doctrinaire neglect, of condescension and prejudice, of dedication and payola, of talent, trash, and many turns of taste, but in an overall view, of the development of an amazingly varied and appealing body of song that has gradually moved away from the cliché towards a more realistic and artistic expression of human values. It is a more vulgar, but also a more vital, body of song than the genteel arbiters of taste would have it — and its influence abroad is so great precisely because it has been so spontaneous and unashamed in embodying the romantic dreams, the anxieties, the fulfillment and the frustrations, as well as the crazy fads and playful moments, of the American people, or, more specifically, of each courting and dancing generation of the American people."[1]

---

[1]Lang, Paul Henry, ed. *One Hundred Years of Music in America.* (New York: G. Schirmer, Inc./Macmillan Publishing Company), p. 140. (Originally published by G. Schirmer, Inc., 1961.)

Classical vs. Popular Music

Traditionally, Americans have made a general distinction between two broad categories of music, "classical" and "popular." Hitchcock suggested the terms are probably poor ones, but they acknowledge the existence of the two major traditions in American music. He calls the two categories "cultivated" and "vernacular," and says,

> I mean by the term 'cultivated tradition' a body of music that America had to cultivate consciously, music faintly exotic, to be approached with some effort, and to be appreciated for its edification, its moral, spiritual, or aesthetic value. By the 'vernacular tradition' I mean a body of music more plebian, native, not approached selfconsciously but simply grown into as one grows into one's vernacular tongue; music understood and appreciated simply for its utilitarian or entertainment value.[2]

American Pop and Classical Separate

At the beginning of the nineteenth century, hardly any difference existed between the two. The songs of the ballad operas and the fuging tunes of the eighteenth century American sacred composers, Yankee tunesmiths, both served as a popular social music for secular entertainment. However, as the nineteenth century unfolded, an increasingly visible attitude toward each other could be distinguished. An eventually profound schism between them began to open up.

This gulf developed quite slowly. During the eighteenth century, the chasm that now exists between classical and popular music was then almost imperceptible. Bernard Shaw once exclaimed, after receiving for review, Herr Meissler's waltzes arranged for flute, *The State Ball Album, The Children's Ball,* and M. deFaye's arrangements of Braga's *Serenata,* "My good sirs: so you think that di Bassetto regards this sort of thing as serious music?!!"[3] Shaw's remarks highlighted a growing eighteenth century attitude toward any music that did not emanate from the pen of a formally trained classical composer. Our present term, "serious music," stems from just this attitude.

In the New World, most of the colonists' musical entertainment was, by necessity, homemade. Knowledge of orchestral music was obtained by playing orchestral arrangements, generally for the piano, but often for other instruments, or for voices. Van der Merwe states, "Recent studies suggest that it

[2]Hitchcock, H. Wiley. *Music in the United States: A Historical Introduction.* (Englewood Cliffs, New Jersey: Prentice-Hall, Inc., 1974), p. 51.

[3]van der Merwe, Peter. *Origins of the Popular Style.* (New York: Clarendon Press-Oxford, 1989), p. 18.

was by such means that an enthusiasm for opera was diffused among the Italian people..., and similar processes were at work all over Western Europe and the United States."[4]

Nineteenth century American arrangements of music by such composers as Handel, Beethoven, Mozart, and Wagner began to appear. Though many of these arrangements were poor, they demonstrated that early American popular musicians had nothing at all against borrowing musical material from their older, more prestigious colleagues. This practice was not new, nor was it confined to just those who composed popular music. Traditional art music composers from the Renaissance, Baroque, Viennese Classic, and early Romantic eras also borrowed quite freely from their popular-music counterparts, though this particular fact is not highly advertised. Although the first generation of European Romantic composers continued to use popular material, after Chopin and Liszt at midcentury, use of the popular idiom by such composers began to fade. By century's end, anything vaguely resembling a popular cliché was studiously avoided in the composition of traditional European art music.

During this period, perhaps because of the loss of the popular-music sound from art music, that small European upper class, the nobility, the clergy, and the well-educated, began losing interest in classical music as a diversion. Classical music was beginning to acquire its present overtones of culture and uplift. Consequently, toward the latter half of the nineteenth century, upper-class Europeans began seeking new musical sounds to divert them, and the older, more traditional classical music was relegated to churches and formal concert-hall settings. Desperately seeking what they saw as true sophistication, those pretenders to gentility inhabiting the East Coast of America emulated their European models.

In the New World, this shift in taste became noticeable during the early decades of the nineteenth century. A vernacular vein of utilitarian and entertainment music continued. This was a music essentially unconcerned with artistic or philosophical idealism. It was a music based on newly established or newly diffused American raw materials, a 'popular' music in the broadest sense. It was unselfconscious, widespread, and naive. A cultivated tradition of fine-art music also continued to grow. This music was significantly concerned with moral, artistic, or cultural idealism. It was a music almost exclusively based on continental European raw materials and models, and was pursued rather selfconsciously. It was, as Hitchcock has said, "...an essentially transatlantic music of the pretenders to gentility, hopefully sophisticated, and by no means widespread throughout all segments of the populance."[5] By century's end, the gulf between popular and classical music was significant.

---

[4]van der Merwe, p. 18.
[5]Hitchcock, p. 52.

When Hitchcock talked about a transatlantic music of the pretenders to gentility, he was referring to the music of the Romantic Era, spawned in early nineteenth-century Europe, and brought to this country by the huge influx of immigrants, some 16,000,000 between 1840 and 1900. Many of these immigrants came from Germany, Scandinavia, Italy, and eastern Europe. Among these transplanted Europeans were many conservatory-trained musicians, who began teaching music here as a livelihood. Their impact and the impact of the music of the Romantic Era on American culture was immense. These continental Europeans were critical in molding a cultivated American. They and their teachings diluted the traditional mainstreams of Anglo-American culture.

The Westward Movement

The extraordinary territorial growth of the nation during the nineteenth century helped to accelerate the split between cultivated and vernacular musical traditions. An ever moving frontier, constantly pushing westward, dominated the entire social and cultural situation. It left behind an ever widening area of newly settled towns, with the old urban centers of the eastern seaboard behind them.

In pioneer settlements such as Horse Creek, Nebraska, musical life was, understandably, vastly different from that of New York or Boston. As the music of cultivated taste began to be taken up by those pretenders to gentility on the East Coast, the music they formerly enjoyed became "both a slightly declassé 'popular' music and part of a vernacular tradition accompanying the westerly push of Americans across the land. By 1853, for instance, a Boston writer remarked of the Yankee singing-school tunebooks, once enjoyed by Bostonians great and small, if used at all, [they] have been crowded to the Far West, out of sight and hearing."[6]

Many of the newly established frontier towns, growing in population, and in stability and ease of life, did have some contact with the eastern seaboard, and wanted even more. However, they had neither the wealth, leisure, urbanity, nor comforting traditions of the eastern cities. Consequently, they envied, feared, and resented East Coast culture. These communities were only one step removed from pioneering, and the men considered any time spent on what they viewed as useless art, wasteful and even effete. Their sensibilities did not need cultivating. Their land did. Music was considered among the most intangible and useless of the arts, and had their special hostility and

---

[6]Hitchcock, p. 53.

The First Theater in St. Louis (from a painting in the Missouri Historical Society, St. Louis).

disdain. They strongly felt that music should be left to the immigrant musicians or to women. From these attitudes developed the American view of music as essentially the province of females, foreigners, or effeminates. The folk of the eastern cities viewed the pioneers as rough, unclean, and ignorant, a class of people to be devoutly avoided. Anything associated with them, including their music, was perceived as highly undesirable among the educated and sophisticated.

Given the nature of these pretenders to gentility, it was inevitable that Romanticism would gain momentum in nineteenth-century America. Under the sway of European music and the immigrant professors, aspiring American musicians affluent enough to do so went to the source of this new music, Europe, to study it in its natural environment. Edward Bailey Birge believed this contributed to a mixed blessing. On the one hand, American musical culture was enhanced and expanded. On the other hand, Americans who had studied abroad began gradually to acquire a feeling of social superiority regarding solo performance in singing and playing. This tended to break down the bonds of social diversion in music, particularly in the home, and ultimately resulted in a distinct loss in the quality of American life. Mixed blessing or not, the growth of private study both here and abroad proved critical to the development of today's popular music. It contributed to the emergence of the solo performer.

By about 1835 or 1840, a rising middle class had become the principal patron of music in Europe and America. The public concert and the public opera had replaced the parties and balls given by the nobility and the upper class, and the sophisticated religious services, as the primary settings for musical performances. Now the fledgling American solo performer had his concert format and his public. He needed only stalwart pioneers in the New World arena to complete his enthronement, a need which was filled almost as soon as it was created. European vocal and instrumental soloists with uncommon technical proficiency began touring the United States in 1843. They were welcomed with open arms by a naive American public who more often than not confused virtuosity with artistry, and flocked to their public concerts, dazzled by their technical abilities. This adulation of the virtuoso emphasized the performer, rather than the composer or even the music. It became commonplace to see a forthcoming concert announced, listing only the name of the performer and none of the music to be performed. This practice has become the trademark of today's pop and rock star.

Household Music and the American Music-Publishing Industry

The rise of the bourgeoisie significantly altered the system of musical patronage throughout the civilized world, and accelerated a professionalism in music. It also created a host of new amateur performers, people with the leisure time to spend on music making and the aspiration to do so. These were people with only modest artistic talent or judgment. Still, they needed music to perform, and the American music-publishing business, begun in the late 1700s, responded to the need. The industry's output reached impressive proportions by the last decade of the eighteenth century and this expansion continued throughout the nineteenth. The publishers' primary output was, of course, music simple enough to be sold in large quantities to amateur musicians across the nation, a music which in a sense would be "popular."

Some of the music published was of the old vernacular tradition. However, many of the songs and piano pieces possessed an aura of pretentious gentility. This music came from and fell into the category of the cultivated rather than the vernacular tradition, though its accessibility to both the performer and the listener kept it closer to the vernacular.

This music was composed by innumerable poetasters (dilettantes), and in reality represented a subdivision of the cultivated tradition. Hitchcock called this genre "household music," a term he derived from the title of an 1850 collection, *Household Melodies, a Selection of Popular Songs, Duets, Trios & Quartets, Arranged to Household Words.* This collection was first issued by W. C.

AN AD FROM 1887 FOR SOHMER PIANOS.

Peters & Sons of Cincinnati and then by other publishers and distributors in St. Louis, Nashville, Cleveland, Pittsburgh, and Louisville.

The term, "household music," appears to be appropriate. "...[It] suggests an analogy with household artifacts of the period such as silverware, ceramics, glass, furniture, rugs, and draperies which although utilitarian were never acquired solely for their utility, but with an eye for their attractiveness and their reflection of the fashionable cultivated taste. The early twentieth century would call such music 'semiclassical' or 'light classical,' thus perfectly describing its ambiguous status."[7] Incidentally, one could speculate, with some

---

[7]Hitchcock, p. 59.

authority, that herein lie the seeds of what we now term "easy listening" or "elevator music," a subdivision of what we define today as "popular music."

Household Music and the Concert Stage

Those 'innumerable poetasters' referred to by Hitchcock were in actuality the first of our American pop composers. They modeled their compositions after the music of the English singers who barnstormed through the eastern half of the nation in the 1830s and 1840s. Though today their music would be laughed out of a pop-music concert, it was the most sought-after music of its day. Among the first of the composers to achieve raging success in the genre was a Presbyterian church organist, Henry Russell. Hitchcock painted the following humorous, though accurate, portrait of Russell and his music.

> Mining the vein of sentiment for the aged that ran so deep in mid-nineteenth century America, Russell concentrated on "old" songs (*The Old Bell, The Brave Old Oak, The Old Sexton,* and many others), for a total he claimed to be over 800 songs. Among the most renowned were *Woodman, Spare That Tree* ("...touch not a single bough,/in youth it shelter'd me,/and I'll protect it now") and *The Old Arm Chair* (MinA, N.123). *The Old Arm Chair,* published in 1840 at the peak of Russell's popularity, illustrates in every detail the genre of the household song. The text is embarrassingly maudlin: the poet gazes on the armchair "with quivering breath and throbbing brow"; religion and filial love are identified ("I almost worshipp'd her when she smiled,/And turn'd from her Bible to bless her child"); the chair itself is an object of sentimental veneration ("I love it, I love it, and cannot tear/My soul from a mother's Old Arm Chair") The cover page, with its lithograph showing Mother and the chair..., is characteristic: nineteenth-century song sheets aimed to be visually seductive as well as vocally attractive. The music is quite simple, the melodic style essentially declamatory, in easy 4/4 rhythms, with an occasional touch of affective chromaticism and a climactic, shuddering, diminished-seventh chord.[8]

This music is characterized by "the cult of the fashionable, the worship of the conventional, the emulation of the elegant, the cultivation of the trite and artificial, the indulgence of sentimentality, and the predominance of superficiality."[9] The music was designed to draw tears and sobs from its original listeners, or to fill them with chills and thrills in its more dramatic moments. Though in the light of the twentieth century, these songs appear ludicrous and pathetic, they cannot be ignored.

Russell, an English singer and ballad composer, came to New York in 1833. He spent almost nine years in America, and during that time, exerted

---

[8]Hitchcock, p. 66.

[9]Chase, Gilbert. *America's Music,* revised second edition. (New York: McGraw-Hill Book Company, 1966), p. 165.

considerable influence on the musical scene of the day. He was well-educated musically. At one time, he had been a student of Rossini in Naples. He must have been a drawing card, for he was usually the featured attraction on any bill, whether appearing with someone else or alone. His American ballads include *The Brave Old Oak, The Charter Oak, The Old Bell, The Ivy Green, Our Way Across The Mountain, Ho Woodman Spare That Tree, The Wreck of the Mexico, A Life on the Ocean Wave, I Love the Man with a Generous Heart, Those Locks Those Ebon Locks,* and many others, including *The Old Sexton.*

Russell related a short anecdote about a friend who confessed that his childhood nurse routinely sang him to sleep with *Woodman Spare That Tree,* and many times as a child, his (Russell's) friend "cried himself to sleep over the simple song."[10] Chase declares this is not a simple song. "It is an artificial song, a concocted song, inflated with a synthetic sentimentality; it does not have the genuine emotion, the organic vitality, the timeless and impersonal quality of, for example, the old folk ballads."[11] This contrast between genuine folk ballads and household music is made merely to emphasize the "vitiating effects of pseudosimple, artificially sentimental songs in forming adult musical tastes through childhood experiences."[12] By "vitiating," Chase meant the degrading, the corrupting, of musical taste. Whether or not this influence is always vitiating is immaterial here. What is important is that music heard in childhood can and does influence musical taste. It is this very influence that has served to create and maintain a huge audience and market for today's popular music.

There were other such composers, such as W. B. Bradbury, who wrote *The Lament of the Blind Orphan Girl* in a style derived in part almost certainly from the Donizetti and Rossini arias he would have heard in New York in the 1840s. *The Lament of the Blind Orphan Girl* was published "as sung with distinguished Applause, by Abby Hutchinson." Abby was the female member of America's most celebrated "singing family" of the age, the Hutchinsons. They were the most famous of several American troupes touring the nation during this period, performing these little bits of authentic American melodrama. On an Albany, New York, program in 1842, the Hutchinsons sang *The Snowstorm,* its concluding verse a classic representative of the popular melodramatic style:

> And colder still the wind did blow
> And darker hours of night came on,
> And deeper grew the drifts of snow.
> Her limbs were chilled, her strength was gone.
> "Oh God!" she cried in accents wild,
> "If I must perish, save my child!"[13]

---

[10]Chase, p. 166.
[11]Chase, p. 166.
[12]Chase, p. 166.
[13]Hitchcock, p. 68.

"It is against this background, of the nostalgic sentimentality of *The Old Arm Chair*, the crocodile tears of *The Blind Orphan Girl*, the hysterical unreality of *The Snowstorm* that one must view the household songs of Stephen Collins Foster." A few of his compositions "so sublimate or mitigate the conventions of the genre, and so transcend the songs of his contemporaries, that Foster must be adjudged America's first great songwriter."[14]

Stephen Collins Foster

Stephen Collins Foster was born in Lawrenceville, Pennsylvania, near Pittsburgh, on July 4, 1826, the same day on which both John Adams and Thomas Jefferson died. He had a childhood typical of his middle-class family, where household music was no stranger. His older sister played the piano, and his father, the fiddle. According to his father, Foster spent all his leisure hours in music, for which he possessed "a strange talent." Nevertheless, Foster received almost no encouragement in his musical pursuits. His brother claimed he "studied deeply and burned much midnight oil over the works of the masters, especially Mozart, Beethoven, and Weber." This apparently was the only musical instruction Foster ever received. Though he struggled for years to understand the theories of composition thoroughly, his music still reflects his lack of formal training.

However, although his music does reflect a lack of formal schooling in composition, his writing demonstrates an obvious and undeniable natural gift for melody. John Tasker Howard believed Foster to be one of the greatest melodists we have yet produced. According to Howard, Foster accomplished melodically what many better and more formally trained musicians had utterly failed to do. He wrote melodies that everyone can understand, melodies so poignant and lovely that one never tires of hearing them. Today, Foster could offer his work without apology or reservation. In a world where transiency is a hallmark, Foster's melodies have remained as fresh and appealing as the day they were conceived.

Many legends and stories have been concocted concerning Foster, many of them untrue. His life was quite tragic. His well-to-do family loved him, did all they could to protect and shield him, and yet failed to understand him. According to Howard, pioneering conditions are almost never kind to those who display artistic tendencies. He believed that Foster was probably born too soon. His family apparently did not understand that Foster's dreaming ways

---

[14]Hitchcock, p. 69.

FROM A PAINTING DEPICTING FOSTER BY HOWARD CHANDLER CHRISTY.

and his indolence may have been his very strength. Not once did they seek to find music teachers for him, though they appeared to recognize his "strange talent for music." Granted, there were few music teachers available. Still, old attitudes prevailed; such diversions were simply not for able-bodied men.

Foster's Youth.   Foster spent his boyhood days in and around Pittsburgh and Allegheny. He attended the local schools, and Athens Academy, located in Athens, Pennsylvania, near Towanda. His first published song, *Open Thy Lattice, Love,* was written at age sixteen. He moved to Cincinnati in 1846 to keep books for his brother. There he again encountered W. C. Peters, a music publisher he had met in Pittsburgh. He simply gave Peters the originals of *Uncle Ned, Oh! Susannah,* and several other songs. Peters published these as *Songs of the Sable Harmonist.* He did not mention Foster's name on the printed copies. Sales of this publication alone earned Peters $10,000. After witnessing such success, Foster gave up bookkeeping and began writing songs for a living.

Foster contracted with Firth, Pond & Company, of New York, to publish his music. The terms of the agreement guaranteed Foster a royalty on every copy of his music published by Firth. Many believe Foster was not well-paid for his works, but this belief is not altogether true. From some of his song publications he received thousands of dollars. Later, when alcohol had almost totally destroyed him, unscrupulous publishers literally stole his music from him. However, in better days, he dealt with reputable firms who gave him the proper royalties from the income his compositions earned.

Foster wrote *Old Folks At Home* in 1851 for E. P. Christy of Christy's Minstrels. Christy had asked Foster to write songs for him that he could sing before they were published, and *Old Folks At Home* was one of these. A clause in the agreement between Christy and Foster allowed Christy to place his own name as composer on first editions of this music. Stephen's brother, Morrison, has been quoted as stating Christy paid $500 for this privilege, but according to Howard, this sum was extremely exaggerated.

Foster had never been south of the Ohio River before the publication of *Old Folks at Home*. All his knowledge about black singing had been gained from black church services and minstrel shows. One of his brothers suggested the name, *Swanee River*, after finding it on a map. Foster used it because it sounded better than his original name, *Pedee*. In 1852, Foster finally took a trip through the South, and gained some little first-hand knowledge of southern life and traditions.

During his childhood and teenage years, Foster continued to display a rare talent for music. Yet countless indications of his talent never once suggested to his loving family his need to pursue a career in music. In fact, his inclinations worried them. However, in 1840, Foster appeared to lose much of his enthusiasm for music. His mother, apparently extremely relieved, wrote a letter to a friend, noting that Stephen had lost much of his devotion to music, while other studies seemed to be more important to him.

Foster Becomes a Professional Songwriter.

Finally, when the songs he had written as a diversion had become popular even beyond the publisher's hopes, Foster realized that music was his true calling. By then, it was too late for him to learn how to write with the mind as well as with the heart. As a result, he had no training to help cultivate his gifts so they would grow into something bigger.

On July 22, 1850, Foster married Jane Denny McDowell, the daughter of one of Pittsburgh's leading physicians. His marriage was a failure, though he appeared to worship both his wife and young daughter. Little is known about his married life. Some historians speculate he and his wife separated several times. Many factors could have contributed to the frequent separations. Love for his parents, the "Old Folks at Home," probably caused Foster to neglect his wife and child, a neglect that was not consciously intended.

A COPY OF THE SHEET MUSIC OF FOSTER'S *MY OLD KENTUCKY HOME.*

Foster never became businessman enough to realize the full earning potential of his best songs. His gift to Peters was typical of his approach to business. Since common-law copyright was not yet established, many of the songs he gave to minstrel performers were published by others. Occasionally, songs were copyrighted by those who had no legal right to them.

Though in 1860 he had contracted with both Firth and with Lee & Walker to produce music under the assurance of a guaranteed income, his drinking problem kept him from producing consistently. He apparently wrote only when he needed money to buy alcohol. According to Howard, he would write a song in the morning, sell it for a pitiful sum by afternoon, and have the money spent by nightfall. Stephen Collins Foster died in New York City, on January 13, 1864, impoverished and an alcoholic.

Like Henry Russell, whom he heard in concert in Pittsburgh, Foster wrote "old" songs. But when Russell used the word "old," he meant simply, "aged." Foster's "old" usually meant "of the past." His music literally drips with nostalgia and lost love, and represents perhaps the best of the household genre. Many of Foster's songs mourned the loss of loved ones through death. And always there is the implication that all the better days have passed forever. Of course, there are a few happy songs among Foster's works; songs such as *Fairy Belle, If You've Only Got a Moustache,* an Irish reel with coy advice to bachelors, and *There's a Good Time Coming.* But for the most part, a sense of loss and nostalgia pervades his music.

In some respects, Foster was like Franz Schubert. He possessed a natural gift for melody that shone precisely because of its simplicity. Though only a dozen or so of his almost two hundred published works are sung anymore, these few are so potent in their charm, they have long since earned their composer's immortality. His strength lay in his limitations, in his very lack of formal musical training. His use of a few basic chords gave his music a directness and simplicity that was utterly charming and always natural. Formal musical training might have destroyed that charm. Many of today's popular-music composer-performers can lay legitimate claim to the same kind of talent, though probably not of the same proportion as Foster's.

Blackface Minstrelsy

Another phase of early American music, blackface minstrelsy, exerted significant influence on the development of popular music. In 1843, four star blackface comedians formed a minstrel band of instruments normally associated with blacks of the period. On February 6 of that year, they premiered as the Virginia Minstrels. They appeared as one of the major attractions of the Bowery Circus. The troupe's New York debut was a raging success. They enlarged their act into a full evening's entertainment of songs, dances, and a parody lecture on locomotives, and opened on March 7 at the Masonic Temple in Boston. The Virginia Minstrels called their show an Ethiopian Concert. It was the nation's first real minstrel show.

Like much of what took place musically in nineteenth-century America, the minstrel show had its British antecedents. It was quite common in eighteenth-century England to see black characters and hear so-called "Negro songs," both "usually of an insufferably patronizing and sentimental character,"[15] included in British dramas and ballad operas.

Contemporary sources in the United States cite the singing of Negro songs here as early as 1769. That year, Lewis Hallam the Younger sang *Dear Heart! What a Terrible Life I Am Led* in Bickerstaff's play *The Padlock* at a New York theater. A Mr. Tyler, a Mr. Dibdin, and a Mrs. Hallam also sang Negro songs in New York concerts during the years 1798-1800, and M. Francisque, choreographer for the Old American Theater Company, performed a Negro dance in 1796.

[15]Hitchcock, p. 107.

A RECORDING OF A MINSTREL SONG.

Blackface minstrelsy basically consisted of white men exploiting the slave's style of music and dancing. Whites blackened their faces with burnt cork, and went on stage to sing Negro songs (also referred to as "Ethiopian songs"), to perform dances based on those of the slaves, and to tell stereotyped jokes about slave life. Two types of black impersonations evolved: One caricatured the plantation slave and his thick accent, and one portrayed the city slicker, a dandy dressed in the latest fashion, whose claim to fame was his exploits among the ladies. The country bumpkin was called Jim Crow, and the city slicker, Zip Coon.

One of the most successful of the early blackface entertainers was George Washington Dixon. As early as 1827, he was singing Negro songs in character. In 1829, he appeared at the Bowery Theatre in New York, where he introduced one of the favorite numbers in his repertoire, *Coal Black Rose*. Foster Damon called it "the first burnt-cork song of comic love."[16] Dixon claimed authorship of another early and highly popular minstrel song, *Long Tail Blue*.

---

[16]Chase, p. 261.

This song was consistently featured in his performances before 1827 on. With the help of other blackface entertainers, such as Barney Burns and William Pennington, *Coal Black Rose* became a standard minstrel number for the next fifty years.

Johann Christian Gottlieb Graupner (1767–1836) came to America from Hanover, Germany, shortly after 1790. He settled in Boston, where, during the nineteenth century, he exerted significant influence on the musical life of early America. Graupner has been called the father of American orchestral music because of his pioneer work in that medium. Interestingly, it is possible Graupner was also the father of the minstrel song. An 1889 New York newspaper article briefly outlined the history of the minstrel show. It quoted Charles White, an old Ethiopian comedian, as having said Graupner sang *The Gay Negro Boy*, in character, on December 30, 1799. According to White, Graupner accompanied himself on the banjo. The song appeared at the end of the second act of what was then called "an Ethiopian entertainment." One can only assume "in character" indicated that Graupner appeared on stage in costume and with blackened face!

In February, 1854, *Putnam's Journal* called attention to a type of musical entertainment gaining a wide following in New York. The article reported that the African opera houses were the only places of amusement where the entertainments were indigenous. These entertainments were described as follows. "...native American vocalists, with blackened faces, sing national songs, and utter none but native witticisms. These native theatricals... are among the best frequented and most profitable places of amusement in New York."[17] The article observed that attempts to establish Italian Opera in New York had ended in bankruptcy even though the wealthiest and best-educated classes supported those attempts. However, " ...the Ethiopian Opera has flourished like a green bay tree."[18]

The Father of Minstrelsy. Known to his contemporaries as "Daddy" or "Jim Crow" Rice, his full name was Thomas Dartmouth Rice. He was born in 1808 in New York City of poor parents, and was trained to be a woodcarver. However, the stage proved a strong lure, and he occasionally took small, non-speaking roles at the Park Theatre. Finally, he left New York and went on the road as an itinerant musician, heading for the frontier settlements of the Ohio Valley. In 1828, he got a job in Louisville, in Ludlow and Smith's Southern Theatre. There he began playing bit parts. In a local drama called *The Rifle*, he played the part of a black field hand. As was done in all theaters of the day,

---

[17]Hitchcock, p. 106.
[18]Hitchcock, p. 106.

whether the play was serious or otherwise, Rice interpolated a Negro song between acts. The song he sang was *Jim Crow*, and, according to Chase, it made Rice famous, and became America's first international pop-music hit.

Rice and publisher W. C. Peters were acquaintances. During a trip to Pittsburgh, Rice got Peters to write down the music to *Jim Crow*. Many editions of *Jim Crow* appeared within a short period of time. Many of these made no reference to Rice. Here is the tune of *Jim Crow* as it was published in Baltimore by George Willig, Jr., with no date, but probably issued around 1828.

JIM CROW.

Though early minstrel performers, such as Dixon and Rice, may have derived their inspiration from hearing blacks sing their own songs, American black minstrelsy in the early years was largely a white man's production. Nonetheless, without the background of the black tradition, American minstrelsy could not have developed. "The songs, the humor, the dances, and the instruments of the plantation [blacks] formed the nucleus out of which grew the first distinctly American type of theatrical entertainment."[19] Gradually, the format of the minstrel show became standardized. It included dialect solo songs, satirical stump speeches and dialogues, burlesques, instrumental numbers and dances, either solo or group, and "walk-arounds," i.e., small-scale

[19]Chase, p. 266.

vernacular *Gesamtkunstwerke* combining solo song, choral song, and dancing to instrumental "symphonies."

After 1865, minstrel companies consisting entirely of black performers began to appear. There were earlier performances of all black troupes, but they were isolated. A troupe calling itself the "Extraordinary Seven Slaves" gave a show in Massachusetts in the 1850s. They were sponsored by northern friends. The most successful of the black troupes formed in the 1860s were Lew Johnson's Plantation Company, and the Georgia Minstrels.

This unique form of stage show had come to represent America's contribution to the world of entertainment. During the latter part of the nineteenth century and the first decade of the twentieth, black and white troupes alike traveled to England and Europe to perform. Some of these companies, such as The Primrose and West Minstrel Company, and Lew Dockstader's Minstrel Company, employed both black and white performers. Actually, neither group had integrated performances, except perhaps in the finales. As a rule, whites presented the first half of the show, and blacks the second half.

By today's standards, these entertainments may appear crude and offensive. However, they served as important support structures of early American popular culture. The minstrels lashed out, in stinging parodies and burlesques, at the arty and pretentious, the foreign and imported. More important to today's popular music, the songs and dances of the minstrel shows formed a part of the compositional base on which the beginnings of black rhythm and blues were founded.

Additional Readings

Chase, Gilbert. *America's Music,* rev. 2nd. ed. New York: McGraw-Hill Book Company, 1966.

Dichter, Harry and Elliott Shapiro. *Handbook of Early American Sheet Music 1768-1889.* New York: Dover Publications, Inc., 1977.

Fisher, William Arms. *One Hundred and Fifty Years of Music Publishing in the United States.* Boston: Oliver Ditson Company, Inc., 1933.

Hitchcock, H. Wiley. *Music in the United States: A Historical Introduction.* Englewood Cliffs, N.J.: Prentice-Hall, Inc., 1974.

Howard, John Tasker. *Our American Music,* revised. New York: Thomas Y. Crowell Company, 1939.

Lang, Paul Henry. *One Hundred Years of Music in America.* New York: G. Schirmer, Inc., 1961.

Ritter, Frederick Louis. *Music In America.* New York: Charles Scribner's Sons, 1884.

Sanjek, Russell. *American Popular Music and Its Business.* Vol. 1. The Beginnings to 1790. New York: Oxford University Press, 1988.

Southern, Eileen. *The Music of Black Americans, A History.* New York: W. W. Norton & Company, 1971.

Selected Recordings

Carr, Benjamin. *Federal Overture.* Musical Heritage Society-3578

———— . *Kyrie Eleison.* Folkways FTS-32381

Foster, Stephen. *Ah! May the Red Rose Live Alway!* Columbia ML-2108

———— . *Beautiful Dreamer.* Angel S-36071

———— . *Camptown Races.* Angel S-36071

———— . *The Glendy Burke.* Angel S-36071

———— . *Jeannie with the Light Brown Hair.* Angel S-36071

The Hutchinsons. *Axes to Grind.* Vox SVBX-5309

———— . *The Bride's Departure.* Vox SVBX-5309

———— . *King Alcohol.* Vox SVBX-5309

———— . *The Pauper's Funeral.* Vox SVBX-5309

Chapter 3 Ragtime and the Blues

Ragtime Arrives

Now the stage was set for the first real fad in popular music in the United States, ragtime. A craze for ragtime music swept through the nation in the 1890s through the media of piano players, player pianos, dance bands, and commercial sheet music. Many threads of earlier American music are embedded in the fabric of ragtime. Probably the earliest was an emphatic use of syncopation by American blacks that was taken partly from African drumming and partly from Afro-Caribbean dance rhythms. A few reports on secular slave music mention the practice of "patting Juba." These reports lend credence to the belief that such a practice included complex rhythmic patterns played against a regular beat, producing a feeling of persistent, constant syncopation. A correspondent, describing the practice in a letter to Edgar Allen Poe, dated 1835, observed that there appeared to be no attempt to keep time to all the notes, but then it [patting Juba] "comes so pat & regular that the cadence is never lost."[1] Such irregularities gave the appearance of rests and grace notes. They were performed so as to "neither hasten nor retard the beat. The time of the bar must be the same, no matter how many notes are in it."[2]

One source couples the Negro dance name *Juba* with the English dance name *jig,* and speaks of "patting" as an intricate rhythmic accompaniment to such a "jig." Another source, a Mississippi planter discussing plantation management in 1851, tells of his slaves' Saturday night dance music; "Charley's fiddle is always accompanied with Ithurod on the triangle and Sam to 'pat.'"[3]

The earliest American music to suggest the intricate and fanciful rhythms of ragtime is probably that of the banjo dances of the early minstrel shows. At least one aspect of these, accentuated rests, related to patting Juba. Minstrel-show banjo tunes were generally referred to as "jigs." So was early ragtime. The terms *rag* and *ragtime* did not gain currency until about 1897. Until then, a pianist or a band that played in ragtime style was called a "jig pianist" or a "jig band."

History is vague concerning the origin of the name *ragtime.* Many believe the name is a shortened version of "ragged time." Such a term would aptly describe the rhythms executed primarily by the left hand in piano rags. Interestingly, these rhythms, which are such an integral part of ragtime, probably did not occur as a deliberate compositional device. Rather, they came about accidentally.

The earliest ragtime pianists were drifters, wandering up and down the Mississippi River and the eastern seaboard. They earned their way playing in cheap restaurants, questionable night spots, saloons, and riverside dives. They played for miserable wages, sometimes just for tips. Their job was providing music for dancing or listening in place of an orchestra. With his left hand, the pianist played orchestral bass. With his right, he played a sharply syncopated melody, altering and embellishing it as he played.

W. C. Handy heard one of these "piano thumpers" while on a visit to Memphis in the late 1880s. As he was walking down Beale Street one night, he heard someone playing a piano with what he described as insistent Negro rhythms, broken patterns of notes played first by the right hand, then by the left. He went into a café where he found a black man at the piano, "dog tired." The piano player told Handy he had to play from seven in the evening until seven in the morning, and in an effort to rest himself, he played with alternate hands.[4]

---

[1]Hitchcock, H. Wiley. *Music in the United States: A Historical Introduction.* (Englewood Cliffs, New Jersey: Prentice-Hall, Inc., 1974), p. 122.

[2]Hitchcock, p. 122.

[3]Hitchcock, p. 122.

[4]Southern, Eileen. *The Music of Black Americans: A History.* (New York: W.W. Norton & Company, Inc., 1971), p. 313.

Ragtime Songs: Vocal and Instrumental

In the early days of the minstrel show, "coon songs" had been a basic stock in trade, but after the end of the Civil War, their importance diminished. However, though their importance had diminished, some coon songs were still being written as late as the 1890s, and these reflected the use of more and more syncopation. Edward B. Marks compiled a list of the 130 most successful popular songs of the 1880s. Only seven of these were coon songs, all written by whites. Of the seven, only one, J. S. Putnam's *New Coon in Town* (1883) used enough syncopation to foreshadow the true ragtime school. According to Marks, the others were mere blackface numbers, written by whites and performed by whites in blackface makeup.

However, during the next ten years, matters changed drastically. Coon songs made a remarkable comeback, primarily because of the song, *All Coons Look Alike to Me,* written and sung by the black actor and singer, Ernest Hogan. This song was published in 1896, and sold quite well in the United States and abroad. Despite its success, the song eventually brought its writer unhappiness. Blacks did not like the title because it was derisive when separated from the lyrics.

Eileen Southern believed the ragtime instrumental pieces created "an excitement and emotional power not previously associated with entertainment music in America."[5] The cross-accented rhythms, resulting from a conflict of rhythmic patterns between the duple-meter bass and the syncopated treble leaning toward a kind of triple meter, were responsible for much of that power. Chromatic melodies and harmony reflected the strong influence of black folk song.

William Krell, a white Chicago bandleader, was first to publish the kind of music black pianists had been playing for years in cheap cafés and riverfront dives. Krell came into contact with folk, ragtime, and other black music during his extensive southern tours. Other black pianist-composers active in or near St. Louis from about 1890 to 1920 included the ragtime pioneer, Scott Joplin, as well as Thomas Million Turpin, James Scott, Arthur Marshall, Scott Hayden, Louis Chauvin, Sam Patterson, and Joe Jordan. There were also a few white ragtime composers, including Charles L. Johnson, Charles Hunter, George Botsford, and Perry Weinrich. A different kind of rag was developing along the Atlantic seaboard, much of it played by excellent pianists. However, only two, James Hubert "Eubie" Blake and the white composer Joseph Lamb, ever found publishers for their music.

---

[5]Southern, p. 317.

Early Rag Composers

Many of the early black songwriters, like so many of the early ragtime pianists, were illiterate. To get their music published, they were forced to play their songs for the professional arrangers of Tin Pan Alley. These arrangers could write down the notes as fast as the musicians could play. Inevitably, most of this music arrived in the hands of the publishers with the arranger's name as composer. Nonetheless, writers, such as South Carolina's Chris Smith and Irving Jones of New York, produced many ragtime pieces around the turn of the century that everyone was singing or playing. The first decade of the twentieth century saw many rag composers: James T. Brymn, Bob Cole, Will Cook, James Europe, Harry P. Guy, Ernest Hogan, J. Rosamond Johnson, Joe Jordan, Cecil Mack, Fred Stone, Charlie Warfield, Bert Williams, and Clarence Williams.

Scott Joplin

Scott Joplin was originally from Texarkana, Texas. He began his career as an itinerant pianist. By 1855, he had migrated to St. Louis, where he played in honky-tonks and sporting houses. For a brief period, he lived in Chicago, and played in the entertainment halls that had sprung up around the 1893 World's Fair. In 1894, he moved to Sedalia, Missouri.

His first rag, *Original Rag*, was published in March, 1899. The *Maple Leaf Rag*, named after a saloon and dance hall in Sedalia, appeared later that same year. *Maple Leaf Rag* was instantly and resoundingly successful. By the time he died, Joplin had published more than thirty original rags, and other piano pieces, songs, and arrangements as well. In 1902, he completed a ballet score called *Rag Time Dance*, and in 1903 the opera, *A Guest of Honor*, unpublished and now apparently lost. In 1911, he published *Treemonisha*, an opera in three acts, at his own expense. The opera is black, and its action is set on a plantation somewhere in Arkansas in 1866. Treemonisha is a black girl who manages to become educated, and overcomes the superstitions and myths that bind her people. Gilbert Chase observed, "The score of *Treemonisha* employs ragtime, but not exclusively. Scott Joplin was trying to create an American Negro opera; he deserves credit for pioneering in that direction."[6]

---

[6]Chase, Gilbert. *America's Music*, revised second edition. (New York: McGraw-Hill Book Company, 1966), p. 439.

The artistic success of Joplin's operas is perhaps questionable, but his rags are most assuredly artistic in every sense of the word. They have been described as elegant, varied, often subtle, and as sharply incised as a cameo. In terms of a native style of dance music, they have been called precise American equivalents of minuets by Mozart, mazurkas by Chopin, or waltzes by Brahms. Technically, they are not easy. They demand a clean, but 'swinging,' performance. In 1908, Joplin published a brief manual containing ragtime exercises. He emphatically stated that all the pieces masquerading under the name of ragtime were not the genuine article. Joplin knew real ragtime of the higher class was difficult to play. He remarked that syncopations are no indication of light and trashy music.

Though St. Louis is rightfully considered the location most important to the rise of ragtime, New Orleans and its contributions must not be overlooked. New Orleans is considered the original center of "ragging" street bands, and of the ragtime dance bands that ushered in jazz. Storyville, a section of the city set aside for "sporting" purposes, was also the center of ragtime piano. The city's leading ragtime pianists were Anthony Jack, and Ferdinand "Jelly Roll" Morton, who modified Joplin's original St. Louis style by adding more swinging rhythms and melodic "walking" bass lines.

New York pianist James P. Johnson marks the turn from ragtime to jazz piano, with works such as *Caprice Rag,* 1914, *Harlem Strut,* 1917, and *Carolina Shout,* 1925. In all these pieces, Johnson's "walking" left hand emphasizes the off-beats and transforms the older two-beat meter into a jazzy four, while his right-hand style dissolves the classic ragtime syncopes into long-breathed runs of even eighths and triplets. This style helped to bring to a close the short, but happy, public existence of ragtime as the current craze, while waiting impatiently in the wings was the era of the blues.

White Composers and Ragtime

Ragtime historian Rudi Blesh considered white songwriter Benjamin Harney to be of historic importance in the development of rag. According to Blesh, Harney was performing rag music for white audiences quite early in its development. This was at a time when blacks were hesitant to play it for anyone other than themselves. Harney, originally from Kentucky, introduced New York audiences to rag in 1896. During that year, he accompanied the buck-and-wing dancing of a tiny black performer called Strap Heel, who was on the bill at Tony Pastor's Fourteenth Street Variety House. Kerry Mills, a white Tin Pan Alley songwriter, composed *At a Georgia Camp Meeting,* a favorite during ragtime's heyday.

Among the great late nineteenth- and early twentieth-century European composers, Debussy was first to notice the new music of black folk origin. In

1905 he wrote *Children's Corner,* a piano suite. One of the movements, *Golliwog's Cakewalk,* progresses in typical ragtime style. There is a syncopated melody in the right hand, and an "um-pah" kind of accompaniment in the left. In 1918, Igor Stravinsky composed *Ragtime,* and *Piano Rag Music.* In 1918, he also wrote the popular *L'Histoire du Soldat,* in which he included a ragtime movement. French composer Eric Satie included a dance in his 1917 ballet, *Parade,* which was in ragtime style. In America, John Alden Carpenter appears to have been the first white composer to use ragtime style in art music. Southern observed, "All of this music reflects the captivating but rather vapid style of the ragtime song rather than the essence of serious rag music."[7] Very few outside the black world of that day had the opportunity to hear rag music played by its legendary composer-performers. That music was too difficult for the average amateur pianist to take home and try out. Instead, the public became familiar with "a pseudo-ragtime style popularized by Tin Pan Alley and exemplified in the playing of white pianist Mike Bernard and his followers."[8]

Black Spirituals

During and after the Civil War, black spirituals began to attract widespread attention and interest. Favorites during those days were *Roll, Jordan, Roll, I Heard From Heaven Today, Blow Your Trumpet Gabriel, Praise Member, Wrestle on Jacob,* and *The Lonesome Valley. Roll, Jordan, Roll,* printed in 1862, was probably the first spiritual ever published. Its publisher was a Miss Lucy McKim of Philadelphia.

A few of the earlier spirituals make reference to emancipation; for example, *No More Peck o' Corn for Me.* A "peck o' corn," along with a pint of salt, made up slave rations. This song is said to have first been sung "when Beauregard took the slaves to the islands to build the fortifications at Hilton Head and Bay point."[9]

NO MORE PECK O' CORN FOR ME

[7]Southern, p. 332.
[8]Southern, p. 332.
[9]Chase, p. 240.

Like the social songs, the postwar spirituals used the forms and characteristics of the old slave songs. However, their content was radically different. It reflected the new status and circumstances that the recently emancipated blacks had achieved. Black folk songs and spirituals began to appear in print early in 1860, though they remained largely unknown to most of the white population of the country. Appropriately, a group of young black singers from Fisk University in Nashville, Tennessee, brought this music to the attention of America and eventually to Europe as well. This group soon became known as the Fisk Jubilee Singers, and since their founding, the choir has made countless United States and world tours.

The Fisk Jubilee Singers

Fisk University opened its doors in 1866. Its first music director was a young white instructor, George L. White. In addition to preparing and conducting the Jubilee Singers, White gave promising students extensive training in musicianship. From the start, the Singers sang both the standard classical repertoire and black spirituals.

White presented a concert to the general Nashville public in 1867. The concert was an overwhelming success. Encouraged, White began taking the choir on short tours to nearby towns and cities. In 1871, he conceived the notion of making a money-raising tour to help with the Fisk building program. This was not an easy decision. His Jubilee Singers did not put on a minstrel show. They told no jokes, danced no dances, sang no catchy tunes. The religious music of the slaves had not yet been presented to the public at large, nor had the public given any indication it was ready to hear such music, partic-

THE ORIGINAL JUBILEE SINGERS, 1873 (FROM A PRINT AT THE TENNESSEE STATE LIBRARY).

ularly in a formal concert setting. Nonetheless, with trepidation and many mis-givings, White began his proposed tour on October 6, 1871. He set out with eleven singers, a young black pianist with significant skill (Ella Shepherd), and a teacher-chaperon (Miss Wells). And he did all this on borrowed funds.

White and his Singers were not immediately successful. In fact, the first newspaper reviews of the initial concerts were rather indifferent. In spite of this, White continued the tour. Then, in Columbus, Ohio, after a sleepless night, White conceived the idea of naming his group. Since slaves had talked for many years about their "year of jubilee," the time when slavery would end, why not name his choir the "Fisk Jubilee Singers"? The name caught on imme-diately. A Boston newspaper reporter wrote that the Fisk Jubilee Singers sang *Home, Sweet Home* with "a power and pathos never surpassed" to an audience that had heard it sung by the renowned Jenny Lind.

In 1872, the Singers were catapulted into fame: the event, the mammoth World Peace Jubilee held in Boston that year. A huge festival chorus, which included the Singers, had been assembled for the occasion. The chorus was scheduled to sing the refrain of the popular *Battle Hymn of the Republic,* with the verses to be sung by the Jubilee Singers. When performance time arrived, the orchestra began the song on too high a pitch level, and the opening failed miserably. Then the Jubilee Singers sang alone. In his book, *The Story of the Jubilee Singers,* J. B. T. Marsh wrote in dramatic fashion that every word rang throughout the building like a trumpet call. The audience was obviously surprised and delighted. Hats were thrown into the air and the audience cheered. The conductor for that concert was Patrick Sarsfield Gilmore. After hearing and seeing the audience response to the Jubilee Singers, Gilmore brought the Singers up from their place just below the orchestra, and put them on his platform to complete the song.

This single event made the Singers' reputation. They went on to sing in places in the United States where the folk music of the blacks had never before been heard. They began traveling to Europe, singing in Germany, Switzerland, and England. Everywhere they went, the Singers won critical acclaim. Within seven years, they raised $150,000, and turned it all over to the university. In gratitude, the university named a new campus building Jubilee Hall.

The Blues

Spirituals and Blues. There is no sharp dividing line between spirituals and the blues. Some spirituals convey the same feelings of hopelessness and despair as do the blues. However, the spiritual is supernal — the blues, worldly. Spirituals are inclined toward more general expression and feeling. They are more group-oriented. Blues are explicit feelings of the individual. In spite of these differences, it is often difficult to distinguish between the two. In fact, many spirituals would have been called *blues* had the term been in vogue during the early days of the spiritual.

The Blues Begin. In attempting to describe the blues, Rudi Blesh made several pertinent observations. According to Blesh, the blues are a complete, complex art form. They "do not happen by the caprice of chance; they are neither arbitrarily created, nor discovered ready-made; they originate and develop spontaneously yet inevitably out of the creative urge in man..."[10] He believed one who heard the blues simply as "barbarous, cruel, or lascivious" music, judged the music harshly and unfairly. Blues are neither the music of "poverty, degradation, and despairing vice," nor are they a "vital and compelling form of folk song."[11] Granted, the blues contain all these elements. They also contain everything from "drunken snores in the barrel-house [and] prostitutes' shrill laughter," to "shivering, ragged poverty singing for pennies on a cold and windy corner."[12] More than this, Blesh believed the blues reflected a lost race in search of a home.

In Gilbert Chase's view, just as black spirituals were the "manifestation of Afro-American folk music in choral singing, the blues are the manifestation of Afro-American folk music in solo singing."[13] When a black river roustabout sang,

> Gwine down de river befo' long,
> Gwine down de river befo' long,
> Gwine down de river befo' long,

Chase believed the roustabout was actually singing "the birth of the blues, with its three-line, twelve-bar pattern"[14]

Blues Characteristics. Blues is an aural music, with few absolute features. By design, it assumes style and shape during its performance, not unlike the improvisation of the Baroque era. The character of a particular piece usually reflects the personal response of the blues inventor to particular events and situations. According to Southern, a blues singer sings about his misery, and by doing so, attains a kind of peace of mind that makes life bearable again.

---

[10] Blesh, Rudi. *Shining Trumpets*, second edition, revised and enlarged. (New York: Alfred A. Knopf, 1958), p. 98.
[11] Blesh, pp. 98-100.
[12] Blesh, p. 100.
[13] Chase, p. 447.
[14] Chase, p. 448.

Most blues have an overriding feeling of sorrow, or "feeling blue." However, they also possess "an undertone of humor, not so much stressed as implied, that gives them a character utterly different from that of the ordinary sentimental song. Indeed, they are not sentimental at all, but combine realism and fantasy in a straightforward projection of mood and feeling."[15] They were compact, but within that compact form, the blues managed to convey a complete mood and situation.

As a rule, spirituals were the manifestation of Afro-American folk music in choral music, and the blues in solo singing. However, there were occasions on which a man or woman alone might sing a spiritual for his or her own comfort, sometimes even humming or chanting it without words. It is very likely the blues were born out of this very kind of lonesome singing, just for the consolation, pleasure, and beauty of the music. *Dark Was the Night* is just the kind of black song performed with guitar accompaniment and without words that blends the spiritual into the blues. Here we find the only real evidence we have of the link between spirituals and the blues.

Another example of this organic link can be found in *Lord, I Just Can't Keep from Crying*, written and sung by "Blind Willie" Johnson. Johnson used guitar accompaniment, and female "helpers" (women's voices as background). This piece is actually a spiritual, but its mood of sorrow is quite close in nature to the beginning of the blues. This particular piece is a unique blend of spiritual and blues in the blues repertory.

After "Blind Willie" Johnson came "Blind Lemon" Jefferson, who froze to death in Chicago in 1930. Then came Huddie Ledbetter, more familiarly known as "Leadbelly." After Leadbelly came William "Big Bill" Broonzy, Leroy Carr from Nashville, Tennessee (jazz historians believe Carr almost completely altered popular blues-singing style), McKinley Morganfield, better known as Muddy Waters, and Sam "Lightnin" Hopkins.

Gertrude "Ma" Rainey was the first of the great woman blues singers. She married at age fifteen, and traveled with her husband's minstrel troupe throughout the South. Then came the "empress of the blues," Bessie Smith. Discovered by a talent scout, she began recording for Columbia Records. She was an immediate success, especially among the black community. She recorded with stellar blues and jazz figures, such as Louis Armstrong, Buster Bailey, Fletcher Henderson, James P. Johnson, and many others. Ferdinand Morton, better known as "Jelly Roll," was a fine blues singer, as well as one of the great early jazz pianists and composers. Jimmie Yancy launched the style of piano blues known as "boogie-woogie." His wife, "Mama" Yancy, was a remarkable blues singer. Clarence "Pine-Top" Smith popularized the term "boogie-woogie." He, Meade Lux Lewis, and Albert Ammons continued this new blues style.

---

[15]Chase, p. 449.

Father of the Blues. Countless musicians, living and dead, helped to transform the blues from a folk song of one region and one group to a type of music recognized throughout the nation. However, one name stands out above the rest: W. C. Handy, the composer of the *St. Louis Blues.* William Christopher Handy was born in Florence, Alabama, November 16, 1873, the son of a Methodist preacher. His father was strongly opposed to Handy's musical inclinations. He once said, "Son, I'd rather follow you to the graveyard than to hear you had become a musician."[16] Apparently, musicians' reputations were little better then than they are now. Despite his father's objections, young Handy managed to acquire the rudiments of music, in school and out, "though," Chase remarked, "scarcely in an orthodox fashion."[17]

By 1909, Handy had moved to Memphis, and had become director of his own group, Handy's Band. The supporters of E. C. Crump, one of Memphis' mayoral candidates for that year, hired the group to help with Crump's campaign. Handy wrote a tune he hoped would not only get Crump elected, but would also be a hit tune for his band. The piece was originally called *Mister Crump,* but was published three years later as *Memphis Blues.* Handy wrote about this composition in his autobiography, claiming the melody of *Mister Crump* as his alone, but, "the twelve bar, three-line form of the first and last strains, with its three-chord basic harmonic structure (tonic, sub-dominant, dominant seventh) was that already used by Negro roustabouts, honky-tonk

W. C. HANDY.

[16]Chase, p. 455.
[17]Chase, p. 455.

piano players, wanderers and others of their underprivileged but undaunted class from Missouri to the Gulf...”[18] Handy was acknowledging that he did not originate the blues. He merely claimed to have developed and exploited the kind of black music with which he had become familiar in his youth.

Handy stood about halfway between the tradition of real black folk music and that of Tin Pan Alley. Although he claimed to have attempted to use all that was “characteristic of the Negro from Africa to Alabama,” he admitted he employed the “low forms” of Negro folk music with fear and trepidation.[19] His reasons for his misgivings point up a condition still in existence today. Handy feared that the “low forms” of Negro music were not considered respectable since they did not come from any sort of formal education in music. Therefore, they must not be of any significant value. Handy fell victim, as many have and continue to do, to the “genteel” tradition train of thought, “genteel” being merely another term for “cultivated.” This attitude toward folk music persists today, not in spite of, but in large part because of, the current attitudes and practices of our university-trained musicians.

The origin of the blues has been lost somewhere in obscurity. The genre probably developed concurrently with the rest of Afro-American folk song in the southern part of the nation. By 1870, it is likely the blues were widespread throughout the southeast, though they were not called “the blues” until much later. The blues were an effective means of transforming Afro-American “hot” music from the vocal to the instrumental idiom through the medium of piano blues and the jazz band. In addition, they were a form of folk song, and later a form of American popular music. The blues are therefore of far-reaching significance in the development of American music.

According to Gilbert Chase, the blues have colored almost every aspect of American music, from folk song to opera, from pop tune to symphony, from stomp to sonata, from spiritual to rock-and-roll, from hot jazz to western and to country music. During the 1960s, the blues became a kind of obsession with modern jazz musicians seeking their roots in the past. The blues reach both into the past and into the future. Chase believed their influence is not limited to American music; their appeal is universal and will endure as long as mankind continues to feel the profound emotions or the ribald moods that they so memorably and uniquely express.

Additional Readings

Blesh, Rudi and Harriett Janis. *They All Played Ragtime.* New York: Oak Publications, 1971.

---

[18]Chase, p. 456.
[19]Chase, p. 456.

Chase, Gilbert. *America's Music*. Rev. 2nd ed. New York: McGraw-Hill Book Company, 1966.

Hitchcock, H. Wiley. *Music in the United States: A Historical Introduction,* 2nd ed. Englewood Cliffs, N.J.: Prentice-Hall, Inc., 1974.

Marsh, J.B.T. *The Story of the Jubilee Singers*. Rev. ed. Boston: Houghton-Mifflin, 1880.

Sanjek, Russell. *American Popular Music and Its Business*. Vol. 1. The Beginnings to 1790. New York: Oxford University Press, 1988.

Southern, Eileen. *The Music of Black Americans: A History.* New York: W. W. Norton & Company, 1971.

van der Merwe, Peter. *Origins of the Popular Style*. New York: Clarendon Press-Oxford, 1989.

Selected Recordings

Blake, Eubie. *The Eighty Six Years of Eubie Blake.* Columbia C2S647

Jefferson, Blind Lemon. *The Immortal Blind Lemon Jefferson.* Milestone MLP 2004

Johnson, James P. *Father of the Stride Piano.* Columbia CL 1780

Joplin, Scott. *Complete Works for Piano.* RCA CRL5-1106

Ledbetter, Huddie. *The Legendary Leadbelly.* Olympic 7103

Rainey, Ma. *Ma Rainey.* Milestone M 47021

Chapter 4
The Growth
of Jazz

Roots

Paul Whiteman, the famous big-band leader of the early 1920s, and a classically trained violinist who had played with the Denver and San Francisco Symphony Orchestras, first encountered jazz in a San Francisco dive. He said that the brazen sounds he heard screeched and bellowed at him from a trick platform located in the middle of a smokey room filled with the smell of stale beer. He called the music crude and raucous, and even unmusical, but he was firmly convinced that it was infectious and uplifting. He admitted that the music hit him hard.

In the eyes of George Gershwin, jazz contributed an enduring value to America by expressing in music that which is essentially American. In 1917, the widely read *Literary Digest,* now defunct, reported that a strange new word, *jazz,* had gained widespread currency among the producers of popular music. The strange word was actually spelled "jass" when first publicly used to designate a dance band. In 1915, Lamb's Cafe in Chicago billed a dance band from New Orleans as "Brown's Dixieland Jass Band."

Jazz is rooted in the cultural, social, and racial environments of the South. No single city can boast that it was the birthplace of jazz. However, the first real strains of what was to become jazz can be found in New Orleans. The late 1700s witnessed the spawning of the Mardi Gras, the New Orleans carnival whose celebration grew to a length of six weeks during the 1800s. Mardi Gras parades begin on the Thursday before Shrove Tuesday, and for well over one hundred years, according to Blesh, these parades have been "symbolic processional tableaux, almost unbelievably elaborate."[1] Traditionally, they have included many floats and bands. It is within these parades, and the music played by the black bands who marched in them, that Rudi Blesh believed the real roots of jazz can be found. Blesh heard the music of those early bands floating through the air like "yellow sunlight." He believed the music of those bands, "with their incomparable elastic, skipping, syncopated rhythms,"[2] were the fountainhead of black jazz.

There has been much speculation concerning the origin of the word *jazz*. Some suggest its roots can be found in France or Africa. The most plausible suggestion seems to be that the word is a corruption of the Elizabethan, *jass*, which has survived in the vernacular of bawdyhouses. The true meaning of the word is unclear. Chase believed that the term carried some kind of sexual connotation. Of primary concern here is the music that emerged as jazz. It was the product of a wide variety of social conditions and ingredients typified by Storyville and its environment, although conditions and ingredients such as those of Storyville were not predominant in establishing the character of jazz.

Jazz Characteristics

Jazz is, in large part, a fusion of ragtime and the blues. In fact, the most salient feature of jazz is derived directly from the blues. Jazz is a vocally oriented music. In instrumental jazz, instruments replace the voice. Instrumental jazz musicians attempt to re-create singing style and blues notes by making their instruments produce sounds in imitation of vocal scooping, sliding, whining, growling, and falsetto effects. Blues performance emphasizes the individual. Jazz performance does the same. Jazz and blues performers are also instantaneous composers, shaping the music, by improvisation, into style and form. In jazz and the blues, there is a preexisting core of basic musical material. This material is usually short, and is used repeatedly. Traditional melodies or

[1] Blesh, Rudi. *Shining Trumpets*, second edition, revised and enlarged. (New York: Alfred A. Knopf, 1958), p. 154.
[2] Blesh, p. 154.

harmonies may serve as this basic material, but it is the improvisational skills of the performer that produces the music.

A jazz score represents a mere skeleton of what takes place during a performance. Each time the basic material appears, it is different, because the players improvise each repeated section. Like folk song, jazz is learned through oral tradition. Those who play jazz learn to do so by listening to it. Jazz also employs an ancient musical compositional device, antiphon. The use of antiphon in jazz implies the use of call and response, or question and answer, between two solo voices or instruments.

Jazz reflects ragtime influence through its emphasis on the use of syncopation, and the presence of the piano in the ensemble. Jazz instrumentation, the roles assigned to each instrument, and the musical texture, all reflect the influence of the brass band. For example, in the classic New Orleans band, melodic roles were assigned to the cornet, the clarinet, and the trombone. Typically, the cornet played lead; the clarinet, a countermelody to the lead; and the trombone, the lower voice of the three.

Early jazz was a synthesis of many different elements: the march/dance beat, the syncopations of ragtime, other syncopated dance rhythms of Afro-Caribbean origin. City blues exerted a particularly strong influence on the development of jazz. Such blues as sung by the classic female blues artists, such as Mamie Smith, Ma Rainey, Bessie Smith, and Ida Cox, tended to be strophic (the same music used repeatedly) in nature, with a characteristic pattern to the text of each repetition. The pattern also extended to the succession of the accompanying harmonies and to the overall musical form. Jazz musicians adopted the musical design of such blues and from that time, jazz, with or without text, meant that design. This design consists basically of a twelve-measure pattern divided into three four-measure phrases. Other lengths can be found, and elaborations of the basic harmonies are, as Hitchcock said, "legion!"

Jazz Pioneers

Charles Bolden. Charles "Buddy" Bolden, a barber who learned to play the cornet in his spare time, was the most colorful figure associated with the beginnings of jazz in New Orleans. In the 1890s, he formed a small band of five-to-seven pieces that became quite popular and was in demand for both dances and parades. His band instrumentation included cornet, clarinet, valve trombone, guitar, bass, and drums. Bolden's band included many of the pioneers of hot jazz. One was William "Bunk" Johnson, a cornet and trumpet player. Johnson was with Bolden from 1895 to 1899.

Bunk Johnson reminisced in his old age about Bolden's musical illiteracy. According to Johnson, Bolden could not read music at all. However, Johnson recalled that Bolden performed well as a lead player. Jazz historian Paul Eduard Miller disputed Johnson. According to Miller, judging from the overwhelming consensus of reports from old-time New Orleans musicians, in addition to his improvisational skills and technique, Bolden could indeed read music. When Bolden was at the height of his fame and success, he was called "King." In 1906, he began to suffer periods of mental derangement. One year later, he was committed to a hospital for the insane.

Freddie Keppard. Another cornet player, Freddie Keppard, inherited "King" Bolden's crown when Bolden became ill. Keppard's celebrated Olympia Band included such jazz greats as Louis "Big Eye" Nelson and Sidney Bechet on clarinet, Willie Santiago on guitar, Zue Robertson on trombone, and Joe Oliver on cornet. Others might also have been heir apparent to the Bolden throne; clarinetist T. V. Baquet and his famous Excelsior Band, with Alphonse Picou on clarinet, Manual Perez on cornet, and John Robichaux on drums. The Tuxedo Band of the Tuxedo Dance Hall was led by cornetist Oscar "Papa" Celestin. The band included Johnny Dodds on clarinet and his brother Warren "Baby" Dodds on drums.

Joseph "King" Oliver. The most prominent and influential of the early jazz pioneers was Joseph "King" Oliver, who moved to Chicago after World War I, where he remained for ten years. He was the first jazzman to make a permanent impact on Chicago.

"KING" OLIVER.

FROM LEFT TO RIGHT: JOHNNY DODDS, CLARINET; "BABY" DODDS, DRUMS; HONORÉ DUTREY, TROMBONE; LOUIS ARMSTRONG, TRUMPET; "KING" OLIVER, CORNET; LIL HARDIN, PIANO. JOHNNY ST. CYR, BANJO (CHICAGO, 1923).

History is vague concerning his place of birth. However, it is certain that he was in New Orleans by the time he was eight or ten years old. In 1899, he was playing cornet there in a children's brass band. By 1907, Oliver was playing with the Melrose, one of New Orleans' better brass bands. Like most black pop musicians of the time, Oliver played his instrument part time. He worked during the day as a butler. Sometime after 1915, he formed his own band, which played for Tulane University's white students and the black patrons of Pete Lala's Café and Café 25. Oliver came into contact with the best bandsmen in New Orleans. Some were already famous, some destined to become so in the future. All these men learned from one another. In 1918, bassist Bill Johnson asked Oliver to come to Chicago to play at the Royal Gardens Café. Oliver never returned to New Orleans.

At different times, some of the best sidemen in the business played with Oliver: Johnny Dodds (clarinet), Jimmie Noone (clarinet), Honoré Dutrey (trombone), Bill Johnson (bass), Warren "Baby" Dodds (drums), and Lil Hardin (piano). Oliver's Creole Jazz Band as a whole was the best of its kind and its time, and made a series of recordings during the early 1920s. The recordings he and the band made for the Gennet, Paramount, Columbia, and Vocalian labels exerted a deep influence on both black and white jazz bands across the nation. And jazz musicians, black and white, flocked to the cafés and halls on Chicago's

South Side, where Oliver played. They came to hear him play and to study his approach to style and technique.

Oliver had several young protégés, one of whom was a talented youngster by the name of Louis Armstrong. Oliver gave Armstrong an old trumpet and taught him how to play. The trumpet was Armstrong's first. Recordings made by the Creole Jazz Band during its early days in Chicago reflect the inventive genius of Louis Armstrong. He alone was responsible for the first significant advance in jazz style. Though Armstrong was to have a glorious and worldwide career in jazz and popular entertainment, he made his most original contributions to jazz in the 1920s.

In 1924, Oliver's bandleading career began to fail. Armstrong and some of his best sidemen began to leave him. Ill health prevented his playing for an extended period. Several times he made poor decisions: for example, refusing an opportunity to play at the new Cotton Club in New York. (The Cotton Club then offered the job to a young man whose name was Edward Kennedy 'Duke' Ellington. Ellington accepted the job and went on to become one of the all-time leading figures in jazz.) Oliver spent his remaining years in Savannah, in poverty and obscurity.

"Jelly Roll" Morton. Jazz historians consider Ferdinand "Jelly Roll" Morton the first true jazz composer. Morton was the first to write down his jazz arrangements in musical notation. He composed many of the pieces that

PICTURE COLLECTION, THE BRANCH LIBRARIES, THE NEW YORK PUBLIC LIBRARY

"JELLY ROLL" MORTON AND HIS RED HOT PEPPERS.

became standards in the jazz repertoire. His arrangement of his own *Jelly Roll Blues*, in 1915, was the first published jazz arrangement in history.

In 1926, Morton and his band, the Red Hot Peppers, made several recordings. Morton planned these sessions carefully, by either writing out the arrangements in advance, or discussing his ideas with each of his players so they would all know exactly what Morton wanted them to do. (Southern notes that the latter is called a "head" arrangement.) Authorities on all sides say these, and some of Morton's jazz-piano recordings, are among the finest examples available of true jazz.

However, by the 1930s, most jazz musicians considered Morton's style outdated. Like Oliver, his career declined during the last years of his life. His last hurrah, as it were, occurred in 1938, when Alan Lomax, then the curator of the Music Division of the Library of Congress, brought Morton to Washington to record his unique jazz style for the Archives of American Folksong.

Satchmo. Throughout most of his career, Daniel Louis Armstrong was called "Satchmo," a contraction of "Satchel Mouth." He came to Chicago in 1922 to play in King Oliver's Creole Jazz Band. By then, Satchmo was already an accomplished musician, and fully capable of assuming the duties of solo trumpet. His music career had begun in the streets of New Orleans, singing for pennies with other children. In 1914, local authorities sent him to the Colored Waif's Home just outside New Orleans for firing his stepfather's pistol in celebration of New Year's Eve. While there, he studied music with black musician and instructor Peter Davis. He learned to play several instruments, and moved from tambourine to lead cornet. Eventually, he became director of the home's brass band, a band often called upon to play for private picnics and join parades through the streets of New Orleans.

Armstrong's first music job was playing in a honky-tonk in the red-light district. His favorite occupation during his free time was going from one honky-tonk to another to listen to the blues played by the local musicians. He took Joe Oliver's place in Kid Ory's Band for a brief period during 1918. Also, for a short time during this period, he played with Fate Marable's Band on an excursion steamer, the Sydney, that sailed up and down the Mississippi. This period was particularly memorable for Armstrong because David Jones, a member of the Marable band, taught him to read music.

Storyville had closed down by the time Armstrong grew up, but he never forgot its music. In his autobiography, *Satchmo*, he wrote about hearing that music on every street corner. Armstrong considered it well worth the little salary he earned during that time to go into Storyville to listen. There was one musician in particular who, by Amrstrong's own admission, could keep him spellbound. That musician was trumpet player Joe Oliver, a man destined to play a major role in Armstrong's life and career.

Armstrong thought Joe Oliver's playing was the strongest and most creative, but Bunk Johnson's tone was the sweetest. Armstrong's playing reflected the best of the great horn players who preceded him, and were either his spiritual or his actual mentors. Armstrong was jazz's first great soloist. He was also one of jazz's most creative stars. His genius has remained untouched by the rise of commercialism and so many other popular styles. During his entire lifetime, Satchmo never went out of vogue. Both his trumpet playing and his singing invited many imitators.

Armstrong left Oliver in 1924 to join Fletcher Henderson's band in New York. He returned to Chicago in 1925 to play with a succession of bands, and make recordings with his own groups, the Hot Five and the Hot Seven. He gained international recognition and fame during these years.

As his fame grew, Armstrong's musical activities expanded to include appearances on television and in Hollywood movies, such as *Pennies from Heaven, The Glenn Miller Story, High Society, A Man Called Adam,* and many others. His first of many tours to Europe came in 1932, when he played the Palladium in London. Because of his work abroad, his worldwide acclaim, and his warm, personal touch in all that he did, he became known as America's "ambassador of good will."

In 1957, Edward R. Murrow produced a film, *Satchmo the Great,* documenting Armstrong's travels. A four-volume record set was released that same year, entitled *Satchmo, A Musical Biography.* It included narrations and some of his old recordings. His autobiography, *Satchmo: My Life in New Orleans,* was published in 1954.

Like all popular music, jazz was ever changing, even in the 1920s. During that year it began to take on new aspects. Bands and orchestras grew in size, and new instruments were added to the traditional voicing. Such large groups prohibited collective improvisation and head arrangements. Many of the younger black jazz musicians entering the field had received their musical training in a college or conservatory, rather than in the field, as had the pioneers. For many of these, entertainment music became a full-time profession that brought both financial rewards and social prestige.

New Orleans

Rudi Blesh reported that blacks had their own New Orleans street bands much earlier than originally thought. As support for his belief, he points to the 1881 funeral ceremonies for President Garfield, which included a huge procession filled, as usual, with bands. More than thirteen permanently organized black bands, representing fraternal and benevolent organizations, labor unions of longshoremen, teamsters, and cotton yardmen, took part in the ceremonies. At least one of the participating black bands was founded around 1871. There is reason to believe the Perseverance Benevolent Society, an organization that supported one of the permanent bands, was founded even earlier. Its building, constructed in 1853, stands on North Villeres Street, near Annette Street.

Many people unquestioningly believe jazz originated in Storyville, the red-light district of New Orleans. The district was named after the alderman who sponsored the ordinance to set aside this section of the city for organized vice. The brothels of Storyville, many marked by garish splendor, flourished from 1887 to 1917, a period that coincided with the rise of jazz. Then, in 1917, pressure from the War and Navy Departments brought about the demise of Storyville. During its heyday, many musicians found work in its brothels, bars, and cheap cafés, where there was plenty of cash, prejudices were rare, and the demand for entertainment, never ending.

Many factors, common to broad areas of the South, contributed to the conception and birth of jazz: American folk music containing remnants of African music, the lively rhythms of the camp-meeting gospel songs and spirituals, the blues inflections and form, the improvised "washboard" bands, the marching brass bands that played for funerals, parades, and picnics. The Midwest and the Southwest produced many early ragtime musicians who exerted a strong influence on the beginnings of jazz. However, many still refer to New Orleans as the cradle and nursery of jazz. It was there, more than any other place, where a combination of geographic, economic, demographic, and social factors created a cultural climate favorable to the emergence of jazz.

Chicago

Around the end of the 1800s, jazz began spreading to other centers. The great packet days of the riverboats were over. Those boats that survived were converted into the famous showboats that plied the Mississippi and its major tributaries during the first decades of the twentieth century: the Capitol, the Syndey, the St. Paul. These excursion steamers and others carried passengers up the river to Memphis, St. Louis, Cairo, Davenport, and even St. Paul. Some made their way east, following the Ohio to Pittsburgh. Some followed the Missouri northwest to Kansas City and Omaha. And the onboard entertainment in large part consisted of jazz, furnished at times by such legends as Fate Marable, Louis Armstrong, Baby Dodds, "Pop" Foster, and Johnny St. Cyr.

More than high pay, the need for variety and travel helped to fill the band rosters of these famous old paddle wheelers. In New Orleans, bands could acquire immediate fame and fortune from a black audience well-acquainted with jazz. But the pleasure boats seldom spent much significant time in any city. Consequently, the bands and their music did not leave a lasting impression on the cities they visited. The music was too transient, its visits always too short, to make any deep or lasting impression on these northern cities. Vaudeville also failed to leave a lasting impression on public consciousness, though the early vaudeville tours of the Original Creole Band carried jazz across the nation from California to New York from about 1912 to 1917. It was dancing, not theater appearances, that finally attracted the ears of the public on a national scale and led to the wide acceptance of jazz.

Jazz was not taken seriously in the casual appearances it made outside New Orleans on the riverboats and in vaudeville. However, when visitors heard it in its native setting, jazz somehow sounded different. As a consequence, jazz, and the magnetism of the city, left permanent impressions on many people. In 1914, Frisco, a cigar-chewing vaudevillian of the day, heard a white band, the Dixieland Players, at the Tom Brown Club in New Orleans. According to Blesh, Frisco was profoundly impressed, at least by the entertainment possibilities he perceived. Frisco carried news of this new music to Chicago, and the Dixieland band soon began receiving offers from clubs there. In June, 1915, the band accepted an engagement at Lamb's Café. The band included Ray Lopez on cornet, Tom Brown on trombone, Gus Mueller on clarinet, Arnold Loyocano on bass and piano, and William Lambert on drums. The spread of jazz had begun, even before the closing of Storyville.

THE ORIGINAL DIXIELAND JAZZ BAND AT HAMMERSMITH, LONDON. FROM LEFT TO RIGHT: BILLY JONES, LARRY SHIELDS, NICK LA ROCCA, EMILE CHRISTIAN, TONY SPARGO.

In Chicago, jazz attained the same sensational aspects it had acquired in New Orleans, though after a less-than-spectacular beginning. Sensation and success both came in a rather peculiar manner, around which a legend has grown. The Dixieland Players entered the Chicago scene without proper clearance from the local union. In retaliation for such a sin, the union spread the rumor this was "jass," or "whorehouse music." Instead of acting to suppress the band's success, the story acted as a magnet. The public flocked to hear them. The band was, of course, delighted. A new sign appeared on the Lamb's Café billboard: "Added Attraction–Brown's Dixieland Jass Band, Direct from New Orleans, Best Dance Music in Chicago."

Black jazz did not come to Chicago in force until about two years after the arrival of the Brown band. Then, Joseph "King" Oliver arrived in Chicago in 1918, and until about 1924, he dominated black jazz there. His Chicago band stood for classic jazz in one of its purest manifestations. In 1920, the Dreamland offered Oliver a permanent and exclusive contract. Oliver accepted and renamed the band there the "Creole Jazz Band." As has already been mentioned, it became the finest band of its day. In that same year, the New Orleans Rhythm Kings came to Chicago. After World War I, they were perhaps the most important Dixieland band in Chicago They were led by the New Orleans trumpet player, Paul Mares.

New York and Dixieland

Dixieland music is usually described as jazz played by white musicians in a manner more or less approximating that of early New Orleans Negro jazz. George V. Laine, a white musician from New Orleans, is credited with having started the trend that became Dixieland. Laine, commonly called Jack or Papa, formed his first band in 1888, and began to play rags by composers such as Scott Joplin. Jack Laine's Ragtime Band consisted of cornet, trombone, guitar, bass, and drums (played by Laine).

The Chicago-based Original Dixieland Jazz Band, an all-black New Orleans group, introduced jazz to Chicago. Therefore, when white musicians, in Chicago and in New York, began playing their interpretations of the new music, it was only natural for them to call what they were playing "Dixieland jazz." Since white musicians had access to a far larger audience than black groups did, a false emphasis on white jazz arose. Blesh noted that this group of white musicians played only a very poor imitation of real jazz. According to Blesh, they had either failed to notice the music of the Original Creole Band, or considered it unacceptable to the white audiences for whom they played.

This imitative school has been called "New York Dixieland." It centered around several bands, each of which recorded under several names. Probably the best-known of these groups was the Original Memphis Five. At various times, this band also called itself the Cotton Pickers, Ladd's Black Aces, and several other names. The group began recording New York Dixieland in 1922, and continued to record, on several labels and with numerous personnel changes, through 1932. Band personnel normally included Phil Napoleon on trumpet, Miff Mole and Vincent Grande on trombones, Jimmy Lytell on clarinet, Frank Signorelli on piano, and Jack Roth on drums.

The Memphis Five played much of their music in a sweet and sentimental style, reflecting the European influence on white American musicians, an influence not seen in the hot style of black jazzmen. Their kind of quasi hot music lasted until about 1926. By 1924, Memphis Five recordings had begun to reflect the extent of the intrusion of the European element into jazz. Formally harmonized and completely written out arrangements of jazz began to appear.

Though he conceded the usefulness of certain elements of European style in larger ensembles, Blesh believed such adoptions were not needed in small jazz groups. Nonetheless, the European influence could be heard routinely in the music of small, all-white jazz bands, and for Blesh, the moment this occurred, the music acquired a sweeter, less aggressive, sound. It lost that basic quality of hot music, barely under control, the one element essential to authentic jazz. He saw this practice as natural to white jazz musicians. The result, he said, was just lukewarm.

Bix Beiderbecke

Leon Bismark "Bix" Beiderbecke was one of the most important and influential jazz musicians of the age. David Ewen called him one of jazz's true aristocrats. Bix was soft-spoken and cultured. He was nearly as familiar with the music of Debussy and Stravinsky as he was with that of his jazz idols. He played very much in a classical style. His playing was always disciplined and under complete control. Bix was born in 1903 in Davenport, Iowa. When he was fourteen, he taught himself to play the cornet. During his high school years, Bix played with several jazz bands. After spending a year at Lake Forest Military Academy just outside Chicago, he took his first full-time professional assignment playing with a band on a Lake Michigan excursion boat.

In 1923, Bix joined the Wolverines, one of the first major jazz ensembles to come up in the Chicago tradition. Bix became the band's heart and soul. He had studied the music and styles of such black greats as King Oliver, Louis Armstrong, and Jimmie Noone, and, in turn, he influenced other players, black and white. According to Leonard Feather, Beiderbecke was probably the first white musician in jazz history to be admired and imitated by black jazz musicians.

BIX BEIDERBECKE.

PICTURE COLLECTION, THE BRANCH LIBRARIES,
THE NEW YORK PUBLIC LIBRARY

Bix and the Wolverines came to New York in the fall of 1924. The week they arrived, Louis Armstrong and Fletcher Henderson opened at New York's Roseland Ballroom. Beiderbecke created as much sensation among white musicians as Armstrong did among the black groups. The Wolverines' recordings were already beginning to influence other musicians. Although the rhythm section may have been a bit weak, a bit unconvincing, it was nonetheless a complete band that only played jazz. By this time, the New York Memphis Five were playing heavily arranged dance music, and were regarded as a novelty group. Such musicians as Trumbauer, Artie Schutt, the Dorseys, and Nichols were all featured soloists in sweet bands. On the fast songs they customarily played a total of about sixteen measures as solo. The Wolverines played nothing but jazz, which consisted almost entirely of solos. Even with its obvious weaknesses, the band was a revelation to New Yorkers. Though just beyond his twenty-first birthday, Beiderbecke was rapidly becoming a jazz legend.

There is considerable confusion surrounding the date Beiderbecke left the Wolverines and his reasons for leaving. He did remain in New York for a time after his separation from the group; then he returned to the Midwest. He enrolled in the University of Iowa, hoping to study music. Like so many young, talented jazz musicians of his day, he was self-taught and painfully aware of his musical deficiencies. He could barely read music. He had learned what little he knew by listening to the early recordings of the Original Dixieland Jazz Band. The University of Iowa would not let Bix take the courses he wanted. As a result, he withdrew and took a job with Charlie Strait's Orchestra in Chicago.

Most white musicians performing jazz in New York during that period tended to view jazz as merely a musical novelty to be used strictly for momentary entertainment. Consequently, the music they played lacked the spontaneity and creative excitement of black jazz artists. Beiderbecke's music exuded an exuberance atypical of any other white jazz musician of that period. Charters and Kunstadt believed Beiderbecke's music contained an emotional intensity equal to that of jazz's most creative musicians.

New York had other premiere Dixieland jazz bands. One, in particular, is noteworthy because of the white jazz musicians who occasionally played with it. The Five Pennies Band was formed by Ernest Loring "Red" Nichols and ostensibly consisted of five members. However, in most sessions the group actually consisted of six to ten players, including some of the most notable white jazzmen of that era: Jimmy Dorsey (clarinet and alto sax), Benny Goodman (clarinet), Eddie Lang (guitar), Miff Mole (trombone), and Joe Venuti (violin).

Bebop

By the early '40s, jazz had arrived at an explosive state. Gifted jazz musicians with original ideas were becoming restless under the dominance of big-band swing, and were eagerly searching for something new. Then, in early August, 1942, because of a dispute with the licensing agencies, the musicians' union imposed a nationwide ban on recording. The ban lasted until the fall of 1943, and effectively "put a lid" on the explosion brewing with the jazzmen, who continued to develop their new ideas. However, these developments did not immediately reach the large sector of the public, who got their jazz primarily from recordings. According to Chase, when the union lifted the recording ban, neither the public nor the critics were prepared for the new jazz sound that struck them almost like a blow. Most of the critics were hostile toward the new music.

This new jazz, called *bebop* or simply, *bop,* originated at Minton's Play House, an upper Manhattan nightclub. Around 1940, a group of progressive jazz musicians started gathering at Minton's to experiment with new approaches to jazz rhythm, harmony, and melody. Jazz legends Charlie "Bird" Parker, and John Birks "Dizzy" Gillespie were the new style's leading exponents. Parker was destined to become the most influential figure in modern jazz, an influence not restricted to his own instrument, the alto saxophone, but an influence that permeated all areas and all media of jazz expression, including composition and arranging. Gilbert Chase called him a creative genius. However, drugs and addiction created excessive instability in his life, and eventually destroyed him. He and Gillespie met in New York in 1939, and afterward were closely associated in the rise of the new jazz.

In the early '40s, Gillespie and Parker both played in a band led by Earl "Fatha" Hines. Had the union not imposed the 1942 ban, Hines probably would have made the first bebop recordings with his band. However, the relatively conservative Coleman Hawkins assembled a band in February, 1944, that made the first recordings of bebop. Band personnel included Dizzy Gillespie, and the man most responsible for organizing the session, Albert "Budd" Johnson on tenor sax. Johnson was a key man in the transition from swing to bop through the music he wrote and arranged for the large bands of Earl Hines, Woody Herman, Billy Eckstine, and Dizzy Gillespie.

The art of drumming was also important in the transition from swing to bop. Jo Jones, Kenny Clarke, and Max Roach pioneered the new drum style. They abandoned the consistent use of the old sock cymbal, and emphasized, instead, the use of the top cymbal in a light, subtle manner. With the steady rhythm now assigned to the top cymbal, the bass drum could be used for special, and often unexpected, punctuations. This new technique allowed the drummer to produce a legato sound that contained greater variety and subtlety.

Another characteristic feature of bop was the increasing importance of the string bass. This characteristic has made a significant impact on modern jazz. Jazzman Jimmy Blanton originated its use in this medium. His unprecedented skill, boldness, and inventiveness made him the first true master of the string bass in modern jazz.

Charlie Parker and Dizzy Gillespie firmly established the vogue of the new music for the public through the recordings they made with a quintet in 1945. By this time, New York's 52nd Street had become the center for the progressive movement. Musically, it was the most important street in America. It was called "the street of swing," and in the '40s, clubs located there, such as the Famous Door, Jimmy Ryan's, Downbeat, Three Deuces, the Yacht Club, and Kelly's Stables, housed the best jazz musicians in the world.

Post-Forties Jazz

Since its inception, the elements of jazz have remained fluid. Part of the genre's charm is its ever-changing timbre, brought about by dropping and adding instruments, and bits and pieces of musical elements such as rhythm, melody, and harmony. In the beginning, jazz ensembles obviously did not include the piano since the early bands either rode or marched when they played. During the days of early New Orleans jazz, "standard" ensembles included string bass, guitar, clarinet, trumpet, trombone, and drums. During the swing era, jazz adopted the standard swing-band rhythm-section instrumentation: piano, guitar, bass, and drums. During the bop era, the guitar was abandoned as a regular ensemble instrument, and used only occasionally for solo work. By 1952, use of the piano in jazz ensembles had become standard practice.

Jazz Becomes Cool. Gerry Mulligan, a highly innovative and successful 1950s jazz artist, did not include a piano in his quartet. He noted that the concept of a jazz band without a piano was not new, and argued that reducing an instrument with such extraordinary capabilities to accompaniment for the solo horn was unthinkable. Mulligan considered the string bass a foundation upon which solos could be built. He felt that the bass provided the main thread around which the two horns could weave their contrapuntal interplay. This approach to harmonic fill was not new. J. S. Bach had led the way into this arena by clearly demonstrating with his inventions that two voices placed against a bass line are quite capable of implying chords or chord series.

This change in instrumentation, combined with following the Bach practice of implied harmony, led to what Joe Goldberg, in his book, *Jazz Masters of the Fifties,* called "the era of cool jazz." Mulligan and his quartet, along with Miles Davis, Gil Evans, and John Lewis, all made significant contributions to this genre. There were critics who believed this kind of jazz was less substantive than its predecessors. They called it less sophisticated and compromising music. They believed its followers could listen to it at a superficial level without becoming unduly involved. Other critics readily conceded that cool jazz was easy to comprehend, but not because its composers wrote silly, simple, superficial music. They saw cool jazz as a bold new step, calling for a reexamination of form, construction, and meter. Cool jazz employed many of the formal elements of European concert music. It often drew hearty criticism for this practice. However, the finest examples of the cool-movement music are those that reflect most clearly the European influence.

Despite many weaknesses inherent in cool jazz, the influence it has had on later jazz developments cannot be disregarded. In particular, two of the most important influences on jazz of the '50s and '60s sprang directly from cool jazz: Miles Davis and the Modern Jazz Quartet. Miles Davis is one of jazz's most intriguing and interesting figures. Though in the view of many, he possessed only a modicum of real talent, his intelligence and strong personality helped make him one of the major figures in jazz. Other than John Coltrane and Charlie Parker, no musician has exerted more influence on the development of jazz than Davis.

Miles Davis. Davis was born in Alton, Illinois, in 1926. Shortly after his birth, his family moved to St. Louis. Davis played trumpet in his high school band, and studied privately. By age sixteen, he was playing with a local jazz band. When Billy Eckstine and his band came through St. Louis in 1944, Davis asked Eckstine for permission to sit in with his band. Eckstine gave his permission, though in later years he commented that at the time, Davis sounded awful.

Davis graduated from high school in 1945. He wanted to go to New York to become a musician. His parents wanted him to attend college. A compromise was reached. Davis agreed to attend Juilliard, in New York City. However, as soon as he arrived in New York, he sought out Charlie Parker and moved in with him. James Lincoln Collier, in his book, *The Making of Jazz,* observed that no one seems to know exactly how Miles accomplished this stunt. At that time, Parker was one of the leading figures in jazz, and Davis was just a kid with a dream, who played trumpet poorly.

Parker began working with Davis, and gradually Davis improved. Parker allowed Davis to play on a few of his early bop recordings. Then, in 1947, Parker hired Davis to play trumpet in the Parker group. Over the next two years, Davis developed into a competent and reliable musician. In 1949, he broke with Parker. He was still not an accomplished lead player, but he was learning.

Davis now began performing with Gerry Mulligan, Gil Evans, and Ramsey Lewis. These men and Miles played key roles in the advent of cool jazz. As he worked in this and other jazz genres, Davis' lead abilities grew. His early recordings of cool music with Mulligan, Evans, and Lewis helped establish his reputation in the profession.

The public displayed little interest in cool-music recordings. However, the record companies began to see a potential jazz star in Davis. He was beginning to develop his own very personal style. He used short, clipped phrases, dropping out of the ensemble for long phrases, or holding single notes over two or more measures at a time. His sound was soft and rounded. He confined his playing to the trumpet's middle registers. He employed a small microphone inside the bell of his instrument, and often played his horn muted. Davis sketched in sound, rather than painting completed pictures. The effect was stunning.

In 1968, Davis began experimenting with rock. In 1969, he recorded *In a Silent Way.* This recording was Miles' response to the urging of Clive Davis, president of Columbia Records, to deal directly with the challenge of rock music. *In a Silent Way* employed one of rock's primary tools, electronic instruments, and included John McLaughlin, a guitarist more associated with rock than with jazz. The record was only moderately successful. Miles' next attempt at a rock crossover was more successful. *Bitches Brew* sold a half-million copies during its first year, and Miles became the star of a new genre, jazz-rock, or, as it has been called more recently, *fusion music*. By the late 1950s, cool jazz as a force in music was essentially dead. But during its brief reign, it had created a larger jazz audience than had ever before existed.

By 1956, Elvis Presley and rock had virtually taken over the entire field of pop music. Though jazz continued, in some circles unabated, it lost some of the audience cool music had gained. Its primary proponents were jazz artists, such as the timeless Miles Davis, Ornette Coleman, John Coltrane, Art Tatum, Thelonius Monk, Charles Lloyd, and during the mid-'80s, Wynton Marsalis. Since the mid-'70s, few pure jazz artists have emerged. The trend toward fusion, begun in the early '70s, has continued. Current instrumental pop music contains elements of many different musical genres: rock, rhythm-and-blues, rag, soul, easy listening, and jazz. However, pure jazz still exists and is still being performed for a small, but dedicated, audience.

Additional Readings

Blesh, Rudi. *Shining Trumpets: A History of Jazz*. New York: Alfred A. Knopf, Inc., 1946 (Rev. ed., 1958; Rev. 2nd. ed., 1975, Da Capo).

Charters, Samuel B. *Jazz: New Orleans 1885-1957*. New York: Walter C. Allen, 1958.

Charters, Samuel B., and Leonard Kunstadt. *Jazz: A History of the New York Scene*. New York: Doubleday & Company, 1962.

Coker, Jerry. *The Jazz Idiom*. Englewood Cliffs, N.J.: Prentice-Hall, Inc., 1975.

Goldberg, Joe. *Jazz Masters of the Fifties*. New York: The Macmillan Company, 1965 (reprinted by Da Capo, 1980).

Hadlock, Richard. *Jazz Masters of the Twenties*. New York: The Macmillan Company, 1965 (reprinted by Da Capo, 1986).

Morgan, Alun, and Raymond Horricks. *Modern Jazz: A Survey of Developments Since 1939*. London: V. Golanoz, 1957.

Schuller, Gunther. *Early Jazz: Its Roots and Early Development*. Vol. 1. Oxford University Press, 1968.

Williams, Martin. *Jazz Masters in Transition 1957-1969*. New York: The Macmillan Company, 1970 (reprinted by Da Capo, 1980).

Selected Recordings

Armstrong, Louis. *Louis Armstrong with Fletcher Henderson*. BYG 529086
——— . *Young Louis Armstrong*. Riverside RLP 12-101

Beiderbecke, Bix. *Bix Beiderbecke and the Wolverines*. La Storia Del Jazz SM 3087

Davis, Miles. *Birth of the Cool.* Capitol DT 1974

Gillespie, Dizzy. *The Greatest of Dizzy Gillespie.* RCA LPV-530

Keppard, Freddie. *Freddie Keppard.* Herwin 101.

Morton, Jelly Roll. *The Immortal Jelly Roll Morton.* Milestone MLP 2003

Mulligan, Gerry. *Gerry Mulligan, Tentette.* Capitol M-11029

Oliver, Joe. *The Immortal King Oliver.* Milestone MLP-2006

Parker, Charlie. *First Recordings!* Onyx 221

Chapter 5
The Swing
Era

Swing Characteristics

For years, the aspect of rhythm called *swing* has defied definition, particularly when used in connection with jazz. According to Gunther Schuller, noted composer and Yale University music professor, any definition of "swing" has little to do with swing itself, just as jazz notation has little to do with jazz as it is performed. As a rule, swing suggests an even, steady pulse. More specifically, swing indicates the accurate timing of a note in its proper place. However, even if this explanation completely encompassed swing, most of the music we call *classical* could be said to swing. When swing in jazz is analyzed, two characteristics surface that ordinarily do not appear in classical music: "(1) a specific type of accentuation and inflection with which notes are played or sung, and (2) the continuity—the forward-propelling directionality—with which individual notes are linked together."[1] These two qualities are present in all great jazz, but not necessarily in classical music.

The swing era was unique in the history of popular music. It was the first such period in the United States to develop its own language and style of dress. Hep talk was its slang. The *haute couture* of the day was the zoot suit with its wide lapels and eighteen-inch knees in the trousers, and its dance forms included the Suzie-Q, the Lindy Hop, the jitterbug, and trucking. James Lincoln Collier discussed these swing-era characteristics in detail because they were significant for the art form out of which they grew. The characteristics were evidence of a large, well-developed, dedicated, undiscriminating audience. Collier believed the 1960s bore a striking resemblance to the swing era because it displayed many of the same characteristics.

Swing, which blossomed in the early-to-mid-1920s, was characterized by a strong, even 4/4 beat ("solid" was a favorite adjective of the period). This was in opposition to the tendency of earlier jazz to confine itself to 2/2 meter. Swing music is most closely associated with the Kansas City style of jazz, as played by the bands of Bennie Moten and his successor, William "Count" Basie. Along with Duke Ellington's Band, Basie's was probably the most influential of all in establishing the swing style. Their styles were diffused nationally by the bands of white leaders such as Benny Goodman, Tommy Dorsey, Artie Shaw, and Glenn Miller. This diffusion occurred primarily because discriminatory practices made it nearly impossible for the black bands to get the same degree of exposure to the national audience.

Virtuosos, stars who improvised brilliantly over the background riffs of the big bands' "sidemen," grew up out of the swing style. Any star system normally contains misplaced values, and these were evident in the development of swing. The star players clearly attempted to play as high and fast as possible. As in earlier days, their virtuosity was often mistaken for great art. In fact, this kind of virtuosity has somehow mutated into one of the artistic trademarks of great jazz and great jazz performers.

With such music, and performers to play it, jazz soon attained transcontinental popularity, a popularity bred on radio stations, in recording studios, and on stages of movie houses (where swing bands appeared increasingly in person). As a result of all this popularity and exposure, jazz began to be more than just a functional music for dancing or drinking. It became a concert music as well. In 1938, Benny Goodman's Band appeared in concert at Carnegie Hall. Since that time, jazz as concert music has become commonplace. The balance between its use as utilitarian music and as a new kind of art music has swung increasingly toward the latter.

---

[1]Schuller, Gunther. *Early Jazz: Its Roots and Musical Development,* vol. 1. (New York: Oxford University Press, 1968), p. 6.

Big–Band Beginnings

Some bands and orchestras in New Orleans were probably playing jazz, as it is known today, before the closing of Storyville. However, larger dance and brass bands did not become popular until after 1920. Fletcher Henderson, an Atlanta University graduate in chemistry and mathematics, formed what jazz historians consider the nation's first "big band" of jazz musicians. He and his sideman-arranger, Don Redman, who got his training at the Boston Conservatory of Music and the Detroit Conservatory of Music, are credited with having started the big-band movement in New York, in 1923.

Fletcher Henderson. James Fletcher Henderson came to New York to do postgraduate work, not to play jazz. To supplement his income, he took a part-time piano-playing job with W. C. Handy, but this soon led to a full professional commitment to music. By 1923, he had his own jazz band, which for many years played at the Roseland dance hall. The group was large, and included many of the best sidemen in the business—Louis Armstrong on trumpet and Coleman Hawkins on tenor sax, for example. According to Leonard Feather, this group is historically important because it was the first of the large bands to gain a wide reputation by playing jazz.

During this period, Feather noted, most dance bands concentrated on the commercial success brought about by playing current pop songs in a conventional manner. Commercialism was crowding jazz out. Eddie Condon complained that jazz musicians could play jazz only in their rooms, and just for themselves. It was through the talents and skills of such bandleaders and arrangers as Fletcher Henderson and Duke Ellington that jazz was incorporated into the large-band framework.

Henderson's band employed classic jazz instrumentation except for the addition of alto and tenor saxophones and a tuba. Obviously, the size of the group prohibited improvisation in the New Orleans style. Both Henderson and his sideman, Don Redman, wrote arrangements for the band, alternating solo and ensemble sections, thus allowing for solo improvisation. Not all the arrangements were written. The group often used "head arrangements." Occasionally, there were even sectional improvisations. From 1924 to 1936, Henderson's band often played for white dances at the Roseland. The band led the way for future big bands, black and white, by creating a style that was original.

Henderson wrote arrangements for his own band, and for others. Some of his finest and most popular arrangements were written for Benny Goodman, including *When Buddha Smiles, King Porter Stomp, Blue Skies,* and *Down South Camp Meeting.*

In the '20s and '30s, New York was a hotbed of jazz activity. In essence, it became the new capital of jazz. Several black big bands appeared during these years, led by men such as Bennie Carter, William "Chick" Webb, Jimmie Lunceford, Andy Kirk, Erskine Hawkins, Cab Calloway, Lucky Millinder, Luis Russell, William "Count" Basie, and Duke Ellington. Clarence Love's Orchestra was popular in the Midwest, particularly in Omaha. Others across the nation included Bennie Moten in Kansas City, George Morrison in Denver, Les Hite in Los Angeles, and Erskine Tate and Earl "Fatha" Hines in Chicago.

Bennie Carter. Bennie Carter, a native New Yorker, could play several instruments, including clarinet and trumpet, but became best known for his prowess on the alto saxophone. In 1933, he formed his own big band. After that, he performed with various groups in France, England, California, and New York. Carter wrote arrangements for Fletcher Henderson and Benny Goodman, as well as for his own recording groups.

Chick Webb. Among the first to play at the new Savoy Ballroom in Harlem, "the home of happy feet," was Chick Webb. He presided over the birth of such dances as the lindy hop, and introduced his singing protégée, Ella Fitzgerald, to the entertainment world. During this period, the Savoy was one of the most coveted music engagements in Harlem, and over time, most of the country's top swing bands performed there. Nonetheless, during the '30s, the Savoy was identified with one band, Chick Webb and the Chicks. Though the Savoy hosted such premier bandleaders as Benny Goodman, Fletcher Henderson, Duke Ellington, and Count Basie, it was Little Chick who owned the hearts of the Savoy audience.

Webb was the first drummer to attract a large jazz audience and his style influenced most of the jazz drummers who followed. As a soloist he was exciting, but as an ensemble drummer he was sensational. His strong, steady bass-drum beat drove the band, accenting the rhythm with every part of his drum set. Audiences held Webb in high regard, and he returned their admiration with warmth and affection.

One evening in 1934, Webb dropped by the Apollo Theater, and heard a sixteen-year-old named Ella Fitzgerald make her first public appearance. Though Ella did not fare well with the Apollo audience, Chick liked her voice, and asked the manager about her. He discovered that Ella was an orphan who grew up in the Riverdale Orphanage. Chick hired her, bought her new clothes, and coached her for several months. When he introduced her at the Savoy, she was an immediate success. Ella, and her voice and style, gained even greater popularity for the band. They soon began a series of nationwide tours, and their record sales soared.

Unfortunately for Webb, success carried with it new demands. Chick, frail and not in good health, soon became ill. He was hospitalized in Baltimore in 1939, and underwent surgery for a liver problem. The operation proved too much for him, and on June 16, he died.

Duke Ellington

Edward Kennedy "Duke" Ellington, born April 29, 1899, in Washington, D.C., is the only jazz musician to become a public figure as an artist. Other jazz musicians, such as Louis Armstrong and Dizzy Gillespie, gained national and even international prominence as pop musicians. Ellington, however, is considered by most, even those who know little about music, a genuine artist. He was nominated for a Pulitzer Prize in composition. He celebrated his seventieth birthday at the White House. Collier believed this kind of attention came to Ellington partly because he was a composer, and composing is something artists do, but also because of the kind of man he was.

Ellington acquired his nickname as a youth because of his natty manner of dress. Like many American boys of his time, his mother forced him to study the piano, something he did at first with extreme reluctance. He was more interested in painting. However, as he grew into adolescence, he began to realize there were certain social advantages to playing the piano, and one could also make money at it. He began taking his piano studies more seriously. In addition to his private lessons, he took a music course at school. He also began hanging around poolrooms and bars, where adults played the piano. Ragtime was at its height. He heard rags and popular melodies played with raggy inflections. Jazz had not yet escaped the boundaries of New Orleans. Consequently, he knew almost nothing about it.

Ellington's Early Years. Ellington graduated from high school in 1919, and received a scholarship offer in art from the NAACP. Rather than accepting the scholarship, he chose music as a profession, and began working seriously in and around Washington. He formed his own band, took out an ad larger than any other orchestra's, and soon was able to devote his time completely to music, instead of painting signs part time. His bands, though they included some of the men who were to be with him for years, still were not jazz or swing bands. They were merely commercial bands playing pop tunes and rags for dancing and drinking audiences.

During the winter of 1922, Wilbur Sweatman and his stage band came through Washington. Ellington and two of his band members, Otto Hardwick and Sonny Greer, joined Sweatman and moved with his band to New York. After completing its New York engagement, Sweatman and his band left the city. Ellington and his two friends decided to remain, hoping to find work with another band. They were unable to do so, though Duke did meet several New York musicians, including pianists James P. Johnson, Fats Waller, and Willie "the Lion" Smith. They returned home, and spent several days stuffing themselves on the good cooking of Duke's mother.

Shortly after returning to Washington, they received a call from Elmer Snowden, a young banjo player from Baltimore. Snowden asked the three to join his band, the Washington Black Sox Orchestra, for a summer engagement in Atlantic City. Snowden spent the entire summer attempting to secure the band a New York job, and finally got them into the Hollywood Cabaret, a newly opened basement club. The band opened the first week of September, 1923, with a six-month contract. On November 23, the *New York Clipper* ran a short article on the group. The review was excellent, praising each member of the band. Sometime during this engagement, the band acquired a new name, the "Washingtonians," and added cornet player Bud Miley and trombonist Charlie Irvis to its roster.

Ellington's First Band.

At the end of the band's engagement, the Hollywood announced it had renewed the band's contract for another six months. Snowden and Ellington had not been on the best of terms for several weeks because they were both natural leaders. Snowden left the group to accept an offer to lead another band. This left the Washingtonians without a leader. Somehow, Ellington gradually assumed the directorship of the group. There was no apparent reason for his assumption of the role. Any of the band members were as qualified as he was. Ellington was then just an apprentice musician. His performance on piano was barely adequate, and his compositional skills were still in the developmental stage. According to James Lincoln Collier, Ellington's emergence as leader required extensive diplomatic maneuvers on his part. At first, the majority of the arrangements played by the band were worked out and memorized in rehearsal. During these years, Ellington's leadership probably amounted to little more than setting tempos and making announcements. Members of the band were proud of the roles they played in developing the music. They felt the band belonged to them. However, as time passed, the band became more and more the exclusive property of Ellington.

In 1925, the Hollywood Club closed for remodeling, and the Washingtonians accepted an engagement in Haverhill, Massachusetts. When they returned to New York, the Hollywood had been renamed the Club Kentucky, and Ellington's band was advertised as probably the hottest band this side of the equator. The band, apparently believing their own publicity, left the Kentucky sometime during October or November, and accepted a job at Harlem's new Cameo Club. Unfortunately, they failed to live up to their publicity. In the eyes of the management, they were ill-suited to the Cameo. They were dismissed after just one night. They found some stage work in a revue with Ethel Waters, but several weeks passed before they could return to the Kentucky.

During these early New York years, the band made its first recording, *I'm Gonna Hang around My Sugar*, with *Trombone Blues* on the flip side. Sounding like a unit of the California Ramblers, according to Charters and Kunstadt, they were playing exclusively for a white audience and had picked up all the dated mannerisms of the white Broadway novelty bands. *I'm Gonna Hang around My Sugar* used every compositional device that characterized the "Ellington arrangement" for the next thirty years.

The Cotton Club. The Cotton Club, located in the heart of Harlem, opened in 1922. From the beginning, its owner, Bernard Levy, imposed a strict policy of whites only, despite loud protests from the black Harlem community. He used Negro orchestras and a Negro revue and ran the club as a tourist

PICTURE COLLECTION, THE BRANCH LIBRARIES, THE NEW YORK PUBLIC LIBRARY

A PROGRAM FROM THE COTTON CLUB.

attraction for society people who wanted to see a little of Harlem life. When Andy Preer, the young leader of the band at the Cotton Club, died suddenly, management decided to replace the old group. King Oliver's Dixie Syncopators were offered the job, but turned it down. Oliver considered the pay for ten men a bit low. The Cotton Club then offered Ellington and his smaller group the job. Ellington immediately accepted. When Ellington opened there, management posted guards at the doors to restrict admission to white patrons.

Ellington's style was strongly influenced by his Cotton Club years. His orchestra was a show orchestra, catering to audiences that expected to hear the same slick commercialized style they had heard in the top revues around the city. Unlike most improvisationally oriented jazz groups, Ellington carefully rehearsed his orchestra, by now renamed the "Cotton Club Orchestra." The group contained some of the most talented musicians of the day. They were led by one of New York's most gifted and imaginative arrangers. Still, the group often sounded patronizing and emotionally uninvolved. The Club's nightly audiences probably played a key role in eliciting this sound from the orchestra. The average Cotton Club audience could not in any real sense understand the music of Harlem. To offset this tendency, Ellington had to dazzle his audiences, and dazzle them he did.

Ellington and Irving Mills.

Throughout the '20s and '30s, bands of every description filled Harlem's cabarets. The majority of these billed themselves as jazz bands. Many were as good as, and some were better than, Ellington's band. The competition for a supporting audience and fame was fierce. Why, then, when bands of the late '20s are discussed, is Ellington's Cotton Club Orchestra the only one remembered by most? This is not to imply Ellington and his orchestra were undeserving of their reputation. They were excellent, but so were the majority playing in Harlem during those days. Charters and Kunstadt suggested that Ellington's manager, Irving Mills, was responsible for Ellington's widespread fame and durability.

Mills entered Ellington's life just after Ellington began playing at the Hollywood Club in 1923. Ellington reached the height of his popularity in 1930. During that year, the *New York Age* published the following article on Mills' relationship with Ellington:

> Irving Mills is a white man who is the manager of Duke Ellington and his famous Cotton Club Orchestra. Mills has been in the music business for many years, being a member of the firm of Mills Music, Inc., music publishers. Mills is a songwriter and a singer who has gained considerable fame for himself on the phonograph discs. He discovered Duke Ellington when that personage arrived from Washington, and with a five-piece colored orchestra made his debut at the Kentucky Club in New York City. Mills signed Ellington and after years of work and study he developed this organiza-

tion into one of the most talked of musical organizations in the world; today Ellington and his band rates on a par with Paul Whiteman, Vincent Lopez, Ben Bernie, and many others in the realm of modern music, as a result of Mills' work and managerial ability.

Mills personally supervises every orchestration and arrangement the band plays. He arranges the bookings and directs the exploitation in general. He selects the records made for the various phonograph companies and is master of the destinies of Ellington.

Mills set up the "personality" recordings that brought much fame and popularity to Ellington. It was Mills' contacts in the recording business and his partnership in a music-publishing house that enabled him to do this. Mills brought singer Adelaide Hall into the studio at the height of her popularity to record with the band. She and Ellington recorded an arrangement of King Oliver's *Camp Meeting Blues* they called *Creole Love Call.* Ellington added cabaret singer Baby Cox and blues guitarist Lonnie Johnson to the band for a few specialty recordings when they both were at the height of their popularity. Even the Rhythm Boys, Paul Whiteman's popular vocal trio, featuring Bing Crosby, recorded the hit song, *Three Little Words,* with Ellington in 1930.

Thanks to Mills, Ellington could be heard on a national radio network every night from the club, and the orchestra's recordings were beginning to sell. In 1927, the orchestra made three recordings of a long medley called *Black and*

PICTURE COLLECTION, THE BRANCH LIBRARIES, THE NEW YORK PUBLIC LIBRARY

"DUKE" ELLINGTON LEADING HIS ORCHESTRA AT MAURICE CHEVALIER'S CLUB ON FORTY-FOURTH STREET, NEW YORK CITY, 1930.

Tan Fantasy, the first one in March, the next in October, and the final one in November. This was the first of hundreds of successful recordings made during those first Cotton Club years.

The First English Tour. By 1932, Ellington was growing weary of the Cotton Club and the music business in general. Consequently, when an opportunity arose in 1933 to make an English tour, Ellington was understandably quick to accept. When he reached London, he was surprised to learn England regarded him as more than just a popular bandleader. The British considered him an important composer and a significant figure in a new music movement. They saw *Creole Rhapsody*, an extended Ellington composition covering both sides of a record, as the first real jazz composition. They felt it was the vanguard, indicating the direction jazz would take in the future. James Lincoln Collier saw the tour as a signal success. Of greater consequence, the tour provided Ellington with the sense that his music had an importance which extended beyond the confines of the Cotton Club. Ellington had always taken his work seriously, but now he felt his music had a wider significance. This encouraged him to consider his artistic goals more carefully.

Then, in 1939, significant changes in Ellington's professional life occurred. He and Irving Mills dissolved their longtime partnership. The orchestra changed record companies from Columbia to RCA Victor. Ellington acquired Ben Webster, a much needed, strong tenor saxophone soloist. Jimmie Blanton, a bassist who proved to be a major influence, also joined the orchestra. Blanton completely changed the style in which the bass was played in jazz, laying the foundation for what became bebop, or bop, bass playing. Unfortunately, he had tuberculosis. His illness caused his departure from the orchestra in 1941, and the following year he died.

Many jazz historians see Ellington's 1940s orchestra as the best of his groups. Collier believed this to be a questionable judgment. He saw the 1930s group as fresher and more imaginative, and certainly more innovative. However, the soloists of the later groups were superior to all but those who played with Count Basie. Nevertheless, the '40s witnessed the peak of the Ellington orchestra's prominence. A deterioration in the quality of the group began in the late '40s, with the loss of several key musicians—often in the middle of an engagement, and occasionally, even in the middle of a number.

Duke Ellington died in May, 1974, and like Louis Armstrong, he departed this life full of honors and still active. Ellington stands with only two others of his calibre, Louis Armstrong and Charlie Parker, in leaving his mark on jazz, and, through it, on all of Western music. Ellington's genius consisted of many musical attributes and skills: a marvelous feeling for tone color, a superb sense of instrumental voicing and arranging, an extraordinary understanding of harmony, a remarkable ability to write short, memorable melodies, a unique capacity to overcome the restraints of standard, confining bar forms, and, perhaps as important as any of these, an uncanny ability to locate and acquire instrumentalists capable of consistently producing the sounds he wanted.

William "Count" Basie

William "Count" Basie, more than any other man, made the swing band really swing. Basie was a ragtimer who hailed from Red Bank, New Jersey. Red Bank is just across the river from New York, and Basie was able to frequent the Lincoln Theater, where Fats Waller played the piano. Much of his knowledge about the piano and ragtime came from Waller. When he was twenty-five, Basie got stranded in the Midwest on a road show. To escape, he joined Walter Page's Band, the Blue Devils, out of Kansas City. When Page's Band dissolved, both he and Basie joined Bennie Moten's Band, Basie as the band's third pianist. Moten's brother, Buster, was second behind Bennie, but they both recognized Basie's ability, and featured him as soloist.

When the Great Depression struck, Moten returned to Kansas City, and the public promptly forgot both his band and him. Sometime around 1935, Bennie Moten died, and his brother became heir apparent to the band. Unfortunately, Buster displayed even less business acumen than had Bennie, and the band soon dissolved. At this juncture, Basie decided to try to keep the band together. He managed to get a nine-piece combo an engagement at the Reno Club, a run-down night spot in Kansas City, and the band began playing there in early 1935. Even by Depression standards, the Reno was nothing to write home about. The Reno did have a nightly radio program. An experimental station, W9XBY, was broadcasting over a police-call frequency that barely reached Chicago. However, that little insignificant radio station proved sufficient in establishing Basie as a major jazz figure.

An old friend and longtime Basie fan, journalist John Hammond, was in Chicago in December, 1935, to hear the new Benny Goodman Band play at the grand opening of the Congress Hotel. While driving around late one night, Hammond happened to hear a broadcast from the Reno. He later reported that he almost forgot about Goodman. Basie's band was stunning! Hammond called the first night he heard the band in person the most exciting musical experience of his life. As soon as he heard the broadcast, he began writing articles about the band. Charters and Kunstadt noted that a number of New York agencies suddenly developed a deep interest in Basie and his group.

Basie's First Contract. Hammond persuaded Willard Alexander of the M.C.A. booking agency to hear the band, but M.C.A. declined to issue a contract at that time. Later when M.C.A. went to Kansas City to sign the band, they discovered that another agent, Joe Glaser, had also gone there to see what all the excitement was about. After hearing the band, Glaser decided he didn't like the group, or at least he didn't believe he could sell them to the public. However, he did like "Lips" Page, the trumpet player, and literally stole him away from the group. When Hammond and Alexander arrived, an announcement greeted them, advising that Page was now an exclusive Glaser property and that the band would have to continue without him.

There was an even bigger blow. Hammond had persuaded Brunswick Recording Studio to issue the band a contract that included a good five-percent royalty agreement. Decca Records got to the band first, and offered Basie and the group a contract for $750. After months of painfully low pay at the Reno, $750 looked like a small fortune. Basie immediately signed the contract without reading the balance of the agreement. When he and Hammond read the contract thoroughly, they discovered that the band had contracted to record twenty-four sides for a total of $750; there were no royalties, and Decca had them for three years! The money amounted to about three dollars a man per record side. Basie had been "taken in style." Hammond eventually forced Decca to pay the band at least union scale, but he never got them to pay the group any royalties.

Basie and New York. The band began preparing for their New York debut in October, 1936. By this time, they had new uniforms, twelve new band arrangements, and four new men; Herschel Evans on saxophone, Tatti Smith on trumpet, George Hunt on trombone, and Claude Williams on guitar. Lips Page and Buster Moten had been replaced, Lips by Buck Clayton and Buster by Couchie Roberts. For their first engagement, they were booked at the Grand Terrace in Chicago, following Fletcher Henderson and his band. Charters and Kunstadt described The Grand Terrace as slick and expensive, with a lavish floor show and a highly critical audience. Basie's first afternoon rehearsal was a miserable failure. After the first terrible hour, he and the band tried to quit, but Alexander insisted they continue. The Terrace had a nightly radio broadcast on a national network, and Alexander knew the broadcast would almost instantly familiarize the public with the band's style. He didn't care what the band did to the Terrace's floor show.

At this juncture, Henderson, who had been watching the rehearsal, made a gesture that was unique in the orchestra business, a gesture that Basie never forgot. Henderson gave Basie dozens of his own arrangements for Basie to use. With this music Basie could at least get through the Terrace engagement. This gracious act saved the band, and the radio attracted the attention Alexander believed it would. And though the new band members were having several serious adjustment problems, a distinctive sound was beginning to emerge. Through the broadcasts, the band was creating quite a stir in New York.

In January, 1937, Basie and the band opened at the Roseland in New York, but had difficulty living up to their advanced billing. According to several who attended, Basie's group completely bewildered the audience. That same month, the band began a series of studio recording dates, and after two or three sessions, Basie made some hurried and much needed changes. He replaced two of the three trumpet players and the guitar player, and added another trombone. The band was now ready to try Harlem. It opened at the Apollo Theater on the same bill with popular singer Billie Holiday.

Alexander had been right about the airtime at the Grand Terrace in Chicago. The band's notices were almost as good as those of Billie Holiday. New Yorkers were unaccustomed to Basie's new hot style. Basie's rhythm section drove the band, instead of the tricky fireworks found in the New York arrangements. What the band played was close to the blues, and Basie's men played short, fierce riffs, instead of the popular arrangements that employed an excess of melodic leading. The riff patterns were just sharp, pulsing, repetitive rhythmic figures set against each other in different sections of the band, with the soloists free to improvise against this. By this time, Basie had developed his own distinctive piano style. While the balance of the rhythm section carried the beat, Basie filled in with irregular melodic figures behind the soloists. Since Basie's style was so radically different from that of the New York bands, his steadily growing popularity did not detract from theirs. Basie simply took his place with the others, without deposing any other band.

After just a year, New Yorkers accepted Basie and his band as an integral part of the musical scene. After two-and-one-half years, Basie finally escaped Decca Records and signed with Vocalion. He made a series of recordings with Benny Goodman in 1940 and 1941, after the rumor spread that he might dissolve his own band and join Goodman as a soloist. However, after these recordings, Basie led his band to even greater popularity during World War II, and eventually, the rumors died. In their prominent years, Basie's Band contained at least a half-dozen of jazz's most outstanding musicians. Even given Henderson's and Ellington's bands, Basie's group, from about 1936 to about 1940, included the largest concentration of the most gifted jazz musicians ever assembled.

Other Swing-Era Bands

During the twenties, Tin Pan Alley was a thriving, powerful, money-making concern, similar, in many ways, to a large corporation. It was always searching for new ways in which to merchandise its product, music. The Alley found a major new market in the dance bands that were beginning to appear in dance halls, night clubs, hotels, theaters and public auditoriums, as well as in recordings and over the radio. There were about fifty thousand of these smaller bands, supplementing the music of stellar groups such as those authentic jazz and jazz-oriented bands and orchestras led by Louis Armstrong, Duke Ellington, Fletcher Henderson, Ben Pollack, and Jean Goldkette. These little bands offered popular songs in formalized arrangements for both listening and dancing pleasure. Their growing importance to the music scene could be seen in the number of sheet-music covers that were published with the photograph of a popular bandleader, rather than that of a prominent stage or vaudeville star.

By this time, radio and recordings had invaded almost every home in America. Consequently, social dancing was as popular in the home as it was in dance halls and nightclubs. The period was the Roaring Twenties, a raucous time in the nation's history. Its music, the new jazz, emphasizing beat, accent, and rhythm, called for new kinds of social dances. People wanted dances with more motion and energy than the waltz, the tango, or the various dances that grew out of the popular pre-World War I one-step and fox trot. In the twenties, the favorite dances included the shaking of shoulders and stomachs, body gyrations, arm swinging, and complex, vigorous foot patterns.

There were more than enough dance orchestras to satisfy the demand so long as Americans kept dancing. Among the earliest of these dance bands were those of Ben Selvin and Art Hickman. Hickman and his band traveled to New York to appear in Florenz Ziegfeld's 1920 *Follies*. In 1921, Hickman opened the new Coconut Grove at the Ambassador Hotel in Los Angeles. Hickman retired after this engagement, but his band continued for a number of years under other leaders.

Vincent Lopez. Vincent Lopez, the son of a music teacher, had early aspirations of becoming a priest. However, his powerful attraction to music caused him to choose it as a career. In his youth, he played the piano in Brooklyn beer halls, saloons, and other questionable establishments. In 1917, he began an engagement as pianist and bandleader at the Pekin Restaurant on 47th Street and Broadway in Manhattan. Because of his keyboard prowess, he acquired a nickname, "the piano kid." While at the Pekin, he introduced the piano rag that was to become his signature music, Felix Arndt's *Nola*.

Lopez remained in New York during his entire professional career. His orchestra began an engagement at the Grill Room of the Hotel Pennsylvania on November 27, 1921, an engagement which lasted for almost twenty-five years. For an hour and a half every night, the orchestra broadcast its performances over radio station WJZ. These were the first live broadcasts ever made by a popular band. Every night, Lopez greeted his audience with, "Hello everybody, Lopez speaking." This greeting grew to be as closely identified with Lopez as his theme song.

Fred Waring. Fred Waring began his career in the twenties as a bandleader, though he later became one of this nation's most prominent choral conductors. After leaving college, he formed a traditional dance band, named it the Pennsylvanians, and began touring the college and vaudeville circuits. He soon became a major attraction at the Metropolitan Theater in Hollywood. In the late twenties, his Pennsylvanians began recording for RCA Victor, and around 1930, Waring added a chorus to his band to individualize its performances. Before his career ended, he completely converted to choral music, and his singing Pennsylvanians became a model for all aspiring young choral directors.

Guy Lombardo. Guy Lombardo hailed from London, Ontario. In London, he and his two brothers played in small combos before forming their own jazz band. They brought their band to the United States in 1923, and accepted an engagement at the Claremont, a roadhouse just outside Cleveland. The owner advised Guy to develop a slow, sweet style that would emphasize the saxophones and would punctuate the flow of the melody with the other brasses. Lombardo took this new style to the Granada Café in Chicago, where the band adopted the name it would bear from that time forward, "Guy Lombardo and His Royal Canadians." WBBM, a small Chicago radio station, decided to air the Royal Canadians directly from the Granada for a fifteen-minute spot. However, when the band completed its first show, the Café's manager instructed Guy to keep playing into the microphone. Lombardo played the balance of the evening. As he played, crowds from all over Chicago poured into the Granada. Lombardo's music was described by Chicago critic Ashley Stevens as "the sweetest music this side of heaven." That saying became Lombardo's musical trademark, and his music quickly became Chicago's new "in" sound.

In 1929, Guy took his Royal Canadians to New York for an engagement. They were to remain there seasonally until 1962. Their recordings and their radio broadcasts from the Grill Room gained them national prominence; their New Year's Eve broadcasts became an annual ritual, climaxed by the playing of the band's theme song, *Auld Lang Syne*.

Woody Herman. Woodrow Charles "Woody" Herman founded "the band that plays the blues" late in 1936. Woody began his show-business life as a child prodigy at age six, singing and tap dancing in vaudeville theaters around the Milwaukee area, where he was born. He learned to play the saxophone and the clarinet, and used them both in his act, in which he was billed as "Wisconsin's only professional juvenile." Myron Stewart, who played the Blue Heaven roadhouse just outside Milwaukee, gave Woody his first job with a jazz band while he was still attending St. John's Cathedral Preparatory School. In

1930, Woody enrolled at Marquette University, where he studied music. One semester later, he left college and joined Tom Gerun's Band.

By 1936, Woody was playing professionally with the Isham Jones Band. When Jones decided to disband the group, Woody took some of Jones' key musicians and formed his own group. They opened that same year at the Roseland Ballroom in Brooklyn. Although Woody billed the group as "the band that plays the blues," they also played pop songs and nonjazz instrumentals. However, the blues were their specialty. Herman's band gained national recognition through the blues medium, both with public performances and with recordings. In 1939, Herman recorded his *Woodchopper's Ball* on the Decca label. The recording sold over one million copies and guaranteed the band's ability to get engagements at the country's leading night spots. Herman had earned his place among the nation's top jazz bands.

Cab Calloway. The name Cab (Cabwell) Calloway is almost synonymous with the terms, "hi-de-hi," and "hi-de-ho." Cab soared to national prominence on the wings of *Minnie the Moocher,* which he introduced with his own band at the Cotton Club in 1931. Calloway began his musical career in Chicago in the 1920s as a drummer and master of ceremonies. He acquired his own band, the Alabamians, in 1928. They played at the Merry Gardens, and Calloway

AN AD FOR CAB CALLOWAY AT THE HARLEM OPERA HOUSE.

did the band's vocal solos. In 1929, Calloway made his Broadway theater debut in the revue, *Hot Chocolates.* Now a star in his own right, Calloway made his film debut in *The Big Broadcast* in 1932. He captured the role of Sportin' Life in Gershwin's *Porgy and Bess,* and he was one of the stars of the 1967 all-black production of *Hello, Dolly!* on Broadway.

The Dorseys. There were countless others, such as Wayne King, "the waltz king," and Les Brown and his "band of renown." Kay Kayser became the dean of radio's "Kollege of Musical Knowledge," and Lawrence Welk offered his "champagne bubble music" at the St. Paul Hotel in Minnesota.

Then, of course, there were Jimmy and Tommy, the marvelous Dorsey brothers. Jimmy played the alto saxophone and Tommy, the trombone. Together or separately, they greatly enriched the sounds of their own bands. Their father was a music teacher, and gave the boys their first music lessons. The two brothers began their professional careers playing with various groups, such as those of Jean Goldkette, Paul Whiteman, and Red Nichols. Then, in the 1920s, each brother formed his own band—Dorsey's Novelty Six, led by Jimmy, and Dorsey's Wild Canaries, with Tommy as director. Both groups broadcast over Baltimore's first radio station. In 1934, the Dorseys formed a combined band of eleven musicians, one of whom was a young trombonist who played with Tommy and arranged for the band. His name was Glenn Miller.

The Dorseys had their musical differences. In one of his *Saturday Review* articles, Richard Gehman listed several of these differences. In his view, Jimmy was more ambitious and more agile, musically. Tommy was quieter, more methodical, less spectacular. Jimmy experimented. Tommy was the smoother musician. Together, they were terrific.

Their personalities were completely dissimilar. Tommy, in his glasses, looked like a young college professor or a bookworm. Jimmy resembled a model for a collar ad. Tommy was hyperactive, aggressive, outgoing. Jimmy was shy, gentle, almost soft. These differences, combined with classic sibling rivalry, made an explosion between the two inevitable. It came one night at the Glen Island Casino, when they had a fistfight in full view of the audience. Later that night, Jimmy criticized Tommy's tempo in *I'll Never Say 'Never Again' Again.* Tommy stared for a moment at his brother, then tucked his trombone under his arm and walked off the stage. That incident began a feud that lasted several years.

For a time, no reconciliation took place. Each went his own way. Jimmy began leading the band Tommy had deserted. Tommy formed another band in 1935, and though Jimmy's band was more popular, Tommy's group proved to be more spectacular musically. George Simon believed Tommy's was the best dance band ever. He felt that others may have sounded more creative or may have had more distinctive styles; but for Simon, Tommy's band consistently did more things better than any other band of the swing era.

In 1939, Jimmy and his band completed an engagement at the New Yorker Hotel. That same night, brother Tommy began one at the New Yorker. The occasion brought the quarreling brothers together once again. On stage that night, in front of the audience, a touching reconciliation took place. However, they did not combine forces again until 1953, eighteen years after their spectacular split. They called the group the Dorsey Brothers Orchestra. Sadly, the time for making additional jazz history had passed. The big-band era had ended. And though both were still young, the Dorsey brothers' time remaining was short. Tommy choked to death in his sleep on November 26, 1956, and six months later, on June 12, 1957, Jimmy died of cancer.

Benny Goodman. On the evening of August 21, 1935, swing became *the* thing in jazz. Benny Goodman was appearing at the Palomar Ballroom in Los Angeles, and playing stock dance numbers, called "society music," which quite apparently did not appeal to that evening's audience. In disgust and frustration, Goodman decided if he were going to fail, he would do it his way. With Goodman on lead clarinet, the band struck up *King Porter's Stomp* and several other Fletcher Henderson arrangements. The audience went wild. Later, Goodman said the roar from the audience was one of the sweetest sounds he had ever heard. For the balance of his engagement at the Palomar, Goodman drew heavily on his swing repertory. Radio carried this music to the rest of the nation. By the time Goodman completed the engagement, swing had become the national jazz rage. Some of Fletcher Henderson's 1920s New York performances, and several of his arrangements possessed a swing character; but it was Benny Goodman who first brought swing to the attention of the nation, and it was Goodman who wound up in the catbird's seat in swing.

Benny Goodman was born in 1909 in Chicago. His father, a tailor, overheard a boy's band playing in a synagogue. Upon investigation, Goodman's father discovered one could take music lessons on borrowed instruments for twenty-five cents a lesson. He took four of his sons to the synagogue to study music. Benny was assigned the clarinet because of his size and weight. Within a year, Goodman had purchased a clarinet of his own from a mail-order house, and was studying classical music with Franz Schoepp. At age twelve, he began copying recordings of jazz clarinetist Ted Lewis. During that same year, he won five dollars playing a jazz piece in a vaudeville amateur-night show. This was the first time Goodman ever earned money with his clarinet.

By the time he was fourteen, Goodman had a regular playing job with a band at Guion's Parade dance hall. In 1925, Ben Pollack hired him for the

Pollack orchestra. Goodman made his first recording, *He's the Last Word*, with this orchestra. Goodman left Pollack to try his luck as a freelance musician in New York. In 1930, he made two notable recordings for RCA Victor, *Rockin' Chair* and *Barnacle Bill the Sailor*, with a jazz group organized by Hoagy Carmichael, which included Jimmy and Tommy Dorsey, Bix Beiderbecke, "Bubber" Miley, Joe Venuti, Gene Krupa, and others. By 1934, Goodman had a band of his own. In 1935, Goodman hired Gene Krupa as band drummer. Krupa remained with the band for three years before leaving to form his own jazz group. It was Krupa who transformed the jazz band drummer from a keeper of time to a virtuoso. Goodman recorded *Sing, Sing, Sing* in 1936, a piece that highlighted Krupa in the first long drum solo in the history of jazz.

After his sensational stand at Los Angeles' Palomar Ballroom, Goodman took an engagement at the Congress Hotel in Chicago. The engagement,

PICTURE COLLECTION, THE BRANCH LIBRARIES, THE NEW YORK PUBLIC LIBRARY

A FRENCH ARTICLE ON BENNY GOODMAN.

which was supposed to be three weeks in length, became an eight-month stand. It was here that Goodman's music finally acquired the label, "swing." After this engagement, a *Time* magazine article called Goodman the "king of Swing." During the summer of 1936, Goodman and his band appeared in the motion picture, *The Big Broadcast,* where he and his band performed *Bugle Call Rag* and *Cross Patch.*

Goodman gave his first Carnegie Hall concert on January 16, 1937. It was the first time swing had been presented in a concert setting in Carnegie Hall. The performance was recorded live, and the recording has since become a collector's item. Frank Norris, in a *Saturday Evening Post* article, described Goodman's swing sound in the following manner:

> His chief characteristics are definition and power, the rhythm instruments—piano, drums and bass—sound and sure, solidly thumping out the time, while the melody, carried on by the concerted brasses and reeds, pulses just a fraction ahead to give the urgent off-beat, the brasses a fine strong burr and the reeds swirling with improvisations on the tune. And then, Goodman's clarinet, clear and unhurried and artful, playing a song that was never written and may never be heard again.

Glenn Miller. Among the newer swing bands, Glenn Miller's was the most serious challenger to Goodman's immense popularity. The Glenn Miller Band was also the last of its kind from the big-band era. Miller's sound was characterized by the manner in which his band employed the use of the reeds and the clarinet. The sound charmed and romanticized the late '30s in such unforgettable songs as his theme, *Moonlight Serenade,* as well as *In the Mood* and the enormously successful *Little Brown Jug.*

Before assembling his own band, Miller had achieved significant success as a trombonist and arranger. After playing for a time with Ben Pollack, he joined the Dorsey brothers as arranger and trombonist. In early 1937, Miller formed his own group, with which he made several recordings for Decca. In 1938, internal strife and personal mishaps appeared to be bringing Miller's career as a bandleader to a close, and in January of that year, he disbanded his combo. However, two months later, he assembled another group, this one better than the first. Miller and the new combo played ballrooms around the Boston area and in New York.

Miller's fame soared. His group became one of the most sought-after and highest paid in all of jazz history. Miller was heard over the radio, in public appearances, and in the movies. His fame was at its peak, when, in 1942, during World War II, he volunteered to serve in the armed forces. He entered the Army as captain, and organized an all-star band that toured the country and gave coast-to-coast radio broadcasts. He formed several groups in England which were heard in service camps and over the air. On December 14, 1944, while en route by air from Bedford, England, to Paris to make arrangements for his band's appearance there, his plane disappeared and was never accounted for. The greatest tribute Miller could have been paid can be seen in the number of postwar bands organized to imitate his sound and play his arrangements. In 1954, Universal Pictures released *The Glenn Miller Story,* starring James Stewart as Miller, and in 1956, the Glenn Miller estate approved the organization of a new Glenn Miller Band, to be led by Ray McKinley.

Additional Readings

Corio, Ann, and Joseph DiNona. *This Was Burlesque.* New York: Grosset and Dunlap, 1968.

Dance, Stanley. *The World of Duke Ellington.* New York: DaCapo, 1980.

Ewen, David. *All The Years of American Popular Music.* Englewood Cliffs, N.J.: Prentice-Hall, 1978.

————. *Great Men of Popular Music.* Englewood Cliffs, N.J.: Prentice-Hall, 1970.

Goldberg, Issac. *Tin Pan Alley: A Chronicle of American Popular Music.* New York: Frederick Ungar, 1931; paper, 1970.

McCarthy, Albert J. *The Dance Band Era: The Dancing Decades from Ragtime to Swing.* London: Spring Books, 1971.

Nanry, Charles, ed. *American Music: From Storyville to Woodstock.* New Brunswick, N.J.: Transaction Books, 1972.

Simon, George. *Simon Says: The Sights and Sounds of the Swing Era.* New Rochelle, N.Y.: Arlington House, 1955.

Walker, Leo. *The Wonderful World of the Great Dance Bands.* New York: Doubleday & Company, 1972.

Selected Recordings

Basie, Count. *The Best of Count Basie.* MCA2-4050

Calloway, Cab. *Classics.* Aimez-Vous le Jazz CBS 62950

Carter, Benny. *Coleman Hawkins, 1930-1941.* Aimez-Vous le Jazz 68227

Dorsey, Thomas. *This Is Tommy Dorsey.* RCA VPM-6038

Ellington, Duke. *The Beginning.* Decca DL 7-9224

————. *Rockin' in Rhythm.* Decca DL 7-9247

————. *In a Mellotone.* RCA LPM-1364

Goodman, Benny. *The Golden Age of Benny Goodman.* RCA LPM 1099

———— *Carnegie Hall Concert.* Columbia CL 814/6

Henderson, Fletcher. *The Immortal Fletcher Henderson.* Milestone MLP 2005

Herman, Woodie. *Woodie Herman.* Everest Records FS 281

Miller, Glenn. *A Memorial 1944–1969.* Victor GM 1

Moten, Benny. *Bennie Moten's Kansas City Orchestra.* EMI PMC 7119

Webb, Chick. *King of the Savoy.* Decca DL 7-9223

Chapter 6
The Rise of
the Pop Solo
Singer

Solo artists, vocal and instrumental, are the backbone of today's popular-music industry. Their popular-music roots can be traced to a variety of early American forms of musical entertainment, which, in turn, legitimately claim traditional European models as their parents. American pop solo artists owe their beginnings to those European composers who wrote operas, cantatas, and sonatas from the seventeenth century onward.

History is vague concerning the period of time during which the American pop solo artist actually emerged. Since the 1840s, European solo artists routinely made extended American tours. In 1843, Norwegian violinist Ole Bull made his first American tour, and in 1850, America was introduced to the Swedish Nightingale, Jenny Lind. During the 1840s, when household music became a household word, groups such as the Singing Hutchinsons gained much popularity singing those types of songs that were the forerunners of the sentimental ballad. Most of these groups featured home-grown soloists whose names, like their European counterparts, gained national recognition. During the heyday of Tin Pan Alley, many of the Alley's most talented song pluggers, vocal and instrumental, went on to become famous vaudeville and musical theater soloists.

Jolie

Perhaps the most recognizable of these figures was Al Jolson. In her biography of Jolson, Pearl Sieben said Jolson needed applause the way a diabetic needs insulin. Jolson was supposedly a kind man, sentimental and "charitable to a fault." According to Sieben, however, he was arrogant and surly, a crude, untutored braggart. His one saving grace was as an entertainer. He was perhaps the greatest in the history of American show business.

Jolson is most often remembered as the singer who made the song, *My Mammy*, a household word. He was born Asa Yoelson in 1886 in Lithuania. His father, a rabbi, fled with his family to the United States in 1890. They settled in Washington, D.C. There, Jolson and his brother, Harry, sang in front of the Hotel Raleigh for congressmen and senators. He spent what he earned on trips to the local theaters. To the genuine dismay of his father, the theater was the only life Jolson would ever know, or would ever want to know.

PICTURE COLLECTION, THE BRANCH LIBRARIES, THE NEW YORK PUBLIC LIBRARY

AL JOLSON IN THE TITLE ROLL OF *THE JAZZ SINGER.*

AN AD FOR *THE JAZZ SINGER*.

PICTURE COLLECTION, THE BRANCH LIBRARIES, THE NEW YORK PUBLIC LIBRARY

Jolson spent a large portion of his early career in bars, circuses, burlesque, minstrel shows, and vaudeville. At twenty-three, he entered the world of musical theater as an end man with Lew Dockstader's Minstrels at the Fifth Avenue Theater in New York. The year was 1909. He entered, as Henry Pleasants remarked, in time-honored fashion. He stole the show from the star.

Jolson spent the next two years in New York in vaudeville, playing three houses simultaneously. Amazingly, he did two spots a day in each, which literally caused him to race from one to the other. On March 20, 1911, the Schuberts put him in their show, *La Belle Paree,* at New York's Winter Garden. Jolson had arrived. That same year, he made the first of his almost two hundred recordings.

During his lifetime, Jolson starred in several movies, including *April Showers* (1926), and *The Jazz Singer* (1927), the first feature film with synchronized speech as well as music and sound effects. This film revolutionalized the motion-picture industry and signaled the end of the silent era. Other motion pictures include *The Singing Fool* (1928), *Say It with Songs* (1929), *Mamie* (1930), *Hallelujah, I'm a Bum* (1933), and *Swanee River* (1940). In 1946, the story of his life was filmed as *The Al Jolson Story.* Its sequel, *Jolson Sings Again,* appeared in 1949.

Jolson made many overseas tours of wartime army camps. He made his last such tour during the beginning of the Korean War in 1950. Shortly after he returned from this tour he died, on October 23, 1950. For his service to American wartime troops he was posthumously awarded the Congressional Medal of Honor.

Bessie Smith

B essie Smith, the "empress of the blues," dominated not only her own times, but also profoundly influenced the times that came after her. She made her first recording on February 16, 1923. Before that date, except for her birthplace, Chattanooga, Tennessee, everything about her, including the date of her birth, is vague. All the following have been given at some time as her birth date: 1894, 1895, 1897, 1898, and 1900. Henry Pleasants stated his research supported a date closer to 1890.

There is also considerable confusion surrounding Bessie's first recordings. Her first sessions may have been as early as 1921, for the Emerson Record Company, but, if this is true, Emerson archives do not indicate they ever released the recordings, nor has anyone ever been able to confirm their existence. Eventually, she wound up the recording property of Columbia Record

Cemetery Blues
(Sid Laney)
Comedienne
BESSIE SMITH - Jimmy
Jones at the Piano
13001D   81241

A COLUMBIA RECORDING OF BESSIE SMITH SINGING, *CEMETARY BLUES*.

Company. Her first side for Columbia was *'Tain't Nobody's Business If I Do.* Her second was *Down Hearted Blues,* written by Alberta Hunter and Lovie Austin. Hunter's earlier recording of the song had been a bestseller for the Paramount Race series. Bessie's recording sold 780,000 copies in under six months. Columbia promptly issued her a one-year contract, effective April 20, 1923, calling for twelve sides at $125 a usable side, and guaranteeing her $1,500 with a one-year renewal option for twelve sides at $150. Bessie's career was launched, and from this time forward, until her death, she dominated the field of pop vocal artists. Bessie was fatally injured in a car accident on the morning of September 26, 1937, while traveling between Memphis, Tennessee, and Clarksdale, Mississippi.

Ethel Waters

Ethel Waters was born in abject poverty, the illegitimate daughter of a twelve-year-old girl, on October 31, 1896, in Chester, Pennsylvania. More

ETHEL WATERS IN
ON WITH THE SHOW, 1929.

than any other black singer of the century, including Bessie Smith, Ethel Waters was a true theater personality. Two of her greatest successes came on the Broadway stage in nonsinging roles. She played Hagar in *Mamba's Daughters* (1939), and the black cook, Bernice Sadie Brown, in *The Member of the Wedding* (1950). She also starred in the 1940 film, *Cabin in the Sky*. Henry Pleasants believed these successes had a tendency to overshadow her success and influence as a singer. More than Bessie Smith and even Louis Armstrong, Waters may well have been one of the most significant influences on every generation of pop vocalists that came after her. As a singer, she was a transitional figure, bridging the gap between all that had been accumulated stylistically from the minstrel show, ragtime, and coon song, as well as the jazz-oriented Afro-American characteristics embedded in the swing era.

Bing Crosby

Harry Lillis "Bing" Crosby was another profoundly influential American pop singer. Crosby's style and approach were quite deceptive. He sang everything with apparent careless ease. His stage presence was such that everything he did in performance seemed casual and natural, not in the least staged. Though Crosby achieved real fame and recognition in the 1930s, he was actually a product of the '20s. His generation challenged the conventions and restraints of a pre-World War I social order. Raccoon coats, garish clothing, hip flasks, a vocabulary infused with slang, dancing cheek-to-cheek, cuddling in rumble-seats, old cars, and jazz all became symbols of his day.

Crosby's immense popularity sprang in large part from his essence of middle-America image. He smoked a pipe. Long before he reached middle age, he was thinning on top. He dressed casually and comfortably. He enjoyed golf, baseball (at one time, he owned the Pittsburgh Pirates), hunting, fishing, the racetrack, and his family. In the language of his own generation, he was Joe Average. Bing Crosby was Everyman.

Crosby's career extended well beyond that of just a pop singer. Throughout his life, he starred in countless motion pictures, including such films as *Holiday Inn, Going My Way*, for which he won an academy award, *The Bells of St. Mary*, and *White Christmas*. In this last film, with film score by Irving Berlin, Crosby and three co-stars sang *White Christmas*, the movie's title song. After the movie, the song was released as a single with only Crosby singing. From 1942, the date on which Crosby's single was released, through 1983, the Crosby recording of *White Christmas* had sold more than twenty-five million copies.

Starting in 1940, Crosby began what evolved into a series of movies with comedian Bob Hope. These movies, known as the "road shows," stretched

BING CROSBY.

PHOTOFEST

across twenty-two years through 1962. They were light comedies, with fluff for dialogue and plot. On screen, Crosby and Hope were a delightful team, turning these small bits of high camp into viewing pleasure. The series consisted of *The Road to Singapore, The Road to Zanzibar, The Road to Morocco, The Road to Utopia, The Road to Rio, The Road to Bali,* and *The Road to Hong Kong.*

From the early '30s through 1950, Crosby starred in various radio shows. He began his radio career in 1932 on CBS Radio in New York. In 1936, he joined NBC's Kraft Music Hall as one of its stars, and remained with NBC for ten years. He made his long-awaited television debut in June, 1952, on a telethon with Bob Hope.

Although Crosby was highly successful in several areas of the entertainment industry, he made his most significant contributions as a popular singer. On September 15, 1970 Decca Records presented him with a platinum disc, commemorating the total sales of 300,650,000 discs!

Ella Fitzgerald

Renowned English accompanist Gerald Moore tells this amusing, yet revealing, tale. Immediately following a matinee performance he and German Lieder singer Dietrich Fischer-Dieskau had given in Washington,

D.C., Fischer-Dieskau rushed to Washington's National Airport and took the first available flight to New York. He was on his way to a Carnegie Hall performance by Duke Ellington and Ella Fitzgerald. Fischer-Dieskau exclaimed to Moore, "Ella and the Duke together! One just doesn't know when there might be a chance to hear that again!"

Ella earned her standing in the pop-music world strictly within the bounds of the music she knew best, jazz and pop. Her honors and accolades in these fields are too numerous to recount here. Suffice it to say over the past forty years, the magazines *Metronome, Downbeat,* and *Playboy* have listed her first in either their jazz-singer or their popular-singer polls no fewer than twenty-four times. And in 1958, Ella won three Grammys.

Ella's appeal and longevity stem from a variety of attributes. Among these are a lovely voice, an impeccable and sophisticated rhythmic sense, flawless intonation, harmonic sensibility, and a remarkable improvisational ability and technique. Ella Fitzgerald is a singer's singer.

During her career, Fitzgerald has sold more than twenty-five million recordings. Some of her more famous recordings include *A-Tisket A-Tasket, Stone Cold Dead in the Market, That's My Desire, Flying Home, Oh, Lady Be Good,* and *How High the Moon.*

Frank Sinatra

Francis Albert Sinatra, born December 12, 1915, has had, in essence, two show-business careers in his lifetime. He began his first rise to stardom in 1937. Frank and three instrumentalists formed a group they called the Hoboken Four, and appeared on Major Bowes Original Amateur Hour. In June, 1939, Frank became a soloist with the Harry James Band. He remained with James through the end of the year. In 1940, he signed with Tommy Dorsey. He stayed with Dorsey until September of 1942. It was during this period that Sinatra became America's first teenage heartthrob. Henry Pleasants humorously described the Sinatra of that time as hollow-cheecked and skinny with a golf-ball Adam's apple and jug-handle ears. According to Pleasants, Sinatra's light, appealing voice inspired the term, "Swoonatra," and produced a remarkable effect on American females, which someone during that period dubbed a "Sinatrance."

Sinatra and the Bobby-Soxers. Sinatra created much the same kind of hysteria in the early '40s that the Beatles created over two decades later. Pleasants believed Sinatra and the Beatles possessed a rare and fundamental

FRANK SINATRA
IN HIS EARLY YEARS.

PHOTOFEST

quality, which brought about this craze over them, a kind of wistful, tender, innocent, helpless vulnerability. For about five years, he held absolute sway over the adolescent female population of the nation. Unfortunately for Sinatra, this attraction did not last.

Toward the end of 1947, his career began to skid. Several factors contributed to his demise. His bobby-soxers were growing up, tastes in songs were changing, and a new batch of singers appeared on the horizon to charm the population with new songs: Tony Bennett, Perry Como, Vic Damone, Billy Eckstine, Eddie Fisher, Dick Haymes, Dean Martin, Johnnie Ray, and Mel Tormé.

Frank's troubles were amplified by problems with his throat during this period, hardly surprising when one considers that during 1946 he had done as many as forty-five shows a week, averaging eighty to one hundred songs a day! During a spring, 1950, appearance at the Copacabana, he completely lost his voice in the middle of a show. He was forced to cancel the balance of the engagement. By 1952, his career appeared to be at an end.

Sinatra's Second Career.
Frank began his remarkable comeback with his nonsinging role as Private Maggio in the motion picture, *From Here to Eternity*, a role for which he won an Academy Award. Although he had starred in many movies before this one, none had revealed his extraordinary acting ability like the role of Private Maggio. After *From Here to Eternity*, Sinatra portrayed a heroin addict in the 1956 film, *The Man with the Golden Arm*. He gave excellent performances in *Pal Joey* in 1957 and *The Detective* in 1968.

During this same period, he moved from Columbia to Capitol Records, and changed his image from one that appealed essentially to a population of adoring young females to one that appealed to an audience of all ages and both sexes. The pop-music world began calling him the "chairman of the board," acknowledging his total dominance and control of the entertainment circles in which he moved.

Now Sinatra's singing style came to the forefront. In the early days, people were more concerned with what he was doing to the female population than what he was doing with his voice. Suddenly, the nation discovered Sinatra, the singer. For the first time, people began viewing Sinatra as a serious popular musician, not just a singer of bobby-soxer songs. People began noticing his endless, effortless legatos, his intuitive understanding of phrasing, his feeling for the meaning and music of words, and his warmth and intimacy, all of which conveyed an overwhelming sense of sympathy and sincerity. The combination of his stage presence and singing style was irresistible.

These vocal characteristics brought Sinatra closer to the art of classical music than any other popular vocalist had ever come. In 1723, Pier Francesco Tosi of the Philharmonic Society of Bologna wrote and published his treatise on bel canto singing, *Observations on the Florid Song*. In it, he made these remarks:

> Let him take care that the higher the notes, the more necessary it is to touch them with softness, to avoid screaming.

> Let him learn the manner to glide with the vowels, and to drag the voice gently from the high to the lower notes.

> Let him take care that the words are uttered in such a manner that they be distinctly understood, and no one syllable lost.

> In repeating the air, he that does not vary it for the better is no great master.

> Whoever does not know how to steal the time in singing [tempo rubato] is destitute of the best taste and knowledge. The stealing of time in the pathetic is an honorable theft in one that sings better than others, provided he makes a restitution with ingenuity.

> Oh! How great a master is the heart!

These qualities and nuances as set forth by Tosi are those very qualities and nuances that Frank Sinatra has possessed throughout his entire performing life.

As of this writing, Frank, at age 76, is still performing. However, during the spring of 1971, he announced tentative plans to retire. Though he did not enter retirement at that time, reactions to the announcement were immediate and worldwide. A letter written to the London *Evening Standard* probably best sums up the feeling of Sinatra fans the world over. In her letter, Mrs. Edna Haber remarked it was "sad, sad to learn that the prodigious, phenomenal Frank Sinatra has called a halt." Mrs. Haber, by her own confession, had been "one of those adoring teenagers" many years ago. At the time she wrote her letter, she was a grandmother, and still considered Sinatra to be America's greatest pop singer. With sweet nostalgia, she remembered how in her youth she had collected all Sinatra's recordings, and had pinned his pictures all over her bedroom walls. For her, Sinatra embodied all those memories of her teenage years "which suddenly, today, seem a little more distant." According to Mrs. Haber, there could never be another Sinatra. She closed her letter with, "Thanks, Frank, for wonderful memories and the pleasure you have given me until this day." Pier Francesco Tosi apparently wrote the truth when he penned, "Oh! How great a master is the heart!"

Nat "King" Cole

Nat "King" Cole was born Nathaniel Coles (he dropped the "s" to become King Cole) in 1917 in Montgomery, Alabama. In 1921, his family moved to Chicago, where his father became pastor of the Truelight Spiritual Temple on Chicago's South Side. By the time he was twelve, Nat was playing the organ and singing in his father's church choir. However, by that time, Nat was captivated by jazz. In later life, he told a reporter he always loved show business and was particularly fond of bands. He admitted that as a child he constantly stood in front of the radio, directing bands.

From the start, Cole was a natural pianist. He took lessons only to learn to read music. He began his career as leader of his own band, the Rogues of Rhythm. For three years he worked around Chicago. During this period he spent much time listening to the older, more established stars of jazz, such as Earl Hines and Jimmy Noone.

Cole's band joined a "shuffle along" road company during its run in Chicago, and traveled with it to the West Coast. After the show folded in Los Angeles, Cole worked for a time as a solo performer. In 1939, a nightclub owner, Bob Lewis, invited Cole to form a trio and come into his Hollywood club, The Swanee Inn. Cole recruited bass player Wesley Prince and guitarist Oscar Moore, and the King Cole Trio was born.

At this juncture, it is pertinent and important to recall that Nat Cole began his career as a pianist, though ultimately he was to make his greatest contribution to the pop-music field as a vocalist. Pleasants believed that Cole was one of the potentially great jazz pianists of his generation. However, his promise as a singer was even greater. As a vocalist, he was an original. He and Billy Eckstine were the first black male singers to rise to the top of the profession in the white world.

Perhaps more than any other singer of this caliber, Cole had a way of caressing a word, of enveloping it with his voice. Music and language were so intimately joined when he sang that one almost cannot hear a melody he made famous without memory immediately evoking the words that accompanied the melody; songs such as *Nature Boy, Mona Lisa, When I Fall in Love,* and *Too Young.* Nat King Cole was a delightful pianist, a delightful singer, and according to those who knew him, a delightful man.

Judy Garland

An unidentified critic once wrote, "God made Al Jolson, then he made Judy Garland, and then he broke the mold." On the surface, this statement appears glib and extravagant. However, a closer examination of the events that occurred across both their careers, and the devotion they inspired in the hearts of millions, leads to quite a different conclusion. Jolson and Garland were two of popular music's most gifted and most enduring stars.

Like Jolson, Judy never had a real childhood, nor did she go through any kind of adolescence in the traditional sense. Ray Bolger, Judy's Scarecrow in *The Wizard of Oz,* once remarked, "Judy was a child who never had a childhood." She went straight from child to woman, and this brought her trouble all her life.

Although Jolson was drawn into show business, Judy was born into it. There were countless parallels in their lives. Both lived for the audience and applause. Performing was the only act through which either could form a satisfactory emotional relationship. Life offstage was a period of excruciating loneliness, emptiness, insecurity, anxiety, fear, and even terror, for both. Marriage was not the answer for either. Nor was an audience, as lover, entirely satisfactory. Pleasants observed that an audience could offer her approval, admiration, and love, but it could not give Garland the companionship she so desperately needed.

During the final months of her life, Judy gave a friend in London a tragic description of her everyday existence away from the stage. She remarked, "Professional happiness doesn't last through the night." Once the curtain rang down, all that remained for her was "the terror of a lonely hotel room." She grew to hate the final curtain applause because in the middle of the night it became completely meaningless. She confessed to her friend that at those times she often wondered, "God, how am I going to make it until morning?"

In her life, Judy made many motion pictures, each elevating her status as a star. And as the pressure increased to complete these pictures, so did the need for stimulants to keep her undernourished and overtaxed body going. Her fifth and final husband, Mickey Deans, watched helplessly as the expensive musicals rolled off the studio assembly line. Although such films heightened Garland's professional status, they added to her insomnia, and caused her to turn more and more frequently to drugs. According to Deans, Garland was eventually existing on a schedule of amphetamines and barbiturates. She was undernourished, overworked, and constantly overstimulated by drugs and alcohol; but no one seemed concerned about the threat to her health and even to her life.

In 1939, Garland played Dorothy in the film adaptation of Frank Baum's *The Wizard of Oz*. In the movie, Garland sang a piece that became her song of songs, *Over the Rainbow*. She was seventeen when the movie premiered. Other movies followed, such as as *For Me and My Gal* in 1942, *Meet Me in St. Louis* in 1944, and *Easter Parade* in 1948. In 1950 and 1951, Garland was ill, and her career appeared to be over. Then she made a comeback in a remake of *A Star is Born*. Most film critics agree that this was the best performance of Garland's life. In 1958 and 1959, illness again appeared to end her career. And once again, she staged an almost miraculous comeback. She starred in a show at New York's Palace Theater, and once again, critics raved. However, this time, the ball was over. She made several attempts at live television appearances, but most of these ended in minor disasters.

Judy was not the most melodically inventive of the great popular singers. Essentially, she sang tunes. She seldom strayed from the notes on the page. She was not a singer given to extravagant embellishments. Her enunciation was impeccable. Like Sinatra, she completely mastered the art of *rubato*. However, none of these factors really explain the phenomenon known as Judy Garland. Probably the one who came closest to explaining it was the composer who once said of Judy, she could sing "not to your ears, but to your tear ducts." Jerry Lewis understood. Pleasants reported, in a moment of nonclowning, Lewis shared with writer Bill Davidson his personal assessment of Garland's special audience appeal. Lewis told Davidson all kinds of people came to see Garland, and each brought his own particular set of heartaches and woes. Somehow, all those people, the overweight women, the rejected lovers, the drug users, the alcoholics, strongly identified with Judy. Lewis believed Garland was singing for all those miserable people. "In a way," he said, "she's singing with a hundred voices."

Additional Readings

Bergreen, Laurence. *As Thousands Cheer: The Life Of Irving Berlin*. New York: Viking Press, 1990.

Dachs, David. *Anything Goes: The World of Popular Music*. Indianapolis: Bobbs-Merril, 1964.

Davis, Sharon. *Motown: The History*. New York: Guinness, 1988.

Ewen, David. *All The Years of American Popular Music: A Comprehensive History*. Englewood Cliffs, N.J.: Prentice-Hall, 1978.

——— . *Great Men of Popular Music*. Englewood Cliffs, N.J.: Prentice-Hall, 1970.

Handy, William Christopher. *Father of the Blues: An Autobiography*. New York: The Macmillan Company, 1941.

Jones, LeRoi. *Blues People: Negro Music in White America*. New York: William Morrow Company, 1963.

Laurie, Joe Jr. *Vaudeville, from the Honky Tonks to the Palace*. New York: Henry Holt, 1953.

Lichter, Paul. *The Boy Who Dared to Rock: The Definitive Elvis*. Doubleday & Company: Garden City, New York, 1978.

Manilow, Barry. *Sweet Life: Adventures on the Way to Paradise*. New York: McGraw-Hill Book Company, 1987.

McFarland, David T. *Development of the Top Forty Radio Format*. New York: Ayer Company Publishers, 1979.

Pattison, Robert. *The Triumph of Vulgarity: Rock Music in the Mirror of Romanticism*. New York: Oxford University Press, 1987.

Pleasants, Henry. *The Great American Popular Singers*. New York: Simon and Schuster, 1974

Simon, George. *Simon Says: The Sights and Sounds of the Swing Era*. New York: Arlington House, 1955.

Waller, Don. *The Motown Story*. New York: Scribner, 1985.

Selected Recordings

Cole, Nat "King." *Honeysuckle Rose*. Decca 8535

——— . *Sweet Georgia Brown*. Capitol 239

——— . *The Christmas Song*. Capitol 311

Crosby, Bing. *Where the Blue of the Night*. Brunswick 6226

——— . *Brother, Can You Spare a Dime?* Brunswick 6414

——— . *Sweet Georgia Brown*. Brunswick 6320

Fitzgerald, Ella. *My Last Affair*. Decca 1061

——— . *It's Only a Paper Moon*. Decca 23425

——— . *A Sunday Kind of Love*. Decca 23866

Garland, Judy. *You Made Me Love You.* Decca 1463
——— . *Over the Rainbow.* Decca 2672
Jolson, Al. *Rock-a-By Your Baby.* Victor 17037
——— . *Swanee.* Columbia A 2560
——— . *April Showers.* Columbia A 3500
——— . *Toot, Toot, Tootsie.* Columbia A 3705

Chapter 7
Country Music

Hillbilly Music

Country music is music from, by, and about the people of the American countryside. The name has survived several popular-music evolutions. At first, it was called "hillbilly." Ralph Peer, an A & R (artist-and-repertorie) man for Okeh Records, coined the term when he asked a young fiddler named Al Hopkins what he called his band. Hopkins told Peer to call the band anything he wanted because they were just a bunch of hillbillies from North Carolina and Virginia, anyway. After that, Hopkins' band became known as the "Hillbillies." The recording industry picked up the cue and began calling the music played by Hopkins' band and others like it, *hillbilly music.*

For several years, country music was called hillbilly music. However, the term was always distasteful and displeasing, particularly to those who wrote and performed the music. They craved a deeper national understanding, and, certainly, greater respect for their music and the country-music business. *Billboard* magazine, which carries music-business news items as well as rating charts, briefly called the music "folk" for southeastern music, and "hot dance" for western swing. Then, *Billboard* coined the term, "country-and-western," a name soon abbreviated to just "C & W." After some time, it became apparent that the terms "country" and "western" were paired illogically. It was like saying "country and Cajun," or "country and bluegrass," when country music implied a much broader musical palette, encompassing western or cowboy music as but one of its many colors. Consequently, "and western" was dropped for the more accurate "country." "Country" it has been for some time now, and since entertainers, fans, and the industry seem comfortable with the term, "country" it will likely remain for some time to come.

For generations, the East Coast rural areas of the United States, particularly the mountain regions, have possessed an oral music tradition brought to this country by early settlers from the British Isles and continental Europe. This transplanted music consisted of authentic folk ballads several hundred years old from Scotland, Ireland, England, France, and other countries, where entertainment in the rural areas was rare and highly prized. Commenting on this Old World music, Douglas Green noted that during the early days of the New World, there was little to relieve the drudgery of daily life, of working and toiling to stay alive. To ameliorate this circumstance, the people sang the storytelling songs of love, adventure, history, and the supernatural, brought with them to the New Land. Green conceded that the performances were rough and unpolished, and the texts sometimes intact, sometimes fragmentary. Nevertheless, the music invoked tears, fright, and laughter, exactly as country music does today. As this music passed from generation to generation in the New World, it underwent a transmutation, gradually becoming a music indigenous to the people and to the region in which it thrived. Because of the inaccessibility of the areas in which it developed, the music remained essentially free from outside influences.

These mountain melodies were simple and uncomplicated. The lyrics told stories about life's everyday events: tragedies, accidents, personal torments, birth, marriage, death. Musical performances were often accompanied by what David Ewen so colorfully described as guttural sounds and rural inflections. This music permeated the very fabric of the society of a people whose daily lives were constructed from the absolute basics of life. Consequently, singing and music making were principal forms of diversion.

Country–Music Instruments

The Fiddle. The violin, or fiddle, as country musicians call it, became the first musical instrument associated with country music. Violins were small and easily transported to the New World aboard the tiny ships that made the rough Atlantic crossing. They came with the earliest settlers, and became firmly entrenched in American folk tradition in the Northeast and the South, and in Canada.

According to Ewen, fiddle music is much more commonplace than vocal music in American folk tradition. Roy Acuff once remarked that he and his fellow musicians rarely considered singing a song outside church. This attitude toward vocal music appears to have been pervasive among early country musicians. As a consequence, vocal music was routinely excluded from the early country-music format. In the beginning, Acuff and his contemporaries were instrumental musicians only. They played for their own entertainment, and periodically provided dance music for their friends and neighbors.

Much of country music, through the years, appears to have possessed a preponderance of, and a preoccupation with, instrumental music. Even so, a definite relationship exists between early instrumental and vocal music in this genre. An examination of the vocal music of the period reveals what Ewen described as a note-for-note imitation of the fiddle accompaniment.

The Guitar. After the War of Independence, America's expansion virtually exploded. This movement left pockets of rural society high and dry, particularly in areas like the remote, virtually inaccessible regions of the Appalachians. These pockets remained untouched for well over one hundred years, when the mixed blessing of railroads and coal mines arrived in the mountains of Kentucky, Tennessee, Virginia, West Virginia, and Georgia. The isolated mountaineer, who had played the same fiddle tunes and sang the same ballads as his or her ancestors, came into abrupt contact with the black section worker, who laid track throughout the southern highlands. These early railroaders brought with them another small, portable instrument called the *guitar,* far better suited to accompany singing than the high-pitched, scratchy, lonesome sounds of the fiddle.

Various parts of America, including the South, were at least vaguely familiar with the guitar before the turn of the century. As early as 1819, Andrew Jackson's daughter-in-law purchased one. This instrument is now housed at the Hermitage, Jackson's estate just outside Nashville. C. F. Martin found enough buyers in 1833 to warrant beginning the manufacture of a line of guitars, which were destined to bring him worldwide fame. However, in those days, the guitar was considered too refined, too cultured, for country music. It was reserved, instead, as a proper instrument for young ladies to study and play in the parlor.

Though the guitar was not entirely unknown in the South and other regions of the country, it had little impact on those isolated mountain pockets of "medieval culture" until the arrival of the black section workers and their guitars. The section workers also brought an African music style that stressed rhythm, a stress that had never been present in Anglo-Celtic musical tradition. Douglas Green observed, "It is interesting in this regard to listen to traditional

Irish records, both foreign, and American-Irish, because the vocal style—accent aside—is pure country music, and the haunting melodies are the very heart of most of this music. And even the instruments - fiddle and concertina, sometimes guitar - are well within country music tradition..."[1]

The Banjo. With the spread of the minstrel show's popularity during the pre- and post-Civil War days, came the popularity of the banjo, an instrument that descended from Africa. Supposedly, a Joe Sweeney invented the five-string banjo sometime during the 1830s. The instrument could be easily tuned to play lonesome, modal sounds. This feature, and its high drone string, made it a favorite among the mountain people. Lester Flatt fondly remembered that in the early days of country music, many bands consisted of nothing more than a banjo and a fiddle. The banjo was usually played in a style alternately called frailing, drop-thumb, or clawhammer. This unique technique included picking

TENOR BANJOS
ALSO FURNISHED IN FIVE-STRING AND BANJO MANDOLIN STYLES

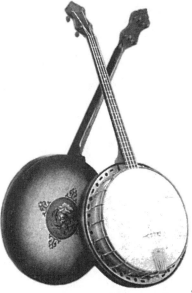

Maple Tenor Banjo
SHADED AMBER FINISH

This excellent Tenor Banjo has a laminated veneer shell with nickel plated flange which also acts as a resonator support. Flange accommodates twenty brackets. Nickel plated straining hoop and calf skin head. Maple neck with ebonized fingerboard having four inlaid position dots. Resonator is of laminated construction and has a diameter of 13½ in. Back of resonator has a floral design decalcomania in colors. The entire instrument is finished in amber and shaded.

No. 780—Each, $22.50

A 1931 WURLITZER AD FOR A BANJO.

---

[1]Green, Douglas. *Country Roots: The Origins of Country Music.* (New York: Hawthorn Books, 1976), p. 9.

the drone string (fifth string of the instrument) with the thumb and brushing the fingers across the other four strings. This style of banjo picking could be either delicate or rambunctious, according to the character of the song, or the mood of the musician.

The Mandolin. Shortly before 1900, several exotic foreign lands opened their doors to American trade, and a decided trend for acquiring the unusual invaded American culture. Americans developed a strong interest in items from the Mediterranean, the home of the mandolin. It was precisely because of this interest that the mandolin found its way first into classically oriented music in America and eventually into mountain music. Orville Gibson, a furniture maker in Kalamazoo, Michigan, altered the design of the Italian mandolin,

A MANDOLIN (FROM A G. SCHIRMER AD IN THE 1930s).

flattening it (more like a guitar or violin), and making the fret board longer. These changes made the instrument sound much better and made it much easier to play. As a result, the mandolin, particularly the Gibson version, became very popular. Mandolin orchestras began to appear. Vaudeville adopted the instrument, and eventually, it made its journey to the mountain people of the highland South.

The Ukulele and the Hawaiian Guitar. In 1898, the Hawaiian Islands came under the control of the United States, and America developed an immense interest in anything Hawaiian. The haunting sounds of Hawaiian music became an overnight stateside success, and exerted an enormous influence on the development of country music. The ukulele and the Hawaiian guitar (a standard guitar—laid flat across the lap and played with a steel bar in the left hand, which slid across the strings, instead of fretting them) became commonplace in vaudeville troupes and other touring shows. By the time the fad

No. 3—3-K

UKULELE—STYLE 3
Mahogany body and neck, finished dark color. Body bound and neatly inlaid with ivory-celluloid. Ebony fingerboard, seventeen frets, pearl position marks, white side dots, ivory nut and bridge saddle, best patent pegs.
Style No. 3—$27.50*
Style No. 3-K
Like No. 3, but body of Koa wood.
$30.00*

A 1931 WURLITZER AD FOR A UKULELE.

had run its course nationally, it was just reaching the mountain areas. Rural musicians, fascinated with the unique sounds produced by the Hawaiian guitar, quickly adapted it to their own brand of music. They combined it with the black slide-guitar style. In its original form, the Hawaiian guitar spoke with a rather subdued voice because its sound traveled upward, not outward. In the mid-1930s the instrument was electrified and amplified, and quickly acquired the name, *steel guitar,* because of the steel bar used to fret it.

Early Recording Artists

Two country fiddlers, Eck Robertson and Henry Gilliland, made the first country-music recording in 1922 for Victor. A year or so later, these two men played two songs they had recorded over radio station WBAP in Fort Worth, Texas, becoming the first recording artists to advertise their own records on the radio. On June 4, 1923, John Carson, a singing fiddler, recorded two songs in Atlanta for Okeh Records. Sales of these two releases were so encouraging that Ralph Peer, an Okeh Record Company talent scout and A&R man, issued Carson a contract. Carson became the first hillbilly artist to be offered a contract for commercial recording, hard evidence that the recording industry believed hillbilly music could be a profitable enterprise.

Professional northern performers and songwriters were quick to recognize the value of hillbilly material. Wendell Hall, "the red-headed music maker," was a vaudeville and radio personality in the 1920s. He added some novelty lyrics to a hillbilly tune, and, accompanying himself on the ukulele, recorded the Tin Pan Alley hit, *It Ain't Gonna Rain No More* for RCA Victor.

Light-opera vocalist Vernon Dalhart turned to hillbilly music in 1924, recording, for Victor, *The Wreck of the Old 97,* and *The Prisoner's Song.* This two-sided hit became, in all probability, the first million-record seller of all time. It is also probable that Dalhart sold more records than any other country star. He recorded under well over one hundred assumed names. Vernon Dalhart was just another pseudonym for Marion Try Slaughter. Slaughter was a Texan who chose the names of two nearby towns in the Lone Star State, Vernon and Dalhart, for his stage name. Dalhart's real home territory was the New York stage, though in a national sense, he was the first hillbilly star.

In the early days, much of the recording emphasis was on groups, despite Rodgers' and Dalhart's success. Authentic mountain and farm people made up the early groups that were recorded, and it was their isolation that helped them preserve the older musical forms the nostalgia-minded record companies so desired. Today, such recordings appear rather simple and primitive. Yet many of these older groups were far more sophisticated than their recordings would indicate. In reality, few of these early bands were as isolated from outside influences as once believed. These simple and primitive recordings are, in actuality, a reflection of the performers' and songwriters' desire to maintain a tradition. They also reflect the desire of the record companies to keep producing a product that would appeal to a rural, middle-aged, nostalgia-oriented market.

In late July, 1927, Ralph Peer, now working for Victor, brought his recording equipment to Bristol, on the Virginia-Tennessee border. This was a red-letter day for hillbilly music. Peer, a folk-song collector, was seeking new country sounds to record. He arrived in Bristol with his wife and two sound engineers, laden with portable recording equipment. He rented a three-story house on the Tennessee side of the border at 410 State Street and set up his equipment on the top floor. For two days, his engineers worked to hang blankets on the walls for baffles, and to build a six-foot platform for the turntable. After Peer and his crew completed the temporary recording studio, they took a weekend break to explore Bristol. They discovered a pleasant city whose population of just over eight thousand people consisted of a strange mixture of rural and urban culture. The city had two newspapers full of wire-service reports, an active Kiwanis Club, a YMCA, a growing upper-middle class that played the bullish 1927 stock market, and a fancy new hotel, complete with a hot jazz band.

Peer decided for several reasons to insert an ad in the *Herald,* a Bristol newspaper. Primarily, it was obvious that the musicians he wished to record would have to come from the nearby hills, not the town itself, which was too sophisticated. In fact, he felt he needed to justify his interest in country music to the townspeople, so in the Sunday morning edition of the *Herald,* he placed this ad:

> Mountain singers and entertainers will be the talent used for record making in Bristol. Several well-known record makers will come to Bristol this week to record. Mr. Peer has spent some time selecting the best native talent. The mountain or "hillbilly" records of this type have become more popular and are in great demand all over the country at this time. They are practically all made in the South.

In no section of the South have the prewar melodies and old mountaineer songs been better preserved than in the mountains of eastern Tennessee and southwestern Virginia, experts declare, and it was primarily for this reason that the Victor Company chose Bristol as its operating base.

On the first day of August, 1927, Peer recorded the Carter Family and the singing of the Mississippi Blue Yodeler, Jimmie Rodgers. Mountain music— the traditional songs, singing style, and instruments of the remote Appalachian mountain region—was the specialty of the Carters. Jimmie Rodgers sang country music that emphasized solo, rather than group, singing. His songs and style had been influenced by many different idioms, including blues, folk, and popular music. Ewen believed that the music of the Carter Family and Jimmie

Rodgers contained the first stirrings of country-and-western music. The members of the Carter Family who made the early recordings were A. P. Carter, who sang bass, his wife, Sarah, who played autoharp and sang most of the solos, and Maybelle Carter, A. P.'s sister-in-law and a guitar specialist, who sang tenor in part singing. The *Herald* advertisement for singers and musicians brought the Carters to Bristol from Maces Spring, Virginia, where for many years they had performed hill-country songs for various organizations and events. Their first Victor recordings were *Bury Me Under the Weeping Willow, Little Log Cabin by the Sea, The Poor Orphan Child, The Storms Are on the Ocean, Single Girl, Married Girl,* and *Wandering Boy.* These first releases sold so well that Victor brought the Carters to their Camden, New Jersey studio in May, 1928, where they made twelve more recordings. One, *Wildwood Flower,* with Maybelle playing guitar, became one of the all-time Carter Family favorites.

After that, the Carters recorded about two hundred fifty more songs, on about a dozen labels. They developed an enormous following from their recordings, their public appearances in schools and theaters, and their radio broadcasts. Their heart songs—songs of love and frustrated love, and simple sorrow songs—were particular favorites of their fans. Supposedly, A. P. Carter wrote most of these. The best were *I'm Thinking Tonight of My Blue Eyes, I'll Be All Smiles Tonight, Meeting Me by Moonlight Alone, Little Darlin', Pal of Mine, Worried Man's Blues, Coal Miner's Blues,* and *Foggy Mountain Top.*

Jimmie Rodgers

Jimmie Rodgers was the first country-music artist to discover that there was a fortune to be made in this pop-music genre. With his high-pitched voice, he created his own unique style, "the blue yodel." Though he is remembered primarily as a blues singer, he also sang country music, western music, cowboy songs, black railroad songs, work songs, hobo songs, and sometimes, even pop tunes. He sold over twenty million records, becoming the most successful of all hillbilly performers. He drove a Cadillac, and purchased a mansion in Texas he named "The Yodeler's Paradise."

Ewen said Rodgers had countless admirers, most of whom knew him only through his recordings. Some of country-and-western's most successful performers of a decade later, including Elvis Presley, Johnny Cash, Hank Snow, Ernest Tubb, Eddy Arnold, Hank Williams, Gene Autry, and Red Foley, acknowledged his strong influence on them. In fact, Ernest Tubb believed that seventy-five percent of the country-and-western stars since Rodgers' time were directly or indirectly influenced by him.

Rodgers spent much of his all-too-brief life in abject misery. He was born in 1897, in Meridian, Mississippi, where poverty was a way of life. In his

FROM A JIMMIE RODGERS ALBUM.

youth, he worked for the railroad as a water boy, and he learned railroad songs and how to play the banjo from the workers. When he was twelve, he won first prize in a local theater's amateur contest for singing *Bill Bailey, Won't You Please Come Home?*, and *Steamboat Bill*.

At age fourteen, Rodgers joined the ranks of railroad workers as an assistant foreman to his father. Within a few months he had become a brakeman on a freight-yard work train. Over the next fourteen years, he held various jobs with the railroad: call boy, baggage master, flagman. He often sang the folk songs he had been gathering for years to his fellow workers, while accompanying himself on the banjo, mandolin, or guitar. Occasionally, he sang with black musicians in nightclubs and honky-tonks around Meridian, and he was also a member of a small jazz group, which played at various functions.

In 1920, Rodgers married, and he and his wife had two daughters. His railroad salary alone was not enough to meet basic family needs. In addition, Rodgers was a chronic, extravagant spender, which added to his financial woes. In 1923, he was in New Orleans searching for a railroad job with a higher salary when his six-month-old daughter suddenly died. In order to attend his daughter's funeral, Rodgers had to pawn his banjo for the fare home.

Rodgers suffered a lung hemorrhage late in 1924. He was twenty-seven years old. For three days, he lay in critical condition in a charity hospital. He spent the rest of his life suffering from tuberculosis. His condition prohibited him from further work on the railroad. He had to find a new livelihood. Apart from railroading, singing was the only vocation he knew. He joined a medicine show touring Kentucky and Tennessee in 1925 as a blackface banjoist and entertainer. In less than a year, he discovered there was not much money in this or similar enterprises. Consequently, he made a futile effort to return to the railroad. However, a tuberculosis flare up brought a swift end to the attempt, and forced Rodgers to abandon that vocation forever.

During this entire period, Rodgers continued to make music. He formed his own group, the Jimmie Rodgers Entertainers. The Entertainers played one-night stands in southeastern fairs and tent shows. Three days a week, they performed on radio station WWNC in Asheville, North Carolina.

In August, 1927, Rodgers saw Ralph Peer's newspaper advertisement for country musicians, and went to Bristol to audition. He recorded *Sleep, Baby, Sleep,* and his first composition, *Soldier's Sweetheart.* Peer paid Rodgers twenty dollars for this session. Victor brought him to their studio in Camden, New Jersey, in November of that year for a second recording session. During that session, Rodgers recorded *Away Out on the Mountain, Ben Dewberry's Final Run, T for Texas,* and the old Tin Pan Alley tearjerker, *Mother Was a Lady.* It was in *T for Texas* that Rodgers used for the first time "the blue yodel," a style for which he became famous, and eventually acquired his nickname, the Mississippi Blue Yodeler.

Rodgers' first royalty check from Victor totaled $27.43. Six months later, his royalty checks were totaling two thousand dollars a month. Two of his 1928 recordings sold a million copies each: *Blue Yodel* (now called *Blue Yodel No. 1*), and *Brakeman's Blues.* He wrote both pieces himself.

Jimmie Rodgers' name was, by this time, a household word. Annually, he earned about one hundred thousand dollars, though this amount would have been much greater had his illness not forced him to restrict his public appearances. This, together with his extravagant spending habits, depleted his money as rapidly as tuberculosis destroyed his body. However, Rodgers continued to record, almost to his last breath. He made his last recording just two days before his death. A lung hemorrhage took his life at the Hotel Manger (later renamed the Hotel Taft) in New York on May 26, 1933.

With his death, his fame became legendary. The year Rodgers died, songwriter Bob Miller wrote *The Death of Jimmie Rodgers*. A society was formed in his name in Lubbock, Texas. In Meridian, Mississippi, his home town, a museum was founded to house his sheet music and personal papers, and his brakeman's kit from his railroading days. In 1954, Meridian erected a monument in his honor. Many notables attended its unveiling, including Adlai Stevenson. The monument was a bas-relief of Rodgers wearing an engineer's cap, a guitar under his arm, and giving a thumbs-up sign. On the monument is the following inscription; "His is the music of America. He sang the songs of the people he loved, of a young nation growing strong. His was an America of glistening rails, thundering boxcars, and rain-swept nights; of lonesome prairies, great mountains and a high blue sky. He sang of the bayous and the cotton fields, the wheated plains of the little towns, the cities, and of the winding rivers of America. We listened, we understood." In 1961, the Country Music Hall of Fame was founded in Nashville, Tennessee, and Jimmie Rodgers was its first inductee. His plaque reads, "Jimmie Rodgers stands foremost in the country music field as the man who started it all... Although small in stature, he was a giant among men, starting a trend in the musical taste of millions."

"Grand Ole Opry"

Atlanta radio station WSB began featuring hillbilly music in 1922. It was probably the first high-powered radio station to do so. Others in the South followed. On January 4, 1923, WBAP in Fort Worth, Texas, offered the first radio barn-dance or square-dance program, directed by a country fiddler, Captain M. J. Bonner. This broadcast elicited such an overwhelming response that after 1927 WBAP established a radio barn dance that aired two or three times monthly. This program was the prototype of many such programs soon to follow throughout America, including the "Chicago Barn Dance." This program was first broadcast in 1924 over WLS in Chicago, and was the brainchild of George Dewey Hay. Later in the 1920s, it became a network presentation under the new name, "National Barn Dance." Hay, who called himself "the solemn old judge," also started another barn dance in 1925 over station WSM in Nashville, the "Grand Ole Opry." "Chicago Barn Dance" and "Grand Ole Opry" became the two most popular radio barn dances of all time.

Though both programs did much to establish the popularity of country music, the name, "Grand Ole Opry," became synonymous with country music. It also became the oldest continuing show in radio history. "Grand Ole Opry" celebrated its fiftieth anniversary on November 11, 1975, with a ninety-minute broadcast from Opryland in Nashville, Tennessee. Country-music stars such as Roy Acuff, Chet Atkins, Johnny Cash, the Carter Family, Loretta Lynn,

Charlie Pride, Marty Robbins, Hank Snow, and Ernest Tubb, participated in the festivities. In 1975, Jack Hurst's *Grand Ole Opry,* a lavishly illustrated book, was published, and that same year, *Fifty Years with the Grand Ole Opry,* a history by Jerry Henderson and Myron Tassin, appeared.

George D. Hay, founder of "Grand Ole Opry," recognized the existence of a large untapped listening audience. He was acutely aware of the demographic composition of the audience toward which he directed "Grand Ole Opry" programming. He deliberately chose the rustic barn-dance setting, and for as long as he was associated with the show, did everything in his power to insure the maintenance of its overpowering nostalgic flavor. During the rapid societal and musical changes of the 1940s, Hay was famous for taking "Opry" members aside, and admonishing them to keep things simple if he thought they were getting too far away from the rural nostalgic image. Hay would remove his glasses, rub the bridge of his nose between thumb and forefinger, and say, "That's nice, boys, but keep it down to earth."

Considering "Opry"'s audience, the request to keep things simple was both reasonable and understandable. Barn-dance audiences consisted of a large number of middle-aged and elderly farm people. Not only did they buy the products advertised on the shows, products such as Royal Crown Cola, Wall-Rite, and Martha White Flour, they also responded positively and warmly to the stranger who knocked at their doors and said, "Hello, I'm from the National Life and Accident Insurance Company, the outfit that runs the 'Grand Ole Opry'..."

Dave Macon

Several country-music stars, both hillbilly and, in later days, country-and-western, gained national—and some, international—fame on the "Grand Ole Opry." Uncle Dave Macon, dubbed "the king of the banjo pickers," and "the king of hillbillies," was the first. He ruled supreme on the "Grand Ole Opry" for fifteen years. Uncle Dave hailed from Readyville, Tennessee, where he had been a farmer, first as a hired hand, then on his own property. He did not become a professional entertainer until age forty-eight. He learned to play a five-string banjo as a boy. While farming, he often appeared at barn dances.

One of Marcus Loew's vaudeville-circuit talent scouts discovered Macon, and invited him to appear at Loew's Theater in Birmingham, Alabama. Marcus Loew was a one-time operator of penny arcades. He opened his first vaudeville theater in the Bronx in 1910, and went on to build theaters all over the nation, becoming the mogul of small-time vaudeville. Macon remained on the Birmingham theater bill for several weeks. He spent the next eight years solidifying his fame by traveling the Loew vaudeville circuit extensively, and by appearing at schoolhouses and various other public auditoriums. In 1927, the "Opry" called him for an appearance. He remained with the "Opry" as one of its brightest stars until his death in 1952.

By 1932, the Great Depression, with its financial burdens, and radio broadcasting, which, in contrast, was enjoying a boom, combined to reduce country-music record sales to ten percent of what they had been in the late twenties. Many fine old record companies dissolved in bankruptcy, including Paramount, Gennett, and the original Columbia. Fear of this specter drove the fledgling industry to seek life-saving solutions to this problem. The answer that materialized was, to many, almost more than obvious: Use new subject matter with traditional instruments and voicings.

During this time, country music began the development of its many commercial branches. It reached out for different segments of its established audience, and for new audiences as well. Singing cowboys came into vogue on stage and screen. Bob Wills and his southwestern dance band, the Texas Playboys, gained new audiences for their dance-hall concerts and for their recordings. However, changes in the business and the music in general came much more slowly to the always traditional and very conservative Southeast. For example, the Vagabonds and the Delmore Brothers were the only two singing groups hired by the "Grand Ole Opry" in the early '30s. Finally, the "Opry" hired the Golden West Cowboys, Pee Wee King's big cowboy band, in 1937. Roy Acuff and Bill Monroe were singer/leaders of traditional, energetic, inventive, refreshing string bands. They both signed with the "Opry" at the end of the decade, Acuff in 1938, and Monroe in 1939.

Roy Acuff

Roy Acuff, the singing fiddler, joined the "Opry" company in 1938. Within two years, he acquired the title, "king of 'Opry,'" from Dave Macon. Acuff, the "Smokey Mountain Boy," was from eastern Tennessee. Early in his life, his vocation of choice was apparently baseball, not music. He had played baseball successfully enough in the minors to interest the New York Yankees in signing him. Just as this signing was about to take place, he suffered a sunstroke that ended his professional-baseball aspirations. After he recovered, he spent much time listening to records and learning to play several hill tunes on the violin. He traveled for two years across Virginia and eastern Tennessee with a medicine show. In 1933, he began making regular appearances on WROL radio in Knoxville. Later he formed a hillbilly group called the Crazy Tennesseans, which became a regular feature on KNOX radio in Knoxville. The group gave concerts across the South, and made records for Columbia. On "Grand Ole Opry," Acuff, accompanied by a string band called *The Smokey Mountain Boys,* became the company's first singing star, performing mountain songs and sacred songs as well.

Acuff earned perhaps the highest income of any country singer to that date. His influence in the business was extensive. Then, in 1942, he extended his influence by forming, with songwriter Fred Rose, the Acuff-Rose Company in Nashville. Acuff-Rose was the first music-publishing house devoted exclusively to country music. Acuff appeared in several movies in the 1940s: *Hi Neighbor, My Darling Clementine, Cowboy Canteen,* and *Night Train to Memphis.* In Tennessee, his popularity won him the 1948 Republican nomination for Governor, but could not get him elected. Acuff was elected to the Country Music Hall of Fame in 1962, becoming the Hall's first living singer to gain this honor. A bronze plaque honoring Acuff was unveiled at the new Grand Ole Opry House in 1972. Its inscription reads, in part: "Roy joined the 'Grand Ole Opry' in 1938. He was its first international star... Truly he has earned the title, the king of country music."

In the South of the '30s, popular music consisted of an odd mixture of sounds. This mixture included the sounds and styles of the old Carter Family, at that time still quite popular with southerners. It also included the sounds of the string band, and, not surprisingly, of family groups, particularly brothers, who grew up with those strange new instruments, the mandolin and guitar. Country musicians learned to match these instruments and their voices to the songs and hymns they had absorbed in their youth. In the early '50s, the sound created by this unique combination became a part of the sound associated with the beginnings of rock-and-roll. The music of Bill Haley and Elvis Presley was strongly influenced by this kind of musical fusion.

This mixture of sounds, groups, and styles has continued in a relatively traditional vein. Any music resulting from such a fusion is still referred to as "old time." During this early period, this genre of country music continued to be called simply "country music." Though names such as "western swing" or "honky-tonk" were applied occasionally to country music, they failed to gain any real and lasting currency. This kind of country music remains to this day firmly entrenched in the traditions from which it came, proudly flaunting its old-fashioned label.

Hillbilly Becomes Country-and-Western

In all probability, the state of Texas is the region most responsible for the sounds and styles that comprise the "western" portion of country-and-western. From the beginning, Texas has exerted strong influence on the development of country music. The list of accomplishments by Texas country-music stars is considerable, including the first country-music recording, the first million-record seller, and five of the thirty members of the Country Music Hall of Fame: Gene Autry, Jim Reeves, Tex Ritter, Ernest Tubb, and Bob Wills. Texas has also produced major stars in every major genre of country music, except bluegrass.

Texas is an ethnic melting pot, with many of its ethnic strains still evident today. Its music incorporated many of those strains, particularly the genre called "western swing." Appalachian music, the foundation of all country music, is the strain most evident. Many of the state's first settlers came from the mountains of the Southeast, bringing their Appalachian music with them. From Tennessee and other southeastern mountain regions came mountain-style fiddling and singing. There has long been a heavy settlement of German, Bohemian, and other central European peoples. These nationalities brought with them their love of polkas, schottisches, and waltzes. Consequently, this music became forever embedded in the music associated with Texas. German and Slavic influences were especially strong in south-central Texas.

Another powerful influence has been the Cajuns of Louisiana, who owe at least the accordion to the immigrant Germans who passed through Louisiana on their way west to Texas. Cajun music is, and always has been, popular in Texas, especially along the southeastern Texas-Louisiana border. Northern Mexico, too, has made its contributions, through its Norteno music.

Although all these ingredients are important, they only serve to add spice to the two basic distinctive sounds of Texas music: the songs of the singing cowboy and square-dance fiddle-band music. Regardless of other influences, past and present, these two types form the foundation of Texas music. They are still dominant today. And it is these different sounds and styles combined with the old-time sounds and styles of the southeastern mountain people that comprise country-and-western.

Ernest Tubb, Hank Snow, Eddy Arnold (the Tennessee Plowboy), Hank Williams, Sr., and Johnny Cash all shared in transforming country music from hillbilly to country-and-western. These men came from the ranks of the "Grand Ole Opry."

Ernest Tubb. Ernest Tubb was born in Crisp, Texas. Before landing his first playing-and-singing job in 1934 with radio station KONO in San Antonio, he served ice cream and sodas in a drugstore, and afterward worked for the WPA. His radio program aired twice weekly for fifteen minutes. Jimmie Rodgers was his hero, and, not surprisingly, Tubb modeled much of his singing and playing after Rodgers. In 1941, he wrote and recorded *Walkin' the Floor Over You,* the first of many of his songs to become million-record sellers. *Walkin' the Floor Over You* established Tubb as a major country artist.

Hank Snow. Hank Snow was a Canadian, born in Liverpool, Nova Scotia, in the same year as Tubb, 1914. His fascination with western movies led to his interest in country music. In his youth, he studied music and listened to Jimmie Rodgers records. Billed as "Hank, the Singing Ranger," he sang over Nova Scotia radio, acquiring immense Canadian popularity. In 1936, Victor offered him a contract, which lasted for several decades.

Initially, Victor released Snow's recordings exclusively in Canada. Consequently, he was virtually unknown in the United States until 1944, when a Dallas disc jockey began playing some of Snow's Canadian recordings. This event led to American radio appearances and bookings, and eventually to a very successful tour. Snow's fame now established, Victor began distributing his recordings in the United States. He continued to make bestselling records and albums into the 1960s.

Eddy Arnold. Eddy Arnold was born in 1918 in Henderson, Tennessee. Until his mid-thirties, he worked as a farmer—hence the name, "Tennessee Plowboy." He became so successful as a pop singer in the 1960s, one forgets that Arnold was an even bigger success as a country-music singer, and member of the "Grand Ole Opry." He was elected to the Country Music Hall of Fame in 1966.

Arnold made his radio debut in 1936 in Jackson, Tennessee, over station WTHS. Within six years, he had become a favorite of Tennessee radio audiences. He went from there to the "Grand Ole Opry," appearing with Pee Wee King's Golden West Cowboys. In 1948, he made his first million-record seller, *Bouquet of Roses*. From that time, he developed into one of country music's major attractions and most successful performers. Between 1948 and 1952, many of his recordings made the top of the charts, five of them in 1948 alone.

Hank Williams, Sr. Hank Williams, Sr. was—and even after his death, continues to be—one of country music's most dominant figures. He became a "Grand Ole Opry" member in 1949, and was one of four musicians to be elected to the Country Music Hall of Fame when it was instituted in 1961. He grew up in several small Alabama communities near Georgiana, a little southern town described by Roger Williams in his biography of Hank as "sixty miles south of Montgomery and 115 miles north of Mobile, meaning practically nowhere." His mother gave him his first music lessons, and introduced him to religious hymns and gospels. By the time he was six, Hank played the organ so well that he was often asked to play in church. When he was eight, he received as a gift his first guitar. His first and only guitar teacher was a black street singer.

In July, 1937, when Hank was just under fourteen years old, the family moved to Montgomery. There Hank acquired a new Gibson guitar and a new pair of boots and cowboy hat. He entered an amateur contest and sang a song of his own, *WPA Blues*. He won the contest, and fifteen dollars, which he promptly blew on nothing in particular. He never learned how to handle money or liquor. Pleasants wryly noted that in future years, Hank would go through immense quantities of both.

In 1937, Hank formed his own band, *Hank Williams and his Drifting Cowboys,* and for ten years they performed over WSFA in Montgomery. By 1946, Williams had settled in Nashville. There, he met Fred Rose, Roy Acuff's partner in Acuff-Rose Publishing. Rose signed Williams to an exclusive contract, and also arranged for Williams to record for the infant MGM Recording Company. His first MGM recording in 1947, his own *Move It on Over,* was a success. This recording secured his invitation to join the "Grand Ole Opry" company in 1949. In his "Opry" debut, he sang *Lovesick Blues.* He virtually brought the house down. MGM released *Lovesick Blues* in 1949. It became Hank's first million-record seller.

No one really knew Hank, not even Hank himself. Only his audiences had any sort of clue as to who he was and what he was like. He would, on rare occasions, reveal at least a portion of himself to them. Allen Rankin once said that Hank had little personality until he sang. Hank had a habit of slouching out on the stage, looking like a limp dishrag. Then he would pick up his guitar and, according to Rankin, undergo a remarkable transformation. Rankin observed that Hank appeared to grow three feet.

Williams was a genuinely sad man all his life. The only time he appeared happy was when he was performing. He left an indelible impression on country music and on the world of popular music. How he accomplished this remains one of show business's mysteries. Measured against any conventional criteria of songwriting or singing, his enormous appeal makes no sense. A writer for the *Alabama Journal* once commented that Hank's singing reminded one of "the whine of an electric saw going through pine timber."

Unfortunately, Hank fell prey to liquor, success, prosperity, drugs, and women, none of which he could handle. He also suffered from marital discord, a chronic bad heart, and a bad back from two slipped disks. He was fired from "Grand Ole Opry" in September, 1952. On January 1, 1953, while en route to a performance in Canton, Ohio, he died in the back seat of his Cadillac.

Johnny Cash. Johnny Cash, another alumnus of "Grand Ole Opry," seems likely, like Jimmie Rodgers and Hank Williams, to become a legend in country music. And, like Rodgers and Williams, early in his career, Cash possessed the same penchant for self-destruction. However, Cash has apparently been able to overcome his problems with drugs, and has become one of country music's most formidable performer/composers.

Cash was born in Kingsland, Arkansas, in 1932. He came from the same kind of poverty and struggle that pervaded the early lives of Jimmie Rodgers and Hank Williams. Cash grew up on hymns and gospel songs. By the time he was twelve, he had begun to write his own music. He made his first radio appearance in Blytheville, Arkansas, while he was in high school. He unsuccessfully auditioned for Sun Records' director, Sam Phillips, who told him to come back when he had better material.

He enlisted in the Air Force, and went to Germany as a radio operator. While in Germany, he tried writing poetry. He left the service in 1954, married Vivian Liberto, a San Antonio girl, and established a home in Memphis. Two of his amateur musician friends saw some of the poems Cash had written, and advised Cash to set one of them, *Hey Porter,* to music. They also proposed forming a combo. They named it *Johnny Cash and the Tennessee Two,* and began appearing at various social events around the city. Again, Cash auditioned for Sun Records, this time with his new combo and some of his own material. Phillips was so impressed with *Hey Porter,* he agreed to record it on the condition that Cash write a second song for the flip side. Cash responded by composing *Cry, Cry, Cry.* The Sun recording, released in 1955, gained a position on the charts in about six weeks. Within a relatively short period, it sold approximately one hundred thousand disks.

Now Sam Phillips was willing to sign Cash to an exclusive Sun contract. In 1956, Sun released *Folsum Prison Blues* and *I Walk the Line,* both of which became gold records and both of which Johnny had written. These were the first two of many. All his recordings between 1956 and 1959 made the top-ten charts in country-and-western music. Cash was the only composer/performer ever to accomplish this. During that period, his records sold over six million copies. In 1959, he left Sun Records for Columbia.

Cash had become a national star by the 1960s. His first three Columbia albums were smash hits. In addition to his recordings, he made appearances on "Grand Ole Opry," gave concerts in the United States (including one at Carnegie Hall) and abroad, made guest appearances on network TV programs, and appeared in several movies. He was approaching the pinnacle of his profession. Then, because of his horrendous performing and business schedule and the domestic problems he had begun experiencing, he began taking tranquilizers and Dexedrine. One night in 1965, he was driving from Mexico, when the border guards seized him for attempted drug smuggling. He spent the night in an El Paso, Texas, jail. That night served several purposes for Cash. In addition to nourishing his long-felt sympathy for prisoners and the lives they spent behind locked doors, it compelled him to take stock of his life as an artist and as a man. He decided to give up drugs and to attempt to put his life back together.

In the fall and winter of 1968, Johnny broke box-office records at Carnegie Hall and Madison Square Garden. In 1969, he became the star of his own ABC network television show. By 1971, his annual income exceeded two million dollars. Cash is still quite active professionally. Whether on national television or live, he always opens his appearances with his warm and forthright, "Hello—I'm Johhny Cash." David Ewen, in describing Cash's concert dress, said, "He wears a personalized costume comprised of an outmoded but stylish frock coat, striped trousers, a vest, and a white ruffled shirt, giving him the appearance, as Albert Govoni wrote, of 'a riverboat gambler, a raffish parson, a card shark out of the Old West… a New Orleans rakehell on his way to a duel over a woman.' "[2]

The 1970s and After

Throughout the 1970s, country music was pulled in several different directions. The trend on Nashville's Music Row was toward a smoother, more popular sound, while in the "Grand Ole Opry," it was business as usual. There was an apparent renewed emphasis on the well-established traditional country music. Though "Opry" stalwarts, such as Roy Acuff and Ernest Tubb, had not had a hit record in several years, the "Opry" itself and all its ritual were flourishing. In Austin, Texas, and other parts of the Southwest, there was an earthier, grittier sound, while in the Southeast, the Allman Brothers and Charlie Daniels were fusing country and rock. In the East, bluegrass became the fad, attracting huge crowds to outdoor happenings.

In October, 1976, David Snow was program director for one of the nation's top-ten country-music stations, located in Buffalo. He made the first of several widely quoted remarks that set the tone for the growing tension over the direction of country music. He observed that his station played middle-of-the-road, easy-listening country music, recorded by such artists as Ray Price, Olivia Newton-John, and John Denver. Management was reluctant to program what Snow termed "drinking songs" by such artists as Hank Snow, Stonewall Jackson, or Buck Owens. Davis admitted he enjoyed the easy-listening artists at home, but he believed they were no longer commercial. During this period, many country-music aficionados apparently believed country music was losing its identity. However, Snow saw the changes as good because, in his view, those changes were bringing more people to country music. He believed that country artists such as Roy Acuff and Ernest Tubb deserved respect for what they had accomplished, but he thought their day had passed. He compared their generation of performers to Babe Ruth, remarking that if Ruth were still alive, no one would play him in a major-league game.

---

[2]Ewen, David. *All the Years of American Popular Music.* (Englewood Cliffs, New Jersey: Prentice-Hall, Inc., 1977), p. 576.

To most country entertainers, this was a gauntlet thrown at their feet, and they responded in different ways. Several days after Dave Snow's remarks, Hank Snow, then still singing in the lean, spare style of Jimmie Rodgers, told a story about playing a date in Kerrville, Texas. He said he stood in nearly waist-deep mud, singing for a hundred people, while just a few miles down the road, Willie Nelson was singing for an audience of a hundred thousand. Snow remarked that his last album had hardly sold three copies. He ruefully admitted that Chet Atkins had warned him to change his style, to "modernize." Snow had refused to believe that the old, familiar country sound and style would ever fail.

Other performers defended the aesthetics and appeal of the more traditional country style. However, an increasing number agreed with a Texas fiddle player and prominent western swing bandleader, Alvin Crow, who said that western music did not sell in Nashville. He believed the Nashville promoters were attempting to sell a watered-down version of country to the nation at large.

Today, country music is a fusion of countless musical elements—hillbilly, traditional mountain country, western, Mexican, folk, rock—and all those elements are blended into a music uniquely American. Country music is, and has always been, in a constant state of change and growth. It will always stir the emotions of many people who have little in common except the universal emotions of pity and fear, love and hate, and the strength to endure.

Additional Readings

Bane, Michael. *The Outlaws: Revolution in Country Music.* New York: Country Music Magazine Press, 1978.

Carr, Patrick. *The Illustrated History of Country Music.* New York: Doubleday & Company, 1980.

Galliard, Frye. *Watermelon Wine: The Spirit of Country Music.* New York: St. Martin's Press, 1978.

Green, Douglas B. *Country Roots: The Origins of Country Music.* New York: Hawthorne Books, 1976.

Grissom, John. *Country Music: White Man's Blues.* New York: Coronet, 1970.

Hurst, Jack. *Nashville's Grand Ole Opry.* New York: Abrams, 1989.

Malone, Bill C. *Country Music U.S.A.* Austin and London: University of Texas Press, 1968.

Selected Recordings

The following recordings are from the New World Recorded Anthology of American Music and are listed by artist, record number within the collection, side number, and band number.

Roy Acuff—#287: s2/3
Eddy Arnold—#207: s1/1
The Carter Family (A. P. Carter)—#287: s1/3, s1/5
Johnny Cash—#207: s2/4
Dave Macon—#270: s2/1
Jimmie Rodgers—#287: s1/2. s1/4
Hank Snow—#249: s2/7—# 207: s1/4

Chapter 8
Broadway, from Vaudeville to Berlin

Early publishers were primarily concerned with the most effective means by which to present new songs to the public. From the evidence, the theater was the most logical and appropriate setting, and in the early 1900s, vaudeville was the most visible theater in the nation.

Tony Pastor and Early Vaudeville

Antonio (Tony) Pastor, born on Greenwich Street in New York on May 28, 1832, is known as the godfather of vaudeville. His early training for the stage began in earnest in 1847 when he became an apprentice with John J.

Nathan's Circus. That fall, Tony made his debut in the circus arena, singing comic songs. When ringmaster Neil Jamison died, Tony succeeded him, becoming the youngest ringmaster among all the circuses active at that time. In 1851, he became ringmaster of the Bowery Amphitheater. There he also acted in dramatic skits for the first time. He became a clown for New York's Nixon Palace Gardens in 1857.

In 1860, Pastor quit the circus and adopted variety as a permanent profession. He made his variety stage debut that same year at Frank River's Melodeon in Philadelphia. He returned to New York as a comic vocalist at the Broadway Music Hall when it first opened on March 22, 1861, and remained there for a year. Then he opened his own business at 444 Broadway. Its name was simply "444." Joe Laurie, Jr. called it a honky-tonk that offered beer, wine, liquor, and a few hostesses. Pastor kept the business until 1865. Then he and Sam Sharply, an old minstrel man, became partners. They took over Volk's Garden at 201 Bowery. They remodeled it, named it *Pastor's Opera House*, and operated it successfully for ten years.

During its first year or two, Pastor's Opera House presented just variety—no vaudeville. Then Pastor decided to organize a variety road show while his house was closed for the summer. He began in Paterson, New Jersey with Tony Pastor's Own Company. It was his first trip as a manager.

A VAUDEVILLE THEATER.

Pastor's traveling show was excellent. It played most of the better theaters, and was always a box-office success. Tony increased his annual tours from three to six months. He played almost every prominent town in the nation.

Pastor opened his Fourteenth Street Theater in the Tammany Hall Building in October, 1881. New York had never seen a theater quite like it. Pastor's October show was straight variety. The theater had actually opened in February of that year, with presentations of Gilbert and Sullivan parodies. However, these proved unsuccessful, so Pastor returned to theater he knew best, variety.

B. F. Keith purchased New York's Union Square Theater in 1893, and converted it to a vaudeville house. It was located only a few blocks from Pastor's, and became fierce competition for his music hall. Keith charged just fifty cents for a good seat in a new and beautiful little theater. He was able to get many headliners and top acts. This combination forced Pastor to lower his admission fees from one dollar to ten, twenty, and thirty cents. He could never again raise his prices. Even with his price reduction, Pastor continued to lose business.

Pastor elected to keep his theater small and intimate. He had no ambition to expand. With so small a house and business, he could still appear occasionally on stage to sing his songs. He was content. Six of the early successful vaudeville managers came from stage backgrounds. Five made fortunes during their lives. Pastor died August 28, 1908, leaving an estate of less than $6,000.

Keith and Albee

Benjamin Franklin Keith and Edward Franklin Albee, two of vaudeville's most enterprising impresarios, served their theatrical apprenticeships in the circus. As a team, they gave a pirated version of *The Mikado* in Boston and on a road tour. While regular performances of *The Mikado* normally cost one dollar and fifty cents, Keith and Albee's show cost only twenty-five cents. In 1885, they purchased their own theater, the Bijou in Boston, refurbished it, and proceeded to make vaudeville history. They began a policy of continuous entertainment (as opposed to the prevailing two-a-day shows) beginning at 11:00 a.m. and running until 11:00 p.m. The Bijou opened with an admission charge of ten cents, later increasing to twenty-five cents. For this sum, patrons could see such vaudeville stars as Weber and Fields, and the Four Cohans.

A booming theater business soon allowed Keith and Albee to extend their theater interests to Philadelphia, first to the Bijou, and then to the Chestnut Street Theater. In 1893, they acquired New York's Union Square Theater and converted it to a vaudeville house, competing with nearby Tony Pastor's Music Hall. Then, during that same year, they built Boston's Colonial House, the most luxurious theater of that time dedicated to vaudeville. This theater, which cost about one million dollars, became the center of a chain that included some four hundred theaters across the East and Midwest, all owned and operated by Keith and Albee. As they spread their influence through the acquisition of theaters, they also developed a vaudeville exchange, the Keith-Albee circuit (later called the United Booking Office). Eventually, this exchange handled the bookings for vaudevillians in over three hundred theaters.

B. F. Keith.

B. F. Keith entered show business through a peculiar back door. It is thought that he was originally a purser on a steamer. Supposedly, he got into show business by way of a candy concession at a circus. E. F. Albee, later his partner for life, was the legal adjuster or fixer for this circus. Sometime around 1883, Keith spent the winter in Boston. During that time, he began a partnership with a Colonel Austin. Together, the two opened a dime museum in an old store. At that time, the dime museum was a popular and profitable attraction.

Dime museums were always the same. There was a curio hall, where the crowd awaited the next show, and a theater, where performances, usually an hour in length, were given. P. T. Barnum had discovered years earlier there was magic in the name, "museum." The very religious customers could salve their consciences by pretending they really came to see the museum, not that abode of the devil, the adjacent theater. The Boston Museum was already giving full-length plays. It eventually became the home of classical drama, and featured two performances a day. For vaudeville, Keith preferred a show an hour.

Keith discovered many would ask when the next show started. When they were told they had to wait half an hour, sometimes more, many patrons simply left. They were apparently unwilling to wait in the dreary curio hall. To combat this revenue loss, Keith advertised a revolutionary new idea in Boston newspapers, continuous performances. Part of the advertisement read, "Come when you please; stay as long as you like."

Excluding holidays, Keith's idea worked well, even given the questionable quality of such endless entertainment. Joe Laurie, Jr. humorously observed that only one with a stout heart and corresponding constitution could endure two hours of one of those Keith productions. As his prosperity grew, Keith improved the quality of his shows by elaborating upon them, and adding a comic troupe. His productions were now primarily Gilbert and Sullivan operettas. Because these shows were in the public domain by then, they were available to him at no cost. His idea worked, but not as well as it should have.

Keith and Albee Join Forces. Keith appealed to his old friend, E. F. Albee, for help. Albee paid Keith a visit. He at once cleaned up the house front, which housed horrible-smelling animal cages. Business immediately increased, so much, in fact, that Albee decided Keith should apply his idea to a deluxe theater. Keith demurred out of parsimony. He failed to see just where the money would come from to build the palatial theater Albee proposed.

Albee, however, was convinced the concept was sound. He decided to join forces with Keith regardless of objections Keith might have to such an arrangement. (Albee's was quite a dominating personality.) Albee arranged to build a theater, primarily with money borrowed from the Catholic Diocese of Boston. To secure Catholic financing, he had to assure the Diocese that performances would be clean and tasteful. In 1893, Keith opened his Boston Colonial Theater.

Given the personalities of the two men, it is odd that Albee, rather than Keith, carried cleanliness and good taste to an almost fanatical degree. Albee hired the superintendent of one of Boston's leading Sunday schools to stand at the back of the theater and monitor all productions. A note was sent backstage when any infraction, regardless of how minor, occurred.

According to Joe Laurie, Jr., Keith was a small man, both in stature and mentality. He was cold and colorless, and petty in small ways about small matters. He had no use for people he could not "buy," and little use and respect for those he could. Variety's famous critic, Epes W. Sargent, once refused a one-hundred-dollar tip offered him by Keith. From that time on, Keith avoided Sargent whenever possible. If Sargent could not be "bought," he was to be feared.

In his later years, Keith gradually withdrew from active participation in the organization. His first wife died in 1910. Keith was devoted to her, and he never quite recovered from her death. He remarried, but suffered a nervous breakdown on his honeymoon, after which he gladly turned control of the business over to Albee. He died shortly afterward while cruising Florida waters on his yacht.

E. F. Albee. E. F. Albee, born in 1857 in Machias, Maine, rose from circus ticket man and legal adjustor to become one of vaudeville's most prominant and shrewdist impresarios. With Keith, Albee built an empire of vaudeville theaters, an empire over which he was one of two rulers. As his job grew, so did his appreciation for the importance of his position. His circus-days stories grew fewer and fewer, until they disappeared entirely. After a time, he forbade even the mention of circus tents in his presence. He was not only the general manager of the expanding Keith Circuit, he was also head of the United Booking Office. He now moved in a new and higher social circle, and wanted to forget his slightly unsavory circus background. When Keith, and later, his son Paul, died, Albee discarded all appearance of acting on Keith's behalf. He assumed full and open command of all Keith-Albee enterprises.

E. F. ALBEE.

In his later years, Albee became somewhat philanthropic. He contributed large sums of money for the building of St. John's Cathedral in New York. He left the Actor's Fund about one hundred thousand dollars. During his active years in show business, he built several stunningly beautiful theaters. Joe Laurie, Jr. remarked about Albee's life and his contributions to vaudeville, "There is no doubt that E. F. Albee took variety out of the kennels and placed vaudeville in the palaces he constructed, but he never seemed to realize that it was vaudeville itself that was more important than the theaters which housed it. The beautiful houses did a lot to dignify vaude, but beautiful theaters can't entertain."[1]

---

[1] Laurie, Joe, Jr. *Vaudeville, from the Honky Tonks to the Palace.* (New York: Henry Holt, 1953), p. 347.

John J. Murdock

John J. Murdock began his theater career in the late 1890s as a stage electrician. Shortly thereafter, he purchased a Cincinnati stock company. He moved to Chicago, where in 1906 he built The Majestic Temple Roof, Chicago's first million-dollar vaudeville house. Murdock was fond of music, and always gave his patrons the best shows currently available. When he could not get top-billing acts, he created them. One of his creations, Grace Akis, "the girl with the auburn hair," later became his wife. Grace was one of the first of the living-picture acts. She became a headliner.

Sometime during the early 1900s, the firm of Kohl, Castle, Middleton and Beck employed Murdock to develop the Western Vaudeville Managers Association. Soon, the Western Association was serving twenty amusement parks with outdoor attractions, bands, and free shows. Shortly after this, Murdock built the Majestic.

Murdock knew how to make vaudeville pay handsomely. He was shrewd, hesitant, and almost never gave a definite answer to any question. His business deals brought theaters into the eastern and western booking circuits on contracts calling for a fifty-fifty division of money earned. He did all the hiring and firing, and booked and charged for the various services that accompany the supplying of attractions. Millions of dollars in income resulted from these arrangements.

Murdock saw the handwriting on the wall in moving pictures. Time and again, he tried to interest E. F. Keith in entering the motion-picture industry, but Keith would not listen. Murdock watched the formation of the Keith-Albee Circuit and saw it become the Radio-Keith-Orpheum. Before he retired in 1926, he arranged the sale of Pathé Pictures, and eventually became its board chairman.[2]

---

[2] The Radio-Keith-Orpheum resulted from a merger between the Film Booking Office of America (FBO), formed in 1922, and the Keith-Albee-Orpheum. FBO was a small film company which produced minor action, melodramatic, and Western movies during the heyday of the silent film, all of highly questionable quality. Joseph P. Kennedy, father of former President John F. Kennedy, purchased FBO in 1926, but the quality of its product remained essentially unchanged. With the coming of sound to the motion-picture industry, David Sarnoff, president of RCA, joined forces with Kennedy, viewing FBO as a suitable vehicle and showcase for his RCA Photophone sound system. Sarnoff and Kennedy then engineered a merger between FBO and the Keith-Albee-Orpheum. This merger provided the newly formed company, renamed the Radio-Keith Orpheum, with theaters in which to display its wares. More importantly, it brought into being RKO Radio Pictures on October 23, 1928. RKO is best known for the Fred Astaire-Ginger Rogers musicals of the 1930s, for the 1933 film "King Kong," for "Citizen Kane" in 1941, and for the Val Lewton low-budget "horror" productions of the early 1940s. In his book, *The RKO Story*, Richard B. Jewell wrote, "RKO generated more than 1000 pictures—some forgettable, some too awful to contemplate, and a handful of the best movies ever made."

Martin Beck

Martin Beck came to the United States as a member of a small troupe of German actors when he was about sixteen. The troupe did not do well and broke up. Beck and another member of the troupe, Charles Feleky, began selling crayon pictures door-to-door and doing odd jobs to keep from starving. In 1893, Beck found a job waiting on tables at the Royal Music Hall in Chicago. His salary was twelve dollars a week plus tips. Soon, because of his knowledge of show business, he was helping out as manager, stage manager, cashier, auditor, and barman. He also continued to wait on tables. Management raised his salary to twenty dollars a week. In 1894, Beck moved to the Engel Concert Hall. His job included essentially the same tasks that he had performed for the Royal Music Hall. After two years, he became a partner in the hall. The Great Depression brought his budding music-hall career to an abrupt end, and he exchanged his apron for a trip West with the Schiller Vaudeville Company.

While in San Francisco, Beck met Gustave Walters, owner of the Orpheum Theater, who offered Beck a job as manager and booker. Beck accepted and was soon promoting the development of a new Orpheum in Los Angeles. Beck negotiated the merger between the Orpheum Circuit and Kohl and Castle in Chicago. The new company became the Western Vaudeville Association. It controlled all the vaudeville bookings in the Midwest.

Beck was primarily responsible for bringing style and class into vaudeville. He offered large salaries to good concert musicians and ballet dancers. These kinds of entertainment were foreign to vaudeville audiences, and often would

THE BELLE OF NEW YORK, 1897.

not fare well. Beck would merely shake his head and say of the audience, "They got to be educated." When asked why he employed that kind of act despite audience disapproval, Beck replied, "Listen, in a vaudeville show everybody on the bill can't wear red noses, baggy pants, and take prat falls. A bill must have variety, change of pace, and have something that appeals to everyone. You know, there are a lot of people [who] like good music. If one man out there liked that fine violinist, I've made a customer!"[3]

In later years, vaudeville began drifting out of style. Beck had begun to move away from an active role in the field, but he attempted to return to a management position and salvage at least some portion of it. Unfortunately, it was too late. Not even his expertise could help. Vaudeville was dying. He then became an adviser to RKO Motion Pictures. Actors remembered Beck fondly, saying that Beck's Orpheum Circuit extended the fairest treatment in the trade.

F. F. Proctor

Frederick Freeman Proctor was born in 1852 in Dexter, Maine. His first foray into show business was as the partner of a foot-barrel juggler. Later, he worked in a circus and in variety shows with various partners. He finally made a successful European tour as a single act under the name of his first partner, Levantine.

In 1880, with H. Jacobs as his partner, Proctor opened his own theater, the Green Theater, in Albany, New York. From 1880 to 1889, he and Jacobs opened theaters in New York, Connecticut, Pennsylvania, and Delaware. In 1889, they opened Proctor's Twenty-third Street Theater in New York City.

After the dissolution of their partnership, Proctor and Jacobs both came to New York, where Jacobs became manager of the Third Avenue Theater. Proctor took over the theater on West Twenty-third Street. Using an idea fostered by Jacobs, Proctor blanketed New York with thousands of one-sheet ads, all shouting, "After Breakfast, Go to Proctor's." This idea worked so well, Proctor was soon able to begin a second theater, the Pleasure Palace on Fifty-eighth Street and Third Avenue. A new era began for Proctor when he acquired George Wallen as his business manager. Wallen convinced Proctor to expand into small New York towns, rather than in the city itself. Proctor took Wallen's advice and became a wealthy man.

Proctor was a man with a colorless personality and few friends. He seldom went backstage to meet any of his acts. However, he was good to his employ-

---

[3]Laurie, p. 362.

ees. He was the first theater owner to provide employees with insurance. He was the first in vaudeville to give dramatic shows with vaudeville inserted between performances, and the first to reduce admission to morning shows. He established full-pit orchestras. He was the first to recognize the value of motion pictures, and the first to present a feature film in a first-tier theater. Proctor was a highly successful man. At one time he owned fifty theaters. He died on September 4, 1929, remembering over three hundred people in his will, and leaving one hundred thousand dollars to the Actors' Fund.

Marcus Loew

At age thirty-six, Marcus Loew was in the fur business. His father had come to America, married a German girl, and become a head waiter. Loew's initial ambition was to be just like his father, quite understandable for someone born in a windowless room on New York's Lower East Side. As a young boy, Loew worked at all types of odd jobs to help with family finances. He finally

PICTURE COLLECTION, THE BRANCH LIBRARIES, THE NEW YORK PUBLIC LIBRARY

"SEEING NEW YORK," C. 1901.

**A VAUDEVILLE
ACT FROM
ABOUT 1927.**

PICTURE COLLECTION, THE BRANCH LIBRARIES, THE NEW YORK PUBLIC LIBRARY/SCHOMBURG COLLECTION

entered the fur business as a salesman. He saved a little money, and purchased an equity in a Harlem apartment house.

David Warfield, an excellent comedian with Weber and Field, also decided to invest in real estate. He invested about fifty thousand dollars in an apartment house just next door to Loew's. Loew visited Warfield and told him his building could be operated in a more profitable fashion. Warfield hired Loew to manage the building. It was a propitious moment. This simple act began a lifelong friendship that reaped both men millions of dollars.

Another of Loew's Harlem neighbors was Adolph Zukor who, like Loew, was also in the fur business. Loew and Zukor became friends. In 1906, Zukor, Aaron Jones, and Morris Cohen bought an old store, and converted it to a penny arcade. Loew and Warfield joined the partnership. Although business was excellent, Loew and Warfield soon decided they wanted an arcade of their own, so they withdrew from the partnership. Mitchell Mark, who later built the first plush motion-picture house in America, joined the Loew-Warfield team. Within a short time, the partners owned four arcades.

Now Loew expanded. He purchased an arcade in Cincinnati and installed a moving-picture machine. The house seated eighty, and Loew charged the going rate of just a nickel a seat. The first week he was open, he made over five hundred dollars. Loew returned to New York and opened a moving-picture house. Within six months, he and Warfield owned forty moving-picture houses, or nickelodeons.

In 1908, Warfield sent Loew an unemployed actor who needed a job. Loew could find nothing for him to do at any of their theaters, so he asked if the actor could recite *Gunga Din* and *The Road to Mandalay*. The actor said yes, and Loew put him on the bill to recite between pictures. Box-office receipts immediately increased, so much so, in fact, Loew decided to install similar acts in all their theaters. This was Loew's first experience with vaudeville.

On the strength of this experience, Loew began booking acts regularly in their theaters. Vaudeville was becoming big business for him. He began purchasing more and larger picture houses, and charging admission rates of ten, twenty, and thirty cents. Business boomed. By 1917, Loew and Warfield had international interests. In addition to their New York theaters, they controlled seventeen in France and several in Germany.

During the early 1900s, Loew purchased their first large theater, a two-thousand-seat house in Brooklyn called Watson's Cozy Corner. Before this purchase, Loew had been accustomed to houses with only two hundred seats. Watson's had been a burlesque house with a questionable reputation. Police had raided it several times because illegal shows bordering on pornography were playing there. Loew's first show was a Shakespeare play performed by an Italian company, Loew said, to remove the stink from the joint. He then reopened the house as the Royal Theater, featuring moving pictures and vaudeville. After a shaky start, business increased almost unbelievably. That season, Loew cleared over sixty-five thousand dollars on the Royal.

Marcus Loew looked more like a prosperous furrier or tailor than a showman. He never wore jewelry, and he dressed conservatively. He was modest and mild-mannered. He treated all actors, well-known stars or otherwise, with courtesy and respect. His reputation in the entertainment industry was sterling. At a testimonial dinner given in his honor, Will Rogers introduced Loew as "the Henry Ford of show business."

During his career, Loew built one hundred fifty theaters, twenty-eight in one year! His favorite was always the New York State Theater on Broadway and Forty-seventh Street. He was loyal to his employees and they were loyal to him. Loew died in 1927 when he was fifty-seven years old. Joe Laurie, Jr. called him a sweet, kind, charitable gentleman. Laurie believed Loew tried to give everyone a fair chance.

Musical Comedy

The 1920s were witness to many major developments in popular music. The era of electronics and technology was born with the establishment of commercial, public radio stations and the development of the electrical recording process (with disc recordings as its product), the public-address system, and the soundtrack for film. Hitchcock noted there was extensive use of microphones and sound amplification. This had significant impact on the nature of orchestration and popular vocal style, and even on the ideas of performers, arrangers, and song writers. During the '20s, New York City was the absolute power center of the popular-music industry. The American lyric theater, which consisted of the declining operetta and the developing musical comedy, was centered around Broadway and Schubert Alley. Tin Pan Alley was the center for the songwriting business, and the still-powerful sheet-music publishers.

The period is particularly notable for the explosion of songs and songwriters. Publishers issued individual songs in enormous numbers. Some achieved immense popularity. However, the songs that, in every sense, achieved the greatest success came from the musical comedy (or just "musical"), the newest popular form of American lyric theater. Combining interpolated songs and dances with a play was not a new idea. This practice had long been a part of the American tradition, and after the minstrel-show interlude, it reasserted itself in the operettas of the late nineteenth century.

The 1920s musicals were different in style and feeling from operettas. They avoided the sentimentality and slightly aristocratic tone that came from the Viennese operetta. American musical comedies were brassy and brash, lively and spicy, colloquial and earthy. They employed more of the elements of dance and music that were identifiably American, and they accurately reflected the optimism and hedonism, the frenetic energy, and the abandoned, carefree attitudes of the postwar-boom era.

American musicals have been compared to the ballad opera of an earlier period. However, "the balance and inter-relationship of its components are vastly different. The ballad opera had been basically a play dotted with occasional songs. The musical, at least that of the 1920s, was essentially a garland of songs, and dances strung on a thin plot line, with occasional spectacular 'production numbers' planned at strategic points..."[4] Masses of people came away from the musicals singing the songs their favorite characters had sung.

Songs, and others like them, were in such demand that they began to appear as single selections on recordings. Nameless singers became well-known recording artists with the music of Broadway. Individual writers, such as Hoagy

---

[4]Hitchcock, H. Wiley, *Music in the United States: A Historical Introduction.* (Englewood Cliffs, New Jersey: Prentice-Hall, Inc., 1974), p. 186.

Charmichael and the Broadway music composers, worked together to create an increasingly large listening and consuming audience for their music. It was this audience and its progeny that became heir apparent to the popular music of the 1950s, a music destined to transform forever the youth of America and eventually the civilized world.

George M

One of Broadway's most famous choruses, *The Yankee Doodle Boy*, came from the musical, *Little Johnny Jones*. George M. Cohan, who wrote the show, played the title role of Johnny Jones, an American jockey who came to England to ride in the derby. This role was Cohan's first Broadway musical success. David Ewen believed when Cohan sang *The Yankee Doodle Boy*, he was "being autobiographical." Indeed, George M. Cohan was a "Yankee Doodle dandy." For several years he insisted he had been born on July 4. According to his birth certificate, he was born on the third. During his day, his fame grew to such heights that his colleagues began referring to him as just "George M."

Cohan was brash and cocky, and completely aware of his own creative abilities. He was not only a true nephew of Uncle Sam, but also a blatantly recognizable American native. He was proud of his country and his heritage. Oscar Hammerstein II once said that Cohan was the kind of American everyone hoped to be when they grew up. There was never an American more indigenous to America than Cohan was to the United States of his day.

Young George. George M. Cohan was the third and last child born to Jeremiah and Helen Cohan. He was born George Michael on July 3, 1878, in Providence, Rhode Island. The Cohan's first child died in infancy. Their second, Josephine, came two years before George. Jerry (short for Jeremiah) Cohan had been performing with various minstrel-show companies when he met Nellie (short for Helen), fell in love, and married her. The year was 1874. Nellie's hometown was also Providence. Before she met Jerry, Nellie had never performed on stage. After she and Jerry married, she joined her husband in a new vaudeville act billed as "Mr. and Mrs. Jerry Cohan." Jerry wrote all their material, did their staging, and served as their manager and advance man. Nellie returned to Providence to have Josephine. As soon as the child was old enough, she joined her parents in the act.

George got only a smattering of schooling as a child. He also took a few violin lessons. He hated school and the violin, and soon deserted them both. The balance of his education came from inside the theater. He made his infant debut as a human stage prop for his father's act. At age eight, he played the violin in the pit orchestra for "Daniel Boone," another Cohan act. He played "Master Georgie" in a Cohan sketch at age nine. By 1888, the vaudeville act had offi-

GEORGE M. COHAN, AGE 9.

PICTURE COLLECTION, THE BRANCH LIBRARIES, THE NEW YORK PUBLIC LIBRARY

cially become the Four Cohans, with Josephine performing skirt dances. By age eleven, George was beginning to contribute some materials of his own. His first was a sketch, "Four of a Kind." When he was thirteen, he toured as Peck in *Peck's Bad Boy*.

His Music.

George began writing songs when he was sixteen. *Why Did Nellie Leave Home* was his first publication. Witmark Publishers bought the piece for twenty-five dollars, then had someone revise Cohan's lyrics. This was the first and only time Cohan ever allowed anybody to tamper with one of his songs. *Nellie* was less than a commercial success for Witmark. Consequently, it was the only Cohan song they ever published.

Cohan became a familiar Union Square figure. He hounded publishers with his songs. According to Ewen, Cohan used the sheer power of his monumental ego and persuasive abilities to wear down publishers' resistance. Cohan's second song, *Hot Tamale Alley*, was only a mild success. His first real hit came in 1898 with *I Guess I'll Have To Telegraph My Baby*. Ethyl Levey, former star of Weber and Fields' extravaganzas, introduced the song to vaudeville. In 1899, she became Mrs. George M. Cohan.

A new age for America and Americans began with the dawning of the twentieth century. George was to become its symbol and spokesman. By that time, he realized he had achieved all his goals in vaudeville. He began thinking about Broadway and musical comedy. In this atmosphere his talents and energies could soar to new heights.

As his first experiment in this arena, George expanded one of his vaudeville sketches into a three-act play incorporating about a dozen songs.

The Governor's Son opened on Broadway on February 25, 1901, starring George, his wife, his sister, and his mother and father. The show was somewhat less than a success. It closed after just thirty-two performances. However, during the next two years on the road, the show did much better. Then it returned to New York. This time, Broadway audiences were more enthusiastic about *The Governor's Son.* For his second show, George expanded another vaudeville sketch, *Running for Office,* into a musical. History repeated itself. Broadway again rejected the show. The Cohans took it on the road, and once again did very well with it. When *Running for Office* returned to Broadway, its audiences were far kinder to it. In fact, one of its songs, *If I Were Only Mr. Morgan,* became a minor hit.

Cohan and Sam Harris. In 1904, Cohan formed a producing partnership with Sam H. Harris. For both men, this was a signal event. The partnership lasted many years, during which time Cohan wrote his greatest stage successes. Cohan and Harris opened an office on Broadway and Fortieth Street. They planned to make their Broadway debut with Cohan's first full musical. *Little Johnny Jones* opened at New York's Liberty Theater on November 7, 1904, featuring George M. Cohan in the title role, of course. All the elements of the production, the cops-and-robber plot, songs such as *The Yankee Doodle Boy* and *Give My Regards To Broadway,* and a recitation with

COHAN AND
SAM HARRIS.

homespun philosophy such as "Life's a Funny Proposition," represented something entirely fresh and new and thoroughly American for the musical theater.

Little Johnny Jones was not an immediate success. Critics did not like it. It was completely different from the elegant operettas to which they were accustomed. They said *Little Johnny Jones* was too brash, too full of ginger. According to one critic, there was more ginger than music. He accused the show of being too Cohanesque. In response to this and to sagging box-office sales, Cohan closed the Broadway production and took to the road once more. Again, the road proved far kinder and more productive. Cohan returned the show to Broadway on May 8, 1905. This time, audience and critic responses were much more positive.

In 1905, A. L. Erlanger paid Cohan a visit and asked Cohan to write a musical for Fay Templeton. Templeton had been a burlesque star for many years, and was now ready to make her Broadway debut. Erlanger asked Harris

GEORGE M. COHAN
IN 1908.

to manage the show, and Cohan to write it. *Forty Five Minutes From Broadway* opened January 1, 1906 at New York's New Amsterdam Theater. Fay Templeton played Mary Jane, a housemaid who became an heiress upon the death of her wealthy employer. The out-of-town production was a smash hit, as was, finally, a Cohan Broadway opening. Box-office sales soared. New Rochelle, New York, became famous as the town "Forty Five Minutes from Broadway." Cohan's reputation was made.

By the time he reached thirty-four, Cohan was one of the wealthiest and most powerful men in the American theater. In 1911, Cohan and Harris had six hits at one time on Broadway. They also owned a controlling interest in seven theaters. Cohan had eleven plays on Broadway between 1910 and 1917. Five were musicals (in three of these, he was the star), five were nonmusicals, and one was a revival, starring, of course, George M. Cohan.

The Congressional Medal of Honor.

When World War I began, Cohan was living on his large, rambling estate in Great Neck, Long Island. On the morning of April 7, 1917, he read in the newspaper that Congress had declared war on Germany. The headlines immediately inspired Cohan to write a song. The result was, David Ewen suggested, probably the most famous American war song ever written. This song eventually won Cohan the Congressional Medal of Honor—Over There.

When Cohan first performed the song publicly, it met with almost total apathy in a place where the reception should have been much warmer—Fort Myers, near Washington, D.C. Cohan sang the song in a show for the troops. Then, Charles King presented the song to a Red Cross benefit audience in the fall of 1917 at New York's Hippodrome Theater. The song appeared to be gaining momentum. A short time later, Nora Bayes used it in her vaudeville act, after which, it grew rapidly in popularity. Leo Feist purchased publication rights for $25,000. For Feist, this proved to a shrewd business move. In just a few months, half a million copies of sheet music had been sold, with two million copies sold by war's end. Additionally, over one million recordings of the song were sold, including one by Enrico Caruso. President Woodrow Wilson called the song a genuine inspiration to all American manhood.

Cohan Leaves Broadway.

On August 7, 1919, the Actors' Equity Association called a strike against all theater managers. The Association took the action to compel owners and managers alike to recognize its legitimacy as the bargaining representative for its members. Cohan was at the peak of his career. The strike immediately closed twelve Broadway shows. Within a month, twelve more were unable to continue operations. These developments caused serious problems at the firm of Harris and Cohan.

Frustration, bitterness, and anger overwhelmed George. He took the strike as a personal affront. He saw many in the front ranks of the Equity forces whom time and again he had personally helped in some way. To George, theirs was an act of treachery. Those who, up to this time, had been friends, he now considered bitter enemies. By the time a new season had begun, the association had won a total victory, but to George, the war was not over. He continued to wage a futile battle against an organization whose position was now invulnerable.

Though George did not leave Broadway at this time, he did lose much of his love for it. He began curtailing his activities. At last, after an unsuccessful run of his play, *The Tavern,* he announced his retirement in late June, 1921. A

COHAN IN
THE TAVERN.

few of the theater's most distinguished personalities appeared to bid him a fond farewell. They heard Cohan make a short, bitter speech in which he declared he had, in essence, lost his self-respect within the theater setting. He advised those in attendance that he might consider returning to the theater should anyone discover a way in which he could do so and still retain his self-respect.

George did return to the profession he loved so much. He ended his retirement on October 5, 1925 with the production of his comedy, *American Born,* at the Hudson Theater. From that time on, he continued to write and produce musicals and nonmusical plays for several years. Occasionally, he would appear in one. However, the name "Cohan" had lost its magic. Now critics routinely mauled him, though they would admit that, regardless of having become sadly outdated in just about every area of the theater, Cohan still had few, if any, rivals as an actor.

Cohan and Hollywood.

Cohan had a disastrous encounter with Hollywood, which left him further embittered. Paramount Pictures cast him in a dual role in a Rodgers and Hart screen musical starring Jimmy Durante and Claudette Colbert. From the beginning, the experience was terrible for George. Paramount gave him a billing below Colbert and Durante. He discovered few with whom he had to work who were aware of his theatrical achievements. Even those few were not impressed. He was forbidden to park his car on the lot because he was not a "star." The ultimate humiliation came when a director tried to teach Cohan—the man who who had originated and popularized flag routines for stage productions—how to perform a flag routine with the song, *Somebody Ought to Wave a Flag.*

After finally completing the picture, Cohan left Hollywood, declaring he would never return. He vowed from that moment on to get his sunshine at the ball park or in Central Park, but certainly not in California. In January, 1933, he returned to Broadway, where he was received as less than a hero. He starred in his own play, *Pigeons and People.* Both he and the play were flops. According to one critic, the whole affair was nothing more than boring.

Nonetheless, there was still one category in which Cohan reigned supreme, acting. In 1933, he starred in the Theater Guild production of *Ah! Wilderness,* a Eugene O'Neill comedy that won a Pulitzer Prize. Four years later, Cohan starred as Franklin D. Roosevelt in *I'd Rather Be Right,* a Rodgers and Hart musical satire. Brooks Atkinson, a reporter for the New York Times, described the evening as a total Cohan triumph. In Atkinson's view, Cohan had never been better; Atkinson wrote that from the opening curtain, the audience belonged, body and soul, to George M.

Hollywood finally paid Cohan its ultimate tribute. It filmed his life story. James Cagney played Cohan in *Yankee Doodle Dandy* and won an Oscar for his performance. Cohan saw the production in a private showing, and was visibly moved. When the film opened in New York on May 30, 1942, the audience of celebrities paid almost six million dollars in war bonds to gain admission.

Cohan's Death. On October 19, 1941, Cohan underwent abdominal surgery, from which he appeared to make an excellent recovery. He spent the following year quietly in New York and West Orange, New Jersey. Then he began to grow weaker. One day he almost forced his nurse to take him by taxi to Broadway. There he stopped by the Hollywood Theater to catch a few scenes of *Yankee Doodle Dandy*, which had portrayed so brilliantly the essence of his life and work. It was as though he were saying goodbye to his street of streets. He never saw Broadway again. He died on November 5, 1942.

Irving Berlin

In 1911, Irving Berlin wrote *Alexander's Ragtime Band*, the song that made ragtime the principal song style of Tin Pan Alley, helped to make ragtime a national craze, and established its composer as king of ragtime. That same year, Berlin began assuming the dominating position in the composition of American popular music he was to hold to the very eve of his death in 1989.

Berlin was born Israel Baline on May 11, 1888, in Temun, Russia. Four years later, his family fled a pogrom, and came to the United States, where they settled in a bleak, cold tenement on Cherry Street in New York's Lower East Side. Most of Berlin's boyhood was spent on the streets. He sold newspapers and held active membership in a street gang. At fourteen, he permanently broke away from formal schooling and ran away from home. For a brief period, he worked as a street busker (strolling street entertainer), singing sentimental ballads in saloons and on street corners for fifty cents a day. Occasionally, he plugged songs at Tony Pastor's Music Hall for Harry von Tilzer's publishing house.

His First Song. In 1906, Pelham's Café on Pell Street in Chinatown gave Berlin a dusk-to-dawn full-time job sweeping floors, waiting on tables, and singing popular songs for the café's patrons. During this period, he wrote his first song to be published, albeit only the lyrics. Two waiters at a rival café, George Ronklyn and Al Piantadosi, had written and published *My Mariuccia Take a Steamboat*. The proprietor of Pelham's Café insisted that his own men follow suit. Nick Michaelson, Pelham's pianist, wrote the melody and Berlin

IRVING BERLIN.

PICTURE COLLECTION, THE BRANCH LIBRARIES, THE NEW YORK PUBLIC LIBRARY

the words to *Marie from Sunny Italy.* Joseph W. Stern & Company published the piece in 1907. Berlin's share of the profits from this venture totaled thirty-seven cents, and it was on this publication that Israel Baline's pen name, Irving Berlin, appeared for the first time.

Berlin on Union Square. Berlin now moved his songwriting career to Union Square, where he worked for a time at Jimmie Kelly's Restaurant, just a few steps from Tony Pastor's Music Hall. After this, he worked for a time plugging songs for Leo Feist. In 1908, a vaudevillian paid Berlin to write some topical verses, and Berlin came up with the song, *Dorando.* Dorando was actually a marathon runner then much in the news for having defeated Johnny Hayes in the Olympic Games. The vaudevillian elected not to use the verses, so Berlin tried peddling them to a Union Square publisher, Ted Snyder. Snyder offered to buy *Dorando,* for twenty-five dollars, but only on the condition that

Berlin supply an accompanying melody. At that time in his career, Berlin was musically illiterate, so he rushed to an arranger to dictate a hastily concocted melody, which Snyder then purchased. Berlin now had written his first melody.

Ted Snyder hired Berlin as a staff lyricist for the princely sum of twenty-five dollars a week. Occasionally, Berlin wrote melodies, mainly for his own lyrics, but periodically for the lyrics of other composers. In 1909, he wrote his first successes, including *That Mesmerizing Mendelssohn Tune,* and *Sadie Salome, Go Home,* a takeoff, employing a pidgin Yiddish, on opera. These songs brought combined sales of several hundred thousand copies.

In 1910, Fannie Brice made her debut in the Ziegfeld Follies with Berlin's *Goodbye, Becky Cohen* and *Doing the Grizzly Bear,* another indicator of Berlin's growing prestige as a songwriter. The Schuberts hired Berlin and Ted Snyder to appear in their revue, *Up and Down Broadway,* where Berlin and Snyder portrayed college students of the day, dressed in sweaters and holding tennis rackets under their arms. They sang *Sweet Italian Love,* and *That Beautiful Rag,* songs they had written for the occasion.

By 1911, several Berlin songs had been adapted for four Broadway musicals, including the Ziegfeld Follies, where Bert Williams sang one of Berlin's specialties, *Woodman, Woodman, Spare That Tree.* That same year, Berlin wrote *Everybody's Doin' It,* a song which almost single-handedly made the turkey trot a national craze, and *The Ragtime Violin,* introduced by Eddie Cantor. It was during this same period that Berlin's *Alexander's Ragtime Band* virtually exploded on the popular-music scene.

Berlin and Ragtime. *Alexander's Ragtime Band* was written for Berlin's own appearance in the Frolics, a revue staged by the New York Friar's Club, which Berlin had just been invited to join. However, he never made his scheduled appearance. The song was released to the Columbia Burlesque on Broadway, and for a time, virtually disappeared. Then, a specialist in coon shouts and ragtime, Emma Carus, performed the piece in her Chicago vaudeville act. The song became an immediate favorite of Chicago. Other star vaudevillians, especially Sophie Tucker, began using it in their acts. Within a few months, *Alexander's Ragtime Band* had sold over one million copies of sheet music, and several hundred thousand piano rolls. Its extreme popularity was nationwide.

On the strength of this popularity, ragtime became an American craze, though *Alexander's Ragtime Band* was not a rag. Everyone wanted a piece of the success; composers began turning out rags by the thousands. Chris Smith's *Ballin' The Jack* was 1913's big ragtime hit. Vaudevillians Billy Kent and Jeanette Warner introduced it, and vaudevillian Eddie Cantor made it popular. Other rags appeared, such as *The Darktown Strutters' Ball,* which was immortalized by Sophie Tucker, and *Dardanella,* which sold over one and one-half million copies of sheet music, and over one million records on the Victor label.

Of all the ragtime composers, Berlin proved to be one of the most productive. In 1913, he appeared at London's Hippodrome, billed as "the ragtime king." During his act, he sang his new composition, *International Rag.* Because of his experience and success in writing rags, Berlin was asked to write his first full Broadway musical score. *Watch Your Step* opened at the New Amsterdam Theater on December 8, 1914, starring international dancing idols Irene and Vernon Castle. An unidentified New York reviewer wrote about *Watch Your Step,* "This is the first time that the author of *Alexander's Ragtime Band* and the like has turned his attention to providing the music for an entire evening's entertainment. For it, he has written a score of his mad melodies, nearly all of them of the tickling sort, born to be caught up and whistled at every street corner and warranted to get any roomfull a-dancing."

Berlin's first successful ballad, *When I Lost You,* was the product of a personal tragedy. He and Dorothy Goetz, the attractive sister of Broadway producer Ray Goetz, married on February 3, 1913. While on their honeymoon in Cuba, Dorothy contracted typhoid fever. Two weeks after they set up housekeeping, on July 17, 1913, Dorothy died. Berlin was devastated. He tried consoling himself by making a trip to Europe with Dorothy's brother, Ray. When he returned to New York, he wrote *When I Lost You,* expressing his intense sorrow at having lost the sunshine and the flowers when he lost Dorothy. After *When I Lost You,* Berlin would prove his mastery of this medium. This was the first of his autobiographical ballads, in which he expressed his inmost feelings. Then came the turbulent period, almost ten years later, that produced the greatest number of his autobiographical ballads.

Berlin met and fell in love with socialite Ellin MacKay, daughter of the wealthy businessman who ran Postal Telegraph. They first met in 1914 and instantly recognized the intense attraction each felt. They knew life for either would henceforth be unbearable without the other. Ellin's father absolutely opposed a marriage that would unite his daughter with a New York Jewish boy who had grown up on the streets and who wrote songs for a living. MacKay did everything in his power to keep the two apart, but his efforts were in vain. On January 4, 1924, Ellin and Irving married in secret at New York's City Hall. They spent their honeymoon in Atlantic City, then took a trip to Europe.

By the mid-1920s, Berlin was a one-man trust in music. He had risen higher in popular music than any man in American history. He had married the daughter of one of the nation's wealthiest men. Show business had made him wealthy. The future appeared secure. Then, for unknown reasons, Berlin's creativity appeared to dry up. Sometime around 1928, he became convinced that his creative powers had deserted him. Between 1929 and 1932 he wrote very little music, and even the music he did write, he considered of little value.

Unfortunately, this period in Berlin's life coincided with the Great Depression. Like most men with money during this period, the Depression simply melted away his financial resources.

In 1932, Berlin's fortunes improved. Two of his old songs, which he had discarded as inferior and had never published, were discovered. Rudy Vallee sang *Say It Isn't So* in a radio broadcast, and recorded it for RCA Victor. Then *How Deep Is the Ocean* began getting airplay. Berlin songs began appearing on the bestseller charts for the first time in several years.

Berlin returned to Broadway in 1932 with a topical musical comedy, *Face The Music,* text by Moss Hart. This show was written about the Depression and some of the lighter, more humorous effects it had on the American lifestyle. For this musical, Berlin wrote *Let's Have Another Cup of Coffee,* a song that became a kind of theme song for the Depression years. He was once again in full stride. He continued to prosper on Broadway. He had traveled to Hollywood by 1935 to create a string of musical hits for the screen. These screen hits began with *Top Hat* in 1935, starring Fred Astaire. Berlin songs were now doing better than ever. He wrote *Easter Parade,* a song that has become an American classic, for the show, *As Thousands Cheer.*

In the late 1930's Berlin once again lifted an old song out of his trunk as he had done with *Easter Parade,* fitted it with new words, and reaped a new financial windfall (though this time not for himself, but for charity). The song was his personal statement summarizing his Americanism, *God Bless America.*

The stream of music from his pen continued unabated. From 1942 to 1966, Berlin wrote 194 songs, five broadway musical scores, and eight film scores.

Berlin's career has no parallel in American popular music. For over seventy years he remained in the vanguard of America's most significant and most widely performed songwriters. He did this despite ever-changing styles and fads and volatile public tastes. No one has ever functioned so productively for so long a time as he. No one has come even close to producing as many standards as he. In the eyes of the world, Irving Berlin is American music.

On September 22, 1989, Irving Berlin died. He was one hundred years old. In 1990, Laurence Bergreen wrote and published Berlin's biography. There could be no more appropriate title than the one it has. Bergreen took the title from one of Berlin's most successful and best-loved Broadway musicals. And Berlin could have no more fitting epitaph than this eloquent, simplistic statement on his life and work: *As Thousands Cheer.*

Additional Readings

Note: These sources generally also apply to chapters 9 and 10.

Bergreen, Laurence. *As Thousands Cheer: The Life Of Irving Berlin.* New York: Viking Press, 1990.

Chase, Gilbert. *America's Music*. Rev. 2nd ed. New York: McGraw-Hill Book Company, 1966.

Ewen, David. *The Life and Death of Tin Pan Alley: The Golden Age of American Popular Music*. New York: Funk and Wagnalls, 1964.

Goldberg, Issac. *Tin Pan Alley: A Chronicle of American Popular Music*. New York: Frederick Ungar, 1931; paper, 1970.

Green, Stanley. *The Rodgers and Hammerstein Story*. New York: The John Day Company, 1963.

Laurie, Joe Jr. *Vaudeville, from the Honky Tonks to the Palace*. New York: Henry Holt, 1953.

McKnight, Gerald. *Andrew Lloyd Webber*. New York: St. Martin's Press, 1984.

Selected Recordings

The following songs are included in the *New World Recorded Anthology of American Music*, and are listed by artist, title, record number, side number, and band number.

Berlin, Irving. *Puttin' on the Ritz* 238: s2/2
——— . *Cheek to Cheek* 238: s2/7
Cohan, George M. *Yankee Doodle Boy* 221: s1/2

Chapter 9
Broadway, from
Kern to the
Gershwins

Jerome Kern

In the early 1900s, Jerome Kern exploded on the American popular-music scene with such force that critic Alan Dale inquired in a 1904 article, "Who is this Jerome Kern whose music towers in an Eiffel way above the average primitive hurdy-gurdy accompaniment of the present-day musical comedy?" Who, indeed, was Jerome Kern? He was born Jerome David Kern on January 27, 1885 in New York City, the youngest of nine boys, only three of whom survived. His parents, Henry and Fanny, were financially comfortable. Henry earned his living as president of a firm that sprinkled city streets with water. He also made profitable real estate investments. Fanny was an excellent pianist, and brought a love of culture and good music to the family.

The Early Years. When he was five, Jerome began studying piano with his mother, who proved to be a severe taskmaster. However, Jerome was quite musical, and his piano lessons came to him effortlessly. Before long, he was spending much time at the keyboard, either practicing or improvising. At age ten, he saw his first Broadway show, Victor Hubert's *The Wizard of the Nile.* It completely captivated him. When he returned home, he sat down at the keyboard and played all the tunes he had heard, by ear.

In 1895, Kern and his family moved to Newark, where he attended Barringer High School. After graduation in 1902, he enrolled in New York's Normal College to prepare for a teaching career. He also enrolled in the New York College of Music, where, for the first time, he received intensive musical training. He studied piano with Alexander Lambert and Paolo Gallico, and harmony with Austen Pearce. During this time, he wrote a piano piece, *At the Casino,* published in September, 1902, by the Lyceum Publishing Company.

Kern spent most of 1903 in Europe, traveling and periodically studying music. His music studies consisted of instruction in theory and composition with private teachers in Heidelberg. He finally settled in London, where the Charles Frohman office hired him for ten dollars a week to play filler materials for Frohman's London productions. One of Kern's compositions, *Mr. Chamberlain,* attracted the lyricist P. G. Wodehouse, with whom Kern was to work so productively in later years. Wodehouse, though only twenty-four at the time, had already published stories and verses in several journals and newspapers. He was also a regular columnist for the *London Globe.* A popular London musical actor, Seymour Hicks, got the two men together for the express purpose of composing a song for him. The result was *Mr. Chamberlain.* Hicks sang the piece in *The Beauty and the Bath,* and Kern had his first hit.

Kern, the Song Plugger. In 1904, Kern returned to the United States. He began plugging songs on Tin Pan Alley for Shapiro-Remick. During that same year, he helped adapt an English musical score, *Mr. Wix of Wickham,* for Broadway. He also contributed four of his own compositions to the score. This was the score—Kern's first for Broadway—that attracted the attention of Broadway critic, Alan Dale.

Max Dreyfus was head of Harms, one of Tin Pan Alley's leading publishing houses. He, too, took strong notice of Kern. Dreyfus, convinced that Kern was a young composer with remarkable potential, hired him as a song plugger for Harms. While he was selling music, Kern kept writing his own songs, some of which Dreyfus published. Thus began a composer-publisher relationship that lasted until Kern's death.

Kern's first American hit, *How'd You Like to Spoon with Me?,* contained lyrics by Edward Laska. A Broadway producer had commissioned Laska to write a song for one of his shows. Many believe the melody Kern finally used was something he had written during his high school days. When Kern completed the piece, the producer who had commissioned it, turned it down because of the word, "spoon," in the title. "Spoon" was the colloquial equivalent of the term, "neck," of a later day. However, the Schuberts liked the song so well they placed it in their show, *The Earl and the Girl*, as a major production number. The show opened at the Casino Theater on November 4, 1905. Two of the show's stars, Georgia Caine and Victor Morley, sang Kern's song, supported by a female chorus couched in swings covered with flowers. The song became the hit of the show.

The early-1900s practice of interpolating individual songs by various composers into a show that was basically the work of someone else was commonplace. This practice gave Kern the opportunity to compose for and be presented in American musical comedies over the next several years. Just under one hundred Kern songs were interpolated into about thirty Broadway productions between 1905 and 1912.

Kern on Broadway. In 1912, Kern wrote his first complete stage score for Broadway, *The Red Petticoat*. The show was a total failure. In 1913, he wrote the scores for two more shows, neither of which did any better than *The Red Petticoat*. Then, in 1914, he wrote his first Broadway success, *The Girl from Utah*, an English import to which Kern contributed about half the score. One of his numbers from the show, *They Didn't Believe Me*, sold two million copies in sheet music. This song became his first classic.

That the song's success on stage was as formidable as its success away from the theater was remarkable. Even more remarkable, however, was the success of something as new and revolutionary as the song was, particularly for its time. David Ewen noted the song's "climax is achieved with a magical (and totally unexpected) change of key: a new four-measure thought is suddenly interpolated in the recapitulation section of the chorus, something that was not being done in the songs of that day. The rhythm is changed from consecutive quarter-and half-notes to triplets without warning. All of this provided continual interest to an exquisite melody, and it continues to catch and hold the ear to this day when well sung."[1] With this composition, Kern opened a whole new world for the popular song.

Kern soon provided a similar service for musical comedy. In 1915, he began an association as in-house composer with a series of musicals known as the "Princess Theater Shows." The New York theater from which the shows took their name was an intimate house, seating only about three hundred. Its

---

[1]Ewen, David. *The Great Men of American Popular Song.* (Englewood Cliffs, New Jersey: Prentice-Hall, Inc., 1970), p. 127.

owner, Elizabeth Marbury, had to find some kind of production that could make use of so small a house. She conceived the idea of producing shows intimate enough to fit the small accommodations, shows economically budgeted and developed as frugally as possible. The 1915 production of *Nobody Home*, the first of these ventures, was a smash hit. It forged a new direction for the American musical theater. This path led away from the large, glittering, expensive shows then in vogue, and toward a different kind of production. This new breed of entertainment was snappy, humorous, and sophisticated. It relied more on script and score content than on such peripherals as sets, costumes, chorus girls, large production numbers, and big-name stars.

Guy Bolton, a young Englishman, adapted *Nobody Home* from an English musical. The show required only two sets, an eight-girl chorus line, a small cast, and a pit orchestra consisting of just ten musicians. The show's high point was the song, *The Magic Melody*. This piece attracted the interest of one of the world's foremost musicologists, Carl Engel. In those days, serious musicologists rarely found anything at all of any value in a popular song. Engel saw *The Magic Melody* as a remarkable change, the beginning of a new regime in American poplar music. He remarked that the song was refreshing, sparkling, and the public loved it.

Very Good, Eddie followed *Nobody Home* that same year. While *Nobody Home* had made only a modest profit, *Very Good, Eddie* was a box-office smash, running for over a year and netting a total of over $100,000. Marbury's 1917 production was *Oh, Boy!*, set on an American college campus. Its run was even longer than that of its predecessor, lasting for 463 performances, 120 more than *Eddie*.

Kern, Bolton, and Wodehouse. P. G. Wodehouse, who several years earlier had collaborated with Kern in writing songs, was on an extended trip to the United States during 1917. He was invited to join the now successful team of Kern and Bolton as a writing collaborator for *Oh, Boy!* Wodehouse had come to the United States primarily to write dramatic criticisms for the magazine, *Vanity Fair.* He agreed to join the team, beginning his collaboration with *Oh, Boy!* Each of the team members had his own responsibilities. Wodehouse was strictly the lyricist, the texts were Bolton's exclusive domain, and Kern composed the music. Wodehouse's lyrics, Kern's melodies, and Bolton's libretto were a perfect combination. Their efforts produced a charming, graceful, and witty show.

Oh, Boy! became a box-office gold mine, as did its 1918 successor, *Oh, Lady! Lady!* In fact, *Lady* did so well, a second production of this show was mounted to play at the Casino Theater at the same time it was playing at the Princess. Perhaps the most notable song to come from *Oh, Lady* was *Bill.* It was dropped from the show before opening night because it proved unsuitable for the voice of the show's star, Vivenne Segal. However, *Bill* was to come into its own as one of the solo masterpieces of *Show Boat.*

Show Boat. By 1927, Kern had become the most influential, successful, and esteemed composer in the American theater. He lived in luxurious ease with his wife and only child (a daughter, Betty, born in 1918) on a palatial estate in Bronxville, New York. Behind him were ten highly successful musicals, all written between 1920 and 1927. Then, in 1927, Kern discovered Edna Ferber's novel, *Show Boat.*

Kern was intrigued by the possibilities the story presented for a fresh new approach to musical theater. Ferber's novel was a rich slice of Americana, set on the Mississippi River during the heyday of the showboat. Kern felt he could fashion a new type of musical from the materials of this book, one with a logical plot line and strong, believable characters and motivations. A musical built on this story would deal with vital social issues as well as personal problems. He realized that old ideas and concepts about musical theater would

PICTURE COLLECTION, THE BRANCH LIBRARIES, THE NEW YORK PUBLIC LIBRARY

A SCENE FROM *SHOW BOAT,* 1927.

have to be abandoned. Ferber's text did not allow for such embellishments as chorus girls, contrived routines and production numbers, synthetic humor, and elaborate dances.

Kern's first task was to win Edna Ferber over to his unique idea. Next, Kern persuaded Oscar Hammerstein II to write the text and the lyrics. Then he got Florenz Ziegfeld to manage production. The prospect of writing such a show enchanted Hammerstein and Kern from the moment they attended a river stage show aboard an old showboat in Maryland. From the beginning, the writing of the show was a limitless joy and exhilaration for both men.

One of the most powerful and beautiful songs ever to come from any musical is *Ol' Man River*. When he began constructing the song's text, Hammerstein told Kern he felt the need to create a first-act song that reflected the impact of the Mississippi on a Negro dock laborer. He told Kern he was considering a song of resignation with a protest implied, sung by a character who is a rugged and untutored philosopher. Kern understood at once exactly what kind of melody Hammerstein required for such lyrics, and began work. The fruit of their combined labor was a song "so eloquent in its emotion, so authentic in style, so deeply moving in feeling, it is often mistaken for a Negro spiritual."[2] Ferber never forgot her initial reaction to *Ol' Man River*. In her autobiography, *A Peculiar Treasure*, she described her reaction the first time Kern played and sang it for her. She said that the music grew and grew until

NORMA TERRIS AS MAGNOLIA AND
HOWARD MARSH AS RAVENAL IN *SHOW BOAT*.

PICTURE COLLECTION, THE BRANCH LIBRARIES,
THE NEW YORK PUBLIC LIBRARY

[2]Ewen, p. 136.

DENNIS KING AS RAVENAL IN *SHOW BOAT.*

her hair stood on end. It brought tears to her eyes, and caused an emotional shortness of breath. For Ferber, it was great music that would live beyond her day and Kern's. She said that each time she heard the song after that day, she experienced an extraordinary emotional surge.

Show Boat opened on December 27, 1927 in New York. It was an immediate sensation. It stunned the musical-theater world. Its artistic and financial success were both immense. Critics branded it an American masterpiece, a triumph, a complete demonstration of the composer's and lyricist's dependence on their basic ideas. The show's initial run lasted about two years, playing almost every night to capacity. Three times it has been on film: first in 1929, in a silent version, then in 1936, the most memorable one, and again in 1951. The number of revivals the show has experienced as a stage production has long been beyond estimate.

Show Boat forged a path to a new era for the American musical theater. A new genre had been introduced: the musical play. All the elements of the musical had been combined into an artistic whole. Like Mozart with opera, Kern had given his players a believable story and believable characters with which to work. Kern's new approach to the Broadway musical exerted strong influence on later collaborators, such as Rodgers and Hammerstein, who always implanted a moral somewhere in their shows, either in dialogue or song. Julie Jordan, the female protagonist in *Carousel,* sang *You'll Never Walk Alone;* while in *Oklahoma,* Aunt Eller advised Laurey to "be hardy" because that was the only way to "deserve the sweet and tender things in life."

Kern in Hollywood. In 1933, Kern produced his last Broadway success, *Roberta*. In this show, the songs were more important than the story line. *Smoke Gets in Your Eyes,* sung by the production's star was a consistent show stopper. In fact, *Smoke Gets in Your Eyes* was one of the main reasons Roberta was a genuine box-office success. After thirty-five years, Kern's Broadway career came to an end. During that time he wrote almost ninety partial or complete scores and over five hundred songs.

Kern now moved to Hollywood, where he spent several years adapting a few of his Broadway hits to the screen, and writing screen musicals. His first original screen score was *I Dream Too Much,* written in 1934. He fell in love with California, and decided he would spend the rest of his life there.

In 1945, Kern traveled to New York to coproduce an important revival of *Show Boat* on Broadway. He was also planning to write a new Broadway score, based on the character, Annie Oakley, to be produced by Rodgers and Hammerstein. However, tragedy intervened. Kern was not to live to see the revival of *Show Boat,* nor was he to complete a single note of a new Broadway score. On Monday, November 5, 1945, he collapsed on Fifty-seventh Street and Park Avenue. He was carried to Doctors Hospital, where he died of a cerebral hemorrhage on Sunday afternoon, the eleventh of November. Only Oscar Hammerstein was at his side. Kern was just sixty years old.

At his funeral, Hammerstein, who delivered the eulogy, said, "We will remember a jaunty, happy man whose sixty years were crowded with success and fun and love. Let us thank whatever God we believe in, that we shared some part of the good, bright life Jerry led on this earth." In a November, 1945 *New York Herald Tribune* editorial, an unidentified reporter eulogized Kern in another manner, "the way most Americans who never met Kern were to remember him for many years to come: 'Genius is surely not too extravagant a word for him... He left us rare treasures.' "

George and Ira Gershwin

Young George. George Gershwin was born Jacob Gershvin on September 26, 1898, in Brooklyn, New York. Brother Ira was born twenty-one months earlier, on December 6, 1896. Eight months after George's birth, the Gershwin family moved to Manhattan's East Side. As they grew up, Ira became the ideal student. He adored reading and sketching, and regularly spent his weekly allowance of twenty-five cents on tickets to neighborhood theaters. George despised study in any form. When he could manage it, he skipped school. He preferred spending his time on the city streets with the neighborhood kids.

No one in the family was musical. George became aware of his own deeply seated musical interests by mere chance. Music rarely came into his life, but when it did, it affected him profoundly. When he was about six, he heard music on an automatic piano arcade, Anton Rubinstein's *Melody in F.* Gershwin later remembered how the unique melodic jumps of the music transfixed him. He said every time after that, when he heard the Rubinstein piece, he would be inundated with vivid memories of his first encounter with the song. Another such instance occurred when the Gershwins lived for a short while in Harlem. By chance, George overheard jazz coming from Baron Wilkin's nightclub. At that time, Jim Europe and his band were playing an engagement there. George was enchanted. After that, each time he got the opportunity, he would roller-skate to the front of the club and sit on the curb, listening for hours.

When George was ten, he was playing ball in the schoolyard when he heard a fellow student playing Dvorak's *Humoresque* on the violin in the nearby auditorium. According to David Ewen, this was Gershwin's most significant boyhood musical experience. Later, Gershwin called the event a flashing revelation of beauty. Incidentally, the violinist George heard that day was a Maxie Rosenweig, who became a violin virtuoso under the name of Max Rosen. George found Maxie and became his friend. For the first time in his life, George learned from Maxie about the world of classical music, about the great traditional composers of the past, and about the ways in which it was possible to make up original melodies.

When George was twelve, the family purchased a piano for Ira, who had already begun to study with his aunt. Ira's musical education lasted just thirty-two pages into Beyer's piano-instruction book. George fell heir to the piano. He began spending all his free time at the keyboard, picking out popular tunes of the day, or concocting melodies of his own. Soon he began studying piano with local teachers, each more inept than the predecessor. Finally, he found Charles Hambitzer.

George Gershwin and Charles Hambitzer.

For the balance of his life, George expressed profound gratitude to Hambitzer, and with good reason. Hambitzer brought George his first real musical awakening. Hambitzer was sensitive, discriminating, and well-trained. He gave his pupil thorough technical instruction at the keyboard and introduced him to excellent piano literature. George's enthusiasm matched his progress. Before long, Hambitzer realized somebody quite special had fallen into his hands. He wrote one of his sisters about his new pupil, stating that George would make his musical mark if anyone would. He proclaimed Gershwin a genius, and said George was no clock watcher. Hambitzer was convinced he could help George become a fine musician.

George began playing the piano in public by the time he was fifteen. He played at school assemblies. He spent one summer playing at a Catskill Mountains resort. He began writing music. His first two songs were a popular ballad, *Since I Found You,* and a piano tango, neither of which was published. Hambitzer didn't discourage Gershwin from writing and playing popular music, but he did insist George continue studying the standard literature of the masters.

During his fifteenth year, George quit high school and found a job in Tin Pan Alley. Remick Publishing hired him to play piano and plug their songs. However, George strongly believed a good popular composer should know everything he could about serious music. Accordingly, he continued to study piano with Hambitzer. He supplemented these studies with instruction in harmony, counterpoint, and orchestration with Edward Kilenyi.

George attracted attention even while plugging Remick's songs. Harry Ruby, who became a successful popular composer in his own right, also plugged songs for a publisher, and often crossed paths with George. He said of George, "Sometimes when he spoke of the artistic mission of popular music, we thought he was going 'high falutin.' The height of artistic achievement to us was a 'pop' song that sold lots of copies. We just didn't understand what he was talking about."[3]

Harry von Tilzer's publishing house bought George's *When You Want 'Em You Can't Get 'Em.* This was George's first publication. He earned a total of five dollars from this piece. Sigmund Romberg used Gershwin's *Making of a Girl* in his Broadway production, *The Passing Show of 1916.* This marked the first use of a Gershwin melody in a Broadway musical.

George left Remick in 1917 and applied for a job with Irving Berlin as his secretary and arranger. Gershwin played his own adaptation of a Berlin song for an audition. Throughout his life, this manuscript remained one of Gershwin's proudest possessions. Berlin told George he could have the job for $100 a week. Then he advised George not to take it. He said George was far too talented to become just an arranger for someone else. Berlin was afraid that George would begin writing like him, and would lose his own spontaneity and original style. Berlin believed that Gershwin was destined to write great music. Gershwin had the courage to turn the job down, a job offering three times the salary he could earn anywhere else.

T. B. Harms and Max Dreyfus.
George found employment with T. B. Harms Publishers. He began work under a most unusual arrangement. Max Dreyfus, head of Harms, hired George for a salary of thirty-five dollars a week.

---

[3]Ewen, p. 172.

George had no set hours. Dreyfus merely required George to write songs and show them to him. Dreyfus' gamble on Gershwin paid off handsomely. Dreyfus continued as Gershwin's publisher for many years, reaping a financial harvest, and gaining deep personal satisfaction by watching his discovery grow into one of America's popular-music giants.

Harms published *Some Wonderful Sort of Someone* as its first Gershwin song. This piece represented a new direction in writing for Tin Pan Alley with its changing tonalities and chromatic harmonies. Other early Gershwin songs contained fresh, new approaches to song structure. *Something about Love* ended in a protracted sequence. *I Was So Young, You Were So Beautiful* extended for twenty-four measures, rather than the more common sixteen.

Broadway. George's first Broadway success for which he wrote the complete score, *La, La, Lucille,* opened in New York on May 26, 1919. This show produced the first Gershwin song of present-day interest, *Nobody But You.* George wrote this song while he was still employed by Remick. He pulled it out of a drawer to use as the main love ballad of the production.

In 1919, Gershwin wrote *Swanee.* Though written for a Ned Wayburn stage show, and given an impressive setting, *Swanee* attracted little attention in its first appearance. Then Al Jolson discovered the song. He sang it in a Sunday evening performance at the Winter Garden. It caused such a stir, Jolson decided to use it in *Sinbad,* the show in which he was currently starring. This song became Gershwin's biggest single piece, in sales and popularity.

Gershwin wrote the music for *Scandals* from 1920 to 1924. *Scandals* was a lavish annual George White revue intended to compete with the *Ziegfeld Follies.* George wrote forty-four songs for five editions of the *Scandals.* Two of these bear the stamp of Gershwin's coming greatness. *Stairway to Paradise,* written in 1922, contains subtle enharmonic changes, bold accentuations, and lovely blue-note writing. *Somebody Loves Me,* written in 1924 and still considered a rare gem, also contained wonderful new harmonic structures and sophisticated, bold lyricism.

By now, Gershwin had become a Broadway luminary. He was earning a large amount of money. Still, he could not settle for the kind of success with which other popular composers were quite content. He continued to seek musical instruction. He hired orchestral musicians to teach him about orchestral instruments. He took lessons in harmony from Rubin Goldmark in 1923.

New Musical Developments. Now Gershwin began exploring new horizons in composition and style. He wrote a lullaby for string quartet whose principal melody was a blues. This was his first attempt to write a serious piece in a popular style. (The Budapest String Quartet discovered this piece many years later. They introduced it to the world in 1967 at a Washington, D.C. concert.) In 1922, Gershwin wrote his first opera, a one-act black opera originally named *Blue Monday*. The work was a total failure. It received just one performance. However, its importance to Gershwin's compositional growth can hardly be exaggerated.

Despite *Blue Monday's* failure, serious musicians began to notice Gershwin. During this period, Beryl Rubinstein was a faculty member of the Cleveland Institute of Music, as well as a renowned pianist. In a 1922 newspaper article, he described Gershwin as a great composer who possessed the spark of musical genius, which was quite apparent in his serious moods. Eva Gauthier gave a November 1, 1923, art-song recital that included a group of Gershwin songs. Gershwin accompanied them for her.

Others began noticing Gershwin. One was Paul Whiteman, noted popular music orchestral director of the day. Whiteman had been the pit conductor for Gershwin's *Blue Monday* during the only performance it received. For some time, he had been searching for ways in which to expand the dimensions of popular-music performance. He saw *Blue Monday* as the perfect work with which to conclude an all-American concert planned for the Aeolian Music Hall. Whiteman asked Gershwin to write the work for his orchestra. Though this was completely in keeping with Gershwin's own goals and ambitions, he refused to promise Whiteman the score. He felt he was not yet ready to undertake such a task. Nonetheless, ideas for such a score began circulating through his brain.

A New York Herald Tribune article, announcing he was at work on a symphony for Paul Whiteman, sent Gershwin to the work table. Within a few weeks, he completed his two-piano version of *Rhapsody in Blue*. Because so little time remained until the scheduled concert, Whiteman asked Ferd Grofé to orchestrate the work. Gershwin's own orchestration of *Rhapsody in Blue* appeared in 1926. It has since become the standard edition for symphony orchestras everywhere.

Whiteman gave his all-American concert on Lincoln's Birthday in 1924. *Rhapsody in Blue* proved to be the highlight of the concert. After its twenty-minute performance, the audience gave it an unusually long ovation. The following day, critics called it a masterpiece. Since its introduction, *Rhapsody* has become perhaps the most famous, the best loved, the most frequently performed, and the most profitable piece of serious music ever written by an American. The initial Whiteman recording for Victor sold a million copies. The slow section of the piece became Whiteman's theme song. *Rhapsody in Blue* was eventually arranged for every conceivable combination of instruments, including a harmonica orchestra and a mandolin orchestra.

This work brought Gershwin wealth and fame. Of greater significance, it brought him due consideration as an important serious American composer, even though jazz style permeated his music. Other innovative Gershwin works

A 1927 PORTRAIT OF GEORGE GERSHWIN BY EDWARD STEICHEN.

followed: the *Piano Concerto in F,* the *Three Preludes for solo piano,* the tone poem *An American in Paris,* the *Second Rhapsody,* the *Cuban Overture,* the variations on *I Got Rhythm* for piano and orchestra, and the folk opera *Porgy and Bess.*

Gershwin withdrew from the 1924 annual *Scandals* revue to return to his first love, pure Broadway musicals. *Lady, Be Good!* opened December 1, 1924 at New York's Liberty Theater. This show had particular significance. It was the first for which George's brother Ira wrote the lyrics. The brothers had intermittently collaborated on a few songs before *Lady, Be Good! The Real American Folk Song* was the first of their combined efforts to be performed publicly. After *Lady, Be Good!,* the brothers remained partners as long as George lived.

Ira.   Ira had displayed deep literary interests from his boyhood on. During his two years at the City College of New York, he wrote sketches and verses for the college humor magazine. He also shared a regular column in the college news-paper. After his college days, Ira worked for several years at various jobs. His free time he devoted to writing. He wrote song lyrics under the pen name Arthur Francis. This name appeared on the sheet music, *Stairway to Paradise,* and on all the lyrics he wrote for his first Broadway show, *Two Little Girls in Blue.* He used his own name professionally for the first time in the 1924 musical, *Be Yourself.* He continued to use his own name throughout his partnership with his brother.

The two brothers worked uncommonly well with one another. Each possessed full sympathy and understanding of the other's idiosyncrasies. Each one respected and admired the other. They stimulated and inspired each other. Yet, in almost every personal aspect of their lives, they were total opposites. George was outgoing, gregarious, the life of the party, a man with his head always in the clouds. Ira was shy, retiring, at times quite naive, and always coldly logical and realistic.

Ira wrote lyrics for George's songs for thirteen years. Ewen believed Ira's lyrics had an inestimable effect on George's music. Though the melody usually came first, the lyrics were always fresh, imaginative, unusual. Ira's writing often

GEORGE AND IRA GERSHWIN.

sparked George's imagination and creativity. Ira possessed a rare insight concerning musical theater. He saw what it should be and could become. As a consequence, he became a powerful influence, leading George down new paths in stage music.

In 1931, *Of Thee I Sing* won the Pulitzer Prize in drama. This was the first Broadway show ever to do so. *Of Thee I Sing* was a skillful, witty, bitter satire aimed at American politics. In this show, more than ever before, music became partner to text in projecting every situation, comment, and aside. The critics proclaimed it a landmark in American satirical musical comedy. This show enjoyed the longest Broadway run of any Gershwin musical.

Porgy and Bess: An American Original.

Porgy and Bess was Gershwin's last stage work. It was also his greatest. It opened in Boston with an all-black cast on September 30, 1935, and in New York on October 10. Though the opera could be be considered a failure at the box office and with the critics, Gershwin knew that at last he had reached new heights in American musical theater. He did not for a moment doubt that *Porgy and Bess* was a masterpiece. Unfortunately, he did not live to see his belief justified. Critics ultimately hailed it as the greatest opera by an American composer, a masterwork.

George Gershwin died on July 11, 1937, from a brain tumor. On July 9, he had been rushed to the Cedars of Lebanon Hospital for surgery. The operation

TODD DUNCAN AND ANN BROWN
IN *PORGY AND BESS,* 1935.

took place on July 10, and mercifully, Gershwin died the following morning. The tumor was attached to that part of the brain which could not be touched. Had he lived, it is probable Gershwin would have been totally incapacitated for the remainder of his life.

For Ira, the loss of his brother proved nearly insurmountable. However, readjustment did come. In later years Ira worked with and wrote lyrics for Jerome Kern, Harold Arlen, Harry Warren, and Kurt Weill. On May 28, 1966, the University of Maryland awarded Ira an honorary doctorate in fine arts. David Ewen, commenting on the occasion, said, "Awesome in dignity though he [Ira] appeared dressed in cap and gown, he could not resist the temptation to whisper to the President of the University: 'Does this disqualify me from playing the horses?'"[4]

Selected Recordings

The following songs are included in the *New World Recorded Anthology of American Music*. They are listed by artist, title, record number, side number, and band number.

Kern, Jerome. *Yesterdays* 216: s1/3
———— . *How'd You Like to Spoon with Me?* 221: s1/7
———— . *That Lucky Fellow* 240: s2/3
Gershwin, George. Strike Up the Band 227: s1/1
———— . *I Got Rhythm* 250: s1/7
———— . *Embraceable You* 271: s1/7

[4]Ewen, p. 186.

Chapter 10
Broadway, from Rodgers and Hart to Stephen Sondheim

Rodgers and Hart

Rodgers' Early Years. Richard Rodgers was born July 28, 1902, into the most fortunate of circumstances. His father, William, was a successful physician with a love for books, music, and the theater. All his life, William had nursed a secret ambition to be a writer. William was a handsome man with wonderful manners and a marvelous wit. He was loved and admired by all who knew him, particularly, his immediate family. Richard's mother, Mamie, was a lovely woman who took more interest and greater pride in cultural achievements than in social matters. She was an excellent pianist. On Sunday evenings, the family would gather around the piano. Mamie would play and William would sing famous opera arias and the song hits from operettas. From this special family activity, Richard acquired an enduring love for music.

Richard and his family lived in a gracious town house on Lexington Avenue in New York. When Richard was one year old, his father purchased a larger, more spacious four-story brownstone in uptown New York. This became the setting of his early childhood. It was the place where he was first attracted to music.

By age four, Richard was using the piano to pick out Victor Herbert songs he had heard his father sing. Two years later, he was playing quite an extensive repertoire of songs, with both hands and all by ear! He studied piano first with an aunt, but secretly, he was dissatisfied with her. Without telling anyone, Richard enrolled himself in a music school near his home, where he studied piano for two years. Richard hated formal practice. He preferred to sit at the keyboard and improvise. However, an exceptional ear and a keen intelligence helped him successfully through his lessons.

Rodgers Disovers Musical Theater.
Something else no less significant than his first piano lessons happened to Richard when he was six. He saw his first musical, *Pied Piper,* starring De Wolf Hopper. In later life, he recalled that this event transported him into a glamorous and beautiful world with which he was entirely unfamiliar. From that time forward, he would attend almost every Saturday matinee. According to Ewen, Richard fell in love with the theater and everything connected with it, including Marguerite Clark, one of the stars of a theater production of *Snow White.* He was then nine years old.

In 1916, Richard saw Jerome Kern's *Very Good, Eddie.* It was a turning point in his experiences with the theater and in his songwriting aspirations. Young though he was, Richard recognized the significance of what was occurring on stage. He knew he was watching a real American musical, with American characters and lifestyles. He also knew he was witnessing, at times, sheer magic. Kern became Richard's hero. This adoration of Kern significantly influenced Richard's future compositional skills and techniques.

Rodgers was now producing popular music as well as listening to it. He played the piano constantly: at home, at school assemblies, at his high school graduation exercises. In 1917, the Akron Athletic Club, of which his brother Mortimer was a member, decided to produce a show to raise funds to buy cigarettes for American soldiers. The club drafted Richard to write the music.

Rodgers contributed seven compositions to the show, which was entitled *One Minute, Please.* Six were written expressly for the show, and one, *The Auto Show Girl,* had been written earlier. The production was a resounding success as a fund-raiser and as a showcase for the musical talents of the young Rodgers. A second amateur group now asked for Richard's song-writing services. *Up Stage and Down,* written for charity, was mounted in the grand ballroom of New York's Waldorf-Astoria Hotel, and contained not less than twenty Rodgers songs. Three of these became the first Rodgers compositions to be published, *Twinkling Eyes, Love by Parcel Post,* and *Love Is Not in Vain.* This show also gave Rodgers his first conducting experience.

Rodgers Meets Hart. One of the Akron club members, Philip Leavitt, recognized Rodgers' uncommon gift for melodic composition and was convinced that the boy needed a permanent and exclusive lyricist. Leavitt was acquainted with such a man, Lorenz Hart. Leavitt introduced Rodgers to Hart at Hart's home on a Sunday afternoon in 1918. Rodgers was sixteen years old. The result of that meeting made theatrical and song history.

Initially, the meeting was not a resounding success. Rodgers was at first in awe of Hart, who was seven years older, quite well-educated, and well-traveled. Then, Hart's cat entered the room, and Hart made some droll comment concerning the cat's lazy approach to life, which sent Rodgers into gales of laughter. The ice was broken. From that moment forward, they were able to exchange ideas, ideals, and experiences volubly. Before the afternoon was over, Rodgers and Hart had become friends and songwriting partners.

Within a few weeks, they wrote fifteen songs together. The lyrics and melodies of these songs had a snap and sparkle that could not be found even in a P. G. Wodehouse–Jerome Kern collaboration. Of the original fifteen, one piece in particular stood out from the rest: *Any Old Place with You.* This piece became their first published song, and marked the real beginning of the Rodgers and Hart career. This piece was also their first venture into the musical theater.

In the fall of 1919, Rodgers entered Columbia College. He had hardly arrived on campus when he became obsessed with the idea of writing the score for Columbia's next annual varsity show. Rodgers and Hart wrote and submitted a score to the Player's Committee at Columbia. The committee's membership included Oscar Hammerstein II, then attending Columbia Law School.

The committee liked the songs, but not the text. They suggested Rodgers and Hart use their songs with a text submitted by another applicant, Milton Kroop. The result of this happy combination, *Come Fly With Me,* was produced at the Astor Hotel on March 24, 1920. The production included thirteen Rodgers and Hart numbers. All were published. The production's music drew high praise from S. Jay Kaufman, a *Globe* reporter with a wide and impressive reputation.

Rodgers and Hart also made a strong impression on Lew Fields, one-time vaudeville star and at that time, a Broadway producer. He recruited the pair to contribute several numbers to a new musical currently in the planning stage.

Rodgers and Hart would be working with a real Broadway veteran, Sigmund Romberg. When *Poor Little Ritz Girl* opened July 28, 1920, it was Rodgers and Hart's music, not Romberg's, that the critics praised.

Now Rodgers and Hart felt they were ready for a real Broadway show of their own. They soon discovered, to their dismay, that gaining entrance into that realm was not so easy. They presented their songs to several publishers and producers. They got little encouragement and no work. They wrote a show with Herbert Fields, Lew Fields' son. However, as David Ewen noted, even Lew's love for his son could not persuade him to produce a bad show. Finally, Rodgers paused to take stock of himself. He was still attending Columbia College, taking subjects, such as physics and mathematics, in which he had no interest. He persuaded his parents to allow him to leave Columbia and attend the Institute of Musical Art. He spent two years studying harmony, ear training, and music history. While at the institute, he got an annual opportunity to write music for shows produced by the school. He was becoming a well-trained musician.

In June, 1923, he left the institute, and rejoined Hart in writing songs. Once again, the team found breaking into that elite world of Broadway writers and composers trying and difficult. After one particularly sleepless night, Rodgers decided to give up his pursuit of a career in music and enter the business world. He persuaded a family friend to give him a job in sales at a salary of fifty dollars a week. His new employer guaranteed him rapid advance in the organization if he showed any aptitude for the business.

Fortunately, Rodgers never launched his retail-sales career. The evening before he was to begin selling children's underwear, Benjamin Kaye, a family friend, called him. Kaye had been working for several months with a group of young people associated with the Theatre Guild, at that time the most powerful and significant producer of serious theater in New York. The Guild was putting together a musical revue for which Kaye wanted Rodgers and Hart to write the music. At first Rodgers was reluctant. He had given up this frivolity called music to become a rational, sober, respectable member of the business community. At last Kaye convinced Rodgers to come to that evening's guild meeting. Rodgers attended, and was enchanted with plans for the proposed revue. He recognized the show as a vehicle that could take full advantage of Rodgers and Hart music. He also recognized that an affiliation with the Theatre Guild, even if only a distant one, was not something to be taken lightly. The guild possessed a powerful voice on Broadway. One word from them could open even the tightest of closed doors for Rodgers and Hart.

Their First Broadway Success.

On May 17, 1925, *The Garrick Gaieties* opened for the first of its two scheduled performances. A program note helped set the prevailing mood and unconventional, slightly impudent

RODGERS AND HART'S
THE GARRICK GAITIES, 1925,
STARRING PHILIP LOEB,
STERLING HOLLOWAY, AND
ROMNEY BRENT AS THE
THREE MUSKETEERS.

PICTURE COLLECTION, THE BRANCH LIBRARIES,
THE NEW YORK PUBLIC LIBRARY

tone of the entire evening's entertainment: "*The Garrick Gaieties* is distinguished from all other organizations of the same character… in that it has neither principals nor principles. *The Garrick Gaieties* believes not only in abolishing the star system; it believes in abolishing the stars themselves. The members of *The Garrick Gaieties* are recruited, impressed, mobilized, or drafted from the ranks of… Theatre Guild productions—a few rank outsiders being permitted to appear; proving we do not intend to become a monopoly."

The show was an unqualified smash. Robert Benchley called it "the most civilized show in town," while Gilbert Gabriel praised it as "witty, boisterous, athletic chowchow." The guild put on four additional performances. All sold out completely. On the strength of this display of popularity, the guild decided to place the show on a regular run, which began on June 8, 1925, and continued for twenty-five weeks.

For Rodgers and Hart, success was never so sweet. They now had their first regular income from show music they had composed. That same year, they saw their new musical comedy, *Dearest Enemy*, come to Broadway. The following year, Broadway witnessed the mounting of five Rodgers and Hart musicals. Between 1925 and 1931, Rodgers and Hart had twelve musicals on Broadway, and three in London. Frequently, Herbert Fields served as librettist. These three young men immeasurably influenced the development of a golden age of musical comedy, and helped musical theater reach adulthood in the 1920s.

Rodgers and Hart Encounter Trouble.

Though theirs was a perfect marriage of words and music, the personal relationship between Rodgers and Hart was filled from the beginning with strife and dissent. Rodgers was very much the family man. He doted on his wife and two daughters. He kept regular hours, adhered to a strict daily schedule, and was meticulous about meeting deadlines. He was a fastidious man—conservative, practical, and quiet.

In every way imaginable, Larry (Lorenz) Hart was Rodgers' opposite. He was a constant bundle of nerves in constant motion. He was flighty, disorganized, indifferent to system or regulation. He was a man who apparently enjoyed clutter. His bachelor apartment was always in total disarray. He despised details. He never knew how much money he earned or spent. He was perpetually late to appointments. Larry's lifestyle was a constant source of irritation to Richard.

As the years passed, Hart became increasingly difficult. He sank further and further into his lackadaisical way of life. He was a lonely man, envious of Rodgers' family. He began drinking heavily, and keeping company with questionable characters. In 1943, Rodgers decided to revive *A Connecticut Yankee,* first produced in 1927. He had hoped this show, which had been such a wellspring of enthusiasm for Hart during its writing, would once again spark some measure of Hart's verve and creativity. And for a brief time, Hart did respond as Rodgers had hoped. All too soon, however, Hart lost his new-found enthusiasm, reverted to drink, and fell back into old habits.

Hart now urged Rodgers to find someone else with whom to work. On the night *A Connecticut Yankee* opened in Philadelphia, Hart went on a drinking binge. When the revival came to New York, he wandered back and forth in the auditorium, muttering to himself. After the final curtain, Rodgers searched the theater for him, but could not find him. Two days later, Hart was found in a hospital, unconscious, with pneumonia. He died there on November 22, 1943.

David Ewen believed that alcohol and pneumonia were not the only factors involved in Hart's death. Several months earlier, Rodgers had told Hart he had taken his advice, and would be working with a new partner, Oscar Hammerstein II. Hart realized then and there that his career was definitely over. The final blow came when Hart sat through the March 31 New York opening of Rodgers and Hammerstein's new 1943 musical, *Oklahoma!* This show was initially offered to Rodgers and Hart. It was eventually written by Rodgers and Hammerstein. Hart recognized this show as a remarkable, revolutionary kind of Broadway musical. After the performance, he went to Sardi's Restaurant to congratulate Rodgers on a brilliant achievement. Then he disappeared into the night. Though he died several months later, Ewen believed that from the time he saw *Oklahoma!* until his death, Hart was merely going through the motions of living.

Rodgers and Hammerstein

When Richard Rodgers finally took Lorenz Hart's advice to find another partner, one magnificent era in his career ended, and another, more glorious than the first, began. Oscar Hammerstein II more than adequately filled the shoes vacated by Hart, but he stepped into those shoes reluctantly. Rodgers visited Hammerstein at the Hammerstein farm in Doylesville, Pennsylvania, to discuss the problems he was having with Hart. At that time, Rodgers and Hart planned to write a musical based on an original text by Ludwig Bemelmans. (This musical never materialized.) Rodgers was consistently experiencing excessive difficulties with Hart concerning the writing of this show. Because of this, he decided to call in another lyricist-librettist to work with him on this project. Hammerstein was very interested, but declined because he didn't wish to harm Hart. However, he made an offer quite out of character for most of his profession, but quite in keeping with the individual. He told Rodgers to get Hart to agree to the project, and should Hart lapse into old ways, Hammerstein promised to step in quietly and finish the project without anyone knowing he had done so.

Rodgers displayed unflagging faith and courage in Hammerstein's talent by seeking him out as a collaborator. At that time, Hammerstein's fortunes were at their lowest ebb. Broadway was certain that Hammerstein had "written himself out," and that his career was over. Rodgers believed otherwise. He knew that a man with Hammerstein's monumental talent could not possibly be finished. Rodgers believed that all Hammerstein needed was the proper vehicle with which to rejuvenate his creative powers. That vehicle came in the form of *Green Grow the Lilacs,* an American folk play the Theatre Guild wanted Rodgers and Hart to make into a musical. Lorenz Hart at once turned the commission down. Rodgers felt that this was the time to recruit Hammerstein.

Oklahoma!   Rodgers invited Hammerstein to lunch to discuss the writing of the musical. Hammerstein knew the play well, and was enthusiastic. Before lunch ended, the two men had agreed on some portions of the adaptations

THIS PHOTO OF RICHARD RODGERS APPEARED IN THE NEW YORK P.M. TO COMMEMORATE THE **2,000**TH PERFORMANCE OF *OKLAHOMA!*, WITH RODGERS CONDUCTING THE ORCHESTRA.

necessary to convert the play into a musical. As a team, Rodgers and Hammerstein coalesced almost immediately. Later, Rodgers described this collaboration as almost chemical. When the right elements are put together, he said, an explosion occurs. *Green Grow the Lilacs* opened March 31, 1943, at New York's St. James Theater, as *Oklahoma!* It was an historic moment. Broadway and the world of musical theater were forever transformed. The opening-night audience stood and cheered at the final curtain. *Oklahoma!* enjoyed the longest run in Broadway history to that date. It lasted an amazing five years and nine weeks for a total of 2,212 performances. It was the first of many brilliant Broadway hits written by this stellar team.

Hammerstein. Oscar Hammerstein II, like Lorenz Hart, was seven years older than Rodgers, but this was the only similarity between the two lyricists. Hammerstein was tall and gangling. Hart was small and graceful. Hammerstein was a man at peace with himself and the world. He was slow and deliberate. Hart was restless and in constant nervous motion. Hammerstein led a well-regulated life, full of routine. He always kept promises and appointments. Hart's was a life completely without routine and regulation. He rarely kept promises or appointments. In almost every respect, Rodgers and Hammerstein were entirely compatible. There was only one way in which they differed. While melodies flowed from Rodgers spontaneously and with uncommon ease, Hammerstein labored long and hard over lyrics. He often devoted weeks to just a single phrase. Nonetheless, the end product of this hard labor was always a grace and simplicity that bore all the trappings of utter spontaneity.

Hammerstein came from a family with a distinguished theater background. His grandfather, for whom he was named, was a highly successful opera impresario. Oscar Hammerstein I established New York's Manhattan Opera in the early twentieth century. It became a formidable competitor of the Metropolitan Opera. He also built and opened New York's Victoria Theater, a vaudeville house active during this same period. Oscar II's father, William, managed the Victoria, and his uncle, Arthur, successfully produced Broadway plays and musicals.

The family directed the second Oscar toward a career in law, not in the theater. Hammerstein attended Columbia College for three years, then entered its School of Law in the fall of 1915. While at Columbia, he occasionally wrote lyrics and sketches for varsity shows. He appeared as a performer in a few of these productions. In 1917, he decided he would rather pursue a career in theater. He left Columbia and persuaded his uncle to give him a job as the Victoria's stage manager and general handyman for one of Rudolf Friml's operettas, *You're in Love.*

From mere assistant, Hammerstein quickly progressed to full manager of the theater. He also began writing more. His first song lyric appeared in a show produced by his uncle. His first musical comedy, *Always You,* appeared in the early 1920s. It was produced by his uncle and the music was written by Herbert Stothart. A *New York Times* reporter found Hammerstein's lyrics quite clever. As a complete show, however, *Always You* was a failure. Hammerstein's next show, *Tickle Me,* enjoyed only limited success. However, *Wildflower,* in 1923, was a smash. With the title song, and *Bambalina,* Hammerstein was catapulted into the Broadway arena of success.

Over the next fifteen years, Hammerstein became one of Broadway's most successful and most prolific librettists and lyricists. He wrote *Show Boat* with Jerome Kern. He wrote the operettas *Rose-Marie* with Rudolf Friml, and *The Desert Song* and *The New Moon* with Sigmund Romberg. All three of these are among the most successful American operettas ever written.

Then, for reasons that are not entirely clear, Hammerstein suddenly went out of vogue. He experienced failure after failure on Broadway and in London. Hollywood proved equally disastrous. In light of this, his collaboration with Rodgers on *Oklahoma!* became all the more crucial in his and in Rodgers' career.

Rodgers and Hammerstein met for the first time in 1915 at Columbia University. Four years later, they collaborated on several songs for an amateur production. After one other amateur show for Columbia, they did not work together again for almost twenty years. Then came Rodgers's problems with Hart, and his collaboration on *Oklahoma!* with Hammerstein. In 1944, Rodgers and Hammerstein wrote the score for the screen musical, *State Fair,* which starred Dick Haymes and Jeanne Crain. Two song classics were created for the movie, *It's a Grand Night for Singing* and the Academy Award winning *It Might As Well Be Spring.*

After *Oklahoma!* came several of Broadway's greatest and most enduring theater works: *Carousel* in 1945, *South Pacific* in 1949, *The King and I* in 1951, *Flower Drum Song* in 1958, and *The Sound of Music* in 1959. All these shows eventually enjoyed enormous success as motion pictures, especially *The Sound of Music,* which grossed the largest box-office receipts to that date in the history of the motion-picture industry. For these productions, Rodgers and Hammerstein won a Pulitzer Prize in drama (for *South Pacific),* two New York Drama Critics Circle Awards for the best musical of the year (*Carousel* and *South Pacific),* twenty-five Donaldson Awards, and seventeen Antoinette Perry Awards.

For several years before the writing of *The Sound of Music,* Hammerstein had periodically experienced intense stomach pains. In late 1959 or early 1960, they began again, this time more severe than ever. A physical examination revealed he was suffering from stomach cancer. Only three people were told: his wife and Richard and Dorothy Rodgers. Regardless, Hammerstein soon knew he did not have long to live. His one wish was to die at home, not in the hospital among strangers. His wish was honored. On August 23, 1960, Oscar Hammerstein II died at his home in Doylestown, New York. Howard Lindsay presented part of Hammerstein's eulogy. He said,

> We shall not grieve for him. That would be to mourn him and he would not want that. On the occasion of Gertrude Lawrence's services he [Hammerstein] said in so many words: "Mourning does not become the theatre. Mourning is a surrender to an illusion that death is final."[1]

Rodgers was inconsolable. His only comment was, "I am permanently grieved." However, this simple statement reflected a hurt from which Rodgers would never recover. He did not withdraw from the theater. It was too much a part of him, as much, Ewen said, as his heart and lungs. Over the next several years, he made several abortive attempts to establish a partnership with a new lyricist. All ended in disappointment. Finally, in 1965, after such a failure with Stephen Sondheim, Rodgers gave up, and withdrew from Broadway.

---

[1] Ewen, David. *Great Men of American Popular Song.* (Englewood Cliffs, New Jersey: Prentice-Hall, Inc., 1970), p. 296.

Cole Porter

A Background of Wealth. Cole Porter was born on June 2, 1892, in Peru, Indiana, into extravagant wealth. Cole's grandfather had made investments in coal and timber in West Virginia, which had brought him an estimated seven million dollars by the time his only grandson was born.

Cole had a rather solitary childhood. His mother, intent on raising a gentleman, would never allow him to play with other children. Consequently, Cole was forced to invent pastimes suitable for just one participant. He made up little productions with a toy theater. Occasionally, he went to the circus, since Peru served as the wintering grounds for the Great Wallace Shows. When he was ten, he began writing music. His first composition was an operetta containing just one song, *The Song of the Birds*. Next he wrote *The Bobolink Waltz*, a piano piece written just after he had heard a bobolink sing outside his window. His mother paid a Chicago publisher one hundred dollars to publish *The Bobolink Waltz*. In his childhood, only one place, Peru's Emric Theater, left a lifelong, indelible impression on him. David Ewen described the Emric as depicting a gondola floating on the Grand Canal in Venice. For some inexplicable reason, this scene awakened the boy's imagination.

Since Cole's mother, Kate, had attended fashionable eastern schools, she insisted Cole do the same. When he was thirteen, Cole left his family to attend Worcester Academy in Massachusetts. He remained there for three years, for some unknown reason, never returning once to visit his family. Nor did any of his family travel to Worcester to visit him.

At school, he was a loner. He made few friends. He spent most of his spare time at the piano he had brought with him. After two years of this self-imposed solitude, he began to thaw. His fellow students found him most agreeable and quite likable. He became very popular, and was elected to offices and positions in several school organizations. Of all the things he did, Cole was most admired for the songs he constantly wrote. Many of them were humorous little ditties about members of the faculty.

Porter graduated from Worcester Academy in June, 1909. That summer he made his first trip to Europe, a gift from his grandfather for passing the Yale entrance examinations. Travel across France, Switzerland, and Germany during this summer brought Cole a love for Europe and travel, which lasted his entire life.

The College Years. Cole attended Yale from 1909 to 1913. His university colleagues remembered him as a young man who smoked Fatima cigarettes, drank Scotch, gin, and champagne, was always meticulously groomed and socially poised, and adored luxurious living. Cole continued to write music prolifically. At Yale, as at Worcester Academy, many of his songs contained satirical verses describing events at his school. One of the songs written at Yale, *Bridget*, was published by Remick in 1910. It was his first publication.

After Yale, Cole entered the Harvard Law School, where he roomed with Dean Acheson, the future secretary of state under both Franklin D. Roosevelt and Harry S. Truman. Cole's heart was not in law, as Dean Ezra Thayer of the law school recognized. He had seen a school production in which Porter had been a performer and for which he had written the songs. Thayer consulted with Porter and urged him to seek a career in music. Porter, of course, had wanted this from the beginning. On Thayer's advice, he entered the Harvard School of Music, where he spent three years studying piano, theory, orchestration, and music history. Though the course of study he followed was designed to prepare a student to enter the world of serious music, Cole continued to follow his heart's dream of becoming a popular songwriter. In 1915, two of his songs appeared in two Broadway musicals, *Two Big Eyes* in *Miss Information* and *Esmeralda* in *Hands Up*.

Porter's First Musical. His chief ambition in life was, of course, to write the score of a Broadway musical by himself. He realized this ambition when *See America First* premiered on Broadway on March 26, 1916, score by Cole Porter. The production was a miserable failure. Critics advised their readers to *See America First* last. The show lasted for fifteen pitiful performances. Only one item was salvageable from this wreck, Cole's song, *I've a Shooting Box in Scotland*. (Fred and Adele Astaire liked the song well enough to revive it for use in their vaudeville act. Fred Astaire used the song again in an NBC television special on February 7, 1968.) Cole believed he was disgraced for life because of the flop. He sneaked back to the Yale Club, walked quickly through the lobby, and hid in his room. He dropped from sight for a time by studying composition with Pietro Yon.

During World War I, Cole enlisted in the First Foreign Regiment of the 32nd Field Artillery Regiment and was stationed in France. In 1919, he left the Army, and rented an elegant apartment in Paris with the intention of continuing his studies in music. He enrolled at the renowned Schola Cantorum, where he became a pupil of Vincent d'Indy. He attended many fashionable parties and events, slowly becoming a member of the international set. Friends invited him to the wedding of two of Paris' social elite. At the ceremony he met one of the most beautiful and most distinguished women in Paris, Mrs. Linda Thomas. Linda was a Kentucky girl who had married and divorced a wealthy newspaper owner. She was wealthy in her own right when she met Cole. She and Cole began dating, inevitably fell in love, and married quietly in a civil ceremony on December 18, 1919, despite strenuous objections from Cole's grandfather.

COLE PORTER.

PICTURE COLLECTION, THE BRANCH LIBRARIES,
THE NEW YORK PUBLIC LIBRARY

Broadway Beckons. Cole continued to write songs that appeared with increasing frequency in Broadway musicals. His first book-musical (as opposed to just a revue) came with *Paris*. It opened on Broadway in 1928, with Irene Bordoni as its star. According to Ewen, Porter's real musical personality emerged for the first time in this show. An unidentified critic for *The New Yorker* wrote, "No one else writing words and music knows so exactly the delicate balance between sense, rhyme, and tune. His rare and satisfactory talent makes other lyricists sound as though they'd written their words for a steam whistle."

A second book-musical, *Fifty Million Frenchmen*, contained songs that excited even Irving Berlin. After seeing the show, Berlin bought an ad in several New York newspapers and wrote about it, "The best musical comedy I have seen in years. One of the best collections of song numbers I have ever listened to."

By 1930, Cole's style of composition had reached full maturation. During that year, he and Linda left Paris and moved permanently to New York. In the first half of the 1930s, Cole wrote the songs that gave him his own place in American popular music: *Night and Day* from *The Gay Divorceé* in 1932, *All Through the Night*, *You're the Top*, *Blow, Gabriel, Blow*, and *I Get a Kick out of You*, all from *Anything Goes*, in 1934, and *Begin the Beguine* from *Jubilee* in 1935.

Tragedy Strikes. By this time, Cole was becoming a significant contributor to screen music. He wrote his first original screen score for *Born to Dance*, an MGM production starring Eleanor Powell and James Stewart. From the abundance of evidence, Cole had now reached the top of his profession. Then, tragedy struck. Cole was horseback riding at a house party when his mount shied at some bushes. The horse reared and fell, pinning Cole underneath. At first Cole did not think his injury was serious. However, when help arrived and he was removed from beneath the animal, he became delirious and went into shock.

In the hospital, Cole's doctor, a bone specialist, found that the fall had shattered both his legs, each in several places. His doctor told him he would have to undergo a series of excruciatingly painful operations to save his legs. Even at this juncture, Cole's sense of humor did not desert him. He laughingly named each of his broken legs, calling the left one Josephine and the right, Gertrude. However, the accident and its probable consequences were certainly not a laughing matter. Within a period of just a few years, Cole went to the operating table over thirty times. By the summer of 1938, his legs had been broken and reset seven times. Most of the time, he was in almost unbearable pain. He was confined to a wheelchair for almost five years, and the terrible pain continued for several years beyond that.

Porter Returns to Broadway. After periodically suffering from severe depression for almost three years, Cole began to fight back. In 1938, he not only wrote the songs for the musical, *Leave It to Me,* he also helped to rehearse the production. Cole's career shifted into high gear in the first half of the 1940s with four Broadway smashes, *Panama Hattie, Let's Face It, Something for the Boys,* and *Mexican Hayride.*

In the midst of all this success, Cole's career took a sudden and inexplicable nose dive. He found himself completely undesirable among the Broadway producers. A few of his friends suspected that the many trips to the hospital for operations and his constant struggle with pain had finally taken their toll, creatively as well as physically. Some believed his career was over. However, it was at this point in his life that Cole produced his masterpiece, *Kiss Me, Kate.* It was by far the best work he had ever done, and one of the finest works of its kind by any composer.

Kiss Me, Kate opened December 30, 1948, and became the only Porter musical to exceed one thousand performances in New York. However, this was only the beginning of the show's glorious history. The national company opened in Los Angeles in 1949 and toured for three years. The show was translated into eighteen languages for performances around the world. There were two significant firsts for this show. It was the first American musical to play in

Vienna, Berlin, and Warsaw, as well as in Yugoslavia, Hungary, Czechoslovakia, and Iceland; and it was the first American musical comedy ever produced by the renowned European opera house, the Volksoper. It remained in the Volksoper's repertoire for more than ten years. Since Porter's musical-comedy career had begun with two shows about Paris, it was only fitting that his career end in the same manner. His last two musicals, *Can-Can*, in 1953, and *Silk Stockings*, in 1955, had Parisian backgrounds. Both shows were box-office smashes. Porter had written an appropriate and triumphant ending to his thirty-nine years on Broadway.

Cole again began experiencing severe pain with his old leg injuries. During the spring of 1958, doctors discovered a bone tumor on his right leg. They recommended removal of the leg. After the operation, Cole tried for a short while to acclimate himself to an artificial limb. Sadly, he seemed unable to cope with the effort of learning to use the device. He completely rejected the use of the limb, and thereafter had two valets carry him about his apartment.

From this point forward, Cole withdrew further and further into isolation. Despair set in. He had lost his mother in 1952 and his beloved Linda in 1953. Now it appeared he had lost his will to live. In June of 1964, he summoned the energy to make his annual voyage to his California mansion. There, as in New York, he simply remained a recluse. The changed setting did not end his self-imposed isolation. In October of 1964, he was taken to Santa Monica Hospital for the removal of a kidney stone. The operation was quite routine, and there were no complications. Nonetheless, two days after surgery, Cole simply stopped breathing. His doctors believed he just did not want to live any longer. He was buried exactly where he wanted to be; between the two people who had meant the most to him in life, his mother and his wife.

Stephen Sondheim

Help from Hammerstein. Stephen Sondheim was born on March 22, 1930. When he was ten, his parents divorced. He and his mother moved to a farm in Doylestown, Pennsylvania, about three miles from the family residence of Oscar Hammerstein II. He and Hammerstein's son, Jimmy, quickly became close friends. Sondheim spent many hours in the Hammerstein home when Hammerstein was in the process of writing *Oklahoma!* with Richard Rodgers. Sondheim had sporadically displayed rare musical talent from age seven, and this saturating exposure to musical theater left a deep and abiding impression on him.

When he was fifteen, Sondheim and two classmates wrote a musical about campus life at the Quaker-run George School he attended. The musical was entitled *By George,* and Sondheim firmly believed it to be a masterpiece. He took the work to Hammerstein and asked him for a truthful assessment. And according to Sondheim, Hammerstein did exactly as Sondheim asked. He told Sondheim the work was terrible. In Hammerstein's view it reflected talent, but it was still terrible! Sondheim remembered Hammerstein thoroughly dismantling every stage direction, song, scene, and line of dialogue. Sondheim confessed he probably learned more about songwriting and the musical theater in just one session with Hammerstein than most people would ever learn in a lifetime. In the course of a single afternoon, Sondheim got the distillation of thirty years' experience.

Hammerstein began that day teaching Sondheim the art of writing for the musical theater. He outlined a course of study for Sondheim to follow over the next six years, one that included the writing of four musicals. For the first musical, Hammerstein told Sondheim to pick a play he admired and turn it into a musical. Sondheim chose *Beggar on Horseback,* by George S. Kaufman and Marc Connelly.

Sondheim's final assignment was the writing of an original musical. He named his final project *Climb High.* He had just finished reading the musical, *South Pacific,* which in its entirety was ninety pages long. *Climb High's* first act was ninety-nine pages, and the second over sixty. He sent it to Hammerstein for critique and evaluation. When Hammerstein returned it, Sondheim could find only one comment: a circle around ninety-nine, and one word, "Wow!"

Study with Babbitt.

Sondheim graduated from Williams as a music major. As an honors graduate, he won the Hutchinson Prize, a two-year fellowship which he used to study with avant-garde composer Milton Babbitt. When he began his study with Babbitt, Sondheim expressed an explicit interest in musical theater. Plainly, he did not aspire to become a composer in the classical vein. However, with Babbitt, he spent much time analyzing the music of classical composers, such as Mozart and Beethoven.

Writing for Television.

In 1953, Sondheim attended a dinner party, where he met George Oppenheimer, whose pilot film, "Topper," had just been accepted for production as a TV series. The TV studio advised that they would require the production of scripts in rapid succession. They suggested he seek the services of a collaborator. Oscar Hammerstein had attended the same dinner party. When he learned of Oppenheimer's need, he suggested Sondheim as the collaborator. After reading some of Sondheim's material, Oppenheimer offered him the job. Though writing for television shows was not Sondheim's first love, it did begin his career and give him his independence.

During a 1955 audition for a possible musical adaptation of the James M. Cain novel, *Serenade,* Sondheim met playwright Arthur Laurents. For the audition, Sondheim played music from *Saturday Night,* a score he had previously written. Though the stage version of *Serenade* never materialized (shortly after the audition, Warner Brothers announced the production of a screen musical of *Serenade,* starring Mario Lanza), the meeting between Sondheim and Laurents proved significant for both men.

Sondheim Comes to Broadway.   About six months after the audition, Sondheim attended a party, where he again came into contact with Laurents. Laurents told Sondheim he was currently working on a musical version of *Romeo and Juliet* with Leonard Bernstein and Jerry Robbins. Sondheim asked who was writing the lyrics. Referring to the score he had heard at the audition six months earlier, Laurents said he never considered Sondheim, though he thought Sondheim's lyrics were excellent. However, in his view, Sondheim's music left a little to be desired. Laurents invited Sondheim to play for Bernstein. Sondheim again played portions of his score from *Saturday Night.* Bernstein was so impressed that he immediately offered him the job. Sondheim accepted, though with some trepidation. Two years later, in Washington, *Romeo and Juliet* opened to rave reviews as *West Side Story.* Sondheim's career took wings.

On September 26, 1957, *West Side Story* opened at the Winter Garden Theater in New York. The rave reviews continued. John Chapman of the *Daily News* proclaimed it, "a new, bold kind of musical—a juke-box Manhattan opera—the skills of show business are put to new tests—as a result a different kind of musical has emerged—a perfect production." John McClain of the *Journal-American* declared, "Young Mr. Sondheim has gone all the way with the mood in his lyrics. His ballads are the lament of the sincere and he can come up with the most hilarious travesty of our times—*Gee, Officer Krupke*—a plaint which should settle the problem of juvenile delinquency forever."

Next came *Gypsy,* a musical based on the memoirs of Gypsy Rose Lee. By this time in his career, only projects that allowed him to write music and lyrics interested Sondheim. However, Jule Styne had already accepted the job of writing the music for *Gypsy,* so Sondheim was only offered the job of lyricist. At first, Sondheim refused. He carried his frustrations to Oscar Hammerstein, who advised him to accept. Finally Sondheim capitulated, though with grave misgivings and considerable reluctance.

Before *Gypsy,* Sondheim had been writing a musical based on plays written by the ancient Greek playwright, Plautus. In early 1958, he was nearing the completion of a first draft of *A Funny Thing Happened on the Way to the Forum* when he became involved in *Gypsy*. Now, six months later, he was able to return to the first musical for which he was to write both lyrics and music. During the six months he spent working on *Gypsy*, several negative events occurred. Leland Hayward, who had initially agreed to produce *Forum*, had become disenchanted with the project, and David Merrick picked up the option. Phil Silvers, for whom the musical was written, had read the first act and had lost interest in the show. He said it was "old shtick." He apparently did not comprehend that the writers intended the show to be "old shtick." Then director Jerry Robbins withdrew from the project. Joshua Logan agreed to direct the show on the condition the authors rewrite the book to his taste. The authors refused, and Logan withdrew. The production appeared doomed.

His First Broadway Hit.
Finally, Hal Prince agreed to produce the show. Then, Zero Mostel accepted the lead male role, after much subtle pressure from his wife. Other pieces began falling into place. George Abbott agreed to direct. Jack Gilford and David Burns joined Mostel to head up the cast, and rehearsals began. The show opened in 1962 in New Haven, Connecticut, to disastrous reviews. After several attempts at repairing the show, Jerry Robbins was called in to play doctor. He told the cast and director the show needed a new opening number that provided the audience with a synopsis of the upcoming evening's entertainment. The original opening song, *Invocation*, had done exactly that. Director Abbott had removed it because he thought the show needed a "hummable" opening song, and in his opinion, *Invocation* was not "hummable."

Sondheim wrote *Comedy Tonight*, and Abbott agreed to use it. *Comedy Tonight* opened the show's first New York preview. It brought the house down, and suddenly *Forum* was a smash. It opened in triumph at Broadway's Alvin Theater on May 8, 1962. Though box-office receipts reflected a slightly slower-than-expected start, by the eighth week of the Alvin run, the house was selling out every night. Ticket sales were further enhanced when *Forum* collected several Tony Awards, including best musical of the year. Though *Forum* was a raging success with the Academy of Arts and Sciences, Sondheim was not nominated for either his music or his lyrics.

Later Broadway Successes.
Sondheim was now recognized as one of Broadway's premiere composers, as well as one of its top lyricists, though his next two ventures were less than raging successes. *Anyone Can Whistle*, which opened in April, 1964, was innovative, but, by most reports, confused. Its short life, only eight performances long, was plagued with hostile notices, a bit

of audience booing, a fire, and two deaths. After *Whistle* came *Do I Hear a Waltz?*, in March 1965, with music by Richard Rodgers and lyrics by Stephen Sondheim. Sondheim was reluctant to accept this task, but did so because he had once promised Rodgers he would write the lyrics should Rodgers ever come to him with an appealing show.

Unlike *Whistle, Waltz* managed a respectable run, 220 performances. However, the show was still considered a flop. It opened in New Haven to mixed reviews, and future reviews reflected little or no improvement. Of all the criticisms, however, the single most devastating appeared in *Newsweek:* "To make a musical comedy without dancing is plausible, to make one without comedy is possible, but to make one without music is, it would seem, unthinkable. Yet this is what Richard Rodgers and Stephen Sondheim have unaccountably tried to do in *Do I Hear A Waltz?*. Rodgers has written songs, all right, but they add up to the flattest score the old master has produced in years."

Sometime in late 1968 or early 1969, an actor friend of Sondheim's, George Furth, asked Stephen to read a series of eleven one-act plays he had written. He wanted Sondheim's professional opinion. After reading them, Sondheim gave them to Hal Prince, who found the writing to be superior, and thought this series of plays would make a grand musical. He asked Furth in to discuss the project, and out of this meeting emerged the elements of *Company.*

Company opened in Boston to mixed reviews. There were rough spots that required smoothing over, and songs that needed altering. By the time the production reached Broadway, the show was considerably improved. It opened on April 26, 1970, at the Alvin Theater, to rave reviews. Douglas Watt of the *Daily News* proclaimed, "*Company* is so brilliant it passes over one like a shock wave." *Time* and *Newsweek* both called it a landmark in musical theater. However, not all reviews were so positive. Clive Barnes of the *New York Times* thought the show contained characters who were extremely unpleasant—"the kind you go out of your way to avoid at cocktail parties." Michael Bennett, who choreographed the show, said he loved *Company,* regardless of the critics' remarks. *Company* was a show he was proud of, and he declared that no review in the world could spoil it for him. So much for mixed opinions!

Follies premiered in early 1971 in Boston. Most of the initial reviews were negative. The *Boston Globe*'s Kevin Kelly said, "*Follies* is in trouble." Elliott Norton of the *Record American* wrote, "When it sings and dances, Harold Prince's new *Follies* is generally exuberant and exhilarating, ingenious and extraordinary entertainment. When it talks, however, when its four principals thrash out the follies of their lives, it is bitter and shallow." Only Samuel Hirsch of the *Herald Traveler* came to the show's rescue: "There's a magic feeling that comes over you when a new musical opens and lets you know all's well… it happens rarely. It happened last night." *Follies* opened at the Winter Garden in New York on April 4, 1971. Again the reviews of a Sondheim show were mixed. Some critics loved it, some hated it: there appeared to be no middle ground. As with *Company*, Clive Barnes of the *New York Times* wrote a scathing article on this Sondheim/Prince production. His review concluded, "I know of no better lyricist in show business than Mr. Sondheim—his words are a joy to listen to, even when his music is sending shivers of indifference up your spine." In the end, though it collected seven Tony Awards (Sondheim for music and lyrics) and the Drama Critics Award for year's best musical, *Follies* lost its entire $800,000 investment.

Then, on February 25, 1973, *A Little Night Music* opened at New York's Schubert Theater, and Clive Barnes more than compensated for his extremely negative reviews of *Company* and *Follies*. His *New York Times* article read, "At last a new operetta... heady, civilized, sophisticated, and enchanting... It is Dom Perignon... the real triumph belongs to Stephen Sondheim, who wrote the music and lyrics... Good God!—an adult musical!" Within six months, *Night Music* repaid its investment, and Hal Prince began receiving offers for European productions of the show. It garnered a host of awards, including the Drama Critics' Award for best musical of the year, the Tony Award for best musical of the year, Tonys for best music and lyrics (Sondheim), best book (Hugh Wheeler), best costumes (Florence Klotz), best actress in a musical (Glynis Johns), and best supporting actress in a musical (Patricia Elliott). Sondheim had his first unqualified smash.

Since *Night Music*, Sondheim has been prolific, writing a full-blown musical about every two to three years. He wrote *Pacific Overtures* in 1976, *Side by Side by Sondheim* in 1977, *Sweeney Todd, the Demon Barber of Fleet Street* in 1979, *Merrily We Roll Along* in 1981, *Sunday in the Park with George* in 1984, and *Into the Woods* in 1988. For more than three decades now, Stephen Sondheim has been a significant force in musical theater.

Selected Recordings

The following songs are included in the *New World Recorded Anthology of American Music*. They are listed by artist, title, record number, side number, and band number.

Rodgers and Hart. *My Romance* 204: s2/1

———— . *We'll Be the Same* 240: s1/1

Rodgers and Hammerstein. *Happy Talk* 298: s2/2

Porter, Cole. *You Do Something to Me* 227: s1/2

———— . *Anything Goes* 272: s2/2

———— . *Begin the Beguine* 298: s2/3

Sondheim, Steven. *Anyone Can Whistle* 272: s2/7

Chapter 11
The Recording Industry

Edison's Tinfoil Recording Machine

By the time he had attained senior citizenship, Thomas Alva Edison had become a national treasure. During this period of veneration, he delighted in escorting visitors through his West Orange, New Jersey, laboratories. When asked about the inventive process and how it took place, Edison would reply that it was neither a matter of pure logic nor a matter of pure luck. It was a combination of both. He would draw an imaginary line with his finger and say, "Look, it's like this. I start here with the intention of reaching here—in an experiment, say, to increase the speed of the Atlantic cable; but when I have arrived part way in my straight line, I meet with a phenomenon and it leads me off in another direction, and develops into a phonograph."[1]

---

[1]Gelatt, Roland. *The Fabulous Phonograph,* 1877–1977. (New York: St. Martin's Press, 1978), p. 17.

So it was with the phonograph, a "leading off in another direction." From the age of eighteen, Edison had tinkered with telegraphic repeaters, devices that record messages at one speed and transmit them at a much greater speed. During the summer of 1877 he was working on an instrument that would transcribe telegrams by indenting a paper tape with the dots and dashes of the Morse code and later repeat the message any number of times and at any speed required. Edison used a steel spring to hold the tape in proper adjustment. He noticed that when the tape ran through the instrument at high speeds, the dots and dashes indented on it made a light, musical, rhythmic sound resembling indistinct human speech. This phenomenon started Edison thinking about ways in which to reproduce telephone as well as telegraph messages.

That same year, 1877, Edison had invented a carbon transmitter for Alexander Graham Bell's year-old telephone. It was only natural, then, that his thoughts often turned to the telephone. While he was pondering ways in which he might invent a small, inexpensive machine with which anyone could record a spoken message, he remembered a makeshift device he had used in his work on the carbon transmitter. By the time he began work on the transmitter, Edison was already going deaf. He could not trust his hearing to judge the loudness of a voice signal coming over the telephone receiver. To overcome this difficulty, Edison attached a short needle to the diaphragm of the receiver, on which he lightly rested his finger. As the signal came over the line, he could judge its amplitude by the strength of the pricks.

Edison believed that the pin could prick a paper tape, indenting it with a record of the human voice as easily as it had pricked his finger. He decided to experiment with this concept. On July 18, 1877, he wrote in his notebook that he had just tried an experiment in which he had held a diaphragm with an embossing point against rapidly moving paraffin paper. He spoke through the diaphragm and the paper became well indented with what Edison called "speaking vibrations." When he saw how well the vibrations had been imprinted on the paper, he concluded that he could indeed store and automatically reproduce the human voice at will.

Edison now set about the task of designing a machine to execute his theory. The instrument he built consisted basically of a metal cylinder with a fine spiral groove cut into its surface, and two diaphragm-and-needle units. One unit was used for recording, and the other for reproducing. Edison mounted the cylinder, wrapped in tin foil, on a screw so that turning an attached handle would cause it to revolve and to move from left to right. When the cylinder was rotated, the recording needle tracked vertically in the spiral groove, imprinting the foil with a pattern of hills and valleys that represented the sound vibrations being directed through the diaphragm mouthpiece. Theoretically, when the cylinder was played, the reproducing needle would convert the indentations on the foil into sound.

Edison drew a sketch of the instrument, and gave it to his most trusted mechanic, John Kruesi, who returned with the completed device, supposedly within thirty hours. Edison promptly wrapped the cylinder with foil, set the machine to record, and shouted into the mouthpiece the nursery rhyme that begins, "Mary had a little lamb." He then reset the sound-reproduction device and again turned the crank. What came back to him was a recognizable reproduction of his own voice. He was, by his own admission, thoroughly dumbfounded.

There is considerable confusion concerning the actual date on which this momentous event took place. The one officially adhered to is August 12, 1877. This date was selected because of a rough sketch Edison made of the instrument and on which he scrawled the words, "Kruesi—make this—Aug. 12/77." However, the selection of this date was made arbitrarily, many years after the advent of the phonograph. In an earlier edition of *The Fabulous Phonograph*, Roland Gelatt expressed doubt that such an instrument could have been produced less than a month after Edison's initial experiments with spoken sound. He expressed even greater doubt that Edison would have waited four months to file a patent for a device that actually reproduced spoken sound. Recently, researchers have discovered another sketch more likely to have been the one John Kruesi used to construct the first tinfoil phonograph. This one is dated November 29, 1877. According to Gelatt, this date seems much more plausible, considering the patent-application date. Edison received his patent on February 19, 1878, less than two months after he applied. According to Gelatt, there was nothing in the patent-office files that remotely resembled Edison's machine.

Commercial Recording: The Early Years

Commercial recording began in 1890. At its birth, the industry suffered from three severe problems, the first of which was pitiful sound-reproduction quality. The playback rolls were now made from a hardened wax, capable of catching only a minute portion of the tonal spectrum. Consequently, the sound coming from the ear tubes barely could be heard. Music reproduced on the wax rolls bore little or no resemblance to live performance.

Playing time was the second problem. The wax cylinders were capable of reproducing a maximum of two minutes of sound, hardly long enough to reproduce even the shortest musical pieces. (Here are the seeds of the record length that would so dominate the popular recordings of later years, particularly the first several years of the rock-and-roll era. This time limit helped bring about the development and marketing of the 45-rpm singles disc, so popular in the early days of rock-and-roll.) The third, and most critical, problem was the lack of a method by which to duplicate the wax cylinders. Because of this, each cylinder was a custom-made product, a kind of first edition.

However, Edison was unwilling to pursue the entertainment potential of his little invention. As far as he was concerned, he had designed his machine with a more "noble" purpose in mind, aiding those who were visually impaired. Consequently, the industry was forced to adapt to recording and reproduction conditions which were vastly inferior. Because the tonal spectrum was limited, the industry recorded only types of entertainment whose sound requirements generally fell within the restricted capabilities of the phonograph. Music was either composed or altered to fit the two-minute limitation of the cylinders. Finally, the industry hired musicians willing to play the same music time and again to fill reproduction requirements.

In these early days of recording, none could compare to the Columbia Phonograph Company, an offshoot of the American Graphophone Company, for range and extent of repertoire. It had signed John Philip Sousa and the United States Marine Band to an exclusive contract, and had begun recording numbers of marches that eventually were to become the most popular cylinders in America. Columbia issued a catalogue of its recordings in 1891, tiny in format and just ten pages long. There were, of course, several recordings of Sousa's Marine Band. John Y. Atlee, famous artistic whistler, was Columbia's next ranking artist. He whistled and sang his way through an assortment of popular songs. A variety of artists, all anonymous, produced the remaining selections.

Early phonographs bore a frightfully large price tag. Edison's 1893 Electric Motor Phonograph, with batteries, ear tubes (antiquated earphones), blanks, and various other items sold with the machine, cost $190, an inordinately large sum in 1893. Columbia Phonograph Company advertising and sales personnel were constantly searching for sales pitches with which to soften the blow of such a purchase. Some of the ideas they hatched were, at the least, quite inventive. One real barnburner salesman suggested using the machine to advertise itself. Accordingly, the company cut cylinders that included spoken advertisements interspersed with musical selections.

Another enterprising Columbia idea-man issued an appeal to the illiterate businessman. Instead of writing grammatically incorrect business letters, he suggested the illiterate businessman use the phonograph to record his letters, and mail the cylinder itself to the addressee. The company stressed the concept that poor writers and spellers could use a phonograph to communicate by mail without displaying their educational shortcomings.

By the mid-1890s, the phonograph was moving inexorably into the field of entertainment. Columbia's catalogue had grown to thirty-two pages by 1893. Speaking records were in real demand. Singers were also very popular during this period, building reputations through their recordings. Among

A GIFT IN A HUNDRED

the Latest Columbia ELECTRIC Record Player

59/6

No. 229 (A.C. only) adds another 100 per cent. to the programme of entertainment from a radio set. It is complete, compact, ready to use—a gift in a hundred ! Size 15 in. by 13½ in. by 6¾ in. Ask for free demonstration.

THE LATEST COLUMBIA PORTABLE GRAMOPHONE MODEL No. 206 (in Black) is a perfect instrument for perfect enjoyment. Its quality and tone give it value which make its price inexpensive. Beautifully finished, embodying all the latest scientific improvements in gramophone sound reproduction, this model is well suited for being a Gift of which one can be proud—a gift in a hundred. Complete, £5 12s. 6d.

Other Columbia Record-Players and Portables are obtainable from your dealer, who will be pleased to let you hear them and to supply full particulars.

MAKE MERRY WITH A COLUMBIA PLAYER AND RECORDS

PICTURE COLLECTION, THE BRANCH LIBRARIES, THE NEW YORK PUBLIC LIBRARY

AN AD FOR A COLUMBIA RECORD PLAYER.

them was Will F. Denny, a tenor who sang effectively in the maudlin style so popular during the period. Len Spencer specialized in Negro songs and sentimental recitations. There were many others, including tenor George J. Gaskin and Dan Quinn, a music-comedy specialist.

There was, however, a significant and noticeable lack of recordings by celebrated traditional opera stars and symphony orchestras of the day. The press had been predicting that, from 1878 on, the phonograph would play a vital and much needed role in the spreading of musical culture. Unfortunately, the predictions of the press were not to be fulfilled for several generations. The tonal and time limitations of the early machines made them simply incapable of reproducing acceptable recordings of traditional art music. And even had they possessed the capability, the music probably would not have sold. For more than ten years after the advent of the phonograph, pop singers, marching bands, elocutionists, and monologists dominated the recording field.

Regardless of the ultimate artistic value of these early recordings, the performers who created them succeeded in casting the phonograph in its rightful role. For years, Edison had opposed its use for what he considered "mere" entertainment. His goals for the machine were far loftier. He thought his invention should be used to benefit the visually and aurally impaired. Nonetheless, by 1894, the success of cylinder sales and public demand for machines that would talk and play music forced him to alter his opinion.

Emile Berliner and His Disc

In 1870, a nineteen-year-old German immigrant, Emile Berliner, landed in New York, virtually penniless. He spent his first three years in America clerking in a Washington, D.C. store. After that, for three years he drifted about the country, working at various jobs. During this period, he worked for a time washing bottles in the laboratory of Constantine Fahlberg, the creator of saccharin. While working for Fahlberg, Berliner spent his free evenings in the library of New York's Cooper Union Institute, educating himself. There he acquired a taste for things scientific. He concentrated his studies on the basic principles of chemistry and physics.

His studies in science whetted his appetite for invention. He built a laboratory in his boardinghouse room, and began practical experiments in the two fields that most interested him, electricity and acoustics. He aimed his specific experiments toward improving Alexander Graham Bell's newly invented telephone.

Berliner worked out a method to improve the telephone transmitter. He applied for a patent and took his transmitter to the Bell company. He arrived at a most propitious moment. Edison had also recently developed an improved telephone transmitter and had sold it to Bell's largest competitor. Bell, forced to seek an improved transmitter of its own, purchased Berliner's invention in 1878 for a large sum, and placed him on retainer to continue his research.

Berliner's association with the Bell Telephone Company did not last for any length of time, nor was it very fruitful. In 1881, he took an extended leave of absence, and he and his brother Joseph went to Hanover, Germany. There they set up the Telephon-Fabrik Berliner to manufacture telephones. Two years later, Berliner returned to the United States, completely severed his connection with Bell, and began working on his own.

Berliner's Gramophone. The date on which Berliner began his work to improve the phonograph is not clear. In 1857, Edouard-Léon Scott de Martinville, a French amateur scientist, had developed an instrument to transcribe a visual record of sound vibrations on lampblacked paper. Scott called the instrument a "phonautograph." Its chief use during its brief lifetime was as a laboratory instrument to measure and analyze sound. By Berliner's day, it had become an artifact in a Washington museum.

Berliner was attracted to the laterally moving stylus of Scott's device. He believed he could construct a talking machine that would use the lateral zigzag movement of the Scott machine, instead of the "hill-and-dale" system then in

OAK

$35.

MAHOGANY

$40.

THE STANDARD.—The Standard Cabinet as made for a clockwork motor Graphophone, has two rows of drawers, with pegs to hold 200 records or cylinders, besides space for other attachments. The cabinet has a roll-top cover. The Standard intended for a Graphophone with an electric motor differs from that described and illustrated above in having a closet on one side for holding the battery. The drawers in this cabinet will accommodate 100 cylinders.

Standard Cabinet in oak finish, . . . **$35 00**
" " *in mahogany finish,* . . **40 00**

AN AD FOR A GRAMOPHONE CABINET.

use. Berliner covered a heavy plate-glass disc with lampblack and placed it on a revolving turntable touching a stylus. He mounted the stylus on a feed screw to create a spiral pattern when the turntable revolved. When the stylus was set into motion by sound waves, it vibrated laterally and left a visual tracing on the lampblacked disc. Berliner applied varnish to the disc to set the delicate tracing, and then had the disc photoengraved in metal. When the "record" was played back through a stylus-and-diaphragm reproducer, the original sounds were re-created. Though the sounds were of less-than-acceptable quality, they still were sufficient for Berliner's first patent application, September 26, 1887, ten years after Edison had patented his own tinfoil phonograph.

Berliner called his machine a "gramophone" to differentiate it from its predecessors. Today the names "gramophone" and "phonograph" have become synonymous. This was not so in the nineteenth century. Then, "gramophone" referred specifically to a talking machine using lateral-cut discs, "phonograph" to a talking machine using vertical-cut cylinders.

Berliner's Experiments with Discs.

In 1888, Berliner began engraving zinc discs with acid. The improvement in sound quality was immediate and significant. On May 16 of that year, he presented his gramophone to members of the Franklin Society in Philadelphia. Throughout this demonstration, Berliner did not mention using his machine for any purpose other than home entertainment. He described the day when mass distribution of excellent musical recordings would be technologically and economically feasible.

Of course, various problems concerning the marketing of Berliner's machine lay ahead. Chief among these problems was the question of record duplication. Berliner soon devised a far more feasible method by which to duplicate recordings. He began making a reverse metal matrix from the original acid-etched zinc disc, and stamping "positive" records in some suitable material, much the same as a metal seal makes an impression in molten sealing wax. This concept provided for an almost limitless number of duplicates from one master recording, and became the cornerstone on which a vast industry was built.

By 1893, after several years of refining and perfecting his machine abroad, Berliner felt the gramophone was ready for the American marketplace. With a few friends and relatives, Berliner formed the United States Gramophone Company. The company manufactured three types of machines. The cheapest and most popular model was the Seven-Inch Hand Gramophone with a manually rotated turntable. It sold for twelve dollars, making it by far the lowest priced talking machine on the market.

For a time, Berliner could find no financial support for the marketing of his gramophone. Finally, he hired B. F. Karns, a former Methodist preacher, to promote his invention. In the autumn of 1895, Karns was able to establish a syndicate of Philadelphia businessmen who invested a total of $25,000. The syndicate named the new company "the Berliner Gramophone Company," and incorporated it in Philadelphia on October 8, 1895. Thus began a struggle between gramophone and phonograph for control of the growing record market, a struggle that remained in doubt for several years.

Sagging sales required the newly formed company's immediate attention. The gramophone, with its manually operated turntable, appeared to the public to be no more than a novelty. In fact, it looked like a toy, and also sounded like one. Even the most experienced operator could not keep a constant revolution rate. Consequently, the pitch alternately soared or tumbled as the operator wound the turntable faster or slower. Berliner obviously needed a spring-operated motor for his machine.

There was an ample supply of spring motors, but all were noisy, inefficient, and relatively expensive. If it was to compete successfully with the Columbia Company and Edison, Berliner Gramophone had to offer a superior product at a lower price. The company tried several motors. All proved unacceptable. Among those designers who made an unsuccessful bid for Berliner's business was a twenty-nine-year-old mechanic, Eldridge R. Johnson. When his design proved impractical, Berliner turned his motor down, and gave the matter no further thought. However, the gramophone bug had now bitten Johnson. He was not one easily entrapped by novelty. He saw the gramophone as something other than just another new invention passing through his shop. He continued to work on a drive motor for Berliner's gramophone. Finally, he built a product that satisfied him. In the summer of 1896, he presented it to the Berliner directors. The demonstration so impressed them that they issued Johnson an order for two hundred of his drives. To be sure, the order was not very large, but at that time, neither was the Berliner Gramophone Company.

The new motor-driven gramophone arrived on the market just in time for the 1896 Christmas rush. At twenty-five dollars each, it far outdistanced its nearest competition, which sold for almost twice as much. Orders began arriving faster than the company could fill them. The company took out large advertisements, apologizing for its inability to keep up with the orders. It explained its steady expansion of its manufacturing facilities, and courteously asked the public to bear patiently with the situation.

Eldridge Johnson's design had succeeded beyond the company's wildest dreams. Sales rose at such a rate that the company began ordering motors by the thousands. By mid-1897, Johnson had designed a better drive motor and had improved the sound box. This improved model became the most familiar piece of talking equipment the world has ever known because of a picture in which a "chubby black and white fox terrier… peers wistfully into its horn and listens to 'His Master's Voice.' "[2]

---

[2]Gelatt, p. 87.

ONE OF THE MANY COLUMBIA RECORDINGS IN THE LATE '20S.

Matrix-making was the step most critical to the duplication of discs. By now, the discs were manufactured from a hard, vulcanized rubber, and were advertised as virtually indestructible. Roland Gelatt remarked, "Unfortunately, the rubber records tended to flatten out in spots, and this would send the needle skidding across the disc." In late 1897, Berliner changed from rubber to a shellac composition. While this product had its own unique problems, it did hold the stamper's impress and was relatively cheap.

The Demise of the Phonograph. Since 1895, the struggle between Berliner and Edison for supremacy of the talking-machine market had continued unabated. While Berliner invented and marketed his disc, Edison and the rest of the industry kept up their efforts to perfect the cylinder. Finally, in 1901, a successful method for molding duplicate cylinders from a negative matrix was perfected. Unhappily for Edison and his colleagues, the process came too late. Though the cylinder was to linger until about 1929, the death knell of the phonograph had sounded (although the industry had adopted the term "phonograph" to denote sound-reproduction equipment). Berliner and his disc

IN THE LATE '20S EDISON PRODUCED RECORDS THAT COULD ONLY BE
PLAYED ON EDISON EQUIPMENT.

had won. The foundations for the distribution of popular music, both in
America and abroad, had been laid. An infant industrial giant, the record
industry, had been established, and waiting in the wings was the advent of the
rock-and-roll era.

The 1940s

By the early 1940s the record disc had become the world's accepted medium
for mass sound reproduction, with a standard speed of 78 revolutions per
minute. Edison's cylinder had become obsolete, and the principal players in
sound reproduction were Columbia and RCA Victor. On a Friday afternoon in
June, 1948, Columbia Records summoned members of the press to a suite in
New York's Waldorf-Astoria Hotel. There they announced a revolutionary new
record product, an unbreakable microgroove disc with a playing time of 23
minutes per side. Columbia named it the LP (long-playing) record.

Many reporters present had heard all this before. Neophone in 1904 and
Victor in 1931 each had attempted to manufacture such a disc. Both had failed

dismally. This time, however, was to be radically different. Edward Wallerstein was spokesman for the new product. He took a symphonic record from a stack of conventional recordings nearly eight feet high, and played it for four minutes, the average length per side for conventional recordings. The record played until the usual break, squarely in the middle of a movement. Then he took a microgroove recording of the same symphony from an LP stack barely 15 inches high containing every recording in the eight-foot-high stack of conventional recordings. He played it on an LP attachment the Philco Corporation was manufacturing to sell for under thirty dollars. This time, there was no trace of a break, and the sound quality had not suffered in the least. In fact, some of those present believed the sound was actually better. A new chapter in the history of the record industry had been opened.

There are only two ways in which a flat disc can be made to play longer: Slow down the revolutions per minute, or diminish the width of the record's grooves and increase their numbers. All those who had previously made unsuccessful attempts to manufacture a long-playing record had relied on one or both of these principles. Columbia was no exception. The only difference was that Columbia's attempt worked, almost flawlessly. Columbia's LP disc played for 23 minutes a side, employed 224 to 300 grooves per inch, and was pressed in vinylite, an unbreakable plastic. The turntable used to play the disc rotated steadily at 33⅓ revolutions per minute.

Columbia set aside a separate division in its Bridgeport, Connecticut, factory in which to press the new records, and Philco's Philadelphia factory tooled up to manufacture the new turntables. During all this activity, the LP remained a well-kept secret. In April, 1948, Columbia felt it was ready to demonstrate its newest product to its largest competitor, RCA Victor. Columbia called a meeting between the highest executives of the two companies. David Sarnoff, then the president of RCA Victor, implied that Victor would be willing to adopt the new 33⅓-rpm speed. But, as Roland Gelatt noted, after the meeting, RCA remained silent on the matter. Columbia waited for what to them seemed an appropriate length of time. Then its administrators decided to proceed without Victor's adoption of the new system. In June, 1948, Columbia launched the LP Microgroove Record.

Many years earlier, Columbia had anticipated the advent of the LP. They had begun preparing a backlog of masters on acetate transcription blanks capable of containing at least 23 minutes of unbroken recorded sound. By 1948, Columbia possessed a large and valuable library of high-quality, noise-free recordings readily transferable to LP discs. The LP made its market debut amid these favorable conditions during the summer of that year. However, the record-buying public did not immediately flock to the new format. The initial recordings were by no means uniform in quality and excellence. The problems inherent in the new recordings encouraged the majority of America's fifteen million record buyers to continue to cling to their prized collections of time-proven, standard-speed recordings. Nevertheless, a small group of enthusiasts saw the immediate advantages and the future promise of the LP. By the end of 1948, Columbia noted with satisfaction that 1,250,000 copies of the new record format were in circulation.

Then, the fortunes of the LP appeared to change. Sales began declining, almost at an alarming rate. The explanation lay in Victor's strange silence throughout the introduction and marketing of the LP. Victor had developed a microgroove record of its own, one that played at a 45-rpm disc speed. Victor's new product consisted of sets of records made from seven-inch vinylite that, according to the advertisements, would fit on bookcase shelves. There was also a compact turntable unit on which to play them. Thus began the battle of the speeds. Columbia's marketing was apparently directed toward the discriminating listener who wanted the continuity that LPs provided. Victor appeared to disregard that market and favor, instead, a larger and less particular record public. Regardless of the markets addressed, clearly Columbia and Victor had combined to sign the death warrant of 78-rpm discs.

The battle between Columbia's 33⅓-rpm disc and Victor's 45-rpm disc continued until the summer of 1949. By this time, Columbia had offered rights to the LP process to all companies. Many recognized the handwriting on the wall and began adopting the new format. Victor, however, continued to pursue its 45-rpm disc. Record buyers grew wary of this war. Record sales began to decline. The public decided to wait until the smoke had settled and the battle had been decided. Fortunately for the record industry, the slump did not long endure. Within eighteen months, almost every record company in the nation had begun production of its own LPs. There was one notable exception, RCA Victor.

By midsummer, 1949, the 33⅓ disc had begun steadily edging ahead in sales. The battle appeared to be at an end, when on January 4, 1950, Victor, mustering a token display of dignity, announced its entry into the long-playing record market. However, Victor refused to abandon its 45-rpm format. It continued to advertise the 45 disc as the one having the preferred speed for popular music. This record's short playing time posed no particular disadvantages in this area, and possessed the added advantage of being unbreakable. Victor's stubborn clinging to the 45 brought it enormous and unexpected financial dividends in the decade to come.

1950 to 1955

Rock. In 1950, no record company in the industry could have predicted the extraordinary events that were to occur in American popular music beginning in 1955. Roland Gelatt marked the year as a turning point in phonographic history. The year 1955 brought about new directions in music and new methods of marketing so radical that the record business was permanently transformed beyond all recognition. In 1953, Bill Haley and the Comets recorded *Crazy, Man, Crazy,* and in 1955, *Shake, Rattle, and Roll* and *Rock Around the Clock.* Though historians cannot agree on the song or the artist that introduced rock-and-roll, they all agree that Haley and his Comets brought the new style of music to national consciousness. Then, in November, 1955, RCA Victor purchased, from Sun Records, the contract and all unreleased recordings of a young Memphis truck driver. In January, 1956, Victor released the first five recordings by this young man. Among those recordings were *I Was The One,* and *Heartbreak Hotel.* The phenomenon called "Elvis" had been born. The rock revolution had been launched.

The Advent of the Record Club. In 1954, Harry Scherman, founder of the Book-of-the-Month Club (BOMC), began a test run of a new concept, a record club operated primarily on the same basis as the BOMC. He called the new organization the Music Appreciation Record Club. Initially, the club produced its own records, but in early 1955, it began purchasing them from Angel Records. The record club marketed its merchandise through the BOMC, which had a membership of about 200,000. In June, 1955, Columbia's contract with the Metropolitan Opera Company expired, primarily because many of the Met's stars were under contract to other record companies. Immediately following the contract's expiration, Harry Scherman announced the formation of BOMC's Metropolitan Opera Club.

Other record clubs began to appear. By late 1955, twelve clubs existed, with a combined membership of one million subscribers. Annual sales totaled over $20 million. In the beginning, RCA Victor and Columbia both refused to join the record-club craze, but late in the summer, Columbia decided to start a club of its own. The company had made an abortive attempt to begin a club in early 1954. This time its marketing techniques and advertising campaigns were more successful. Finally, in 1956, RCA Victor entered the record-club arena. In March, 1960, *Reader's Digest* tested the market with a record club of its own. Eventually, this club became the largest mail-order record company in the world.

1955 to the Present

In January, 1955, Victor announced a new sales plan. All 45s were priced at eighty-nine cents. All 78s were raised to eighty-nine cents in an effort to eliminate that faltering market completely. Victor was employing every means at its disposal to create a two-speed market, 45 rpm for all popular singles, and

33⅓ for albums. During the preceding five years, over 200 million 45s had been sold, and Victor meant to increase the 45 rpm's share of the market to three out of every four units sold within the next five years.

At first, sales of singles appeared to be unaffected by these changes. Then came Elvis, and rock-and-roll. When Victor purchased Elvis' contract from Sun Records in 1955, it was not prepared for what was about to occur. Within a year after Victor released Presley's first single, sales of his records alone forced Victor to change its total sales operations and its initial contract with Elvis. During that first year, Elvis sold over ten million records. Seven reissued singles from the Phillips and Sun label days were each selling at the rate of 12,000 copies a day. Presley's first LP release initially sold over 300,000 copies, breaking all previous sales records of first-release LPs.

Long-playing record sales dominated the market in 1955, with only a slight increase in 45-rpm sales. Seventy-eights were steadily declining. Because the 78 represented a decreasing percentage of money earned in record sales, manufacturers were slowly phasing it out. Forty-fives could be produced more cheaply and earned a higher profit margin. Neither 45s nor 78s are a vital force in the market anymore.

From 1955 to 1979, the record industry boomed. In 1955, it released a total of 1,615 LP albums, and 4,542 pop singles. By 1967, the industry had passed the billion dollar mark in annual sales. In 1968, it issued a total of 6,540 singles, and recorded a total of 183,000,000 singles sales through retail stores, jukebox operators, and other sales outlets. That same year, the industry released 4,057 LPs, which grossed over $1 billion. A total of 196 million LPs were purchased. Ten years later, record sales peaked at $4.1 billion gross. (This figure was no doubt aided by the enormous sales of *Saturday Night Fever*. This album alone legitimately sold over 25 million copies.) Statistically speaking, during this period, practically every man, woman, and child in the nation could have purchased one LP and several singles in 1979. However, statistics can be deceiving.

During the first fiscal quarter of 1979, record sales actually decreased significantly. R. Serge Denisoff noted a drop in industry growth of eleven percent a year, beginning in 1979. To combat this alarming decline, record companies began diversifying and cutting back their releases. The Recording Industry Association of America (RIAA) reported a total of 7,625 releases for 1982. The year 1978 had been a boom time for the recording industry. About 295 albums had gone gold and platinum, and 71 singles had done as well. By 1982, these numbers had decreased significantly. The number of gold and platinum albums fell by 40 percent, and only 24 singles achieved gold status, the lowest number since 1966. Eleven recipients of the gold trophy were new acts such as Stray Cats, Men at Work, and Tom Tom Club. The superstars still managed respectable years, but were not doing as well as they had been.

MTV. MTV was essentially the brainchild of four men, all of Warner Amex Satellite Entertainment Company (WASEC): John A. Schneider, president and CEO of Warner Amex, John Lack, executive vice president, John Sykes, vice president, and MTV's "operationalizer," Robert Pittman. Schneider oversaw the development of the concept. It was MTV's intent to reach an untapped 12-to-34-year-old audience. MTV's executives believed the entertainment industry was ignoring this particular body of young people. This target group fit demographically between the offerings of Nickelodeon and The Movie Channel.

John Lack was the self-proclaimed rock-music connoisseur who formulated the bulk of the MTV concept. In October, 1979, he hired Robert Pittman to implement the project. As a sociology major in college, Pittman was more than aware of the usefulness of number crunching. He was somewhat of a broadcast Wunderkind, coming to prominence as a research director at radio station WDRQ-FM in Detroit. After spending several productive years in radio at WPEZ-FM in Pittsburgh and WMAQ and WKQX in Chicago, he took over WNBC-AM in New York as program director. There he went head-to-head with the Top 40 flagship, WABC. Using a format having fewer commercials and void of jingles, and playing songs lasting three or more minutes, he successfully challenged the Top 40 giant. However, Pittman, who was becoming increasingly disenchanted with formatted radio, received a Warner offer "he could not refuse."

During his rise up the major-market ladder, Pittman had used psychographics as an increasingly important survey addition to basic demographic data. Radio consultant Rob Balon defined psychographics as a method of categorizing people by their professed attitudes, their overt life styles, and their psychological characteristics. According to Denisoff, psychographics tries to discover the factors that cause individuals and groups to watch particular television shows. This calls for thinking in terms of predisposition, rather than age. Psychographically, an album-oriented rock listener can be either a 30-year-old male executive or a high school sophomore. Using information gathered by psychographic means, MTV intentionally targeted a highly specific demographic sector. Pittman told many reporters that MTV's core audience was the generation that grew up on TV and rock music.

Having solved the problem of a market, Pittman now directed his energies toward piecing together a library of video clips that would serve as his broadcast material. In the early 1980s, American rock-genre videos were virtually nonexistent. As Pittman quickly discovered, much of the early history of rock initially captured on video tape had been either discarded or destroyed. Other than tapes of his appearances on the "Ed Sullivan Show," Elvis Presley's early television material was unavailable. Materials from Dick Clark's "American Bandstand," constituting a treasure chest of "golden oldies," were not only badly dated, but were unavailable. As Denisoff noted, only a handful of concert clips and movies were left. Experience had shown that concert videos fared badly on the 25-inch screen. Pittman turned to the English, who had pioneered the rock-video clip, the lifeblood of music television.

In the 1960s and 1970s, English television consisted of two networks, the BBC and the commercial outlet, ITV. ITV pioneered the vanguard pop-music TV programs called "Ready! Set! Go!" ("RSG"), "Beat Room," "Thank Your Lucky Stars," and "That's for Me." Of these, "RSG" was the most popular. It did not confine itself to the safe favorites, but featured, instead, a wide and progressive playlist. Cathy McGowan was the show's video jockey (*veejay*). British critic Nick Cohn described her as an uncomfortable amateur stumbling on lines.

"RSG" was in many ways shaped by the powerful British Musicians Union. Early in the development of British music videos, the union banned lip-syncing on "RSG". This action forced "RSG" to begin live broadcasts. Live broadcasting on "RSG" launched the careers of the fledgling Rolling Stones, the Who, the Kinks, the Animals, and several other future British rock celebrities. "RSG" filled additional airtime with experimental film clips, which were often set to music. Denisoff believed these "far-out shorties" were the primitive prototypes of contemporary video clips. This description applied equally to "RSG" and its future American counterpart, "MTV." The format employed by both emphasized one song, though the song may have been taken from an album. A well-done video aids cost-conscious fans in deciding whether or not to purchase a song from a specific album.

"MTV" premiered August 1, 1981, 12:01 a.m., EST. It began its career with the 1979 hit, *Video Killed the Radio Star*, by the British group, the Buggles. Its final format was modeled after a type of programming pioneered by several legendary radio-broadcast personalities. It consisted of the same kind of DJ patter and recorded music, but excluded the radio-broadcast practice of periodic news breaks, public-service announcements, and weather.

Five veejays were selected to staff the programs: Nina Blackwood, an actress and model with some broadcast experience; Mark Goodson, a teen-idol DJ from Philadelphia and New York; J. J. "Triple J" Jackson, the lone black veejay, with television and radio experience in the Los Angeles and Boston areas; Martha Quinn, with extensive experience in radio and TV advertising; and unemployed actor Alan Hunter, who, according to a television critic, looked like "a sophomore on his way to class."

The final look was a fantasy setting for kids that included posters, albums, stereo equipment, and other current status symbols of the generation. Normal television lighting and teleprompters were gone. All veejays were instructed to ad lib. *Rolling Stone* magazine described the look as casual, thrown together. The written dialogue sounded as though it were being made up as the show proceeded. The well-constructed format appeared to move from one event to the next in a completely random order. The show included well-trained actors who looked and sounded like people one would meet at a campus party. Above all, there was a pervasive attitude of perfection in bringing about a "what-the-hell—let's boogie mood." This was the exact air of calculated "laid-backness" Pittman was striving to achieve.

By 1984, just under two and one-half years after it had begun, MTV had become a giant in the music industry. The young giant had its problems, to be sure. Nonetheless, it had become a true giant with all the attendant power and influence necessary to alter the course of popular music throughout the world. In 1991, MTV's power and influence is unabated. In fact, it is gaining in popularity and prestige. Some prophesy MTV will eventually replace radio as the prime disseminator of the popular-music culture.

The Future: The Compact Disc and Digital Recording

In 1982, Japan introduced the compact disc (CD) to the recording industry. The following year, the compact disc made its debut in Europe and the United States. The CD is the most significant new audio configuration since the advent of the cassette tape. United States manufacturers' shipments in 1984 totaled 5.8 million units, valued at $103 million. In 1986, manufacturers shipped a total of 53 million units with a suggested retail value of $930 million, over nine times the dollar amount in 1984! In 1986, the dollar value of CD sales surpassed that of vinyl LPs for the first time. Since its introduction, the price of CDs has been declining. Industry experts believe this decline will continue as the number of American CD-manufacturing facilities increases. However, for the moment, the cassette tape remains the undisputed format king of the industry.

Perennial dramatic change within the recording industry has been its hallmark since Edison first wrapped a cylinder in tinfoil and reproduced the sound of the human voice. The most recent innovation has been digital recording. RIAA, in the 1988 edition of their annual publication, *Inside the Recording Industry: An Introduction to America's Music Business,* remarked that, during the '80s, digital recording impacted profoundly on the recording industry and the music business. Digital-recording techniques are employed in producing compact discs. They are also now being applied to the production of cassette tapes. These are the tape equivalent of the compact disc, and are appropriately called "digital audio tapes." Digital sound reproduction yields far superior recordings than those produced by the older analog methods, whether on disc or tape.

While digital-recording techniques do produce a tape similar in quality to CDs, tapes wear down over time because they must physically pass across a playback head to produce sound. Compact discs are read by laser beam.

Nothing touches them to wear them down. Consequently, as a medium for the most faithful reproduction of sound, the compact disc is by far the most superior devised to date.

During 1989, cassette-tape sales flattened out. This promoted the belief and rumor that the cassette tape as a recording medium was on the decline. Sales figures for the first half of 1990 strongly disputed this rumor. The RIAA News Release, dated October 1, 1990, reported that cassettes were still the consumers' format of choice. Shipments of cassette tapes rose 5.19% to 222.27 million units, and the suggested list-price dollar value rose 7.52% over the sales figures from the preceding year. The total topped the 1.6 billion dollar mark. The RIAA also reported that the compact disc continued its steady climb. Its sales increased by 36.35% to 132.08 million units. Since their 1983 introduction, CD sales have risen to impressive heights. Sales data from the first half of 1990 show CDs claiming 31.17% of the total prerecorded music unit sales worldwide. In this same report, RIAA noted the continuing decline of vinyl LPs and singles; LP unit shipments fell 67.92% and singles slipped 34.67%.

For the present, the cassette tape still offers one major advantage over the CD. Consumers can purchase blank tapes with which to make their own recordings. The RIAA believes CDs will be able to do this in the near future. Phillips, the Dutch-based electronics company, has been conducting research on this capability for several years. Though not much information is available concerning the manner in which such recording can be accomplished on the compact disc, some believe a single laser beam will read, erase, and rewrite recorded material. The breakthrough may hinge on new compounds under investigation by the Phillips scientists.

Additional Readings

Bowers, David. *Put Another Nickel In.* New York: Bonanza Books, 1966.

De Long, Thomas A. *The Mighty Music Box: The Golden Age of Musical Radio.* Los Angeles: Amber Crest Books, 1980.

Denisoff, R. Serge. *Solid Gold: The Popular Record Industry.* New Brunswick, N.J.: Transaction Books, 1975.

————. *Tarnished Gold.* New York: Transaction, 1986.

————, and Richard A. Peterson, eds. *The Sounds of Social Change: Studies in Popular Culture.* Chicago: Rand McNally, 1972

Douglas, George H. *The Early Days of Radio Broadcasting.* McFarland & Company, 1987.

Ewen, David. *The Life and Death of Tin Pan Alley: The Golden Age of American Popular Music.* New York: Funk and Wagnalls, 1964.

Gelatt, Roland. *The Fabulous Phonograph, 1877-1977.* 2nd Rev. ed. New York: Macmillan, 1977.

Johnson, R. Fenimore. *His Master's Voice Was Eldridge R. Johnson.* Ardmore, Pa.: Gold Star Publishing Co., 1974.

Keith, Michael. *The Radio Station,* 2nd ed. Boston: Focal Press, 1989.

McFarland, David T. *Development of the Top Forty Radio Format.* Ayer Company Publishers, 1979.

Sklar, Rick. *Rocking America: How the All-Hit Radio Stations Took Over: An Insider's Story.* New York: St. Martin's. Press, 1985.

Stanley, Robert H. *The Broadcast Industry.* New York: Hastings House, 1975.

Tobler, John, and Grundy, Stuart. *The Record Producers.* New York: St. Martin's Press, 1982.

Chapter 12
Tin Pan Alley

Origins of the Name

Around 1903, songwriter and journalist Monroe Rosenfeld visited New York's music-writing district, 28th Street. He was preparing an article for his column in the *New York Herald,* and needed some specific material pertaining to popular music. While meeting with renowned songwriter-turned-publisher Harry von Tilzer, Rosenfeld heard someone playing a peculiar-sounding upright piano. Von Tilzer had wound strips of paper through the strings of the piano to produce a tinny effect he liked. Those sounds gave Rosenfeld an idea for his article's title. He called it "Tin Pan Alley." The name caught on, and almost from the date the article was published, the nation began calling 28th Street and the American popular-music industry "Tin Pan Alley." In later years, von Tilzer claimed that he, not Rosenfeld, had coined the phrase as a title for Rosenfeld's article. This may have been true, for Rosenfeld was not above filching the ideas of other people. Nevertheless, Rosenfeld was responsible for first giving the name circulation.

Alley Foundations

The sentimental ballad served as the foundation material on which Tin Pan Alley was built. In 1892, Charles K. Harris wrote the song that marked the climax of his career and became the hallmark of Tin Pan Alley's early history, *After the Ball*. When he was twenty-five, Harris attended a dance in Chicago, at which he witnessed a scene filled with poignancy. Near him, a young couple was arguing. Angry words ensued. The young man left in a huff. Harris was left pondering the thought that many a heart is aching after the ball. And thus, the idea for a ballad was born.

Harris returned home to Milwaukee, and based on the argument he had seen, developed this story line; A young man sees his sweetheart kissing a stranger at a ball. He becomes convinced she is unfaithful, and leaves the ball before his sweetheart can explain. He never sees her again. After many years, he discovers the man his sweetheart was kissing was her long-lost brother. The song ends with the untrusting lover, now an old man, describing this episode to his little niece in an effort to explain why he has never married.

Immediately after Harris completed the song, vaudevillian Sam Doctor came by to see him, seeking a new slow waltz for his act. Harris handed him *After the Ball*. Doctor introduced the piece to vaudeville audiences in 1892. What followed was a minor disaster. In the middle of the premiere performance of the piece, Doctor forgot the words. He stood on the stage, silently floundering in embarrassment, while the audience roared with laughter. The introduction of Harris' ballad was completely destroyed.

Despite the unfortunate circumstances surrounding the introduction of the ballad, Harris was able to place *After the Ball* in Charles Hoyt's extravagant show, *A Trip to Chinatown*. He simply paid the show's singing star, J. Aldrich Libbey, $500 in cash and a percentage of the song's royalties to perform the piece. According to Ewen, this was one of the earliest examples of the infamous 1950s practice called "payola." Harris completed this "shady" transaction by slipping the orchestra leader, Frank Palma, a box of fine cigars to orchestrate the song.

Hoyt did not place the song in a position of much relevance within the production. He put it in the second act, considered to be the less important of the two acts of the musicals of that day. However, regardless of its unimportant position in the show, the song was an immediate and overwhelming success.

This led Harris to believe he had a solid hit, particularly when Witmark Publishing's Isidore Witmark offered him the then-unprecedented sum of $10,000 for publication rights. Harris respectfully refused the offer. A few days after the sheet music was completed, the Oliver Ditson music store in Boston placed an order for seventy-five thousand copies. This order forced Harris to purchase a printing press, rather than using a local printer to produce his sheet music. When orders began pouring in from across the country, he had to purchase additional presses. Within a year, the Harris publishing house was earning as much as $25,000 a week from *After the Ball*. John Philip Sousa played his own arrangement of the ballad at Chicago's 1893 World Columbian Exposition. This instrumental version grew so popular that Sousa was almost forced by public demand to include it in almost all his future programs.

Over the years, *After the Ball* sold more than five million copies of sheet music. This sale was without precedent in the annals of American popular music. In his autobiography, Harris stated that the song eventually earned him over ten million dollars. Single-handedly, this song made Charles K. Harris a power in the music-publishing business, and one of the most celebrated writers of sentimental ballads in the 1890s.

Though he wrote many songs after his giant hit, Harris was never able to duplicate the success of *After the Ball*. However, he did go on to become quite a successful figure on what was the future Tin Pan Alley. When he opened his first publishing office on Grand Avenue, he hung out a shingle, reading, "Charles K. Harris—Banjoist and Songwriter—Songs written to order." David Ewen believed the phrase, *Songs written to order,* was well worth italicizing. According to Ewen, Tin Pan Alley emerged virtually the moment Harris hung out his shingle. Ewen observed, "By advertising that he was in the business of manufacturing songs to order, Charles K. Harris of Milwaukee had become the father of New York City's Tin Pan Alley."[1]

Sentimental ballads prospered in the Tin Pan Alley of the 1890s primarily because the era itself was sentimental. David Ewen painted a touching and an accurate portrait of the nostalgic, whimsical innocence of the age.

[The 1890's] was essentially a sentimental era. It paid lip service to morality, virginity, and basic virtues in unctuous phrases. It regarded the home, the wife, the family, as sacrosanct; the mother, as a boy's best friend; a sister or a daughter, beyond the touch of sordid realities. Man was the sovereign of his domain. He made the rules that his womenfolk obeyed. He might invade places forbidden to his wife, daughter, or sister. He might toast—with champagne in slippers in fancy restaurants—women who lived on the other side of respectability; he might even consider it the ultimate in sophistication to cavort with the glamorous stars of the stage. But this in no way interfered with, or was regarded as a contradiction to, his sanctimonious attitudes at home. His wife lived in a world of her own. Possibly as a reaction to the way in which her husband entertained less moral companions away from home, his wife made a fetish of

[1]Ewen, David. *The Life and Death of Tin Pan Alley.* (New York: Funk and Wagnalls Company, Inc., 1964), p. 19.

respectability. She swathed herself in a multitude of garments, her skirt floating atop layer upon layer of petticoats; her corset strapped around her body like protective armor; her peek-a-boo shirtwaist and mutton sleeves permitting little flesh to be seen. To her, the women of the night spots—for all their finery and diamonds—were unfortunate, to be regarded with a mingling of pity and contempt, because so few of them would ever know the blessings of marital life, children, and the security and peace that respectability brought.[2]

Union Square and the Popular-Music Publishing Business

Throughout most of the nineteenth century, Union Square in New York had been the entertainment seat of the nation. Just before 1890, music publishers began moving north, toward the Square. Willis Woodward and M. Witmark and Sons led the way. Others soon followed. Howley and Haviland moved to Broadway and 32nd Street, and Leo Feist moved his offices to 37th Street. However, most of the other publishers congregated on a single block, 28th Street between Fifth Avenue and Broadway. M. Witmark and Sons were first, opening offices in 1893 at 49 West 28th Street. Joseph W. Stern and Company, Jerome H. Remick, F. A. Mills, and Shapiro-Bernstein, all from Union Square, soon followed suit. Broder and Schlam from San Francisco and Charles K. Harris from Milwaukee also joined the 28th Street gang. By 1900, the largest representation of music-publishing houses found anywhere, had gathered along both sides of 28th Street. For the first time, the popular-music publishing business, formerly scattered all across the nation, became centralized. This concentration of music publishers comprised the real beginnings of Tin Pan Alley.

There were sound practical reasons for the centralization of the music-publishing industry in and around Union Square. Publishers were eager to be near their potential markets, and the Square embraced a host of entertainment centers. Tony Pastor's Music Hall, featuring many of vaudeville's most glamorous stars, was there, along with the Dewey Theater, favored home of burlesque shows, Theiss' Alhambra, featuring a variety of live entertainments, and a proliferation of other burlesque and sporting houses, beer halls, penny arcades, and restaurants. Across the street from the Alhambra stood the street's most famous restaurant, Luchow's. Just a short distance from the square, several theaters were clustered, housing regular performances of minstrel shows and

---

[2]Ewen, pp. 37–38.

variety troupes. Close to Irving Place and fashionable Gramercy Park were two hotels, the Trafalgar and the Academy. Though both were run down and weather-beaten, they still served as home to visiting entertainers.

By 1890, in Union Square, as elsewhere throughout the United States, the minstrel show was dying and vaudeville was on its way to its peak. Of all the branches of musical theater, vaudeville contributed the most significantly to the birth and growth of the Tin Pan Alley of the 1890s and early 1900s. Consequently, the histories of vaudeville and the Alley are inextricably intertwined.

New music publishers were constantly springing up on or near the square. These newcomers frequently had little capital and even less experience. Nonetheless, they possessed initiative, energy, and drive, and these qualities served them well in place of experience and money. They contributed significantly to the business by instituting many of the songwriting, publishing, marketing, and promoting procedures that eventually became the heart and soul of Tin Pan Alley.

Stern and Marks

Joseph W. Stern & Company numbered among those new arrivals who made significant contributions to the Alley. Joseph W. Stern and Edward B. Marks organized the company in 1892. Before its formation, Marks had sold sewing hooks and eyes and whalebone, while Stern had sold neckties. Neither man had any musical training, nor experience in the music-publishing business.

Marks occasionally wrote verses for weddings or birthday parties. He remembered he even occasionally won little prizes for some of his verses. One day, Polly Holmes, an Irish character comedienne, then appearing at Tony Pastor's, asked Marks to write her a comedy number. He responded with *Since McManus Went Down to the Track*. He asked George Rosenberg, an active arranger/composer on the Alley, to add a melody to his lyrics. Holmes sang the number at Pastor's and received a hearty round of applause. Marks' career as a lyricist had begun.

On the advice of a publisher, Frank Harding, Marks sought out and established a collaboration with then-popular vaudevillian Will H. Fox. Through his act, Fox had become the first successful piano-playing comic in vaudeville. The collaboration was a complete failure. Marks' first genuine success came with *December and May*, a sweet, sad love story about an elderly bachelor and his young sweetheart. This was one of the Alley's earliest "December-May" songs. In 1893, William Lorraine set the lyrics to his music, and Frank Harding published the piece. Lydia Yeamns introduced the number that same year at Tony Pastor's. It was a huge success, and became a permanent part of Yeamns' repertory for the next twenty-five years.

The Sentimental Ballad. After measuring his own profits against those realized by his publisher, Marks decided to enter the publishing business himself. While selling on the road, he had crossed paths a number of times with Joe Stern, who sold neckties and enjoyed writing melodies. The two men began a friendship and, shortly after, a writing partnership. One day in 1894, a blinding rainstorm stranded them at their Mamaroneck, New York hotel. While reading a local newspaper to pass the time, they stumbled upon a poignant news item. A policeman had found a lost child wandering through the city streets. The policeman turned out to be the little girl's long-lost father. This was obvious grist for the music-writing mill of the 1890s. Stern and Marks scurried back to the hotel parlor, sat down at a piano, and wrote the words and music of *The Little Lost Child.*

Marks and Stern were convinced that the wisest course of action was to publish the piece themselves. They rented a small office in the basement of a building on Fourteenth Street and Second Avenue, and hung out a new sign reading, "Joseph W. Stern & Company." (Marks was the "& Company." In the beginning he was not thoroughly convinced he should quit his "day-job" just yet.) They used all their capital, about $100, to purchase a desk and chair, and make a deposit with a local printer. On the day the printer delivered the new song, Della Fox, a well-established Broadway star, happened along, and noticed the shiny sign, advertising Stern & Company. She saw that the company was new, and thought she might be able to get some fresh material for her Broadway act. Stern and Marks completely charmed her with their newly delivered *The Little Lost Child.* Fox took the piece and introduced it to Broadway. It was an immediate success. However, the song's immense popularity really began when Lottie Gilson began singing it in vaudeville. Ewen reported that she invariably stopped the show with the song, and on any number of occasions, the audience persuaded her to repeat the refrain several times before it would let her continue.

Stern and Marks made many contributions to the Alley in addition to producing a sensational ballad that sold between one and two million copies. As salesmen, both men realized they could merchandize sheet music in the same manner as neckties and whalebone. They became the first Tin Pan Alley publishers to use a salesman to visit all the local shops and distributors that handled their music. For as long as they continued to travel, selling neckties and sewing hooks, they carried a supply of their latest publications along with their other samples. When *The Little Lost Child* made it possible for them to leave their outside jobs permanently, they continued to travel several times a year around the country, carrying a full sample case of their latest products.

Joe Stern and Edward Marks became the first publishers to issue orchestrations as well as piano scores of their publications. Before this new and unorthodox practice, performers who wanted to use a new number in their acts were forced to pay for its orchestration. By issuing orchestrations for their publications, Stern and Marks broke down the performers' reluctance to try out new materials, and significantly increased the sales of their publications. When it was financially possible, they hired George M. Rosenberg full-time to orchestrate every Stern song.

Though Stern and Marks occasionally issued songs by other composers, by far their biggest hits were their own compositions. Their single most successful endeavor came sometime in 1896, about two years after *The Little Lost Child*. A news item had inspired *The Little Lost Child*. *Mother Was a Lady* was inspired by an actual episode witnessed by both Stern and Marks. They were dining with Meyer Cohen, a singer of popular ballads, in a German restaurant on Twenty-first Street when they overheard two young women at a nearby table harassing a waitress. The waitress exclaimed through tears, "My mother was a lady!" Then she added, "You wouldn't dare to insult me if my brother Jack were only here!" Cohen remarked, in this incident lay the beginnings of a sensational ballad. Marks "took the cue… and developed a pathetic story about a waitress who was being subjected to insults by a salesman. Only later does the salesman discover the waitress is the sister of his best friend. In atonement for his cruel behavior, the repentant drummer begs the waitress for her hand in marriage."[3]

Mother Was a Lady was a smash. It sold several million copies. Its sales alone enabled Stern and Marks to move to larger publishing quarters a few blocks north of Union Square. Now, even well-established composers began coming to them with songs that reaped both composer and publisher large sums of money. Apart from their own compositions, their largest publishing success came before 1900 with a song supposedly written by Maude Nugent. One day in 1896, Nugent paid a visit to Stern and Marks to sing for them a song she claimed to have written, *Sweet Rosie O'Grady*. Both men liked the piece well enough, but felt the market was saturated with songs whose titles included a girl's name. Nugent grabbed her music from the piano, and left in a huff. According to Ewen, Marks followed her out, shouting, "I'll buy it, I'll buy it." He caught her just as she was about to enter Howley and Haviland Publishing. The two returned to the office, where Marks paid her one hundred dollars in cash for all the rights to the piece.

There were those who felt that Nugent did not deserve even the one hundred dollars Marks paid her for the song, much less any royalties. Many doubted she had actually written the song. These skeptics noted the fact that she had never before produced a successful song, nor did she ever do so again. Also, she was married to Billy Jerome, a very successful songwriter. The skeptics believed Jerome had simply written the song for her and allowed her to sell it as her

---

[3]Ewen, p. 61.

own. To Stern and Marks, the question of exactly who wrote the piece was unimportant. Their interest lay in the profits that kept pouring in from its publication. In 1918, the song spawned an offspring, *The Daughter of Rosie O'Grady*, and in 1943, Betty Grable starred in a screen musical entitled *Sweet Rosie O'Grady*.

Stern and Marks launched the careers of several composers, including one of early Broadway's most famous, John Stromberg. Stromberg wrote many smash ballads in the late 1890s, his most famous—and sadly, his last—was *Come Down, Ma Evenin' Star*. This song was found in his pocket when his body was discovered in 1902 in a New York apartment where he had apparently committed suicide. Lillian Russell, an early Broadway superstar, sang it in the Broadway show, *Twirly, Whirly*. On opening night, she broke down midway through the song, and was unable to continue. After this, *Come Down, Ma Evenin' Star* became her signature song. In 1912, Russell starred in a musical production that employed *Evenin' Star*. Her performance so stirred the audience that by the time the song was over, there was not a dry eye in the house.

Leo Feist

In 1893, Stern & Company published *Those Lost Happy Days*, by Leo Feist, and launched the career of the man who would become one of their fiercest competitors. Feist was a corset salesman turned songwriter. After he tried without success to get Stern and Marks to take him as a partner, he began printing his own songs, found musicians to introduce them, and peddled his music himself to the shops. As soon as he had accumulated $200, he rented a two-room office close to Union Square, and entered the publishing business in earnest.

His first hit came in 1894 with Monroe Rosenfeld's ballad, *And Her Golden Hair Was Hanging Down Her Back*. By the close of the century, Feist was among the most successful publishers on Tin Pan Alley. His became the first house to flaunt a slogan concerning all its publications: "You Can't Go Wrong with a Feist Song."

During the 1890s, other new publishers joined those houses already firmly established on the Alley. Firms such as Shapiro-Bernstein and a Detroit importation, Whitney-Warner, made significant contributions to the growth of the industry and the Alley. At the same time older houses were solidifying their own positions. M. Witmark and Sons was growing into an Alley power, largely through the ballad, *The Picture That Is Turned to the Wall*, by Charles Graham. Like Stern and Marks, Witmark made several significant contributions to the profession. It was the first publishing house to distribute free "professional copies" to performing artists. It hired burlesque-house musician Frank Sadler to orchestrate its popular songs. Sadler introduced the Alley to new instrumental effects and unusual harmonies. Witmark was one of the first houses to become interested in ragtime, and in 1898, it became the first publishing house on the Alley to open a music library. Witmark's ad in the New York *Dramatic Mirror* read, "For sale or hire the largest collection of vocal concert numbers and excerpts in America... music of every description, arranged, transposed, copied, lithographed."

Song Plugging

The younger publishing houses along Tin Pan Alley made their most significant contribution in the field of song exploitation. Through the new and logical concept that song hits were not born but were made, these firms began selling music using a high-pressure method called "song plugging." Through the practice of song plugging, the young houses sold their songs in the hundreds of thousands. Song plugging brought about the million-copy sales of several songs, an achievement considered a phenomenon before 1890.

Demand for Tin Pan Alley's products was enormous, forcing Alley publishers to expand their staffs. Pianists who demonstrated new song products to prospective buyers were assigned cramped working quarters. Arrangers worked with musically illiterate composers, helping them write down their melodies and harmonize them. Orchestrations for instrumental groups were adapted from the original scores, and distributed free to encourage performance of the songs. Publishers employed staff composers and lyricists to produce songs in quantity. In those days of fierce competition, quantity was of greater concern to the Alley than quality.

Songs rolled out of Tin Pan Alley as though they were on a Henry Ford assembly line. Creativity gave way to audience whims, needs, and interests. When the general audience became enamored of new inventions, such as the automobile, the telephone, the telegraph, and the flying machine, Alley songwriters stood ready to produce songs by the literal dozens on these topics. On the Alley, "polite borrowing" was a way of life, and the instant a song containing a girl's name or some common term such as "goodbye" became popular, all songwriters rushed to compose similar songs.

Tin Pan Alley measured its success solely by the number of sheet-music copies sold. Sheet music was the only source of income for publisher and composer. Before the day of the Alley, Charles K. Harris' success with *After the Ball,* and Stern and Marks' with *Mother Was a Lady* and *The Little Lost Child,* proved that a small fortune could be realized with just one song. Now more than ever before, financial bonanzas could be achieved on Tin Pan Alley with just a single publication. Million-copy sales became almost commonplace. About one hundred songs produced on the Alley between 1900 and 1910 sold more than a million copies each. In July, 1913, *Billboard* began publishing a

PICTURE COLLECTION, THE BRANCH LIBRARIES, THE NEW YORK PUBLIC LIBRARY

TWENTY-EIGHTH STREET OFF FIFTH AVENUE, C. 1916.

weekly chart of the week's bestsellers. It was the first such chart ever published on popular music. In the beginning, *Billboard* canvassed one hundred twelve retailers and department stores, but within a few weeks, it was using over five hundred reports to compile its chart. *Billboard's* first top-ten chart included *When I Lost You* and *Snookey Ookums,* both by Irving Berlin, *When Its Apple Blossom Time in Normandy, The Trail of the Lonesome Pine,* and *That's How I Need You.*

Million-dollar sales brought publishers about one hundred thousand dollars each, and if the publisher were also the composer, which often was the case, this sum could easily double. Those who were composers and lyricists, but did not serve as their own publishers, also could earn about one hundred thousand dollars, which was divided between lyricist and composer.

To increase sales potential, Tin Pan Alley now began offering its products to buyers through two new markets, department stores and five-and-dime stores. Sometime during the late 1800s, Siegel-Cooper's, located on 18th Street and Eighth Avenue, became the first department store to install a sheet-music department. They were joined by Macy's, on Herald Square. By the turn of the century, department stores had become a major sheet-music sales outlet. During this same period, sheet-music counters were opened in the five-and-dime stores. Publishers sought to enhance sales by placing "song pluggers" at these counters to sing and play current releases.

Song pluggers became the kingpins of the Alley. Many a new release lived or died by the skill, charm, and ingenuity of the plugger. In Union Square, publishers themselves often served as pluggers for their own products. The art and science of plugging became so sophisticated and specialized on Tin Pan Alley, publishers began hiring trained musicians to fill these positions. Men such as Jean Schwartz, Mose Gumble, Johnny Nestor, Joseph Stanley, and Ben Bloom spent part of their professional careers as pluggers. These men, and others like them, would sometimes stand near their 28th Street offices, looking for stage performers who often came to the Alley, searching for new materials. Like circus-sideshow barkers, the pluggers would attempt to entice and woo the performers into their publishers' respective offices to listen to the newest releases. Other plugging methods were far more complex than this.

David Ewen described in detail the humorous methods employed by Mose Gumble:

> The activity of Mose Gumble, ace plugger, was typical. He was a bald-headed singer who made the rounds of places where people gathered, all the way from Coney Island in Brooklyn to 125th Street in Manhattan, singing the songs he wanted to promote. He enjoyed a huge acquaintance in the trade, cajoling actors with his charm and glib tongue into using his numbers. As a fifteen-dollar-a-week staff pianist for Shapiro-Bernstein, Gumble had demonstrated songs for stars such as George M. Cohen, Nora

Bayes, and Webster and Fields. From demonstrating he went on to plugging. He would sometimes board a horsecar on Broadway and shout out his songs to the throngs in the streets. But initially his favorite stamping ground was Coney Island. From evening to the following morning he toured Coney Island dance halls, restaurants, and other night spots. Many a time he slept on the beach to be on time for the next morning's rehearsals, and thus put himself in a better position to convince a singer to use one of the pieces he was plugging. Single handedly he was responsible for starting Jean Swartz's *Bedelia* on its three million copy sale.[4]

During the early 1900s, nickelodeons began installing "flickers" (hence the name "flicks" or the "flick" for motion picture shows). By 1907, some four hundred of these theaters were in operation. Here was still another outlet for the song plugger. He placed songs with the house pianist, who played background music for silent movies. Pluggers themselves would often appear as live stage entertainment just before the presentation of the film, and during intermission. The nickelodeon soon became such a productive setting that many pluggers routinely worked as many as eight of these theaters an evening and several more on weekends. Sammy Smither (one-time baseball player turned plugger) once boasted he could plug a song fifty times in a single evening.

Song Slides. Other means were also employed to plug songs. One such highly popular method included using a photographic product called "stereopticon slides." When such slides accompanied a song, they were called "song slides." George H. Thomas, a Brooklyn theater electrician, conceived the notion of song slides. The theater where he worked was presenting *The Old Homestead,* a play in which the ballad *Where Is My Wandering Boy Tonight* was sung. The theater manager produced an unusually dramatic effect during the performance of the song by dimming the house lights and flashing a picture on a screen depicting a drunk at a bar, with his head resting tiredly on his arm. Observing the effect this produced on the audience gave Thomas the idea of dramatizing other popular songs by showing a series of slides on a screen during performances. He carried his concept to Joseph W. Stern & Company, and convinced them to apply the treatment to the newly released *The Little Lost Child.* Stern and Marks paid a photographer to shoot the slides in a Brooklyn police station, where the different episodes of the ballad were depicted. Thomas' wife played the lost child's mother, a real policeman played himself, and a child actress was recruited to play the part of the little lost girl.

Stern and Marks showed the slides for the first time during the intermission of an 1894 minstrel show. May Allen sang the ballad. The gimmick

---

[4]Ewen, pp. 128–129.

worked far beyond the wildest expectations of anyone connected with it. Soon, song slides began appearing all over the nation. They influenced the sale of sheet music to such an extent that within a remarkably short period of time, all sheet-music publishers were rushing pellmell to have their songs dramatized by stereopticon slides. The De Witt C. Wheeler Company became heavily involved in the production of song slides. Singers started specializing in this field. Many vaudeville and musical-theater stars, including Georgie Jessel, Fanny Brice, and Eddie Cantor, began their careers as song-slide actors.

In the beginning, publishers gave the slides away to any theater who wished to use them. However, song slides rapidly became a basic part of the show, and audiences eagerly sought those shows that used them. Consequently, publishers concluded that they could charge a modest fee of from five to ten dollars for a set of slides. On some occasions, there were as many as one thousand sets of slides of a single song simultaneously rented to theaters all across the nation.

The Demise of the Alley

Until 1914, life on Tin Pan Alley was relatively simple and straightforward. Songs poured out of the Alley in number. They were advertised by the pluggers and in vaudeville. White Americans purchased the bulk of the popular music published for use with the home piano or guitar. Alley publishers profited from the sale of their sheet music, composers received royalties from the sales, and artists collected gifts or a cut of the royalties in return for plugging the songs in vaudeville. The Alley was one big happy family.

Then, the Copyright Act of 1909 appeared, and life on the Alley began changing dramatically. The Copyright Act gave publishers and composers the right to collect royalties on songs that were performed publicly. However, merely acquiring the right to collect these royalties did not guarantee that publishers and composers would, in fact, receive the money mandated. At the time the act was inaugurated, those who had legitimate claim to such income had no viable means by which to collect these royalties. In 1914, publishers and composers took concrete action to alleviate this problem. They formed ASCAP, the American Society of Composers, Authors, and Publishers, an organization dedicated to the enforcement of the 1909 Copyright Act. The Society immediately sued Shanley's Restaurant in New York for nonpayment of ASCAP royalties. In 1917, after an extended court case and trial, Supreme Court Judge Oliver Wendell Holmes ruled in favor of ASCAP. Restaurants, hotels, and ballrooms were forced to pay royalties on live performances.

Radio and the Alley. Since just after the turn of the century, radio as a popular-music source of entertainment had been gaining strength and popularity. By the early 1920s, radio had sounded the death knell of vaudeville, and was seriously eroding Alley sheet-music sales by replacing sheet music and the piano as the principal source of home entertainment. Radio's biggest sin was its refusal to pay royalties on the music it used. Once again, ASCAP sued for non-payment of royalties, and won. The fledgling broadcast industry was ordered by the court to pay a percentage of its profits for use of ASCAP material.

Radio created a gap between consumer and performer. Vaudeville artists came into close contact with their audiences. The audience told them, by its reactions, whether they were succeeding or failing. Vaudeville audiences were small, and the shows they saw invariably included enough variety to satisfy everyone present. Radio shows were impersonal. Their audiences were significantly larger, and were always isolated from the performer. Programming was obviously limited to aural experiences only. Radio widened the gap between audience and artist by spawning a small number of "stars," such as Kate Smith, Russ Colombo, and Rudy Vallee, with whom its patrons had no direct contact.

Songs written for vaudeville and those written for radio differed significantly. A vaudeville song needed to appeal to only a small number of people to insure its success. During vaudeville days, a song could be expected to remain popular for well in excess of a year, and often longer, thus producing profit over an extended period. If songs targeted at radio audiences were to be profitable, they had to appeal to everyone, almost immediately, since the same program went into every home. Radio could make a hit in seven days and kill it in sixty merely because of its access to so many homes across the country. The backbone of vaudeville and Tin Pan Alley had been the sentimental ballad that most often told a tragic story. Songs heard over the radio of the late '20s and early '30s tended to paint pictures, rather than to tell stories. As this new genre grew in popularity, sentimental ballads slowly faded into the past. The stage was being set for the destruction of the Alley.

The ASCAP and BMI War. Hollywood contributed significantly to the Alley's demise. Like radio, it, too, came between audience and performer. The combination of Hollywood and radio encouraged the rise of the big isolated star, and created a totally different market for popular-song composers. Songs from Broadway musicals and other sources replaced the music of the older, more traditional, Tin Pan Alley composers. In all, by 1920, the changes wrought by the advent of radio broadcasting, Broadway musicals, and Hollywood took a serious toll on the fortunes of Tin Pan Alley. The Alley managed to survive, but in noticeably altered and much damaged form. Many of its publishing houses had been badly affected, and by the late 1920s, many had been taken over by the big Hollywood movie companies. The war between ASCAP and Broadcast Music, Incorporated (BMI) which began with the formation of BMI in 1939, and culminated in ASCAP's defeat in 1941, ultimately dealt Tin Pan Alley its deathblow.

After the formation of ASCAP, and the consequent suits against the radio industry, radio and Tin Pan Alley declared a shaky, uneasy truce, lasting well into the 1930s. This arrangement continued even after Hollywood had acquired several ASCAP publishing houses. Despite the instability of the ceasefire, both sides remained at least quiescent as long as they each were making money. Then the swing era arrived, and began adversely affecting Hollywood. Radio could easily profit from swing by arranging hookups from theaters and dance locations where swing was being performed, by playing swing recordings, and by hosting live swing radio shows. Hollywood was not so fortunate. Movies were the only means by which it could bring swing to the public, and movies took a long time to write, film, and market. Also, their costs were much greater than the comparatively simple radio shows. As a direct consequence, decreasing numbers of people visited movie theaters, and Hollywood profits took a nose dive.

Hollywood fought back through ASCAP. It planned an incredible increase in radio royalties, an increase designed to produce one of two results. If radio could not afford the new rates, it would have little popular music to play, and paying customers would once again fill movie theaters. If radio could afford them, Hollywood would not suffer any noticeable financial loss.

However, ASCAP and Hollywood made one serious miscalculation. They both believed that white America would prefer only music that ASCAP owned. This proved incorrect. Late in the 1930s, the radio industry learned of ASCAP's plans, and began quietly building a library of popular music not covered by ASCAP copyrights. By the time ASCAP announced its new rates in January, 1941, BMI owned a significant library of music.

Radio refused to pay the increase, which was almost double the old amount. As a result, no ASCAP music could be broadcast. This was potentially crippling for all radio stations. Nearly all the song writers whose music they had been programming for years belonged to ASCAP. To keep its radio audiences, BMI was forced to purchase and play music by black composers, who wrote in a more vernacular, less sophisticated style than the white composers who belonged to ASCAP. Music written by these black composers had always been considered by ASCAP unsuitable for white city dwellers. Consequently, such composers were barred from ASCAP membership. This resulted in the broadcasting of music that did not originate with white urban composers, and the creation of a market for a new kind of music.

People did not return to theaters in significant numbers, nor were radio stations forced to play only ASCAP-controlled music. America continued to listen to the radio, and BMI's new and, by then, extensive library of music. ASCAP lost the battle and the war. In October, 1941, it capitulated, and settled with the radio companies.

However, the damage to the Alley had been done. The listening habits and preferences of much of the nation had been forever altered. BMI's library included an abundance of country-and-western, and rhythm-and-blues. Programming this kind of music led to a national preference for these two genres. In particular, the listening public appeared to prefer the rhythm-and-blues of the black community, a genre of music that eventually played a major role in the development of rock. The day of the Alley was at an end.

Additional Readings

Burton, Jack. *Blue Book of Tin Pan Alley.* 2 vols. Watkins Glen, New York: Century House/American Life Foundation, 1962.

Ewen, David. *The Life and Death of Tin Pan Alley: The Golden Age of American Popular Music.* New York: Funk and Wagnalls, 1964.

Goldberg, Issac. *Tin Pan Alley: A Chronicle of American Popular Music.* New York: Frederick Ungar, 1931; paper, 1970.

Marcuse, Maxwell F. *Tin Pan Alley in Gaslight.* American Life Foundation. Watkins Glen, N.Y.: Century House, 1959.

Pleasants, Henry. *The Great American Popular Singers.* New York: Simon and Schuster, 1974.

Stein, Charles W., ed. *American Vaudeville As Seen by Its Contemporaries.* New York: Knopf, 1984.

Selected Recordings

The following songs are included in the *New World Recorded Anthology of American Music.* They are listed by title, record number, when known, side number, and band number. Also where the artist is a well-known figure, his name has been included.

Armstrong, Louis. *Ain't Misbehavin'* s2/7
Crosby, Bing. *Brother, Can You Spare a Dime?* s1/1
Stormy Weather 248: s1/1
All of Me s1/4
Shoe Shine Boy s1/7
When My Dreamboat Comes Home s2/3

Once in a While s2/4
In the Still of the Night s1/4
Love Walked In s1/5
The White Cliffs of Dover s2/8
Dinah 279: s1/4
Yes Sir, That's My Baby s2/3
Mississippi Mud s2/4

Chapter 13
The Folk-Music Revival

Revival Roots

During the week of November 17, 1958, the number-one position on the *Billboard* top-five chart was occupied by the Kingston Trio's recording of *Tom Dooley*. This song was a century-old Blue Ridge Mountain folk tune, originally entitled *Tom Dula*. Dula was a mountain man who was hanged for murder in 1868. Fred Bronson marked this recording as the beginning of the folk-music revival, which took place in the late fifties and early sixties. According to Bronson, the Kingston Trio started the modern folk movement in the rock era. They set the stage for Peter, Paul and Mary, Bob Dylan, Joan Baez; Judy Collins; John Denver, and Gordon Lightfoot.

Dave Guard, Bob Shane, and Nick Reynolds all were college students in the San Francisco area in the mid-fifties. Guard, Reynolds, and two other singers were playing as Dave Guard and the Calypsonians at a San Francisco club called the Cracked Pot. Frank Werber, a publicist for the Purple Onion nightclub, saw the group and was duly impressed. However, he thought dropping the bass player would improve the group. Soon after, the bass player left, and Bob Shane joined the group. Werber then offered to manage them. He sent them to a vocal coach, put them through extensive rehearsals, and helped them select a new group name, one that would retain a calypso flavor and still sound collegiate. The result was the Kingston Trio. The trio's first engagement under Werber was at the Hungry i in San Francisco. (Their most successful album was entitled *The Kingston Trio: From The Hungry i*.) When Phyllis Diller canceled an appearance at the Purple Onion, Werber used the trio to fill in for her, and they went on to work the Purple Onion for seven straight weeks.

During this engagement, Bob Hope's television agent, Jimmy Saphier, saw the group. He told Voyle Gillmore of Capitol Records about them. Gillmore flew to San Francisco and signed the trio to a recording contract. One night, while at the Purple Onion, the trio heard a vocalist sing *Tom Dooley* for a club audition. They liked the song and included it in their first Capitol album, released June 1, 1958. Its resulting popularity forced Capitol to issue the song as a single. Many believe that this song launched the modern folk-music revival.

Folk-music purists argue that the style of music performed by the Kingstons and groups like them was just an insipid, vague imitation of genuine folk music. Most folk-music authorities believe the revival started much earlier. Sandy Paton is a collector and producer of traditional folk music and folk-music recordings. He pointed to the work done by John and Alan Lomax as the single most significant factor in bringing folk music to the attention of the public at large. During the early part of the 1930s, these two men set out with cumbersome equipment to record authentic American folk music from across the nation. That body of songs became the nucleus of an immense collection of folk music now housed in the Library of Congress' Archive of American Folk Song. According to Paton, the pioneering work carried out by the Lomaxes marked the true beginning of the folk revival. In 1934, the Lomaxes brought Huddie Ledbetter, known worldwide simply as "Leadbelly," to sing for audiences in Washington, Philadelphia, and New York. Paton believed Leadbelly was probably the first genuine folk artist to touch urban Americans with his personality and the raw power of his music.

In different sections of the nation, other stirrings were taking place that contributed significantly to the awakening national interest in folk music. Bascom Lamar Lunsford began the annual American Folk Festival in Asheville, North Carolina, in 1928. The White Top Festivals in the early 1930s introduced thousands of visitors to the traditional music of Appalachia. Sarah Gertrude Knott organized the first National Folk Festival in St. Louis in 1934. At all these events, the music performed was the authentic folk music of rural America, and the audiences that heard it were, for the large part, urban Americans.

Woodie Guthrie arrived in New York in 1939, performing first as a solo artist, then with the Almanac Singers. In the late forties, a group called "The Weavers" brought a dressed-up kind of folk music to the nation. They were remarkably successful. Still, folk music, traditional or otherwise, had not yet attained the popularity that it would experience in another ten years. During the late forties and early fifties, folk music experienced a slight decline in popularity, but with the appearance of the Kingston Trio, it suddenly blossomed again. Sandy Paton contended that the New Lost City Ramblers were probably more instrumental in this apparent reawakening than the Kingstons. Regardless of the cause, or who was responsible, after the release of *Tom Dooley*, it quickly became quite clear America had indeed discovered a new sound.

America Comes Back to Folk Music

With its new-found interest in folk music, America again discovered the guitar. Pete Seeger, internationally known folk-music composer/singer, believed there were several reasons for this revival of interest in the guitar. In Seeger's view, after World War II, Americans began digging in earnest for their roots. They began studying their country's heritage. As evidence of this interest, Seeger pointed out the number of historical recreations around the country, magazines such as *American Heritage*, and the movies and novels about American life that appeared after the War.

According to Seeger, post-World War II Americans were again becoming a nation of doers, rather than passive participants in American life. They began participating in a host of do-it-yourself activities: boating, skiing, bowling, photography, weaving, hot rodding. Americans by the millions rediscovered the guitar just when folklorists, such as John and Alan Lomax, were digging out and presenting to the nation some of the world's best folk music.

Seeger believed that perhaps a certain sophistication was required to sing hillbilly songs without worrying about being called a hillbilly, or to sing spirituals without fear of being called an Uncle Tom. He suggested that people were incapable of choosing confidently between good and bad in such music until they had been separated from their past for several years, a point of view with which this writer entirely agrees!

Folk music is a gutsy, raw-boned, honest expression of everyday human emotions and events, the very kinds of emotions and events John Dewey and many others believe contain the roots of aesthetic expression and experience. According to Seeger, most popular music is, after all, rather banal. People turn to music, seeking to use the art to express their innermost thoughts and feelings when their own expressive abilities seem somehow inadequate. For them, music becomes an extension of their own inner emotions and selves. During those periods, triviality most assuredly begs the question.

To Seeger, folk songs contained the real elements from which human life is made: outlaws, heroes, murderers, broken-hearted lovers, fools, villains. Folk songs were and are tragic, sentimental, scandalous, giggly, and cute. But more than any of these, for Seeger, folk songs were straightforward, honest depictions of life. He believed art songs were too concerned with erudite matters, and pop songs with being clever. Folk music is more than a collection of old songs about people, places, and events. It is a process whereby significant topics and events in the lives of a people have historically been preserved. It is a process that continues today, with little real change.

Hootenanny: Hallmark of the Folk-Music Revival

Webster's *New World Dictionary* defines the word "hootenanny" as "a meeting of folk singers, as for public entertainment." Webster may have derived its definition from the event with which the term has been associated since at least 1940. During that summer, leaders of a Seattle Democratic Party group were planning a series of fund-raising social events. These gatherings were not planned specifically as dances, dinners, or formal stage entertainments, but as a combination of all these, and more. In searching for an appropriate name for such an event, the field of choices was eventually narrowed to "wing-ding" and "hootenanny." "Hootenanny" won. Bertha and Terry Pettus, editors and publishers of the Seattle group's political paper, the *Washington New Dealer,* probably coined the term in a July, 1940 notice, advertising the first of these social events.

Uncertainty has always surrounded the term "hootenanny." Historical sources cannot satisfactorily explain the manner in which the term acquired its present-day meaning. However, by 1946, "hootenanny" was widely used to designate such musical pastiches. Regardless of its origins, when the modern folk movement took wings in the late '50s, musicians quickly adopted the term to describe any folk-music gathering, large or small. By then, increasingly large groups of folk singers across the nation had begun gathering in parks and other public places to sing and play their music. As the crowds increased, so did the alarm of the residents who lived close to these gathering places. The events attracted nonconformists and "queer, devious characters," and, after 1957, beatniks. After a time, these gatherings alarmed even the police. Walter Winchell, nationally syndicated columnist and news reporter, commented in his July 4, 1961 column, "An officer stopped a stroller near the [Washington] Square [New York]: 'Whatcha doin' here?' the law demanded. 'I'm looking for someone to mug,' admitted the man. 'Sorry,' the law apologized, 'I thought you were a folk singer.' "

Perhaps the best-known and most popular gathering place in the nation during the heyday of the hootenanny was the dry fountain in Washington Square Park, located in Greenwich Village. In early April, 1961, Parks Commissioner Newbold Morris issued an order banning singing sessions and rallies in the park without a permit. A permit previously applied for by folk singers had been denied, based on an old law that prohibited use of musical instruments in the park. The folk singers who routinely gathered there elected to disregard the ban. On April 9, 1961, a large group entered the park after police warned them not to use musical instruments on the grounds. When singing, accompanied by musical instruments, began, the police ejected the crowd and arrested seven of the folk singers. The singers and their followers moved to the steps of nearby Judson Memorial Church. For the next thirty days, the church steps became a sanctuary. From there, the group made general protests, began a defense fund for the arrested singers, and formed the Greenwich Village Right-to-Sing Committee. During this period, city officials offered the group use of the more formal amphitheater in East River Park. The offer was refused. The State Supreme Court upheld the Parks Commissioner's decision. In early May, authorities allowed singers to return to Washington Square. On the day they did, the singers stood with their instruments draped in black crepe and sang an out-of-tune version of *The Star Spangled Banner*. They followed this with a very low-volume pledge to the flag.

Early Folk Singers

Leadbelly. Among those first musicians who wrote and performed folk music, several names emerge as legitimate giants, including Huddie "Leadbelly" Ledbetter, Josh White, Woodrow "Woody" Guthrie, Burl Ives, and Earl Robinson. Ledbetter was born in 1885 in Mooringsport, Louisiana. Like his family, he picked cotton for a living. He learned to play the guitar at an early age. Leadbelly was often involved in brawls, and at age 33, served a seven-year term in a Texas prison. He was again incarcerated in Louisiana, this time for four years, beginning in 1930.

John A. Lomax, pioneer folk-music collector and compiler, discovered Huddie while Huddie was serving his Louisiana State Prison sentence. After Huddie left prison in 1934, he worked as a chauffeur for Lomax. Lomax promoted Huddie as a folk singer in colleges, prisons, left-wing organizations, and on records. Toward the end of his life, Leadbelly sang at the Village Vanguard and other nightclubs in Greenwich Village. He spent his final days in poverty and sickness. He was on relief when he died in Bellevue Hospital in 1949.

Had he lived just one year longer, Leadbelly would have attained comparative affluence. The Gordon Jenkins orchestra, and the folk-music group, The Weavers, combined to revive an old song Leadbelly had written while in Louisiana State Prison, *Goodnight, Irene*. After this, the song was recorded by Frank Sinatra and other big-name stars. *Goodnight, Irene* became a several-million disc seller, and would have brought Huddie the financial resources with which to live out his remaining days in comparative comfort. In addition to *Goodnight Irene*, Leadbelly wrote *Easy Rider, Rock Island Line, Gray Goose, Good Morning Blues, The Midnight Special, Whoa Back Buck, Keep Your Hands off Her, Fannin Street*, and *New York City*.

Josh White.

Josh White sang the blues and songs about lynching, slums and poor housing, and Jim Crow. These kinds of songs first found favor with radical groups in the late thirties, even before White achieved national fame as a folk singer. Throughout his life, White remained true to songs of social significance.

White was born in 1908, the son of a Greenville, South Carolina, preacher. His parents named him Joshua, hoping he too would become a preacher. When he was very young, he learned to sing and play the guitar. As a boy, he traveled around the country with two blind minstrels, Joel Taggart, and one of the early blues legends, Blind Lemon Jefferson. From them, he gained a rich repertory of folk songs. Occasionally, he would accompany Taggart and Jefferson on his guitar.

Josh was only eleven years old when he made his first recording. Several years later, in about 1933, he began recording spirituals for Columbia Records. He called himself "the singing Christian." He also recorded blues, work songs, and songs of protest under the assumed name, Pinewood Top. He gained national exposure singing with a folk group, the Southernaires, over the NBC television network.

Josh cut his right hand severely on a broken milk bottle, and for three years, he was unable to play the guitar. By 1940 he had regained complete use of his hand, and was able to resume his folk-music career. His major successes began in the 1940s with his participation in the Broadway theater. Josh played a minor part in the 1940 production, *John Henry*, starring Paul Robeson. He also appeared in *Blue Holiday* and *A Long Way from Home*.

During this period, Josh also sang on the radio, made several recordings, and played in several nightclubs, including Barney Josephson's Café Society

JOSH WHITE.

Downtown, where he made the first of many highly successful appearances. He made the first of three appearances at the White House in 1940. The Federal Government sent him on a goodwill tour of Mexico, and he made several successful trips to Europe. In 1966, Josh was involved in a serious automobile accident, and as a result, became largely inactive. He died in 1969 in a hospital in Manhasset, Long Island, while undergoing heart surgery.

Woodie Guthrie. Woodrow Wilson Guthrie was born July 14, 1912, in Okfuskee County, Oklahoma. His parents named him in honor of the Democratic presidential candidate of that year, but he lived his entire life as "Woody." He grew up on songs and tales told by his grandmother, Mary Tanner. During the first two decades of this century, Oklahoma was still pioneer country. Consequently, the songs he heard his grandmother sing were

PHOTOFEST

WOODIE GUTHRIE.

about wildcats, panthers, coyotes, and wolves, and about the settling of Okfuskee County.

Woody's family was financially secure until a series of disasters struck. His father's land-trading business went bankrupt. Fire and cyclones destroyed three family houses. His sister died in an oil-stove explosion, and as a result of this, his mother suffered a mental breakdown and had to be institutionalized. From that time on, Woody literally fended for himself. He took just about any job that presented itself. He soon left home to roam the nation, earning his way in large part by singing folk tunes learned at his grandmother's knee, and songs of his own composing.

Woody sang to his guitar accompaniment at rodeos, carnivals, and dances. In California, he began making appearances over several radio stations. Then he began performing with actor Will Geer for labor unions, with whom, Ewen said, Woodie became a favorite during the 1930s. Alan Lomax sought Woody out to record for the Archive of American Folk Songs of the Library of Congress.

For a time during the early '40s, Woody sang with the Almanac Singers, a group that included three of early folk music's premier performers—Lee Hayes, Pete Seeger, and Millard Lampell. For several years after that, Woody continued to record and sing all across the country, until a serious hereditary nervous disorder, Huntington's chorea, permanently hospitalized him. He died in 1967 at Creedmore State Hospital in Queens.

Burl Ives. Burl Icle Ivanhoe Ives was born in Hunt Township, Jasper County, Illinois, in 1909. Ives' American ancestry reached back to the seventeenth century. His father was a tenant farmer in Hunt County.

Everyone in the family sang. Burl learned folk songs from his grandmother, songs such as *The Blue Tail Fly, Barbara Allen, Lord Thomas and Fair Eleanor,* and *The Wayfaring Stranger,* all of which later became part of his permanent repertory. He once told a reporter he couldn't remember when he started to sing.

As a child, Ives' chief ambition in life was to become a preacher. At about age nine, he became a boy evangelist. Then, he heard a jazz band at a school dance. He saw people dancing to the music. Later in life, Ives said, "There they were, a'dancin' and a'singin' and a'laughin'. I said to myself, 'Boy this ain't religion. It's music.' And I decided not to become a preacher."[1]

During his high school years, Ives occasionally sang for the local Rotary Club, accompanying himself on the banjo. After graduation in 1927, he enrolled at Eastern Illinois State College (now Eastern Illinois University) at Charleston. There he played football (in high school he had been an all-conference guard), sang in the college quartet, and played the banjo in the college jazz band. After two years, he dropped out to "bum around" the country. He was curious to discover what America looked like. He found out the hard way. He traveled across every state but Washington and Oregon, earning his way by waiting on tables, washing dishes, preaching, and singing folk songs, many of which he learned during his travels. He went back to college in 1931, but again the urge to wander overtook him, and once more he took to the road. In 1933 he settled briefly in Terre Haute, Indiana, and took a job singing on a local radio station.

By that time, Ives had made his way to New York, where he lived and worked as a busboy at International House, near Columbia University. On Sundays, he sang solos at the Riverside Church and the Church of St. Mary the Virgin. Occasionally, he sang American folk songs and ballads in bars, cafés, and night spots in Greenwich Village.

By 1938, Ives was drifting toward an acting career. During that year, he performed with the Rockbridge Theater, a Carmel, New York, stock company. He also appeared in the small part of the tailor's apprentice in the Rodgers and Hart Broadway musical, *The Boys from Syracuse.* After World War II and his release from the Army, Ives got a radio series over CBS, "The Wayfarin' Stranger," began making records, and was a principal in the 1944 Broadway musical, *Sing Out Sweet Land.* This show consisted of a score made up exclu-

---

[1]Ewen, David. *All the Years of American Popular Music.* (Englewood Cliffs, New Jersey: Prentice-Hall Inc., 1977), p. 420.

sively of American folk songs. His success in this production helped to convince Ives that his future lay in acting. In March, 1955, Tennessee Williams' *Cat on a Hot Tin Roof* opened at Broadway's Morosco Theater, starring Ives as the character Big Daddy. This production enjoyed a run of 694 performances. Ives played Big Daddy in the film version as well, which also starred Elizabeth Taylor and Paul Newman. He was outstanding in both versions.

Earl Robinson. During the latter part of the 1930s, Earl Robinson became the singing champion of the radical left. He was a musician thoroughly trained in traditional music. He held a Bachelor of Music degree from the University of Washington, and he studied composition privately with Aaron Copland. He wrote his music in the style and structure of folk songs, but all his music was exclusively his own. In 1940, he received a Guggenheim Fellowship in music to write a setting for Carl Sandburg's *The People, Yes.* However, during the 1930s Robinson become convinced that writing abstract music designed exclusively for concert-hall aesthetic appeal was not a responsible pursuit. He believed a socially conscious composer had an ethical and moral obligation to aim his efforts toward the pertinent issues of the times, to write a simple and uncomplicated music capable of direct communication with the masses.

In the late '30s, Robinson allied himself with the Communist Party. In 1938, he wrote two ballads that became popular with the radicals, *Joe Hill* and *Abe Lincoln. Joe Hill* was written to glorify the labor movement's hero and to propagandize unionism. *Abe Lincoln* aligned itself with the Communist popular front, which appealed to the antifascist and prolabor liberals for support. The chorus in *Abe Lincoln* proclaimed Robinson's interpretation of Lincoln's beliefs: The people who inhabit America own it and its institutions. They can exercise their constitutional rights to amend its government or their revolutionary rights to overthrow it.

In 1942, Robinson wrote another tribute to Lincoln in the form of a threnody, *The Lonesome Train*, text by Millard Lampell. Directed by Norman Corwin, *The Lonesome Train* premiered over CBS; it was so successful that it brought Robinson a Hollywood contract. Also, during that same year, he wrote another document praising American democracy and pleading for tolerance, *The House I Live In*, text by Lewis Allen. Robinson himself introduced this song in a socially oriented Broadway revue, *Let Freedom Sing* (1942), which had a run of about a week. Frank Sinatra discovered the song, and added it to his repertoire. He sang it for the first time in 1945 at a high school assembly in Gary, Indiana. Sinatra later starred in a movie short built entirely around the song. The short won a special award from the Academy of Motion Picture Arts and Sciences, and promoted Sinatra as a crusader for tolerance.

The Folk-Music Revivalists

During the 1940s, the popularity of folk music and its singers began to spread. Of limited appeal a decade earlier, The National Folk Festival, begun in St. Louis in the early '30s, appeared in Washington, D.C. in 1942, in New York City in 1943, and in Cleveland in 1947. It became a several-day event, and included performances by amateurs and professionals alike in front of audiences that numbered literally in the thousands. In 1959, this festival set up national headquarters in Washington, D.C., as the National Folk Festival Association Incorporated.

During the mid-1940s, hootenannies were held in New York City to raise money for the founding and publishing of the first magazine devoted exclusively to folk music, *People's Song.* Folk singers and their music spread out across the nation. Motion pictures began featuring folk songs in increasing numbers. By 1947, folk music was being played regularly over radio stations nationwide.

Pete Seeger. With this exposure came greater and greater recognition for an increasing number of folk singers. Names such as Pete Seeger, Oscar Brand, and Susan Reed gained household familiarity. Like Earl Robinson, Pete Seeger openly and courageously espoused strong leftist and socially conscious convictions. These convictions made Seeger a favorite with the left-wing movement.

PETE SEEGER.

They also brought him into open conflict with the House Un-American Activities Committee. In 1955, this committee indicted him on ten counts of contempt of Congress (the United States Court of Appeals overturned these indictments in 1962). However, for several years, Seeger was blacklisted on television stations. Regardless of this, his popularity and importance rose significantly above the political and social setting. According to David Ewen, Seeger, more than any other folk singer of the '40s, except Burl Ives, attracted a huge audience for folk music.

Peter R. Seeger was born in New York City in 1919. He was the son of Charles Seeger, a distinguished composer, musicologist, and professor of music. His stepmother, Ruth Crawford Seeger, was also a nationally renowned composer and musicologist. His half-brother, Mike, and his half-sisters, Peggy and Penny, were professional folk singers.

Pete grew up steeped in the classical-music tradition. When he was sixteen, he attended a folk-music festival in Asheville, North Carolina with his father. This was his first contact with folk music. The experience left an indelible impression on him. After high school graduation, he attended Harvard University for two years. In 1938, he abruptly left school for good. He traveled all over the nation, either hitchhiking or riding the rods (holding on to the rods underneath freight-train cars). He gathered folk songs and sang them in migrant camps, hobo colonies, and saloons during these Depression years. During his travels he met and became friends with Woodie Guthrie, Leadbelly, John A. Lomax, and Earl Robinson. All these men encouraged Pete in his folk-music collecting and singing.

Between 1942 and 1945, Seeger served in the special services division of the armed forces, entertaining American troops at home and in the Pacific theater. After his tour of duty, Seeger helped found People's Song, Inc., a union of songwriters and a clearinghouse for folk music. He also became the union's director.

Seeger's real fame with the general music public began in 1949, with The Weavers. The group made its debut at the Village Vanguard in New York's Greenwich Village in 1949. Success was instantaneous. Demand for the group for nightclub appearances, concert halls, colleges, recordings, and radio was enormous. By the time the Weavers disbanded in 1952, they had sold over five million records.

After the breakup, Seeger continued to perform across the United States. In 1963, he made a world tour. Two of his early 1960s compositions, both rooted in the folk-song tradition, were genuine hits: *Where Have All the Flowers Gone?* and *And Quiet Flows the Don. If I Had a Hammer*, written with Lee Hayes, became a bestseller as recorded by Peter, Paul and Mary, and also by Trini Lopez.

Oscar Brand. Oscar Brand was a Canadian, born in Winnipeg in 1920. He came to the United States when he was seven. His family settled first in Minneapolis, then in Chicago, and finally in New York. Brand's entire family was musical, and from his parents and grandparents, he acquired a deep love for music and singing. After graduating from Brooklyn's Erasmus Hall High School in 1937, he spent several years hoboing around the country, picking up farm jobs as he went. During these years, he collected folk songs and learned to sing them to his banjo accompaniment.

Brand returned to Brooklyn to attend Brooklyn College, where he became active in the drama department. He graduated in 1942 with a degree in abnormal psychology. After serving in the armed forces from 1942 to 1945, he settled permanently in New York City with the intention of becoming a professional folk singer. Over the next several years, he recorded more than fifty albums for various record companies. His own composition, *A Guy Is a Guy*, became a bestseller in 1952, as recorded by Doris Day for Columbia Records.

Susan Reed. Susan Reed was born in Columbia, South Carolina, in 1927. She was the daughter of the distinguished actor, playwright, and director, Daniel Reed. Susan's father was an aficionado of folk music and often had famous houseguests, such as Carl Sandburg and Leadbelly. (Sandburg was a fine folk musician as well as a poet.) Such an environment was to have a pronounced effect on Susan's later life.

Susan spent much of her childhood traveling with her family. By the early 1940s, her family had settled comfortably in New York. There, Susan began singing in a church choir, and during the war years she entertained wounded soldiers in local hospitals. She began singing professionally after a very successful 1944 appearance at New York's Café Society Uptown. Susan accompanied herself on the zither and the Irish harp, and her repertory included American folk songs, and ballads from foreign countries as well.

Folk music crossed the line into pop in the mid-to-late 1940s. This incursion continued well into the '50s. In 1951, Jimmie Rodgers (no relation to the great country singer of the 1920s) revived an old folk song, *Kisses Sweeter than Wine*, and turned it into a hit. *Kisses Sweeter than Wine* was an adaptation of an old Irish folk song, *Drimmer's Cow*. The Weavers had furnished the old tune with new words, and Leadbelly had adapted the music. In 1956, Eddie Fisher recorded *Cindy, Oh Cindy*. That same year, Johnny Mathis' recording of *Twelfth of Never* made the charts. This was an adaptation of an older Kentucky folk tune, *The Riddle Song*. In 1957, Harry Belafonte recorded *Jamaica Farewell*, Johnny Horton recorded *The Battle of New Orleans*, and, in 1958, the Kingston Trio cut *Tom Dooley*. All these songs were either direct adaptations of, or based on, American folk songs. Folk songs continued to appear on the pop-music charts until the end of the '50s.

Additional Readings

DeTurk, David A., and A. Poulin, Jr., eds. *The Folk Scene: Dimensions of the Folksong Revival.* New York: Dell, 1967.

Ewen, David. *All the Years of American Popular Music: A Comprehensive History.* Englewood Cliffs, N.J.: Prentice-Hall, 1978.

Hatch, David, and Millward, Stephen. *From Blues to Rock: An Analytical History of Pop Music.* New York: St. Martin's Press, 1987.

Suggested Recordings

The following recordings are listed by artist, song title, record company, and record number. (For a more detailed discography of this era, see *The Billboard Book of Top 40 Hits,* by Joel Whitburn.)

Baez, Joan. *The Night They Drove Old Dixie Down.* Vanguard 35138

Chapin, Harry. *Cat's in the Cradle.* Elektra 45203

Collins, Judy. *Both Sides Now.* Elektra 45639

——— . *Cook with Honey.* Elektra 45831

——— . *Send in the Clowns.* Elektra 45253

Guthrie, Arlo. *The City of New Orleans.* Reprise 1103

Kingston Trio. *Tom Dooley.* Capitol 4049

——— . *Where Have All the Flowers Gone.* Capitol 4671

——— . *Desert Pete.* Capitol 5005

Chapter 14
Prelude to the
Rock Era

What Rock Is and Is Not: An Explanation

Since its advent in the early 1950s, rock music has been worshipped as the new sound by its advocates, and decried as a prostitution of the art by the more learned of our musical society. Few on either side have paused to consider exactly what rock is, and is not. Those who have, generally have not been heard, or simply did not say anything that satisfied rock proponents or art-music aficionados. Occasionally, however, a voice of reason has been raised in an attempt to define not only rock, but its place in musical society. One such voice is Carl Belz, who, in 1972, was a Professor of Fine Arts at Brandeis University. Belz introduced his excellent book, *The Story of Rock,* by describing rock music as a folk art.

Belz believed that rock is an integral part of a long, continuing tradition of folk music across America and throughout the world. At first glance, his thesis appears to be simple and obvious. However, it is actually constructed from many elements, including several complex issues surrounding art history, the connection between folk art and fine art, and the manner in which the creative act is perceived, regardless of its origin. Because rock originated in the realm of pop art only, its connections to folk and fine art are blurred, and the complexities of such connections are intensified.

During the 1960s, distinguishing between folk, fine, and popular art became increasingly difficult. Indeed, many questioned the validity of making such distinctions. As a direct consequence of this kind of questioning, some of best artistic statements since the late 1930s and early '40s emerged. According to Belz, at least a part of the complexity of this situation was due to what he described as the pop-art phenomenon, a fine-art style generated by the popular or mass culture. Billboards, comic strips, advertising, and supermarkets inspired significant numbers of pop paintings and sculptures, which occasionally bore a striking resemblance to the objects that inspired their creation. New types of theater experiences, such as the "living theater," "happenings," and "environments," contributed to the idea that all of life can be viewed as a work of art. When all these things were considered, distinguishing between art and non-art objects, and even between the different classifications of art objects, became less important than describing a situation in which anything and everything can be called art. However, for the art historian and art critic, such distinctions were fundamental. Since rock's inception, it has variously been called popular art, fine art, folk art, and even non-art. Rock music has posed a particularly thorny problem for the critic-historian.

Belz believed that the huge, current interest in rock could be viewed in part as a reaction to pop art. During the 1960s, the adult population began taking an interest in art materials previously considered alien and embarrassing by the critics of modern American civilization. When rock began developing in the mid-1950s, there was an absence of such appreciation. Rock did not emerge as a result of a sophistication and art appreciation gained from art galleries, museums, and periodicals. It emerged, instead, as a response to a series of vital needs and changing social values. It was a youth movement and a lifestyle radically different from the one that had existed prior to 1952. This new music addressed the new values and new lifestyle of the youth who found it so appealing. However, this new sound possessed an important characteristic that had never before been present in art music. According to Belz, rock spoke as the voice *of* the people. All previous art music had simply spoken *about* people from a detached and self-determined vantage point. On every level, rock was a direct confrontation with reality. Art music was a confrontation with art. Belz believed that this distinguishing characteristic made rock a folk art rather than a fine art.

Belz stressed that the differences between the functions of fine and folk art must not be regarded as clear-cut or absolute. It can be argued that all art reflects a response to vital human needs, and a lifestyle that changes with each new generation. Belz believed that, generally speaking, all art is a reflection of reality. Consequently, on the surface, folk and fine art share similar characteristics. It is when one considers the elements that are significant in the creation and the appeal of each that dissimilarities begin to appear.

Modern fine arts display an increasing awareness of their special characteristics and uniqueness. For example, modern painting has consistently addressed questions concerning "the intrinsic nature of its expression: its flatness, its shape, its opticality, and so forth."[1] Answers to these "questions" have evolved into a specific content. The most prominent and successful examples of this kind of fine art force the consumer to acknowledge that the art object he or she is experiencing is a *reflection* of life, not life itself. Belz said, "To put it another way, fine art declares itself as being different in kind from life."[2] Belz did not believe that fine art ignored life or was not concerned with reality. Rather, he believed that all fine art always reflects life, at least in part, and finds its meaning in that reflection. He concluded that fine art is conscious of its own existence, and generally conscious of art.

According to Belz, folk art does not reflect this concern with art for art's sake. Folk art concerns itself with the immediacy of life and the most expedient manner in which to express life issues. Folk art does not concern itself with the elements from which it is constructed. Fine art uses the different elements from which it is constructed as entities in themselves, to be directly confronted, and by which one may assess the value of the work. Folk art uses its elements indiscriminately to accomplish its prime objective: a direct, overt confrontation with life. According to Belz, "The work of folk art says of itself, 'this is reality,' while the work of fine art says, 'this is a picture of reality.' "[3] Belz concluded that this did not imply that one form of expression was superior to the other, merely different.

According to Belz, rock has, since its inception, related more to folk art than to fine art. This relationship can be seen in the media that surrounded it from the beginning, and in the responses of its consumers. One of the principal events of the television show, "American Bandstand," directly reflected this relationship. A panel of three or four teenagers routinely reviewed new record releases. The host of the show played the record, the audience danced, and the panel then discussed the merits of the song. Their discussions never included an assessment of the artistic qualities of the recording or of the song. They did not review the song's structure, its various elements, such as melody, harmony, or rhythm, or its contents. In short, they did not discuss any of the issues central to an assessment of a piece of fine-art music. Those who appreciated and understood rock never expected such questions to be discussed because such

---

[1] Belz, Carl. *The Story of Rock*. (New York: Oxford University Press, 1972), p. 8.
[2] Belz, p. 8.
[3] Belz, p. 8.

issues were and are not a part of a response to folk music. The response to folk music is spontaneous. To folk-music consumers, the art is reality. There is no need for the existence of such questions because there is no "aesthetic distance" between art and consumer.

Rock in the 1950s was condemned by the nation's adults and the press specifically because they did not understand that the music they heard was not fine but folk art. Teenagers appeared to understand the nature of rock from the beginning. They never attempted to impose fine-art standards on it. They simply accepted it as it was, a music that employed all the elements found in fine-art music unconsciously, rather than as deliberate devices to achieve specific artistic effects.

Belz thought that the difficulty in identifying rock as a folk art lay in the fact that it was so closely related to the huge and complex world of commercial music, while traditional works of art decidedly were not. Consequently, rock critics have accused promoters of foisting off on a gullible public a music conceived in completely bad taste for purely mercenary purposes. Additionally, rock critics believe that rock artists are interested exclusively in financial gain, and are essentially unconcerned with artistic merit or quality.

Belz believed that these kinds of suspicions were based on the flawed assumption that art quality and salability are mutually exclusive. However, he realized that simply proffering such a theory did not immediately allay such suspicions. He admitted that countless rock stars have made enormous sums of money from the sales of their records, but he questioned whether such evidence provided "any meaningful explanation of why rock came into being in the first place, or why it has continued to exist."[4] Various rock artists have won and lost vast sums of money, but rock itself has continued unabated.

Popular art succeeded, according to Belz, by selling what appeared to be reality, rather than reality itself. However, although rock music did emerge in that larger genre called "popular music," it cannot be considered simply as popular music. Attempting to do so occasionally proves too problematic. As a case in point, Belz cited the work of Elvis Presley, whose music he thought underwent a transformation from folk art to popular art. Nonetheless, Belz was convinced that the distinction between the two art genres is usually quite clear.

In the final analysis, all music, like all art, regardless of the category to which it is arbitrarily assigned, comes from the same wellspring of human creativity. It reflects, in some form and to some degree, however slight, the human condition. All the arguments for and against the viability of any music cannot negate this fact. Music in any guise serves a basic human need. It explicates man's emotions. In this writer's opinion, Charles Leonhard best described music's ability to do this when he said, "The art of music is a gestalt consisting

---

[4]Belz, p. 10.

of a variety of styles, all of which have one thing in common: they illuminate our life of feeling and have a profound effect on our human potential."[5]

The Importance of Elvis and the Beatles

Across the history of the development of popular music in the United States, many individuals have influenced trends and directions; Thomas Dartmouth Rice, Scott Joplin, Joseph Oliver, Louis Armstrong. None, however, have displayed the strength or longevity of either Elvis Presley or the Beatles. From 1956 through the early 1970s, Presley and the Beatles shaped the development of pop music worldwide. Every pop artist striving to attain stardom did everything possible to emulate either Presley or the Beatles.

This text concerns itself with the development of American popular music. Accordingly, by far the largest portion of artists and issues addressed are native to America. This is by design. However, the Beatles exerted such immense influence on the development of American popular music that any history of American pop would be incomplete without at least a section devoted to them.

Since the Hellenistic period, well-established rules and regulations have governed the construction of Western Hemisphere music. Such rules and regulations are usually referred to as music theory, the systematic description of the materials and patterns of musical composition. Since the days of Pythagoras, theorists have studied the music of the masters of the different ages in an effort to discover the manner in which those masters manipulated the materials and patterns of sound available to them. Theorists found that in solving most musical problems, these composers consistently applied the same treatment to recurring musical problems. Consequently, when manuals of instruction were derived from such writings, these treatments became the rules and regulations governing music composition in the style of a given period. If newly composed music is to sound like the music of a particular period, it must be constructed according to the theory of that period. Across the ages, certain composers have epitomized the musical characteristics of their respective periods: des Prez, Palestrina, and di Lasso in the Renaissance; Vivaldi, Bach, and Handel in the Baroque: Mozart and Beethoven in the Viennese Classic and early Romantic. It is composers of this caliber that the theorists have studied in greatest detail. And it is composers of this caliber who, across the ages, have been emulated by those of lesser ability.

---

[5]Shetler, Donald J., ed. *The Future of Musical Education in America.* Reston, Va: MENC Press, 1983. "The Future of Musical Education in America: A Pragmatist's View." Charles Leonhard. (Used by permission.)

When fledgling composers study such manuals in order to learn the craft of composition, they are, in a sense, learning to compose by formula. Theory manuals instruct the student to follow the rules and regulations faithfully, to employ certain materials in a definite order. Only when the new composer has absorbed these rules and regulations completely, and has demonstrated a certain mastery over them, is he or she allowed to begin breaking the rules to seek new and untried manipulations of musical materials and sound patterns.

Like the traditional art music of Western Europe, American pop music is, and has always been, written to a kind of formula: The more original, arresting, and appealing the formula, the more popular the music. Musical genius is assessed, at least in part, on the originality and appeal of the formula. Those considered to be masters, past and present, are those who created the formulas (wrote the music from which theoretical rules and regulations were derived) by which others composed music that sounded like the masters, but fell just short of the originality required to produce the formula. Once a successful formula has been created, other, less talented writers can merely "plug in" musical bits and pieces and arrive at something very like the original. However, those kinds of compositions usually lack this intangible quality that gives great music its durability and longevity.

Much of the music produced by Elvis Presley and by the Beatles has demonstrated a durability resembling that of the music of the seventeenth-, eighteenth-, and nineteenth-century master composers. This comparison is not intended to equate rock music with the masterpieces of traditional European art music. Each of the two genres serves an entirely different purpose and consumer group. A multitude of differences exists between them. However, the two musics do posses one common trait: The composers who are the most durable and successful are those who create the formulas.

Granted, Elvis Presley did not write his own music. Still, he possessed such extraordinary charisma and audience intelligence that one must place him among those who create the formulae. Presley developed a stage presence so compelling and so successful that almost all pop solo artists after him attempted to emulate his style. Even the Beatles, after they had become international stars in their own right, were, by their own admission, in awe of Presley during the first few minutes of their first meeting. Elvis Presley and the Beatles created and developed most of those characteristics desirable in rock stars. Accordingly, they have been allotted separate chapters.

Additional Readings

Belz, Carl. *The Story of Rock.* New York: Oxford University Press, 1972.

Chapter 15
Elvis

Childhood and Early Years

Elvis Aron and Jesse Garon Presley were born on January 8, 1935, in Tupelo, Mississippi. They were the twin sons of Vernon Elvis and Gladys Smith Presley. Jesse, though perfectly formed, was delivered stillborn just minutes after Elvis. He was buried the following day in an unmarked grave in the Priceville Cemetery. Gladys and Vernon adored their surviving son, and treated him as though they somehow sensed that destiny had chosen him for something special in life.

Elvis was born into abject poverty. His parents had met and married in 1933, during the Great Depression. Vernon was a farm worker and Gladys worked at the Tupelo Garment Company. Their twelve-hour workdays began at 6:00 a.m. and their combined weekly wages totaled twenty-six dollars. In 1934, Gladys discovered she was pregnant. She had to quit her job and Vernon took a second job driving a milk truck.

A tornado struck Tupelo when Elvis was one year old. It ripped through the heart of the little city, leaving hundreds dead and more homeless. The tornado

ELVIS.

PHOTOFEST

missed the Presley home by just one mile. Tupelo would spend the next several years attempting to recover. Elvis would spend the first years of his life amid this chaos and ruin.

Elvis exhibited a love for music when he was two years old. His family belonged to the First Assembly of God Church, located one block from their home. During the severity of the Depression years, this church became a sanctuary for the Presley family and a center for most of their social activities. Throughout his childhood and adolescence, he and his parents sang at camp meetings and revivals, but only as part of the congregation.

Elvis' fifth-grade teacher, Mrs. J. C. Grimes, remembered him well. Mrs. Grimes thought Elvis was a good student. She considered him sweet and average. One morning, Elvis sang *Old Shep* for Mrs. Grimes. She was so taken with Elvis' voice that she asked the school's principal, Mr. J. D. Cole, to hear him. Cole was so impressed that he entered Elvis in the talent show of the Mississippi-Alabama State Fair. Elvis sang *Old Shep,* and won second prize, which was five dollars and free admission to all the fair's amusement rides.

When he was thirteen, Elvis' parents gave him a guitar. It became one of his prized possessions, and he took it everywhere. He listened to radio shows and tried to copy the sounds he heard. His favorites were Jimmie Rodgers (the

Mississippi Blue Yodeler), Otis Spann, B. B. King, Howlin' Wolf, Arthur Crudup, and Muddy Waters. Elvis combined the sounds these singers made with the sounds of the spirituals he learned as a child. Even then, he was developing that unique mixture of sounds destined to alter the course of popular music worldwide.

When Elvis began his high school years, he wore his hair quite short. When he was sixteen, he developed a need to be different. He let his hair grow long, and he began combing it high in front and sweeping side hair back into a style that eventually became known as a "ducktail." His style of clothing became wild. He would wear unlikely colors, such as pink or Kelly green. Paul Lichter said that Elvis wanted attention and he got it.

Through most of his childhood and adolescence, Elvis was painfully shy. Then, during the latter part of his senior year, the self-confidence and strength of personality that would become one of his trademarks began to emerge. He began dating and spending time with his buddies. Elvis received his high school diploma June 14, 1953.

Early Successes

Sun Records and Sam Phillips. In 1953, Elvis began driving a delivery truck for Crown Electric Company in Memphis. While making his rounds one day in September, he passed the Memphis Recording Service, a division of the Sun Record Company. He decided to take his lunch break that day to record two songs for his mother's birthday. The fee was four dollars, the total amount he had in his jeans pocket. No one could possibly have recognized this as a historical moment filled with enormous import and consequence.

The two songs that Elvis recorded that day were *My Happiness* and *That's When Your Heartaches Begin.* Sam Phillips, owner of the record company, entered the studio in which Elvis was recording shortly before he completed his session. After Elvis finished, Marion Keisker, general manager of the studio, found a note Phillips had left on her desk. It read, "Elvis Presley… Good ballad singer. Save this."

Several months later, Elvis returned to Sun Records to make a second private recording. Sam Phillips engineered this session. Elvis recorded *Casual Love Affair* and *I'll Never Stand in Your Way.* (To this day, the public has never heard these two recordings.) Later, on a trip to Nashville, Phillips bought a demo record of a ballad entitled, *Without Love (There Is Nothing).* Though he liked the song and thought it had real potential, Phillips could not identify the black vocalist who had made the recording. He returned to Memphis, and called Elvis.

Elvis made several attempts to produce a good recording of *Without Love.* Each attempt failed, probably because at that time the musical material in

Without Love was beyond Elvis' vocal capabilities. Nonetheless, Phillips was so fascinated with Elvis' voice and style that he asked him to keep singing. Elvis spent the next three hours singing every song he knew.

Phillips put guitarist Scotty Moore and bass player Bill Black with Elvis to form a trio. For the next several months the trio rehearsed diligently, but the sound Phillips wanted failed to materialize. Then, during one rehearsal session, while the trio was taking a break, Elvis began singing *That's All Right, Mama.* It was the sound for which Sam Phillips had been searching. The pounding beat, the freshness, the vocal modulations, all the vocal emotions of the black vocalist were there. Phillips recorded *That's All Right, Mama,* and an old country stand-ard, *Blue Moon of Kentucky,* was chosen for the flip side.

Sam Phillips asked Dewey Phillips, top disc jockey at Memphis' radio station WHBQ, to play the dub of the recording. Dewey had been playing so-called "race" music for several years before the advent of rock-and-roll. Dewey con-sented to give the record airplay.

During the first seven days following the initial airing of *That's All Right, Mama,* Sun Records received more than five thousand orders for this recording, for which Phillips had not yet pressed a commercial record. However, he did recognize the phenomenon taking shape. He took *Blue Moon of Kentucky* to Sleepy Eye Joe, Memphis' top country-and-western disc jockey on radio station WHHM. Sleepy Eye played the record, didn't like it, and decided not to give it any airtime. However, the day afterward Sleepy Eye left for a vacation. His sub-stitute found the demo record on a turntable, and apparently thought Joe meant the recording to be aired. *Blue Moon of Kentucky* got airtime.

Disc jockeys were unable to pigeonhole Elvis. Country-and-western dee-jays thought his music fell into the category of rhythm-and-blues. Rhythm-and-blues disc jockeys thought Elvis' records belonged in the country-and-western genre. Elvis' music faithfully reflected all the influences from his childhood experiences: the upland white southern gospel sounds of the rural South, strongly flavored with black gospel and black rhythm-and-blues, and Nashville's traditional country music. This sound, called rock-a-billy, originated with early rock groups such as Bill Haley and the Comets, but it was Elvis' music that was responsible for the worldwide spread of this unique blend. And it was this sound that became so strongly associated with rock during its first ten years. Sam Phillips decided to market Elvis' records himself.

Presley's First Manager. Bob Neal, head of a Memphis booking agency, was organizing a show featuring Carl Smith and Slim Whitman. The show was scheduled for the Overton Park Shell auditorium August 10, 1954, with Dewey Phillips as M. C. Sam secured a spot on the show for Elvis. For the afternoon show, Elvis sang *Old Shep* and *That's When Your Heartaches Begin.* The audience was polite, but apparently unimpressed. Elvis discussed this with

Dewey and Sam. Dewey suggested Elvis sing *That's All Right, Mama* and several other "rocking tunes" on the night show. That evening, when Dewey introduced Elvis, the curtains parted, and Elvis, standing center stage, was quite a spectacle. He wore a black sports coat trimmed with pink darts and black high-rise pants with pink pocket flaps and pink lightening bolts lining the outside seam of the leg. This was the show in which Elvis acquired his nickname, "the Pelvis." Elvis stood there for a moment, then began slowly rotating his hips, and even before he sang a note, the audience began screaming. The audience was his. That night, he almost literally brought the house down.

Bob Neal now began handling Elvis' career. He put the trio on the road, billed as "Elvis Presley, the Hillbilly Cat, and his Blue Moon Boys." A typical week's schedule would include dates in New Orleans on Friday, Shreveport on Saturday, Memphis Auditorium on Sunday, Ripley, Mississippi on Monday, and Alpine, Texas, the following Friday and Saturday nights.

Sun released Elvis' second record, *I Don't Care if the Sun Don't Shine*, with *Good Rockin' Tonight* as the flip side. Simultaneously, Sun released his third single, *Milkcow Blues Boogie*, backed by *You're a Heartbreaker*. It was late in 1954, and Elvis was the hottest pop-music commodity in the South. His personal appearances were the catalyst.

During this period, the Memphis *Press-Scimitar* ran the following headline on its front page: "He's Sex!" The brief article also featured an accompanying three-column picture of Elvis. It described Elvis as "sexy, lazy, tough, and good looking." This article added to the momentum of Elvis' career. Before the appearance of this story, only Dewey Phillips played Elvis on his radio show with any consistency. After the article, all the stations began playing Elvis' records. For the first time, Memphis began to realize it had a genuine home-town phenomenon.

Tom Parker. Early in 1955, Bob Neal realized the immensity of the task of managing Elvis. Elvis' career had attained such proportions that Neal could no longer continue as Elvis' manager, and be a husband and father. He chose to relinquish his managership. Thomas Andrew Parker, "the Colonel," now entered Elvis' life. Parker grew up traveling with his uncle's carnival show. He lost both his parents by the time he was ten. By seventeen, Parker had his own circus act, which featured a pony and a monkey. Later he became a press agent for several traveling shows. He made his entry into the pop-music field as Gene Austin's manager. Austin recorded the hit song, *My Blue Heaven*. By the time he first came into contact with Elvis, he had already made stars of Eddy Arnold and Hank Snow.

Parker first saw Elvis at a matinee performance in Texarkana, Arkansas. As he watched Elvis work his magic on the audience, he became convinced that whatever Elvis had, it was real and vital. According to Paul Lichter, when the poor boy from Mississippi and the old carney met, show-business history was made.

When Elvis signed with RCA, both Sam Phillips and RCA officials conceded that the money involved represented the largest amount ever paid for a contract release. Elvis, still just twenty years old, had only one year left on his contract with Sun. *Billboard* reported the payoff amounted to $40,000. RCA acquired the rights to five singles released by Sun and to all unreleased masters recorded by Sun. Tom Parker, Sam Phillips, Bob Neal, and Coleman Tiley III were all involved in the arrangement. Parker also established Elvis Presley Music, a publishing company, in collaboration with Hill and Range Music, Inc., of New York.

On January 10, 1956, just ten days after his twenty-first birthday, Elvis entered RCA's Nashville studios to record the first side for his new label. *I Got a Woman* was his first song put on tape. Elvis followed it with a song he had heard while touring the South, *Heartbreak Hotel.* Since his Sun recordings, his voice had matured noticeably. It was much deeper and he and his style were much more assured. For the first RCA recordings, guitarist Chet Atkins, drummer D. J. Fontana, and pianist Floyd Cramer joined Scotty Moore and Bill Black. The following day included another session and a momentous event. The southern gospel quartet, the Jordanaires, sang backup for Elvis. It was their first session with Elvis.

No one in the industry, not even Tom Parker, was prepared for the events that occurred following the release of Elvis' first RCA record. Within a year, sales of his records alone forced Victor to change its total sales operations and

THE HUGH JONES COLLECTION

ONE OF THE MANY ELVIS PRESLEY ALBUMS.

its initial contract with Elvis. During that first year Elvis sold over ten million records. Presley's first LP release initially sold over 300,000 copies, breaking all previous sales records of first-release LPs.

To this point, Elvis' name was familiar only to southern pop-music audiences. Colonel Parker persuaded a close friend, the general manager of Edward B. Marks Music Corporation, to carry recordings of Elvis to New York. Parker told his friend that no one north of the Mason-Dixon line had heard Elvis. However, by then, Elvis was the hottest pop-music commodity to storm the South in many years and Parker believed Elvis would produce the same startling effect on radio audiences across the nation. Elvis merely needed exposure to that nation-wide audience, and Parker believed New York was the place to start.

Parker's friend carried recordings of Elvis to Bill Randle, a disc jockey who had a New York show on Saturday night as well as a Cleveland show during the week on WERE radio. Randle felt Elvis would be too much for his New York audience, but he agreed to play Elvis in Cleveland. The result in Cleveland was immediate and overwhelming. Thousands of callers told Randle that Elvis was terrific. As a result of the airtime Elvis received, Parker began receiving calls from all the New York record companies that had listening posts in Cleveland.

Presley and National Television

Parker arranged six appearances for Elvis on "Stage Show," the CBS television show featuring Jimmy and Tommy Dorsey, and presented by Jackie Gleason. During this period, *Billboard* and *Cashbox* both named Elvis the most promising new country-and-western singer of the year. Elvis made his first appearance on national television on January 28, 1956. For each of his six appearances, Elvis received $1,250. For his debut, he sang *Blue Suede Shoes* and introduced the nation to *Heartbreak Hotel.* His national TV debut caused quite a sensation, to say the least. Phone calls and letters swamped CBS.

Jackie Gleason was apparently somewhat incensed by Elvis' performance antics. He accused Elvis of behaving like a sex maniac on national television. There was even some talk about canceling his remaining appearances. However, nothing came of this suggestion, and Elvis made his second appearance on February 4, 1956. He sang *Tutti Frutti* and introduced the flip side of *Heartbreak Hotel, I Was the One.*

During this period, Elvis' popularity experienced a significant shift. No longer was he considered just a country-and-western star. He was now also a rhythm-and-blues *and* pop star. *I Was the One/Heartbreak Hotel* sold faster for RCA than any record in its history. *I Was the One* became number one on

Memphis radio stations literally overnight. *Heartbreak Hotel* achieved number-one status much later. By the time Elvis made his sixth appearance on the Dorsey Brothers' show, he was a legitimate and significant new rock superstar.

When RCA released Elvis' first album, it immediately rose to the top of *Billboard*'s charts. This album contained several unissued tracks from Sun Records, and new materials as well. In just one month, it sold more than 362,000 copies, breaking all previous RCA sales records. According to Paul Lichter, its sales were three times the total of RCA's previous best sellers.

From his first national television appearances, Elvis became a controversial figure. Lichter said Elvis' personal appearances only added to the controversy. Fans fought for the opportunity to see him perform. In San Diego, two packed audiences of over 5,000 each paid $15,000 to hear him sing eight songs. The manager of the San Diego Arena was forced to call in the police and a platoon of Naval shore patrol to protect him from the frenzied mob that literally chased him to his dressing room. Elvis told reporters about one girl who grabbed at him and clawed his side rather badly. One reporter who saw the show wrote, "He's fascinating!—like a snake." Parents the nation over began to perceive Elvis as the Presley menace. A fourteen-year-old girl from Long Island told reporters that her parents locked up her Elvis records and broke her record player.

Parker booked Elvis into the New Frontier Hotel in Las Vegas for a two-week stand, beginning April 23, 1956. Elvis suffered his first and last failure as a professional entertainer there. This particular audience did not respond well to him. After he completed his two weeks, one Las Vegas newspaper compared Elvis to a jug of corn liquor at a champagne party. The reporter claimed that Elvis hollered his songs and made embarrassingly direct bodily movements. He further claimed that everyone in the room breathed a sigh of relief when Elvis finished his act. Elvis refused to view his two weeks at the New Frontier as a failure, saying that the New Frontier didn't keep failures for two weeks.

Elvis appeared twice on Milton Berle's national television show. On April 3, 1956, the nation saw him live from the flight deck of the U.S.S. Hancock. This TV appearance was perhaps the wildest Elvis ever gave. The critics responded with cries of "lewd" and "obscene." Approximately forty million people watched the show, and regardless of how they viewed Elvis or his act, they probably never forgot the experience.

Elvis' second appearance on "The Milton Berle Show" came on June 5, 1956. He appeared with Arnold Stang, Irish McCalla (Sheena, Queen of the Jungle), and Debra Paget, the lovely young Hollywood star who would costar with him in his first movie. During this appearance, Elvis introduced *Hound Dog*. This performance was even wilder than his first one. Morning papers asked, "Is He a Fad? Or the Beginning of a Long Line of Entertainers? Is He a Good Influence? Or Bad? Is He Dangerous?" Jack Gould noted, whatever else Elvis might be, he was certainly, by any reasonable standards of success, big business.

Elvis had now become a "corporation." Colonel Parker employed Hank Saperstein to manage all the different Presley enterprises, by then grossing annually between nineteen and twenty-four million dollars. With some of his new-found wealth, he bought his parents a beautiful ranch home on Audubon Drive in Memphis. His parents were thrilled with their son's success and their new home. However, with Elvis' unprecedented popularity came a heavy penalty. Frantic fans, attempting to catch even a glimpse of their idol, caused huge traffic jams. The Presley's neighbors began complaining. Elvis began searching for a more suitable location for a family compound, one offering much greater privacy. In early 1957, he purchased the house and the accompanying thirteen-and-three-quarter acres that would become known to the world as "Graceland." The acquisition cost him one hundred thousand dollars.

Hollywood

Elvis received a visit from Hal Wallis, one of Hollywood's premier producers, during his April, 1956, Las Vegas engagement. Parker and Wallis arranged a Hollywood screen test for Elvis, who together with veteran actor Frank Faylen, read a scene from *The Rainmaker.* Response to the screening was overwhelming. Elvis signed a three-picture contract with Wallis and Twentieth Century Fox.

Love Me Tender, the first of the three films, opened at New York's Paramount Theater to capacity crowds. Demand for this motion picture caused Fox to make and ship more copies of it than any other film in the studio's history. Regardless of its success, reporters nationwide wrote scathing reviews of the movie and of Elvis. The movie's title song became Elvis' sixth million-seller. It was backed by his seventh, *Any Way You Want Me.*

Elvis' second film was *Loving You.* His third, MGM's *Jailhouse Rock,* became number three in the top-grossing films of 1957. Paul Lichter believed Presley's performance in this movie caused one to be strongly reminded of the late James Dean. The title number, *Jailhouse Rock,* was the standout scene in the entire movie, and perhaps the best musical production number of his career. Elvis had now begun to live the life of an immensely rich, extravagantly popular, and attractive young star. He lived at a Hollywood hotel along with an entourage of six friends from Memphis, three musicians, three personal assistants, and five secretaries.

According to Presley, his favorite movie was *King Creole,* based on the Harold Robbins novel, *A Stone For Danny Fisher.* Twentieth Century Fox had purchased the rights to the screen version of the novel for James Dean. Following Dean's death, the studio had shelved it. After much persuasion from Hal Wallis, Michael Curtiz, director of several Hollywood classics, including

Casablanca, reluctantly agreed to direct Elvis. He had at first refused because he was accustomed to working with stars who possessed a certain dignity, and in his opinion, Elvis Presley and dignity were not exactly roommates. Ultimately, Wallis prevailed, and Curtiz agreed to direct the film with the provision that he would have Elvis' complete cooperation.

During his first meeting with Presley, Curtiz discovered that Elvis was not a typical self-centered rock star with an overinflated ego, but a warm, humble, and genuinely good person. He pushed Presley hard, and when the picture was complete, Curtiz remarked he was proud of the dignified performance given by Elvis. *King Creole* was Elvis' last film for more than two years. It left his critics crying "Oscar!" Shortly after its completion, Elvis entered the army. He had given his fans a performance he would never duplicate.

The Army Years

Elvis was drafted into the army in March, 1958. His salary dropped from several hundred thousand dollars a year to seventy-eight dollars a month. Paul Lichter remarked that the United States Government lost $500,000 a year in income taxes when it made Elvis Pvt. US53310761. During August of that year, Gladys, Elvis' mother, was hospitalized with acute hepatitis. While in the hospital, she suffered a massive heart attack and died. Her death was a blow from which Elvis never quite recovered.

After Elvis completed basic training, the Army assigned him to overseas duty. He arrived October 1, 1958 in Germany and was greeted by fifteen hundred fans. While in Germany, Elvis met a pretty, petite teen-ager. She was an armed forces brat, the daughter of an Air Force captain. Her name was Priscilla Beaulieu. This girl would someday become Mrs. Elvis Presley.

Elvis left very little unreleased music at the RCA studios when he entered the Army. In 1959, RCA did release an LP entitled *Elvis Sails* and two sound-track recordings of *King Creole*. The two King Creole recordings remained bestsellers for over eighteen months. In March 1959, RCA released a new Presley single, *A Fool Such as I / I Need Your Love Tonight*. It quickly became his nineteenth consecutive million-seller. In June, RCA released the final song Elvis had recorded before his entry into the army, *A Big Hunk o' Love*. This song, like its predecessors, sold over a million copies, and became a national number-one hit.

As just another kid serving his country, Elvis managed to win the grudging respect and admiration of his fellow soldiers. Throughout his service tenure, he remained good-natured and cheerful. He performed the tasks assigned to him without complaint. By the time Elvis completed his tour of duty, he had accomplished something as an ordinary foot soldier that had eluded him as a civilian millionaire. By depositing his dominating personality in a foot locker and becoming a number, he had earned a badge of respectability from the world at large.

Return to Civilian Life

In March, 1960, Elvis returned to America, and was discharged from the Army at Fort Dix, New Jersey. Despite inclement weather, more than two thousand fans greeted him when he arrived from Germany. Television crews, newsmen, and photographers gathered at the airport en masse. One reporter noted that Elvis' discharge was the most publicized return of a soldier since the return of General Douglas MacArthur.

Back to Work. On March 26, ABC taped the Frank Sinatra TV special, "Welcome Home, Elvis," in the Grand Ballroom of the Fontainebleau Hotel in Miami Beach. The network admitted the audience by invitation only, about seven hundred guests in all. The show featured Frank Sinatra, his daughter, Nancy, Sammy Davis, Jr., Joey Bishop, and Peter Lawford. Nelson Riddle and his orchestra furnished the accompaniment. During this performance, Elvis was on stage for just six minutes. His salary for this engagement came to one hundred twenty-five thousand dollars.

In the last days of 1960, Elvis made a new motion picture, *Flaming Star.* In it, he played a role originally written for Marlon Brando. Two additional films followed in 1961—*Wild in the Country* and *Blue Hawaii.* Elvis' roles in *Flaming Star* and *Wild in the Country* were both dramatic roles, and his reviews from each were quite good. However, both movies suffered at the box office because Elvis' fans were apparently unwilling to accept him in such roles. *Blue Hawaii* was quite another matter. This film became the most financially successful of all the Presley movies. Its soundtrack recordings alone brought revenues in excess of six million dollars. Once again fans saw Elvis in a setting more familiar to them, their idol with guitar in hand and a song to fit every occasion.

In 1961, Elvis made his last live appearances for almost eight years. The entire world of entertainment was begging for personal appearances at any price. Elvis and the Colonel chose instead to do three charity shows, the proceeds of which benefited the needy. On February 25, 1961, Elvis performed for nine thousand people during two sold-out performances at Ellis Auditorium in Memphis. During the evening, RCA presented him with a plaque, honoring him for a phenomenal sales figure, 76,000,000 records! Dick Clark presented him with the American Bandstand award for top male vocalist. Elvis appeared next in Hawaii, where he helped raise sixty thousand dollars for the U.S.S. Arizona War Memorial.

By 1962, Elvis had settled into a routine. He made three motion pictures a year, and most of his records came from the soundtracks. He had formed his famous entourage, referred to by the newspapers as the "Memphis Mafia." Entourage personnel consisted of four men. Joe Esposito was a former Army companion who handled Elvis' business affairs as competently, Paul Lichter declared, as the Colonel himself. Red West served as a bodyguard. He had been with Elvis since the beginning, and had written several of Elvis' most successful songs, including *If Every Day Was Like Christmas* and *If You Talk in Your Sleep*. Sonny West, one of Red's cousins, also served as a bodyguard. Charlie Hodge handed Elvis his scarves and water when Elvis was on stage. Offstage, he was possibly Elvis' closest friend.

In January, 1965, Elvis celebrated his thirtieth birthday. Radio stations around the nation featured his records. "Shindig," a national TV show, paid him tribute as he watched from Memphis. During this year, he completed two movies, *Harum-Scarum* and *Girl Happy*. He reportedly earned one million dollars for each of these films, plus fifty percent of the profits. Elvis continued to share his wealth by giving the Motion Picture Relief Fund the largest single donation in its history, fifty thousand dollars.

By the time 1966 arrived, Elvis had garnered sixty-four gold records. That year, for the first time, his motion pictures failed to draw the record crowds and box-office receipts earlier movies had drawn. Paul Lichter observed that in view of the quality of the scripts for *Frankie and Johnnie, Paradise-Hawaiian Style*, and *Spinout*, such dismal box-office returns were quite understandable. Fans were becoming increasingly disenchanted with Elvis' films. Record sales were also beginning to show signs of fan dissatisfaction. In 1966, several singles were released: *Tell Me Why* (recorded in 1957), *Blue River, Joshua Fit the Battle, Milky White Way, Frankie and Johnnie, Love Letters,* and *Spinout*. By any commercial measure, all these records flopped. Every indicator pointed to a much needed change.

Presley Weds. For several years, Elvis' name had been romantically linked with countless females from Hollywood and everywhere else he had encountered them. In 1967, Elvis silenced all gossip, at least for a time. On May 1, that year, Elvis and Priscilla Beaulieu, the teenager he had met while in the army in Germany, married in absolute secrecy in Las Vegas. After the wedding and the reception, Colonel Parker held a brief news conference to announce the happy event. On February 1, 1968, Priscilla gave birth to a six-pound, fifteen-ounce baby girl, who was named Lisa Marie.

After the birth of his child, Elvis returned to Hollywood to begin work on *Live a Little, Love a Little*. During 1968, he made three additional films, *Charro!, Change of Habit,* and *The Trouble with Girls. Charro!* was an excellent motion picture, according to Paul Lichter, perhaps one of Elvis' two best. The other two were barely average. Fans rejected them all.

A Remarkable Comeback

At this juncture in his life, Elvis displayed all the earmarks associated with the ending of a professional show-business career. Then, in 1968, he began one of the most remarkable comebacks in entertainment history. During that year, NBC television announced it had signed Elvis for his first TV special. The show was scheduled to air in December. Tom Parker wanted Elvis to come out on stage, greet his audience with, "Good evening, ladies and gentlemen," sing twenty-six or so Christmas songs, bid his audience a Merry Christmas and a goodnight, and leave the stage. The show's musical producer, Steve Binder, did not agree. He felt the television special was a crucial moment in Elvis' professional life. He wanted Elvis to return to the format that had been so successful in the early years. Binder won his point.

The show was taped during the last week in June. The studio admitted two hundred people to the taping. Elvis was nervous. It had been eight years

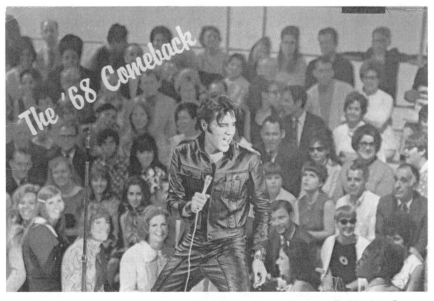

THE HUGH JONES COLLECTION

ELVIS RETURNS.

since he had sung to a live audience. However, from the moment he stepped onto the stage, he owned it and his audience. Reporters would later say this was the Elvis of old, the man who set and broke every record in the entertainment industry. NBC edited the four hours of tape to fifty minutes. On December 3, 1968, the show aired nationally. It made television history. A song written especially for the event, *If I Can Dream,* became Elvis' first million-seller in almost four years. The soundtrack album rose to the Top Ten and sold consistently for over a year. For the first time in his career, all the critics praised him. Suddenly, he was everyone's favorite. Elvis had come back.

During the late summer of 1970, Elvis completed a highly successful Las Vegas engagement. At this point in his life, no entertainer anywhere on the globe could claim greater fame. Elvis Presley was the embodiment and definition of the term, "superstar." However, this stellar position had exacted its price. Elvis suffered much of his life from chronic insomnia. He spent countless nights with Dewey Phillips and others, talking until five or six o'clock in the morning, particularly after a show. After he became an established superstar, Elvis spent hundreds of thousands of dollars, renting entire entertainment centers such as theaters for his exclusive use. On these occasions, he and his entourage would spend all night watching movies, or entertaining themselves and guests. His stardom and personal lifestyle were beginning to take their toll.

His Death

Elvis' battle with insomnia eventually included the use of pharmaceutical drugs. At first, he took only those drugs designed to help him sleep. Then, as the doses of these drugs increased, he resorted to the use of drugs to help him awaken. Gradually, his tolerance of these substances grew. And gradually, he increased the amount he was ingesting on a daily basis. During 1970, Elvis was troubled with a recurring eye problem, later diagnosed as glaucoma. He took drugs for the pain. His substance dependency was increasing.

For several years, Elvis and Priscilla had been drifting apart. By the summer of 1973, it was obvious to the world their marriage was over. In October, after months of rumor, Elvis and Priscilla divorced. Following the divorce, Elvis' health and physical appearance deteriorated significantly and noticeably. He was hospitalized several times for a variety of reasons, most of which actually could be attributed to his growing drug problem. Negative reviews of his records and live performances began accumulating. Nonetheless, interest in the man and the legend continued unabated.

In January, 1974, RCA executed a master stroke, placing Elvis at the top of the money-making pile for years to come. It released a single-record album called *Elvis - A Legendary Performer, Volume 1.* The album was a collection of

Elvis' finest recordings, spanning his entire career. Almost immediately after its release, it became a gold record. Eventually the series included volumes two and three. All sold extremely well.

By 1976, drugs and a destructive lifestyle had taken an extensive toll on Elvis' health. He began losing control, physically and emotionally. In February, Elvis participated in a seven-day recording session for RCA. The recordings reflected his failing strength and health. In the weeks that followed, Elvis tried to reassert control. He worried about his blossoming weight. He went on fad diets and a sleep cure. Nothing worked for long.

America celebrated its bicentennial in 1976, and Elvis scheduled several tours for that year. Somehow he managed to make them all, a remarkable feat, considering his physical condition at the time: a twisted colon, a raging nutritional imbalance, drug side effects, glaucoma, a severe kidney problem, an enlarged heart, hypoglycemia, hypertension, arteriosclerosis, and lupus. Every date was sold out. And every performance must have been sheer agony.

By July, 1977, Elvis' physical and emotional problems had combined to destroy his public image. Fans and reporters alike deserted him in droves. His reviews were pitiable. Reporters called him a fat, over-the-hill old man. At the end of July, the first copies of the book, *Elvis: What Happened,* appeared. Written by three of those closest to him, the book exposed Elvis' abuse of drugs. Jerry Hopkins reported that the book portrayed Elvis as a fat and aging rock star, hooked on drugs, neurotically hiding away in his southern mansion, emerging only on rare occasions to attend a movie theater kept open from midnight to dawn for his personal use, living out his life according to the numbers in his numerology book. Hopkins saw the biography as a bitter distortion lacking perspective or compassion, written by people who wanted to get rich and get even for some wrong, real or imagined, done them by Presley.

Elvis was deeply wounded by the book. He called his former wife because he was worried about what his daughter, Lisa Marie, would think should she ever read it. Elvis was planning a tour at the time, and he asked if Lisa Marie could visit him before the tour. Priscilla agreed.

Lisa Marie arrived at the end of July. On August 7, Elvis planned a special treat for his daughter. He rented Libertyland, a theme park, for the evening, and invited close friends and their children. Hopkins said his friends remember him that night as a solemn, but proud and funloving father who followed his daughter to each ride with the other children.

Sometime during the morning of Tuesday, August 16, 1977, Elvis died, sitting in a chair in his bathroom at Graceland. He was in the midst of selecting the music for the tour he was planning. Members of his household discovered his body sometime around 1:30 in the afternoon. They immediately summoned an ambulance, and all the way to Baptist Hospital, medics kept attempting to resuscitate him. All attempts failed. Officially, Elvis' death was attributed to an erratic heartbeat. The medical examiner reported his death as natural, caused by several health problems. He also told reporters that because the physical problems were so many, the exact cause of Elvis' death might never be determined.

During his lifetime, Presley compiled an amazing list of statistics. He holds either the number-one or number-two position in the four major categories of achievement in popular music: most charted records, 107; most number-one records, 18; most Top-Ten records, 38; and most weeks holding the number-one position, 80!

Additional Readings

Dunleavy, Steven. *Elvis. What Happened?* New York: Ballantine, 1977.

Hopkins, Jerry. *Elvis: A Biography.* New York: Simon & Schuster, 1971.

———— . *Elvis: The Final Years.* New York: St. Martin's, 1980.

Lichter, Paul. *The Boy Who Dared To Rock: The Definitive Elvis.* Doubleday & Company: Garden City, New York, 1978.

Selected Recordings

The following recordings are listed by artist, song title, record company, and record number.

Presley, Elvis, *All Shook Up* RCA 5870

———— . *Are You Lonesome Tonight* RCA 7810

———— . *Don't Be Cruel/Hound Dog* RCA 6604

———— . *Heartbreak Hotel* RCA 6420

———— . *I Want You, I Need You, I Love You* RCA 6540

———— . *Its Now or Never* RCA 7777

———— . *Jailhouse Rock/Treat Me Nice* RCA 7035

———— . *Love Me Tender* RCA 6643

Chapter 16
The Beatles

John

J ohn Winston Lennon was born on October 9, 1940, during one of those massive air raids with which Hitler devastated Great Britain during World War II. Like so many couples during a time of impending crisis, his parents, Fred and Julia, were married on a whim, in December, 1938. Their marriage began hastily and tenuously. Fred's vocation, ocean-liner steward, merely added to its instability.

John was born when Fred was at sea. Before John's birth, Fred had grudgingly, but routinely, sent money to Julia. However, when John was eighteen months old, the money stopped. A short time later, Fred disappeared from the ship, probably leaving at one of its many ports.

When John was five, his father suddenly appeared, and attempted to take John to New Zealand. At the last moment, Julia blocked the attempt, but only because her older sister, Mary Elizabeth, had insisted. Once more Fred disappeared from John's life, this time for several years. The effects of this kind of trauma so early in childhood were mirrored throughout John's life in almost everything he did, particularly in the music he wrote.

Mary Elizabeth, or Mimi, as she was called, and her husband, George, were childless. She had intervened on John's behalf because she wanted John for herself. She recognized Julia's indifference to John, and believed that Julia would willingly give John up. She was correct. Soon after Fred's second disappearance, Mimi began caring for John, and Julia made no objection to the arrangement. Mimi and her husband were the only real parents John ever knew. By the time John was old enough to be involved with school and friends completely, Julia had stopped even the infrequent visits she had originally made.

From the beginning of his schooling, John was a slow student with an inordinately cruel personality. By his third year at Quarry Bank School, a small, strict grammar school not far from his home, he had been demoted to the bottom of his class. One of his teachers believed John merely wasted other students' time.

Early in his life, John developed a quick and corrosive wit. He took obvious pleasure in lacerating hapless victims with his scathing tongue. He and three neighborhood friends indulged in increasingly dangerous pranks. With John as ringleader, the boys stole candy and toys from local stores. As John grew older, he began stealing to order, setting up a brisk black-market cigarette business. Then he began stealing from Mimi. Regardless of the action she took, nothing stopped him.

In 1956, three musical events significant to John occurred. The first was a fad called "skiffle." Skiffle was a form of the American washboard-and-tin-can band. Anyone with either or both of these items could play skiffle. Peter Brown and Steven Gaines believed the song, *Rock Island Line,* began the entire skiffle craze. It was sung by Lonnie Donnigan and it became a teenage anthem. During this period, the American movie, *Blackboard Jungle,* appeared, romanticizing teenage rebellion. Its theme song, *Rock around the Clock,* by Bill Haley and his Comets, was unlike anything ever before heard in Great Britain. Then came the musical and physical embodiment of rock, Elvis Presley, the first rock superstar. Bill Haley was a kind of father figure. Presley decidedly was not.

From the moment John heard Elvis, he wanted to be like him, dress like him, sing like him. He began combing his hair like Elvis and wearing the same style clothing. He developed Elvis' swagger. Most of all, he wanted a guitar like Elvis'. Mimi bought him one, a small Spanish model with cheap wire strings.

John became obsessed with playing his guitar. He practiced until his fingers bled. His mother, Julia, taught him a few banjo chords, and John began with those. Mimi watched him spend hour after hour practicing. Ultimately, she heartily regretted having purchased the instrument. She warned John that he was wasting his time, that he would never earn a living with the guitar.

Paul

John called his first group "The Quarrymen," after his high school. The band appeared in several competitions and at high school dances. They played for street fairs and church dances. On July 6, 1957, Ivan Vaughan, a member of the group, invited a young friend to a church dance where the Quarrymen were playing. Vaughan's young friend was Paul McCartney, then fourteen years old.

During the afternoon, after the group had played for a time, Paul borrowed a guitar from one of the band members, and began playing. To the Quarrymen and the immediate audience, Paul sounded like a genuine virtuoso. The Quarrymen were particularly impressed not only with Paul's facility on the instrument, but also with his ability to tune a guitar, a skill that none of them had yet been able to master.

George

George Harrison was born on February 25, 1943. His father was a city bus driver and his mother, a contented housewife and mom to all the neighborhood kids. By the time he was fourteen, George was completely infatuated with the guitar. His mother purchased him a deluxe model, and became his strongest support in learning to play the instrument.

George met John Lennon and the band, which was using the name "Johnny and the Moondogs" at that time, during the winter of 1959. When he first met John, George had not yet quite mastered his instrument. Consequently, when he played his best number as an audition for the band, no one in the group was very impressed. Nonetheless, George began traveling with the band to all its engagements, hoping one day they would invite him to join. Periodically, the band asked him to sit in with them, and on rare occasions, they even allowed him to play his own solo. Quietly, before anyone realized what had occurred, George had become a member of the band. Three of the four young men who so altered the course of the development of popular music and influenced an entire worldwide generation of youth, had now come together.

During the early 1960s, rock music made its presence felt in a significant way in England. Hundreds of rock groups sprang up all over the country. Their stars were young boys who dreamed of filling the void left in the rock world when Elvis Presley was inducted into the army. Every Liverpool neighborhood appeared to have its own band. There were ample opportunities for performances: church halls, ballrooms, town halls, and skating rinks.

The Beatles' First Manager

By this time, Allan Williams, owner of the Jacaranda, a small Liverpool coffee house, had begun managing Johnny and the Moondogs. Williams had become acquainted with Larry Parnes, a moderately successful London manager and promoter. He managed to secure Johnny and the Moondogs an audition with Parnes. For this audition, the group changed its name to the "Silver Beatles." One of the band members had suggested the word "beetles" in response to Buddy Holly's group, the Crickets. John couldn't resist puns. He was the band member who suggested "beatles," as a play on beat music. The "silver" was added to give the name sparkle.

Using Johnny Hutch as a sit-in drummer, the group played their audition. Parnes liked the group and wanted to book them, but without the bass player, Stu Sutcliff. John became angry, and turned Parnes down. One week later, Parnes offered the boys another booking, with Sutcliff as bass player. The Silver Beatles became the backup band for singer Johnny Gentle on a two-week tour of Scotland, an engagement no self-respecting professional London band would have taken. However, the Silver Beatles were in no position to be selective. They were not yet a professional group, and this tour allowed them to launch their career officially.

Allan Williams' unending search for new engagements for the Silver Beatles carried him to Germany, to Hamburg's St. Pauli district. St. Pauli was a neon-lighted night world filled with shady, sleezy night clubs, hookers in doorways, transvestites, pornography shops, and gun stores. There he met Bruno Koschmider, a German businessman who owned several prosperous St. Pauli enterprises, including at least one night club. Williams told Koschmider about the virtually untapped well of entertainment in Liverpool. Koschmider showed some interest, but made no commitments at that time. Williams returned to Liverpool without any bookings, but filled to overflowing with hope.

Several months later, Koschmider and Williams met again, this time in London. Koschmider was looking for entertainment for his club, and Williams succeeded in booking one of his clients, Derry and the Seniors, with Koschmider. Derry and the Seniors were so successful in Hamburg that Koschmider contacted Williams and requested another group. The Silver Beatles were chosen. Excited about leaving England for the first time, in an effort to enhance their image, the band dropped "Silver" from its name, and became simply, "the Beatles."

The Beatles still had not acquired a permanent drummer. In desperation they asked Pete Best, someone they had known for several years, to join the group. Best had only recently become a drummer, and he was not yet very good. Pete's mother ran a night spot called the "Casbah," located in the residential section of West Jersey. The club was located in a basement filled with wooden benches and a dragon painted on the ceiling. The Beatles had helped Pete's mother clean the place up for the opening, and, in turn, had received an invitation to play there.

At the Casbah, the Beatles made a new friend who was to become an integral part of the group, as important as any of its members. His name was Neil Aspinall. Almost immediately, Aspinall began helping the Beatles set up and break down their equipment. His run-down red and white van with a radiator that leaked became the Beatles' official transportation. Aspinall gradually became the Beatles' road manager, though the term "road manager" would not gain coinage for several years.

Hamburg had proved to be a significant catalyst for the Beatles. During their five-month stay, they acquired the polish of professionalism. After their return to Liverpool, they played at the Casbah. It was the first time anyone had heard them since their return. Their audience was thunderstruck. Though they were still somewhat disorganized and quite casual in their approach to the stage, they possessed genuine polish and skill, gained from their five months on the road. The group boasted a stage look entirely removed from the run-of-the-mill rock band. They wore leather pants, cowboy boots, and denim jackets. Their hairstyles featured feminine bangs combed over their foreheads.

Now demand for the Beatles began to grow. About a month after their homecoming concert at the Casbah, they were recommended for an engagement at the Cavern Club. This was considered a plum. The Cavern had recently switched from jazz to beat music, and was attracting packed houses. The Beatles were so popular at the Cavern, they eventually became its house band.

In 1961, the Beatles returned to Hamburg for a second engagement. During their first trip, they had met Peter Eckhorn, owner of the Top Ten Club in Hamburg, and for a brief time, had played there. This Hamburg engagement belonged exclusively to Eckhorn. Because the Beatles had acquired the connection to Eckhorn on their own, they decided they no longer needed Allan Williams as a manager. The bass player, Stu Sutcliff, wrote Williams, advising him he would no longer be receiving his ten percent of their salary. Williams was furious, but helpless. Fire had destroyed the only written contract between the two parties. For years after his dismissal, Williams spoke out quite bitterly about the group. He wrote a short book, *The Man Who Gave the Beatles Away*, in which he described many of the group's early activities.

Brian Epstein

During the autumn of 1961, the Beatles made a significant discovery: Brian Epstein, who would become for them what Colonel Tom Parker had been for Elvis Presley. Brian Epstein was the product of the union of two wealthy Jewish families. He was born on September 19, 1934, in an imposing five-bedroom house in Liverpool's best suburb, Childwall.

From the beginning of his life, Brian was surrounded by wealth. He attended the Liverpool College, an exclusive private school. Liverpool expelled him at age ten for drawing obscene pictures. His mother was certain that Brian had actually been expelled for anti-Semitic reasons. She believed anti-Semitism was everywhere, and she managed to instill this belief in Brian. By the time he was fifteen, he had attended seven schools. Finally he discovered Wrekin, a school in Shropshire with which he was quite happy, at least for a time. While at Wrekin, he became involved in dramatics for the first time. He had at last found a field in which he was genuinely interested.

After an unsuccessful stint in the army, Brian entered the family furniture business. His father opened a new branch for Brian. Despite his unorthodox approach to merchandising, the branch became an overnight success. Within a year, its profits were approaching those of the parent store.

Unfortunately, at least in the opinion of his father and his mother, Brian's interest in the furniture business soon waned. He had always loved the theater, and frequently attended performances at the Liverpool Playhouse. On the casual suggestion of an actor friend, Brian auditioned for the Royal Academy of Dramatic Arts in London. He had decided to become an actor. Much to his surprise, the Academy accepted him.

Though he soon became disenchanted with the Academy and its students, Brian managed to remain for three terms. Then he decided to rejoin the family business. Brian's father was again expanding the business, and he wanted Brian to run the record department in the new store.

In the beginning, the record department occupied just one side of the first floor. However, with Brian in charge, the status quo changed, rapidly and dramatically. By the end of its first year of operation, the department included ten employees and occupied two floors of the new store. The record division became a substantial portion of the family-business income.

On October 28, 1961, a young man named Raymond Jones walked into the record shop, and asked for a copy of *My Bonnie*. Brian asked who had done the recording, and was told by Jones that it was the Beatles, a group with which Jones was certain Brian was not familiar. Upon investigation, Brian discovered the record was a single, cut in Germany by Tony Sheridan, who had befriended the Beatles during their second German engagement. Brian also discovered that the Beatles were playing backup for a group called "the Beat Brothers" at the Cavern, located not more than 200 yards from his store. Brian decided to pay the Cavern a visit.

What Brian discovered stunned him. In the greasy, dank basement setting of the Cavern, four young men dressed in tight blue jeans and leather jackets casually played good-time rock-and-roll music, and joked with one another during the performance. The result was electric. About two hundred youngsters were packed into the small setting, all wolfing down soup and sandwiches and responding wildly to the music and the stage show. Bob Wooler, the club disc jockey, announced that Brian Epstein, owner of the largest record store in the city, had dropped by for a visit. After the show, George Harrison asked why he had come. Epstein could provide no plausible reason for having done so.

Within a short time, Brian had decided he wanted to manage the Beatles, though as yet the Beatles themselves knew nothing of his decision. Epstein ordered two hundred copies of the German recording of *My Bonnie,* and plastered their name all over the front of his store. Epstein began his campaign to manage the Beatles by going to the family attorney for advice. The attorney's advice: Leave the group alone. Next Epstein went to visit the Beatles' old manager, Allan Williams, who gave him essentially the same advice, though much more graphically. Epstein refused to heed either man.

Epstein's first formal meeting with the group came on December 3, 1961. Epstein requested that the Beatles ask club disc jockey, Bob Wooler, to attend the meeting as their adviser. Six weeks after their initial meeting, the Beatles and Brian Epstein signed a formal contract, giving Epstein twenty-five percent of the Beatles' earnings.

From the beginning, it was understood that Epstein would have no say whatsoever over the music. However, he began almost immediately changing the Beatles' image. He insisted that the group stop eating and drinking on stage. He made them plan each show in advance, with a set order for the music, and no talking and mumbled dialogue during performances. Epstein made them abandon their jeans and leather jackets and don identical suits, an idea all but Paul thought ridiculous. Paul, however, possessed a sense of showmanship almost as strong as Brian's, and he supported Brian's concept wholeheartedly. With encouragement from Paul, the group relented, and Brian ordered gray lounge suits with velvet collars from a Liverpool tailor. Now Brian was satisfied. As far as he was concerned, the Beatles were ready to record.

Brian now began a campaign to secure the Beatles an English recording contract. He visited Decca Records, where his name alone as the owner of the NEMS Record Store gained him a meeting with one of the junior executives, Mike Smith. Smith went to Liverpool to hear the Beatles, and was sufficiently impressed to offer them an audition in Decca's West Hampton studio.

The audition took place on New Year's Day, 1962. It was a disaster. All the boys were nervous and frightened. Their voices cracked, they sang slightly out of tune, and their playing was stiff and unnatural. Decca turned them down. Brian was furious and demanded an audience with Dick Rowe, head of Decca's A&R division. Rowe refused. Brian eventually gained a meeting with Beecher Stevens, general manager of Decca's wholesale division. Brian threatened to withhold all his store orders from Decca, who still refused to offer a contract. Brian went to several other record companies. Each visit ended in failure. No record company expressed any interest in the group.

Ringo

In August, 1962, Brian fired drummer Pete Best. Earlier that summer, George Martin of Parlophone Records had offered the Beatles a formal recording contract, and Brian recognized Pete was, at best, a weak, ineffectual drummer. Though he knew Pete had to be dismissed, Brian did not relish the chore. Pete was an important member of the group, particularly where their loyal Liverpool fans were concerned. Nonetheless, Brian recognized the need for a new drummer.

The Beatles recommended Ringo Starr, a drummer they knew well from both the Liverpool and the Hamburg circuit. For several months, Ringo had served as drummer for the most popular and biggest of all the Liverpool groups, Rory Storm and the Hurricanes.

Ringo was born Richard Starkey, Jr., July 7, 1940, the son of bakery workers Elsie Gleave and Richard Starkey, Sr. Ringo grew up in a dockside slum area of Liverpool, called the "Dingle." The tenements located there were known as the "Cast Iron Shore." When he was six, Ringo developed what at first was diagnosed as a severe stomachache. When the pain persisted and grew worse, he was taken to a local hospital in an ambulance. The stomachache was, in actuality, appendicitis. By the time Ringo reached the hospital, his appendix had burst and peritonitis had set in. He was in a coma for ten weeks, and because of various complications, spent the next year in the hospital. By the time he was released, he was so far behind the other children, he couldn't read or write. A sympathetic neighborhood girl taught him what little he was able to learn from that point. When he was thirteen, Ringo developed a cold that turned into pleurisy. He returned to the hospital, this time for a two-year visit. He was fifteen years old when the hospital released him, weak and still only partially recovered. His only job potential was as a messenger boy.

During his hospitalization, Ringo played drums in a hospital-ward band. In 1956, the year he was released, skiffle bands were still the rage in England, so playing drums in a skiffle band was a logical step for him. Eventually, skiffle died out, but Ringo kept up his drumming. His percussion skills grew. It was during his 1959 Rory Storm days that Ritchie became "Ringo" because of all the rings he wore, and Starkey became "Starr," so his drum solos could be announced as "Starr time."

Late in the summer of 1962, George Harrison called Ringo and asked him to join the Beatles. The group placed him on salary at first. If all went well, he would become a full-fledged member of the group, participating equally in all income. Ringo immediately cut his hair to match the rest of the group. Brown and Gaines thought that Ringo was probably the most unlikely candidate imaginable to play the greatest bit part in entertainment history. To them, Ringo was a short, skinny, unassuming twenty-two year old, with sad, blue eyes.

Rising to Fame

EMI Records. Epstein had secured the Beatles a recording audition with George Martin of EMI Records. The session was scheduled for September 12, 1962. When the Beatles arrived with their new drummer, they discovered that Martin knew about Pete Best's dismissal, and had hired a sit-in drummer to play the session. Martin had never heard Ringo play, so he requested a brief audition. After hearing Ringo play, Martin decided to remain with the drummer he had hired. Martin handed Ringo a tambourine and told him when to use it. Regardless of this temporary disruption, the group had finally solidified. The names *John, Paul, George,* and *Ringo* would soon be household words throughout the civilized world.

The Beatles cut just two songs that day, both written by Paul: *Love Me Do,* and *P.S. I Love You.* Prior to this session, the Beatles performed a brand of music that combined skiffle elements with a heavy dose of the rock-a-billy music of the Elvis Presley kind. Martin arranged *P.S. I Love You* to feature the harmonies that would become a Beatle trademark. These harmonies represented a radical and permanent departure from the sound that had dominated successful rock since its inception in 1955. The new sound completely altered the direction of rock, and heavily influenced this music for years after the disbanding of the Beatles. Their first songs were recorded on four-track recorders in monaural, as opposed to the sixteen- and thirty-two-track overdubbings of the later years.

When Martin announced the impending release of a record by the Beatles at an EMI (parent corporation of Parlophone) executive meeting, the executives laughed, thinking Martin was joking. At that moment in England, only American acts, such as Bobby Vee and Del Shannon, were popular. Parlophone released *Love Me Do* on October 4, 1962, during the period when the Twist craze was sweeping America. The music business had conceded the demise of guitar groups in popular music. *Love Me Do* was released and forgotten.

Brian Epstein began a letter-writing campaign to Radio Luxembourg and the British Broadcasting Corporation (BBC), urging them to give *Love Me Do* airplay. After hundreds of requests, Radio Luxembourg played the recording. The BBC followed suit. Suddenly, *Love Me Do* appeared on the *New Record Mirror* charts at number forty-nine. It climbed to number twenty-nine on the *Melody Maker* charts. By now, all Liverpool was talking about the Beatles. By mid-December, *Love Me Do* had climbed to number seventeen on the hit parade.

John Lennon's *Please Please Me,* recorded in February, was the next release. George Martin was so pleased with the recording session, he announced over the intercom from the control booth that the Beatles had just recorded their first number-one hit. His prediction proved accurate. On March 2, 1963, the

PHOTOFEST

AN EARLY BEATLES RECORDING.

Beatles had their first number-one hit, the first of a long line of chart-dominating singles over the next ten years.

The Beatles were now the most sought-after group in England. Despite this and their recording success, the mainstream "Fleet Street" London press continued to ignore them. Brian Epstein made countless attempts to bring the Beatles into mainstream London bookings with exposure commensurate with their recording popularity. His efforts always failed. Epstein blamed this problem on what he saw as a conspiracy.

When the Beatles began showing signs of real success, they were approached by the Leslie Grade Talent Agency, a large, powerful representation-and-booking organization. Brian refused the offer. When the Beatles had difficulty breaking into mainstream entertainment, Epstein became convinced that the agency and its owners were blackballing the Beatles. Finally, in September, 1963, when the Beatles had the number-one single, the number-one album, and the bestselling extended-play recording in England, they received an invitation to appear on one of England's top TV entertainment shows, "Sunday Night at the Palladium." On October 13, 1963, they played to an audience of fifteen million people. Three days later, they received an invitation to participate on the Royal Command Variety Performance during the first week of November, where they would be seen by none other than Princess Margaret and the Queen Mother. On November 4, 1963, the London *Daily Express* headline read, "Beatles Rock Royals." However, the *Daily Mirror* coined the catchword that grew almost overnight into the term synonymous with the Beatles, "Beatlemania."

Now Brian Epstein began his courtship of America. After the Royal Command Performance, he flew to New York to meet with Capitol Records, the parent company of EMI in England. He attempted to sell Capitol the Beatles' *Please Please Me,* but Capitol sent George Martin a polite note of refusal, declaring that the Beatles would not sell in the American market. Epstein was now free to peddle the Beatles to any record company in the U.S. He traveled across the country, pitching them to every label he could find. He finally managed to sell the single to a small label, Vee Jay. *Please Please Me* did exactly as the larger record companies had predicted. It dropped from sight after the sale of only a few hundred records. The Beatles' next single, *She Loves You,* was another number-one hit in England. All the major American labels also turned this one down. Epstein sold it to a record company even smaller than Vee Jay, Swan Records. It, too, completely disappeared the moment Swan released it in America.

Though by now, America was acutely aware of the Beatle phenomenon in England, the Beatles still did not have an American recording contract of any import. Epstein realized that securing such a contract required that America be exposed to the Beatles. He saw the proper avenue of exposure as national television. In 1963, "The Ed Sullivan Show" was the nation's top-rated TV entertainment show. Epstein promptly decided that the Sullivan Show would be the vehicle by which Americans would be properly introduced to Beatlemania. He carried his proposition to Sullivan, who, surprisingly, agreed to air the Beatles. Apparently, Sullivan recognized the value in being the first to expose them to America, even as just a curiosity. Sullivan had been at London's Heathrow Airport the previous autumn when the Beatles returned from a Swedish concert. He had witnessed firsthand their tumultuous reception. Epstein managed to secure not one, but two, appearances on the show. He signed contracts for consecutive Sundays, February 9 and 16, 1964.

America Discovers the Beatles.

The week preceding the Beatles' first Sullivan appearance proved to be Ed's most difficult in the history of the show. He thought he had seen everything the week he introduced the nation to Elvis Presley, but this was dwarfed by the Beatles' appearance. The press followed them constantly, rehearsals for the show were continually interrupted, and Sullivan had received over fifty thousand ticket requests for a theater seating just over seven hundred. Several thousand of these requests had come from VIPs in the entertainment business or in government. Rejecting them became an enormous diplomatic headache.

Finally, the moment arrived. Sullivan stepped out on stage, and shouted over the screams of the audience, screams that continued for the entire five minutes the Beatles were on stage, "America, judge for yourself." Approximately seventy-three million Americans watched the Sullivan show that night. The weather in much of the country was cold and snowy. Families across the nation elected to stay inside and see for themselves this phenomenon called "The Beatles."

Overnight, the Beatles became the most thoroughly discussed entertainment group in the nation. Media pressure forced Epstein to grant a press conference before the Beatles' departure for Washington, D.C., the site of their next concert. More than 250 newspapers, TV and radio stations, and wire services were represented. Even Dr. Joyce Brothers had been invited to assess the psychological ramifications of the Beatles. The conference lasted so long that the Beatles were served a roast-chicken lunch during the proceedings.

Epstein and the Beatles were scheduled to fly to Washington the day after the press conference. However, a heavy snowstorm that morning grounded all air traffic, and the group traveled instead by rail. Three thousand young people stood in the snow at the station, awaiting their arrival. An additional seven thousand appeared outside the Coliseum where they were to perform.

The Beatles returned to England just fifteen days after they had departed. During their brief visit, they had managed to become the entertainment rage of America. They were the cover story of *Newsweek* the day after they left the U.S. They were now in real demand on both sides of the Atlantic.

Following their return to England, the group began work on their first feature film, tentatively called *Beatlemania*. Brian had initiated this project about six months before the American visit. Making rock-music motion pictures was as dangerous as it was glamorous and appealing. According to Brown and Gaines, most movies about rock filmed during the fifties and sixties looked cheap and shoddy, and had ridiculous scripts. Nonetheless, Brian decided to attempt the venture. Elvis had made movies that were successful, and Brian believed the Beatles could do the same.

Sometime during the initial planning stages of the movie, its name was changed to *A Hard Day's Night*. Richard Lester directed, and Alun Owens wrote the screen script. Brown and Gaines contend that the script, along with those for *Blowup* and *Alfie,* was perhaps the most faithful representation produced of Swinging London during that period. With Lester and Owens in charge, the Beatles became a sort of modern-day version of the Marx Brothers. When the film was released, it garnered accolades bordering on hysteria. American film critic Andrew Sarris called *A Hard Day's Night* the *Citizen Kane* of juke-box movies. *Newsweek* proclaimed, "The legitimacy of the Beatles phenomenon is inescapable."

The First American Tour. In August, 1964, Brian Epstein announced the Beatles' first major tour of the United States. The Beatles landed in San

Francisco to the screams of thousands of hysterical girls, a scene that was repeated incessantly for the next four weeks. Everywhere they went, thousands of girls, all screaming, greeted them. The Beatles had hoped to see a bit of America, but all they saw was an endless procession of limousines, hotels, meals served by room service, smelly dressing areas in stadium locker rooms, and thousands of girls, all screaming.

All across the country, the Beatles played only the largest stadiums available. Epstein demanded between $25,000 and $50,000 for each appearance, and about 50 percent of the profits. By booking the Beatles in such large accommodations, promoters could meet Epstein's price, and still sell tickets for a reasonable sum, thus pleasing both the Beatles and their fans. Although Epstein's prices were the highest ever asked for a personal appearance at that time, promoters were competing fiercely for the opportunity to book the group.

With each concert, the reputation of the group swelled to even greater proportions. The Beatles played Milwaukee, Chicago, Montreal, Jacksonville, Boston, Baltimore, and Pittsburgh. Their last appearance of the tour was a charity concert for Cerebral Palsy at the Brooklyn Paramount. They shared the bill with Eydie Gormé and her husband, Steve Lawrence. Toward the end of September, an exhausted Beatles and road crew boarded a flight out of New York for England and home.

Home Again. Eighteen days after returning to England, the Beatles were again out on tour, this time on a grueling five-week sweep of Great Britain. And they were expected to spend the two weeks before the tour in EMI's Abbey Road studios, cutting their fourth album, *Beatles for Sale.* Though hastily prepared, the album was a slick and polished product. It appeared in time for the Christmas season, and like its predecessors, was a smash hit. It replaced *A Hard Day's Night* in the number-one position on the charts, and gave the Beatles four number-one albums in a row.

During the late winter of 1965, the Beatles began work on their second film, at first called *Eight Arms to Hold You,* and eventually released as *Help!* This film cost nearly three times as much as *A Hard Day's Night,* took twice as long to shoot, and produced far less critical acclaim. Despite its ridiculous plot and lack of box-office success, the movie produced two of the Beatles' most memorable songs, *Yesterday,* and the title song, *Help!*

Yesterday, written by Paul McCartney, resembled, as Paul described it, an egg. It was a seamless, flawless wonder. *Yesterday* became the first Beatles recording to appeal to a wide cross-section of ages and tastes. It validated Paul as a composer, and became the single most recorded song in history, with over 2,500 cover versions appearing by 1980.

John Lennon wrote the lyrics to *Help!* Since the song was written specifically for the film title, no one paid much attention to it. However, the curious lyrics provided deep insight into the person John Lennon really was, a lonely, often frightened young man, with a total lack of self-confidence.

The Beatles Meet Elvis. In August of 1965, the Beatles returned to the United States for a third concert tour, this one far more leisurely than either of the first two. They played just thirteen concerts in nine cities. While in Los Angeles, many Hollywood stars made requests to meet the Beatles. However, the Beatles showed no particular interest in encountering what they considered to be boring movie actors. The only celebrity they had any interest in meeting was Elvis Presley, who happened to be living in Los Angeles that August, filming *Paradise, Hawaiian Style*. Tom Parker, Elvis' manager, arranged a meeting at Elvis' home on Perugia Way.

Though at the time of their meeting, the Beatles were international rock stars in their own right, they were still awed by Presley. For the first five minutes or so, they simply sat and stared at Elvis. Then Tom Parker uncovered a roulette wheel hidden in a coffee table, and the ice was broken. Epstein was an eager gambler, and Elvis and the Beatles began playing music together. As they played, they compared notes on the trials and tribulations of megastardom.

The Beatles spent most of the winter of 1965 and the spring of 1966 in EMI's Abbey Road studios, recording two albums that became minor masterpieces, *Rubber Soul*, released in December of 1965, and *Revolver*, released the following spring. Here the simplistic love songs began disappearing. They were replaced with a bewildering and stunning array of subjects, from the ordinary to the transitory and esoteric. Songs, the likes of which Beatles fans had never before heard from their idols, filled both albums. These two albums were portenders of new directions for the Beatles. Previous albums had been a collection of unrelated songs. *Rubber Soul* and *Revolver* were strung together by a kind of central theme. The Beatles' music had now entered its most sophisticated stage.

THE HUGH JONES COLLECTION

A BIT OF BEATLES MEMORABILIA.

The Religion Controversy. During the summer of 1966, the Beatles began what had become for them an annual event, a world tour. Brian Epstein had been slightly ill during the first portion of the trip and had traveled to Portmerion on the northwest coast of Wales to convalesce. He had been there just four days when he received word that the Beatles were involved in a terrible scandal. Several months earlier, Maureen Cleave, a writer for the English newspaper, the *Evening Standard*, had published a profile on John Lennon. One of the subjects broached during the interview was organized religion, a topic not normally discussed with a rock star. Cleave quoted John as stating that Christianity was dying. At least, that was the meaning American Bible Belt ministers attached to Lennon's statement. John might have been allowed that view unmolested had he not followed it by claiming that Jesus was okay, but his disciples were a bit slow-witted and ordinary.

In Great Britain, the public and the press chose to disregard these comments. However, this combination proved too much for America's religious community. It reacted negatively and violently. When John's comments appeared several months later in *Datebook,* a teen magazine, a veritable firestorm erupted. America's religious leaders rose in arms. John's remarks infuriated the Bible Belt. Throughout the Southeast, Beatles records were burned by the thousands. Southern ministers held church rallies to collect Beatle memorabilia. Record stores and large chain stores began refusing delivery of Beatles records. During the first few days of the controversy, more than thirty-five radio stations completely stopped airing Beatles records. Vatican newspapers, commenting on John's views, warned that some subjects were absolutely sacrosanct, and should not be violated, even by those who were known as "beatniks." Most damaging of all to the Beatles themselves, promoters all across the nation were threatening to cancel upcoming summer concerts.

Epstein, acting in direct opposition to his doctor's orders, flew immediately to New York. He went directly to the office of Nat Weiss, the attorney who acted on the Beatles' behalf in all American transactions. Epstein asked about the possibility of canceling the American tour. Weiss advised that such an action would undoubtedly cost the Beatles millions of dollars. Weiss believed that canceling the tour would be unnecessary provided John would issue a public apology. At this suggestion, John became quite angry. In his eyes, he had simply spoken the truth, and he saw no reason to apologize for having done so.

After much persuasion, John agreed to attempt an explanation at a press conference. When the Beatles flew into O'Hare Airport on August 11, a mob of hostile newsmen and disc jockeys greeted them. Later that night, the press was invited to the hotel for a conference. A pale and nervous John Lennon took the microphone and delivered what he considered an apology. At one point, unsure about what they were hearing from him, one reporter asked, "But are you prepared to *apologize*?" At this, John bristled. He believed he had just apologized. After several additional attempts to explain his exact meaning,

John finally broke down and said, "I apologize, if that will make you happy. I still don't know quite what I've done. I've tried to tell you what I did do, but if you want me to apologize, if that will make you happy, then okay, I'm sorry."[1]

John's apology helped soothe some, but not all, of the troubled waters. A nasty tension remained in the air. The tour went poorly, measured by prior Beatles standards. Performances appeared stilted and tired. In Tennessee, the KKK picketed the Memphis Coliseum. The Beatles completed their San Francisco concert, the last one scheduled for the tour, and immediately flew home to England.

New Horizons

John, Paul, George, and Ringo had now been together almost constantly for ten years. Those ten years had been glamorous, yet grueling. Now they all needed rest, and time away from one another. In September, 1966, each went his separate way. They spent the next four months apart, away from being the Beatles. They had agreed to meet in December to begin work on a follow-up album to *Revolver*. During their time apart, by an odd coincidence, they all grew mustaches and longer hair without consultation with one another. Suddenly, young men everywhere began sprouting mustaches and long hair.

By November, 1966, Brian Epstein had received several nervous phone calls from Arthur Howes, the Beatles' English tour promoter. Howes needed to know about plans for the next tour. Finally, though he thought the idea ridiculous, Epstein phoned Howes to say that the Beatles would no longer accept any bookings. News of this shocking decision leaked out within an hour after Epstein's announcement, and his office was inundated with calls. The following day, newspapers reported that the Beatles intended to exist solely as recording artists, something no entertainment act had ever before attempted. Many articles implied this was the beginning of the Beatles' long-expected demise.

In December, the Beatles began work on their next album, called *Sergeant Pepper's Lonely Hearts Club Band.* They finished recording in early April, and Paul flew to America for a brief vacation. At the time of completion, not one of the Beatles even suspected the magnitude of what they had just created.

As Paul was returning home, he spent time reflecting on the events he had witnessed on his trip. The American hippie movement was at the grass-roots level and was gaining strength on a daily basis. Paul had been overwhelmed by what he had seen. There was nothing like it in London. There, the English counterpart of the hippie movement was totally about wealth, stardom, and

---

[1]Brown, Peter, and Gaines, Steven. *The Love You Make: An Insiders' Story of the Beatles.* (New York: McGraw-Hill Book Company, 1983), p. 213.

the latest fashions. Because of the clothing hippies wore, Paul thought they were merely the American version of the Swinging London set. As he left America, what he had seen convinced him that *Sergeant Pepper's* would be a bestseller. Little did he know that *Sergeant Pepper's Lonely Hearts Club Band* would become the hallmark of one of the most thrilling and turbulent decades in United States history.

The Death of Brian Epstein.

In August, 1967, Brian Epstein died at his home on Chapel Street in London. For several years, Epstein had ingested heavy amounts of all kinds of drugs. Many times, during the course of his years as the Beatles' manager, he had entered hospitals in attempts to free himself from the addiction. During the summer of 1967, he appeared to have made real progress toward rehabilitation. However, his withdrawal was short-lived. Many believed that Epstein committed suicide. This belief was strengthened by rumors of the discovery of a suicide note. While such a note had, in fact, been found, further investigation revealed that the note had been written before a previous suicide attempt, and had simply never been removed from among his possessions. Brian Epstein was buried in Liverpool at Longlane Jewish Cemetery, close to his father's grave. His funeral was conducted quietly and with dignity. The Beatles did not attend. They stayed away to prevent the services from becoming a media circus.

At first, the Beatles were unaware of the extent of their loss. For years, Epstein had managed their incomes and overseen their financial empire. Now there was a sudden void. The Beatles were left to fend for themselves. Paul McCartney apparently recognized the dangers inherent in this kind of drifting ship. Two days after Epstein's funeral, he requested a meeting with the other Beatles to discuss their next project. Paul presented the group with his ideas for a TV special, to be called the "Magical Mystery Tour." According to Paul, the Beatles would write the script for, produce, direct, record, and edit the show. After much grumbling, from John in particular, the group agreed to undertake the project.

"Magical Mystery Tour" was a disaster. When it was finally completed, all who viewed its initial screening shared the same opinion. It was awful. Peter Brown suggested the Beatles junk the film and absorb the 40,000 pounds invested in its making. Paul McCartney disagreed. He believed the public would greet the film as warmly as they had received all similar Beatles offerings. BBC purchased the TV rights, and aired the film on December 26, England's Boxing Day, a day when millions of Englishmen were home celebrating the holidays.

McCartney could not have been more incorrect. English critics pounced on the film, calling it rubbish. In Los Angeles, the *Daily Variety* printed similar headlines: "Critics and Viewers Boo: Beatles Produce First Flop With Yule

Film." Negative press reviews were such that for the first time anyone could recall, an artist felt he had to make a public apology for his work. McCartney apologized the day following the TV showing in an *Evening Standard* article by Ray Connolly. He said, "We goofed. It was like getting a bash in your face... I suppose if you look at ["Magical Mystery Tour"] from the point of view of a good Boxing Day entertainment we goofed really." This immense "goof" managed to gross two million dollars from college rentals. In America, the album grossed eight million dollars during the first ten days of its release. In England, the album climbed rapidly into the number-one position. A lesser rock group would have been destroyed by such a financial disaster!

The Founding of Apple. While Brian Epstein managed their financial affairs, the Beatles never had to concern themselves with their extensive wealth. They were required only to call Brian or sign a bill, and Epstein took care of everything. With Epstein gone, the Beatles were suddenly faced with a significant problem; how to handle their money. Each of them had spent well beyond his means. New British tax laws prohibited them from advancing money from their various enterprises without incurring an immediate tax liability. Expert tax advisors provided them with a simple solution. Expand. A business of some sort was the most logical direction in which to expand.

Though for several months the Beatles had toyed with the idea of a related business, for them the very word, "business," painted dark and dismal pictures. There was something about "business" that reminded them of going to school. They derisively called businessmen "the men in the suits." However, they recognized the need for such a venture, and finally agreed to try their hand. They formed a new company that took one of Paul's puns for a name, "Apple Corps, Ltd."

On May 12, 1968, Paul and John flew to New York, where they met with the other board members of the newly formed Apple to make its founding official. The five-day publicity blitz accompanying the announcement included a board meeting on a Chinese junk anchored in Manhattan harbor, a photo layout in *Life* magazine, and an appearance on the "Tonight" show, hosted that night by Joe Garagiola. John described the Apple concept to approximately twenty-five million people. In his description, he told this vast television audience that the Beatles were, in essence, giving away money to anyone who had a dream and needed financing for that dream. At least, that was the message every con artist, crook, and dreamer in the nation received. The Beatles were so rich they were giving away their money. And all one had to do to get some of this free money was to appear on the Beatles' doorstep with any kind of a plan, regardless of the nature of the project, and the Beatles would say, "Go ahead and do it." John and Paul obviously had no idea of the havoc that would result from their innocent announcement.

Apple eventually moved its headquarters into a beautiful five-story Georgian town house in the heart of London's tailoring district. Apple began its own record label. The Beatles created a new set of releases to introduce the label. These recordings, called *The First Four,* were packaged in a special introductory box, one of which was hand-delivered to Buckingham Palace. Among these new songs was Mary Hopkins' recording of *Those Were the Days.* A George Harrison composition entitled *Sour Milk Sea,* sung by Jackie Lomax, was included, along with a Lennon-McCartney tune called *Thingumybob,* performed by the Black Dyke Mills Band.

The Beatles made two personal contributions to the set, *Hey Jude* and *Revolution.* Paul had written *Hey Jude* to John's young son, Julian. *Revolution* was a John Lennon composition. *Hey Jude* became one of the bestselling singles in England in twenty years. Mary Hopkins' *Those Were the Days* was just as popular. The two songs fought throughout the summer they were released for the top spot on the charts. Eventually, the two sold a combined thirteen million copies.

Approximately five months after the release of *The First Four,* the Beatles released what was to become one of their classic album sets. Entitled *The Beatles,* the public began calling it the white album, or the "double white," because of its elegantly simple white cover, with the words, "The Beatles," imprinted in almost invisible raised lettering. Paul conceived the idea of having each album individually numbered, like fine lithographs. Critics praised it as the Beatles' finest collaboration. *London Observer* writer, Tony Palmer, raved "If there is still any doubt that Lennon and McCartney are the greatest songwriters since Schubert, then... [the *white album*]... should surely see the last vestiges of cultural snobbery and bourgeois prejudice swept away in a deluge of joyful music making... "

Splitting Up

This high praise is quite interesting, since most of the work on the album came from the Beatles as individuals. The album was not a collective effort. For some time, the Beatles had been growing increasingly disenchanted with each other, and the group as an entity. They became quarrelsome, and individual differences broke out. John, Paul, and George all thought Ringo less than a perfect drummer. Paul became increasingly dissatisfied with Ringo's work on the *white album,* and after several sessions, began returning to the studio to dub in Ringo's drum parts. The other Beatles had decided the little man who had come to them by chance was not a good enough musician to be included on much of the album.

At first, Ringo chose to ignore this. Finally, after a particularly unpleasant recording session, he went home to announce that he had quit the group. He declared he was no longer a Beatle. For a few days, he sat home, brooding. Then he decided to return to the group. When he reached the studios, he found his drums buried under several hundred pounds of welcome-back flowers. This delighted Ringo and he forgave everyone. However, the decay had begun. The foundation of the Beatles was irreparably cracked. Nothing could save the group from eventual destruction.

The Final Months. On New Year's Eve, 1968, as in previous years, the Beatles celebrated the incoming year together. Although these gatherings had always been warm and boisterous, that year's was a particularly sad and subdued affair. No one yet realized that a permanent split was in the making, but it was obvious to everyone concerned that all was not going well.

On January 2, the Beatles arrived at a cold, bleak sound stage at the Twickenham Film Studios to begin work on a new album and documentary. Originally entitled *Get Back,* it was later renamed *Let It Be.* Rather than touring to publicize the new film, the group decided to give a single concert at the film's completion. Paul deeply regretted the 1966 decision to end the Beatles' tours. He believed the Beatles had lost contact with their fans. He had broached the subject of another tour with the others, but had met strong resistance to the idea. *Let It Be* was a compromise. It was Paul's attempt to return to the Beatles' roots, to reestablish contact with the fans.

From the outset, nearly insurmountable problems plagued the filming and recording sessions. After discovering Twickenham could not provide the necessary setting in which to make the film, the Beatles moved operations to the new Apple studios, only to discover the new studios were not yet ready to accommodate such a project. In desperation, they decided to move to their corporate headquarters on Saville Row. Though this setting proved more acceptable, there was still an air of hostility pervading all the sessions.

When the Beatles completed the movie, the planned final concert took place, not in some grand location, but atop the Saville Row building, in bitter cold weather. "Braving the bitter cold, they ran through a few numbers, giving a frozen, ironic performance. The noise from the rooftop brought a crowd of pedestrians to the street below, and eventually a bobby arrived and tried to stop it all. But by then it was too late. The Beatles had given their last public performance."[2]

Historians uniformly agree that, for the United States and most of the civilized world, the decade of the sixties was a time of enormous change and turbulence. Though there were still four months left, the decade realistically came to a traumatic close at summer's end, 1969. During that summer, half a million rock fans descended on a farm in "Woodstock, New York, for a week-

---

[2]Brown and Gaines, p. 327.

end rock celebration called by its promoters the Woodstock Music and Art Fair." Brown and Gaines described the weekend as a three-day celebration of music and love. During that summer, Neil Armstrong became the first human to walk on the moon. In Los Angeles, Charles Manson heeded what he believed to be a call to destruction embedded in the Beatles' song, *Helter Skelter,* and with his equally insane followers, he murdered his way into infamy. That same summer, John Lennon formally announced his withdrawal from the Beatles. The disintegration of the Beatles had begun. In April, 1970, Paul McCartney announced his intention to leave. From that time forward, the Beatles were involved for several years in disputes and legal battles over contracts and the disbanding of the group. By 1980, the Beatles essentially no longer existed.

Lennon's Death. In 1980, John Lennon, his wife, Yoko Ono, and their son, Julian, were living in the Dakota apartments on Central Park West in New York City. In the fall of that year, John had experienced a resurgence of his career. He had recorded and released a new album, *Double Fantasy,* which was being critically acclaimed as fresh and upbeat. It climbed rapidly toward the top of the charts. John appeared to have regained much of the direction and momentum lost when the Beatles began breaking up. On Monday evening, December 8, John walked out of the Dakota's entrance gates toward his waiting limousine. A young man named Mark Chapman stepped forward and thrust a copy of the *Double Fantasy* album into John's hands. John obligingly signed the album cover "John Lennon, 1980." He returned to the Dakota later that evening, at 10:50 p.m. As he entered the darkened archway of the hotel, someone called his name. John stopped and turned. Mark Chapman, the young man whose album cover John had signed earlier that evening, was facing him in a combat stance, holding a .38-caliber revolver. Chapman fired five times, striking Lennon with each shot. By the time Lennon arrived at the emergency room of the Roosevelt Hospital, he had lost over seventy percent of the blood in his body. Dr. Stephen Lynn, director of emergency services, said resuscitation was impossible. John Lennon was dead.

Postscript

During their professional lifetime, the Beatles made a significant impact on the development of American popular music, and on the lifestyle of an entire generation of American youth. Like Elvis Presley, the Beatles dominated the musical charts, not for days or weeks or even months, but for more than ten years. In the United States alone, the Beatles hold either the top position or second place in all four major categories of recordings; most charted records, most number-one records, most Top Ten records, and most weeks holding number-one position. The Beatles' music became *the* music to emulate. Their first U.S. number one hit, *I Want to Hold Your Hand,* topped the charts on February 1, 1964, where it remained for seven weeks. In 1986, Fred Bronson wrote, "Today, *I Want to Hold Your Hand* stands as the biggest-selling British single of all time, with world-wide sales hovering near 15 million." Bronson added the importance of *I Want to Hold Your Hand* "cannot be [over]estimated."[3] Bronson believed that it shares the distinction with Bill Haley's *Rock around the Clock* of being the most important single in the rock era. Ringo Starr and Paul McCartney each went on to successful solo careers, as will be discussed in subsequent chapters.

Additional Readings

Brown, Peter, and Steven Gaines. *The Love You Make: An Insider's Story of the Beatles.* New York: McGraw-Hill, 1983.
Davies, Hunter. *The Beatles.* New York: McGraw-Hill, 1968.
McCabe, Peter, and Robert D. Schonfeld. *Apple to the Core: The Unmaking of the Beatles.* New York: Pocket Books, 1972.

Selected Recordings.

The following recordings are listed by artist, song title, record company, and record number.

The Beatles. *A Hard Day's Night.* Capitol 5222
———— . *Can't Buy Me Love.* Capitol 5150
———— . *Come Together/Something.* Apple 2654
———— . *Eight Days a Week.* Capitol 5371
———— . *Help!* Capitol 5476
———— . *Hey Jude.* Apple 2276
———— . *I Want to Hold Your Hand.* Capitol 5112
———— . *Let It Be.* Apple 2764
———— . *Love Me Do.* Tollie 9008
———— . *Paperback Writer.* Capitol 5651
———— . *Penny Lane.* Capitol 5810
———— . *She Loves You.* Swan 4152
———— . *The Long and Winding Road/For You Blue.* Apple 2832
———— . *Ticket to Ride.* Capitol 5407
———— . *Yesterday.* Capitol 5498

---

[3]Bronson, Fred. *The Billboard Book of Number One Hits.* (New York: Billboard Publications, Inc., 1985.) p. 143.

Chapter 17
Rock
Foundations

Prelude to 1955

After World War II, popular music in America underwent a violent up-heaval. Hitchcock said, "With the exception of a continuing undercurrent of sweet, romantic, conservative, virtually 'traditional' song—heard from such older performers as Lawrence Welk (b. 1903), Perry Como (b. 1912), and Frank Sinatra (b. 1917)—American popular music was transformed entirely, from 'pop' to 'rock.' "[1] As had been the case before in popular music, the music of the blacks was the main source of the transformation. This time it was the black rhythm-and-blues dance music on recordings. There were several kinds of music included in this genre. The strong-rhythmed dance music of

---

[1]Hitchcock, H. Wiley. *Music in the United States: A Historical Introduction,* 2nd edition. (Englewood Cliffs, New Jersey: Prentice-Hall, Inc., 1974), p. 257.

the big bands, whose roots were deeply embedded in the Kansas City swing style, was present. The urban blues of the big-city dance halls and auditoriums were included. Its roots could be found in the personal laments or exultations of the self-accompanied country blues singers. Those same roots were deeply anchored in the close harmony of singing groups such as the Ink Spots, the Dominos, the Ravens, the Drifters, the Orioles, and others, whose music was rooted in the gospel singing of rural evangelistic and urban storefront churches.

Another kind of folk music played an important role in the development of the new popular music, the hillbilly style of the southern upland whites. Hitchcock said:

> These two musics—rhythm-and-blues and country-and-western—had some stylistic characteristics in common which made their marriage a potentially happy one: they both emphasized a highly personal, grassroots earthiness of vocal style; they both were based rhythmically on a powerful and danceable instrumental background; and they both tended to favor the guitar, whether the electrically amplified guitar of the urban blues singer, the natural 'acoustic' guitar (long prominent as a rural, folkish instrument) of country blues, or the steel guitar, sometimes amplified, of country-and-western music.[2]

The transformation of American popular music through the marriage of black rhythm-and-blues and white country-and-western music occurred primarily because of a new phenomenon in American society: a self-conscious, self-aware, and economically strong "youth culture" of rebellious teenagers. This generation was born just before World War II or during the baby boom immediately after it, grew up in the postwar economic boom, and reached adolescence in the 1950s.

Early in that decade, rhythm-and-blues records began to attract white teenagers, especially as a music for dancing. A few alert disc jockeys began programming the records for a general audience, not just for the black community. During this period, Alan Freed, a disc jockey at WWJ in Cleveland, hosted a radio show featuring the bestselling records of the day. The owner of a large record shop in Cleveland told Freed that kids, black and white, were purchasing rhythm-and-blues records "by the armful." Freed conceived the idea of attracting youngsters to his program by including rhythm-and-blues. Response to his programming was phenomenal. Freed promptly began programming an exclusive diet of rhythm-and-blues, and began calling himself "Moon Dog." He named his show "Moon Dog's Rock and Roll Party." David Ewen reported Freed chose the term 'rock and roll' because he suspected there was a racial

---

[2]Hitchcock, pp. 257–258.

stigma attached to rhythm-and-blues. Freed found the words "rock-and-roll" in the lyrics of a rhythm-and-blues number. (It is reported he coined the term from the 1947 rhythm-and-blues hit, *We're Gonna Rock, We're Gonna Roll,* by Wild Bill Moore.)

Kids across the entire broadcast area of WWJ loved Freed and the music he played. Freed would often play records and shout in rhythm to the music. He would also bang his fist on a telephone directory, pounding out the beat of the music. In Freed, the kids found a kindred spirit, one who understood them, who backed their rebellion against the domination of their parents and society.

In 1954, Freed moved his rock-and-roll program to WINS in New York, where he became an even greater force in the world of pop music. Clark Whelton, a *New York Times* reporter, wrote, "I'll never forget the first time I heard the Freed show. I couldn't believe the sounds that were coming out of a radio. In 1954 radio was Gruen watch commercials, soap operas and Snooky Lanson Hit Parade music... Alan Freed jumped into radio like a stripper into Swan Lake. He was a teenager's mind funneled into 50,000 watts... In 1954 there was no one else like him."

Soon, record manufacturers were marketing rhythm-and-blues/rock-and-roll recordings to the population in general, not just to blacks. And soon they were employing white musicians to "cover" black hits—to record duplicates, or new (smoother-edged, somewhat diluted, and generally more commercially successful) versions of them. Some were searching for white musicians whose styles were based on, or close to, black music. White rock-and-roll hits, in turn, awakened interest in the black music and musicians they had imitated. Before long, much American popular music was moving in the direction of rock-and-roll. In 1953, a rock-and-roll song appeared on *Billboard*'s bestselling list, the first indication at the national level of changing tastes in popular music. The song was *Crazy, Man, Crazy,* performed by Bill Haley and the Comets, a white group out of Chester, Pennsylvania. What followed was, at the least, a genuine American phenomenon. Rock-and-roll exploded on the popular-music scene.

Rock Arrives

*B*illboard magazine's July 9, 1955 issue listed Bill Haley and the Comets' *Rock around the Clock* as that week's number one single. There was no fanfare surrounding this event, yet it marked the dividing line between all that had come before it and all that would follow. Historians cannot agree upon which song stands as the first true rock-and-roll piece. However, they all agree that *Rock around the Clock* is *not* that song. Many believe Jackie Brenston's Memphis recording of *Rocket 88*, released on the Chess label in 1951, was the first. (The record was actually made by the Ike Turner Band. Brenston was Turner's saxophonist.) Haley recapped *Rocket 88* during that same year, and became the first white artist to make a rock-and-roll recording. While Haley did not invent the term, "rock-and-roll," he did bring rock to the consciousness of America and the world. Though his career did not attain the heights of Elvis Presley, to the world of rock music, Bill Haley will always be the father of rock-and-roll.

William John Clifton Haley, Jr. was born on July 6, 1925, in Highland Park, Michigan. His parents were musical. His father, a textile worker, played the banjo, and his mother, who taught piano, occasionally played organ in a neighborhood Baptist church. His family moved to Wilmington, Delaware,

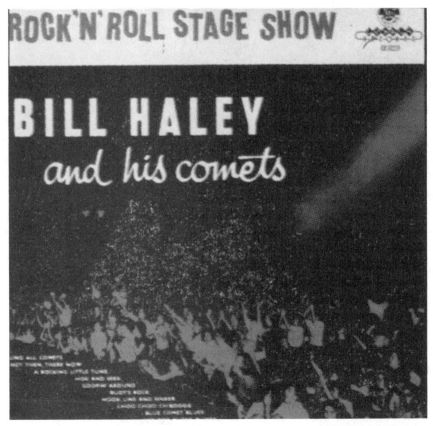

THE HUGH JONES COLLECTION

A BILL HALEY RECORDING.

when he was seven. Soon after this move, Haley began playing his own home-made cardboard-box guitar.

At about age twenty-five, he saw a notice in *Billboard* advertising a singing job. He answered the ad, and a group called the "Downtowners" hired him as a singing yodeler. He left this group to become a disc jockey in Bridgeport, New Jersey, at radio station WSNJ. In 1948, he moved to WPWA in Chester, Pennsylvania. There he formed a singing group, The Four Aces of Western Swing. He disbanded this group in 1949, and began a group called the "Saddlemen." One year later, Haley and the Saddlemen signed a recording contract with Dave Miller and Holiday Records. They recorded *Rock This Joint* in 1952, a song that blended a country sound with rhythm-and-blues.

In 1953, the Saddlemen became the Comets, and recorded their first chart hit, *Crazy, Man, Crazy.* It rose to number 15 on the Billboard chart, the first rock-and-roll record ever to make the chart. That same year, Max Freedman and Jimmie DeKnight (a New York music publisher whose real name was James Myers) wrote a song specifically for Bill Haley. However, because of his dislike for DeKnight, Miller refused to allow Haley and the Comets to record it. When Haley's contract with Miller expired, Haley and DeKnight paid a visit to Milt Gabler of Decca Records. Gabler immediately signed Haley and the Comets, and on April 12, 1954, the group went into the studio to record *Thirteen Women,* and the piece DeKnight had written for Haley, *Rock around the Clock.*

Rock around the Clock was only mildly successful. However, Haley's next single, a recap of Joe Turner's *Shake, Rattle, and Roll,* hit the Top Ten and made Haley a national star. During this time, DeKnight had still not given up on the marketability of *Rock around the Clock.* He promoted the song vigorously by sending copies to everyone he knew in Hollywood, including MGM. MGM released the movie, *Blackboard Jungle,* starring Glenn Ford as a high school teacher confronted by violent students, in the spring of 1955. *Rock around the Clock* was the song heard under the credits.

Both the movie and the song created a sensation. There were riots in theaters. Clare Booth Luce called the film "degenerate." As a result, it was removed from the Venice film festival. *Rock around the Clock* was rereleased and shot to number one. Movie producer Sam Katzman signed Haley and the Comets to star in his 1956 film, *Rock around the Clock.* A new trend had been established in Hollywood, the marriage of rock-and-roll to the silver screen. The way was now paved for the later screen successes of Elvis Presley and other rock stars. Unfortunately, Haley was never again able to attain the success of his only number-one single. He did tour most of the world, and was quite popular in Europe. However, by the '70s, his once immense popularity had disappeared entirely, and he had all but slipped into obscurity. Apparently unable to cope with this, Haley became an alcoholic, and on February 9, 1981, he died of a heart attack at his home in Harlingen, Texas.

American Pop in Transition

The rock era had begun in earnest. However, because the transition from pop to rock, which began in 1953, occurred so quietly and so gradually, it went virtually unnoticed until January of 1956. *Billboard*'s music popularity charts dated July 9, 1955, reflected the odd admixture of tastes in existence when rock first appeared. Although rock-and-roll was beginning to come of age, the cultivated folk-ballad tradition was still very much in evidence. The Top Five songs for the week of July 9, 1955, were:

1. *Rock around the Clock*
   Bill Haley and the Comets
2. *Cherry Pink and Apple Blossom White*
   Prez Prado
3. *A Blossom Fell/If I May*
   Nat (King) Cole
4. *Unchained Melody*
   Les Baxter
5. *Learnin' the Blues*
   Frank Sinatra

Rock continued to gain a foothold in the music industry, while the cultivated offspring of household music continued to thrive. For a time, the two genres peacefully coexisted on the pop-music front. Elvis Presley's *Heartbreak Hotel* was number one on the charts for the week of April 21, 1956, and that same week, the number-three song was Les Baxter's recording of *Poor People of Paris* and the number-five song was *Lisbon Antiqua*, by Nelson Riddle and his orchestra. Both the number-three and the number-five songs were instrumental, and belong to the cultivated tradition currently called "easy listening," or "elevator music."

Throughout much of 1955, the nation's pop-music consumers continued to display the ambiguity reflected in *Billboard*'s July 9, 1955, Top Five chart. For the week of September 3, that year, Mitch Miller's *Yellow Rose of Texas* was number one. Pat Boone's *Ain't That a Shame* followed it. Then came Bill Haley's *Rock around the Clock*, Frank Sinatra's *Learnin' the Blues*, and Boyd Bennett's *Seventeen*.

An unusual, but important, pop-music influence during the 1950s was choral conductor Mitch Miller. Miller was a graduate of the Eastman School of Music. For a time after graduation he played oboe, first in the Rochester Philharmonic Orchestra, then with the CBS Symphony and the Budapest String Quartet. In the 1940s, he became head of pop music for Mercury Records. In 1951, he left Mercury for Columbia Records to become head of A&R (Artists and Repertoire).

In 1958, Columbia released a record album called *Sing Along With Mitch*. The album was a collection of standard pop songs performed by an all-male chorus, directed by Miller. Columbia furnished a complete set of lyrics with each album so consumers might "sing along with Mitch," should they so desire. The album was so successful that it led to a series of similar releases, and an NBC special telecast on May 24, 1960, featuring Mitch and his Mitch Miller Singers in a nationwide sing-along. This concept proved so popular that NBC decided to give Miller his own series, which ran from January, 1961, to September, 1966.

During the week of October 8, 1955, the Four Aces' recording of *Love Is a Many-Splendored Thing* replaced *Yellow Rose of Texas* as the nation's number-one single. It was number one for two weeks and became the theme for a motion picture of the same name. The Four Aces were a male vocal quartet specializing in pop ballads and love songs. This was not the same group as the one formed by Bill Haley, though they were both from Chester, Pennsylvania. Al Alberts was lead vocalist, Dave Mahoney sang tenor, Soc Vaccaro, baritone, and Lou Silvestri, bass. Before the rock era, the Four Aces had placed sixteen songs on the Billboard chart, including *Three Coins in the Fountain*, for which they won an Oscar.

From October 29 to November 25 of that year, *Autumn Leaves*, recorded by pianist Roger Williams, held the top spot on the *Billboard* chart. Then, Tennessee Ernie Ford's *Sixteen Tons* took over, and held the top position for the next seven weeks. Both of these songs are in the older tradition of pop music. During this period, though several rock and rock-influenced songs appeared on the *Billboard* chart, popular music of the older vein still held sway with the nation's listening public. For example, during the week *Sixteen Tons* climbed into the number-one position, four of the five songs listed were of the older, more genteel style. Only one, Gale Storm's *I Hear You Knocking*, was of a definite rock nature, and it was number five that week. However, after the phenomenal success of Elvis Presley's *Heartbreak Hotel*, rock recordings from several artists quickly began to dominate the charts. Individuals such as Gogi Grant, Pat Boone, Fats Domino, and Sonny James, and groups such as the Platters, became regulars in the nation's Top Five club.

Dick Clark and "American Bandstand"

Through the years, many television shows have dealt with rock music. Of all these, one classic has survived: "American Bandstand." This program, aimed primarily at a teen target, was televised nationally for the first time in 1957. It aired during the weekday viewing hours most popular with its target audience, from 3 to 5 p.m.

"American Bandstand" began in Philadelphia in 1952, a remarkably early date for such a show. During its early days, it was called simply "Bandstand," and Bob Horn acted as host. Sometime during 1956, Dick Clark, a young Philadelphia disc jockey who looked like he drank milk and exercised a lot, joined Bandstand as its host. When the network began national telecasts, the program acquired a new name, "American Bandstand."

"American Bandstand" was deceptively simple. Primarily, it gave the appearance of being a teenage dance party that just happened to air routinely on television. The host played records, the audience danced, and periodically, a guest performer appeared on the show. A panel formed by the TV studio assessed new releases, and the host conducted short interviews with the teenagers themselves.

The appeal of "American Bandstand" lay in its simplicity. The program appeared to make no effort to "entertain" the television audience. Since its inception, it had existed solely for the pleasure of the audience that came to the TV studio. In the beginning, a filmed performance of the song accompanied the playing of each record. The teenage audience in the studio spontaneously began dancing to the records as they played. Before long, the entire show had evolved into a televised dance party. Carl Belz remarked that this ultimately provided the program with its *raison d'être*. Everyone was invited to observe a "real-life situation." Routine viewing of the show produced an intimate familiarity with the regulars—those kids who came to the dance several times a week. The TV audience and the kids who danced were the real stars of "American Bandstand." Belz concluded that the show attained an unprecedented popularity because it was allowed to keep its unique qualities, rather than be transformed into popular entertainment designed primarily for a passive TV audience.

Dick Clark's consistently relaxed, controlled, quiet manner and personal style were perfectly suited to the "American Bandstand" experience. Clark introduced new songs casually, unlike many of his radio counterparts. He never sought to dress or behave like any of his teenage guests, nor did he assume their vocabulary or attitudes. He projected the image of an attractive older brother or father. He was a well-known and admired television personality who genuinely liked and understood teenagers and enjoyed their music, but made no attempt to become one of them.

The success of "American Bandstand" lay in the perceived spontaneity of its format and the real spontaneity of its participants. A later imitation, the "Lloyd Thaxton Show," stylized every element of its format. Occasionally, Thaxton himself feigned performing by miming the words to a song or the playing of some musical instrument. Dance contests were conducted that required dancers to become immobile immediately when the music stopped. Any movement beyond the music's interruption automatically removed a couple from the competition. While the results of these and other kinds of deliberate manipulations may have been amusing at times, they were not as spontaneous nor as expressive as the elements from which "American Bandstand" was constructed.

Among other imitators were "Shindig," which originated in 1964 and lasted about one year and "Hullabaloo," which began about the same time, but lasted into 1966, primarily because it included artists who were more popular with adult audiences.

In the late 1960s, several television shows attempted to present rock-and-roll music in a more lifelike context. None achieved the kind of success experienced by "American Bandstand." This imitative type of programming reached a climax in 1966 with "The Monkees," which lasted two years on network television. Its countless commercial aspects were most deliberately and carefully planned. "The Monkees" borrowed extensively and shamelessly from the best-known existing rock groups. This "borrowing" resulted in a slick, polished style. However, the program fell short in its appeal to the teenage audience for whom it was intended. It did not attract older viewers. It appealed instead to kids between the ages of six and twelve. Across the years, since the inception of "American Bandstand," rock audiences had grown more sophisticated.

Payola

Without doubt, the most outrageous and most damaging scandal ever to strike rock culminated in the payola hearings of 1959 and 1960. Oren Harris chaired the House of Representatives Special Subcommittee on Legislative Oversight investigating allegations of misconduct in the promotion practices of songs and records. These investigations produced a 1600-page document entitled *Responsibilities of Broadcasting Licensees and Station Personnel.*

Radio disc jockeys became the primary target of the investigation. They were accused of accepting material bribes, money and other goods, from record producers, distributors, and manufacturers in exchange for heavily promoting certain recordings. Authorities charged defendants with the illegal limiting of business competition and with dictating public taste. Though on the surface this investigation appeared to be a noble cause, Carl Belz believed these hearings were, in reality, an attack on what the committee saw as "bad" music. Committee members believed rock encouraged juvenile delinquency. They thought illegal business activities had foisted it on the American public. Several examples of rock music and artists were cited as support for this view during the hearings. As a result, the discussions often departed from points of legality and drifted into the realm of aesthetics. Belz remarked, "As much as any fact in rock history, this demonstrated that the music had made a profound and revolutionary impact on the American public." Belz believed that had the music been aesthetically pleasing to those on the committee, the hearings would never have taken place.

The payola hearings had a profound impact on the pop-music industry in general, and on several radio personalities in particular. In essence, they ended disc jockey Alan Freed's career. In 1959–1960, he was charged in the payola scandal, and indicted on charges of income tax evasion. The hearings proved neither the artistic deficits nor the merits of rock music.

Young Rock Grows

Buddy Holly. On September 23, 1957, a young group called "the Crickets" slipped into the number-one spot for a week with *That'll Be the Day*. What was to follow would leave an indelible print on popular music worldwide. The

THE HUGH JONES COLLECTION

A BUDDY HOLLY RECORDING.

group's lead singer was a bespeckled twenty-one-year-old named Charles Hardin Holly. His mother called him "Buddy." Holly's impact on popular music was significant. To this day, his music continues to influence both the art and the artists. Fred Bronson wrote, "In the short span of three years, Buddy Holly created a timeless body of work that influenced almost every major artist of the rock era, especially the Beatles, the Rolling Stones, Bob Dylan, Elton John, Linda Ronstadt, John Denver, Bobby Vee, Tommy Roe, Elvis Costello, and a list too long to complete here. No one knows what more Buddy would have contributed if he had lived beyond his 22 years."[3]

On February 3, 1959, Holly and two other prominent rock stars, Richie Valens and J. P. Richardson, "the Big Bopper," boarded a small private plane in Clear Lake, Iowa, for their next concert stop, Fargo, North Dakota. They took off just after 1 a.m. in the middle of a heavy snowstorm. A few minutes later, excessive ice on the wings caused the plane to crash into a frozen Ames, Iowa cornfield on the farm belonging to Albert Juhl. Everyone on board was killed. In 1972 Don McLean recorded *American Pie*, a song whose opening lines commemorated Buddy Holly.

Holly's last studio track, *It Doesn't Matter Anymore* became a posthumous hit. Most of his hits were songs he wrote. Several years after his death, he was acknowledged as a legend in pop music. Contemporary rock stars continue to record his songs: *Everyday, Peggy Sue, Oh, Boy, Words of Love*, and *Raining in My Heart*.

The Everly Brothers. In October of 1957, the Everly Brothers made their top-of-the-chart debut with *Wake Up, Little Susie*. The "rock-a-billy" style and harmonies of these two brothers would influence several generations of rock stars, including Simon and Garfunkel, the Beach Boys, the Mamas and the Papas, and even the Beatles.

Don and Phil Everly were born in Brownie, Kentucky, where their father, Ike, was a coal miner. When the brothers were still quite young, Ike and his family moved to Shenandoah, Iowa, where for a brief period, the family had a half-hour radio show which aired every morning at 6:00 a.m. over radio station KMA. Upon invitation, Don and Phil joined the show for fifteen minutes on Saturday mornings with "The Little Donnie Show." Don was seven.

In November, 1955, the Everly Brothers recorded their first single, *The Sun Keeps Shining*, for Columbia Records. When Columbia failed to renew the brothers' recording option, they recorded *Bye Bye Love* for Cadence Records. By the time the boys had completed a 'tentshow' tour of portions of the Southeast, *Bye Bye Love* had climbed to number two on the national charts.

---

[3]Bronson, Fred. *The Billboard Book of Number One Hits*. (New York: Billboard Publications, Inc., 1985), p. 27.

PHOTOFEST

THE EVERLY BROTHERS.

Then, in 1957, the Everly Brothers recorded their first number-one single, *Wake Up, Little Susie*. This song launched a highly successful career which spanned the next ten years. Their last recording to reach the charts, *Bowling Green*, appeared in July, 1967. During the early-to-mid-1980s the Everlys made several appearances on national television, and seemed to be attempting a comeback. However, this attempt was brief and, by all measures, not highly successful.

By mid-1956, the rock revolution was well under way, and was gaining momentum on a daily basis. Elvis Presley's name continued to appear on the charts with increasing frequency. The week of October 21, 1957, saw his double-sided hit, *Jailhouse Rock* and *Treat Me Nice*, ascend to the number-one spot, where it remained for the next seven weeks. Even during the final week of 1957, *Jailhouse Rock* and *Treat Me Nice* were still listed among the Top Five nationally. When the record finally disappeared from the chart the first week in January, it had been there for a total of ten weeks!

On March 17, 1958, an instrumental group, the Champs, took their place at the top of the chart with their only number-one single, *Tequila*. According to Fred Bronson, the Champs are more famous today for who entered the group after they recorded *Tequila*— Glen Campbell, Jim Seals, and Dash Croft. Campbell went on to become a solo star. Seals and Croft became a duo after forming a group called "the Dawnbreakers."

The First Number-One Novelty Song. For two weeks, beginning April 28, 1958, a novelty tune climbed into the number-one position. It was the first of several such songs scattered across the early years of the rock era. Ross Bagdasarian wrote and produced *Witch Doctor*, and recorded it under the name of his alter ego, David Seville. Work on *Witch Doctor* laid the ground-work for what was to become a multimillion-dollar empire. Bagdasarian came up with the idea of recording and playing back vocals and music at different speeds. This device eventually blossomed into a giant windfall for him, built around three friendly rodents, Alvin, Theodore, and Simon—The Chipmunks—who made their debut with *The Chipmunk Song*. Within three weeks of its release, the song had sold more than 2,500,000 copies. It became the fastest-selling record of 1958. The Chipmunk empire had begun. After *The Chipmunk Song* came *Alvin's Harmonica*, which peaked at number three. On October 4, 1961, "The Alvin Show" premiered on CBS, and ran for a full season. CBS repeated the series on its Saturday morning schedule for three years, beginning in 1964. By 1967, Ross Bagdasarian, creator of the Chipmunks, decided to retire the three comic figures. He wanted the pop-music world to consider him a serious composer, not just a writer of novelty songs.

Ross Bagdasarian died suddenly of a heart attack on January 16, 1972. His Chipmunks, however, lived on, well beyond their creator. They began a come-back in 1980 when a radio station played a recording of rock star Blondie's *Call Me* at a faster speed, and reported in jest that the record was by the Chipmunks. Popular demand for the "new" Chipmunk song was so great that Ross, Jr., and his wife, decided to record two new Chipmunk albums, *Chipmunk Punk* and *Urban Chipmunk*. They also sold a new series of Chipmunk adventures to NBC for their Saturday morning schedule. The new series premiered in September, 1983, and is still being aired regularly. Bagdasarian's pioneer work in novelty songs opened the door for later novelty successes—*Monster Mash, Ahab the Arab,* and *The Streak,* for example. In June, 1958, *Purple People Eater,* a novelty song recorded by Sheb Wooley, was number one on the charts for six weeks. The following month rock again took over the top spot with *Hard-Hearted Woman,* Elvis Presley's tenth number-one hit.

The Hot 100. In August, 1958, *Billboard* introduced the Hot 100, the weekly singles chart that would become the nation's standard to determine the best-selling, most-played records in America. The first song to reach number one on the Hot 100 chart was Ricky Nelson's *Poor Little Fool.* It was his sixth hit single. Even though rock had begun to dominate the charts, other genres of popular music still routinely made their way into the nation's Top Five, and occasionally, into the number-one position. Novelty songs were one such genre. The older, more traditional popular music also appeared on the charts with some regularity. In August 1958, *Volare,* recorded by Italy's Domenico Modugno, took over number one, and held it for six weeks. This was the only record originating in Italy ever to reach number one on the American pop charts.

The Proliferation of Rock

Before April, 1959, only one Top-Five chart had ever been totally dominated by rock. It appeared in December, 1957, and included:

1. *You Send Me*
   Sam Cooke
2. *Jailhouse Rock/Treat Me Nice*
   Elvis Presley
3. *Wake Up Little Susie*
   Everly Brothers
4. *Silhouettes*
   The Rays
5. *Raunchy*
   Bill Justice

The next time such a chart appeared was the week of April 13, 1959. That week the chart read as follows:

1. *Come Softly to Me*
   Fleetwoods
2. *Venus*
   Frankie Avalon
3. *Pink Shoelaces*
   Dodie Stevens
4. *It's Just a Matter of Time*
   Brook Benton
5. *Tragedy*
   Thomas Wayne

This chart appears to mark a turning point in the nation's response to rock music. Never again was the older, more traditional genre of popular music to appear on the charts with any regularity. Only occasionally would a song written in the genteel style rise into the Top 100 chart. When it did, its popularity routinely confined it to a ranking no higher than fortieth. The rock era had begun in earnest.

Innovations in Rock. Before 1958, the only electrically amplified instruments commonly used in the rock arena were the fretted string instruments, such as guitars and electric basses. Electric keyboards had not yet arrived on the rock scene. Then, beginning on May 11, 1958, an instrumental song, *The Happy Organ*, rose to the top of the chart for one week. The song was written and recorded by Dave "Baby" Cortez. Originally, the song was entitled *The Dog and the Cat,* and was supposed to be a vocal number accompanied by piano. The vocal line proved unacceptable to both Cortez and cowriter Ken Wood. The decision was made to make the piece an instrumental arrangement. Cortez changed the melody in the recording studio, and after completing it, used the studio's electric organ, instead of a piano, for the recording session. At this juncture in the history of rock, use of any kind of organ, electric or otherwise, was virtually unknown. Cortez was instrumental in making the electric organ popular in the rock field. Now the stage was set for the advent of future electronic inventions such as the Moog synthesizer and MIDI instruments.

Other innovations in the pop/rock arena began to occur. Marty Robbins opened the year 1960 with his recording, *El Paso.* The song was a landmark for many reasons: It was the year's first number-one single, the first country song to win a Grammy, and the longest single to date to become number one. Before *El Paso,* the common length for all popular singles was two and one-half to three minutes. *El Paso* was five minutes long, and Columbia Records refused Robbins' request to release it as a single. Instead, he and Columbia compromised. *El Paso* was released on an album entitled *Gunfighter Ballads and Trail Songs.* After four weeks of airplay, demand for *El Paso* became so great that company executives agreed to release it as a 45, despite its unusual length.

Early 60s Dance Crazes. On September 19, 1960, Chubby Checker's *The Twist* became number one for two weeks. It is the only recording to become number one in two separate chart runs, first in September, 1960, and again in January, 1962. Its combined chart run of 38 weeks made *Twist* the longest-running number-one single to date. *Twist* was first recorded in 1958 by a Detroit group, Hank Ballard and the Midnighters. Ballard wrote the song after seeing a group of teenagers do a new dance in Tampa, Florida, the twist. He recorded it as the flip side of the Midnighters' first pop hit, *Teardrops on Your Letter,* but it was ignored by DJ's. They favored *Teardrops* instead.

However, the dance itself spread across the country and became the hottest dance on Dick Clark's "American Bandstand." Clark suggested Danny and the Juniors re-record the song, but the group declined. Clark then called Cameo-Parkway Records and suggested that one of their artists record the song. The chore fell to one of their newest commodities, Chubby Checker.

After its initial number-one run of two weeks, the song and its dance faded in popularity with the national teenage crowd. As it was doing so, it inexplicably rose in popularity with adults. A society columnist reported that Prince Serge Obolensky had been seen dancing the twist at Manhattan's Peppermint Lounge. The dance suddenly became a worldwide sensation, and the newest plaything of the international jet set.

National dance crazes associated with a number-one hit continued to appear occasionally. In August 1962, Little Eva's *The Loco-Motion* rose to the top of the chart for one week. Within weeks of the song's release, the entire nation was dancing the Loco-Motion. According to Carole King, the record's coproducer, the dance did not exist until after the song was a number-one hit. When everyone began asking how the dance went, Little Eva was forced to make one up. In early 1974, the group, Grand Funk Railroad, recorded *The Loco-Motion*. Their recording also went to number one, making *The Loco-Motion* one of only three rock-era songs to become number one by two different artists.

Groups and Solo Artists.

In rock, all-male and mixed groups have traditionally been far more common than all-female groups. Nonetheless, through the years there have been several quite notable all-female rock or rhythm-and-blues ensembles. The first of these ever to have a number-one single was the Shirelles, with their recording of *Will You Love Me Tomorrow*. The song topped the chart on January 20, 1961, and held that position for two weeks.

From 1955 through 1962, the rock field was dominated by solo artists, male and female. There were few vocal groups that attained stardom, and fewer still instrumental groups. From May of 1961 through September of 1962, only five vocal and two instrumental groups managed to produce number-one singles. The balance of the number-one singles across the entire period from 1955 to 1962 came from solo artists. Ricky Nelson had produced his first number-one single in 1957, *Poor Little Fool*. The years 1961 and 1962 were dominated by the names of Pat Boone, Roy Orbison, Ray Charles, Chubby Checker, and of course, the venerable and perpetual Elvis Presley.

The Four Seasons.

On September 15, 1962, *Sherry*, the first number-one hit by the Four Seasons ascended to the top position and held it for five weeks. To most people, Frankie Valli appeared to be an overnight success. In actuality, his success was ten years in the making. In 1954, he joined forces with Nick and Tommy DeVito and Hank Majewski, the Variety Trio. The name of the group was changed to the "Variatones." After one year, the group became the "Four Lovers." They made it to the Hot 100 chart with *You're the Apple of My Eye*, a song they performed on "The Ed Sullivan Show."

In 1960, Bob Gaudio, formerly of the Royal Teens, joined the group as a keyboard player. This group auditioned for a New Jersey bowling-alley lounge, but failed to get the job. However, one important change resulted from the audition. The group took the name of the bowling alley, the Four Seasons.

Sherry was the first of a long list of hits for the Four Seasons over the next several years. The group's popularity appeared to spring vocal, rock-oriented groups into the limelight. On November 17, the Four Seasons produced their next chart-topper, *Big Girls Don't Cry.* The Four Season's durability was amazing. Their active career, which began in 1954 and took wings in 1962 with *Sherry,* continued until January 1976, when their last number-one hit, *December, 1963 (Oh What a Night),* topped the charts. As of this writing, Frankie Valli still performs professionally, and occasionally makes guest appearances on national television talk shows, such as "The Oprah Winfrey Show."

Rock Goes International

In December, 1962, a seemingly innocent occurrence took place, foreshadowing events that would reshape the whole of the rock genre and youth culture worldwide. London Records launched the first British group to have a number-one single in America. On December 22, 1962, *Telstar,* by the Tornadoes, rose to number one, and held the position for the next three weeks. England had opened the door and quietly joined the rock revolution. The next international hit, the only number-one hit to date sung in Japanese, was *Sukiyaki,* by Japanese artist Kyu Sakamoto.

Jeanine Deckers, better known as the "Singing Nun," closed out the year 1963 with her number-one hit, *Dominique,* another of the international newcomers. This song, originally recorded in Brussels by Philips Records, eulogized the founder of the Dominican order. That a song of this nature should rise to the number-one position in a world of popular music dominated by raucous rock is unlikely and incongruous. At the least, it was a startling contrast to the chart-toppers of recent years. Nevertheless, *Dominique* did rise to number one on the *Billboard* charts, and by doing so, provided an even more startling contrast to what followed it so closely. In February 1964, America met the Beatles.

Additional Readings

Note: These readings generally also apply to Chapters 18 and 19.

Belz, Carl. *The Story of Rock.* New York: Oxford University Press, 1972.

Bronson, Fred. *The Billboard Book of Number One Hits.* New York: Billboard Publications, Inc., 1985.

Brown, Peter, and Steven Gaines. *The Love You Make: An Insider's Story of the Beatles.* New York: McGraw-Hill, 1983.

Chapple, Steve, and Reebee Garofalo. *Rock 'n Roll Is Here to Pay: The History and Politics of the Music Industry.* Chicago: Nelson-Hall, 1977.

Coon, Caroline. *The New Wave Punk Rock Explosion.* London: Orbach and Chambers, 1977.

Cooper, Al, with Ben Edmonds. *Backstage Passes: Rock 'n Roll Life in the '60's.* New York: Stein & Day, 1977.

Dachs, David. *Anything Goes: The World of Popular Music.* Indianapolis: Bobbs-Merril, 1964.

Dalton, David and Lenny Kaye. *Rock 100.* New York: Grosset & Dunlap Publishers, 1977.

Davies, Hunter. *The Beatles.* New York: McGraw-Hill, 1968.

Davis, Sharon. *Motown: The History.* New York: Guinness, 1988.

Denisoff, R. Serge. *Solid Gold: The Popular Record Industry.* New Brunswick, N.J.: Transaction Books, 1975.

————. *Tarnished Gold.* New York: Transaction, 1986.

Evans, Tom and Mary. *From the Renaissance to Rock: Music, History, Construction and Players.* New York: Paddington Press, 1977.

Ewen, David. *The Life and Death of Tin Pan Alley: The Golden Age of American Popular Music.* New York: Funk and Wagnalls, 1964.

Gillett, Charlie. *The Sound of the City: The Rise of Rock and Roll.* Rev. ed. New York: Pantheon Books, 1984.

Groia, Philip. *They All Sang on the Corner: New York City's Rhythm & Blues Vocal Groups of the 1950's.* New York: Edmond, 1973.

Hatch, David, and Millward, Stephen. *From Blues to Rock: An Analytical History of Pop Music.* New York: St. Martin's Press, 1987.

Hopkins, Jerry. *Elvis: A Biography.* New York: New Rochelle, N.Y.: Macmillan, 1971.

————. *Elvis: The Final Years.* New York: St. Martin's, 1980.

Keith, Michael. *The Radio Station.* 2nd ed. Boston: Focal Press, 1989.

Larkin, Rochelle. *Soul Music.* New York: Lancer Books, 1970.

Lichter, Paul. *The Boy Who Dared to Rock: The Definitive Elvis.* Doubleday & Company: Garden City, New York, 1978.

McCabe, Peter, and Robert D. Schonfeld. *Apple to the Core: The Unmaking of the Beatles.* New York: Pocket Books, 1972.

Makower, Joel. *Woodstock: The Oral History.* New York: Tilden Press, 1989.

Manilow, Barry. *Sweet Life: Adventures on the Way to Paradise.* New York: McGraw-Hill Book Company, 1987.

Marks, J. *Rock and Other Four Letter Words.* New York: Bantam, 1968.

Miller, J. *The Rolling Stone Illustrated History of Rock and Roll.* New York: Rolling Stone Press, 1980.

Palmer, Robert. *The Rolling Stones.* New York: The Rolling Stone Press, 1983.

Rosenman, Joel, John Roberts, and Robert Pilpel. *Young Men with Unlimited*

Capital. New York: Harcourt, Brace and Jovanovich, 1974.

Sanjek, Russell. *American Popular Music and Its Business.* Vols. 1–3. New York: Oxford University Press, 1988.

Shaw, Arnold. *The Rockin' '50's.* New York: Hawthorn Books, 1974.

Sklar, Rick. *Rocking America: How the All-Hit Radio Stations Took Over: An Insider's Story.* New York: St. Martin's. Press, 1985.

Smith, Joe. *Off the Record: An Oral History of Popular Music.* Warner Books, 1988.

Waller, Don. *The Motown Story.* New York: Scribner, 1985.

Whitburn, Joel. *The Billboard Book of Top 40 Hits.* New York: Billboard Publications, Inc., 1987.

Selected Recordings

The following recordings are listed by artist, song title, record company, and record number. (For a more detailed discography of this era, see *The Billboard Book of Top 40 Hits,* by Joel Whitburn.)

Champs. *Tequila* [1]. Challenge 1016
Crickets, The (Buddy Holly). *That'll Be the Day.* Brunswick 55009
———. *Oh, Boy!* Brunswick 55035
Everly Brothers. *Bye Bye Love.* Cadence 1315
———. *All I Have to Do Is Dream.* Cadence 1348
———. *Bird Dog.* Cadence 1350
———. *Devoted to You.* Cadence 1350
———. *Wake Up, Little Susie.* Cadence 1337
Ford, Tennessee Ernie. *Sixteen Tons.* Capitol 3262
Haley, Bill. *Rock around the Clock.* Decca
Holly, Buddy. *Peggy Sue.* Coral 61885
Kingston Trio. *Tom Dooley.* Capitol 4049
McLean, Don. *American Pie—Parts I & II.* United Artists 50856
———. *Vincent.* United Artists 50887
Marvelettes. *Please Mr. Postman.* Tamla 54046
Modugno, Domenico. *Nel Blu Dipinto Di Blu* (Volare). Decca 30677
Platters, The. *Only You.* Mercury 70633
———. *My Prayer.* Mercury 70893
———. *The Great Pretender.* Mercury 70753
Prado, Prez. *Cherry Pink and Apple Blossom White.* RCA 5965
Presley, Elvis. *Heartbreak Hotel.* RCA 47-6420
Riddle, Nelson (and his orchestra). *Lisbon Antigua.* Capitol 3287
Robbins, Marty. *A White Sport Coat (and a Pink Carnation).* Columbia 40864
———. *El Paso.* Columbia 41511

Seville, David (a.k.a. Ross Bagdasarian). *Witch Doctor.* Liberty 55132
———— and the Chipmunks. *The Chipmunk Song.* Liberty 55168
Shirelles. *Will You Love Me Tomorrow.* Scepter 1211
———— . *Soldier Boy.* Scepter 1228
Sinatra, Frank. *Learnin' the Blues.* Capitol 3102
Tornados. *Telstar.* London 9561
Wooley, Sheb. *The Purple People Eater.* MGM 12651

Chapter 18
Rock in Its
Adolescence

Prelude to Internationalism

Bobby Vinton ushered in 1964 with his sedate number-one hit, *There! I've Said It Again,* a saccharine-sweet love ballad reminiscent of Tin Pan Alley's heyday. There was nothing particularly remarkable about the song or the artist. Yet this recording is one of the most significant of the rock era because it signaled the end of an age. Fred Bronson called the years from 1960 to 1963 "innocent years." He believed that by 1963 rock-and-roll had somehow become less threatening, less offensive than when it first appeared on radio stations in 1955. Elvis and his gyrations had faded into the background, and the motion picture, *The Blackboard Jungle,* released in 1955, was at best a dim memory.

During the early 1960s, songwriters such as Gerry Goffin, Carole King, Neil Sedaka, Howard Greenfield, Barry Mann, and Cynthia Weil wrote hit after hit. Their music was softer, less raucous, and less animated than that of earlier years. Instruments traditionally associated with the symphony orchestra, such as violins, began appearing with increasing frequency in rock recordings. Such additions to rock instrumentation were greeted with mixed emotions. Those who considered themselves rock purists resented what they saw as an unwelcome intrusion of the "establishment." Others applauded the new orchestration because it made this rough, loud, new genre more acceptable to them. Rock was beginning to acquire an air of naive sophistication.

American artists, such as Bobby Vinton, dominated the charts. From the days of Haley's *Rock around the Clock* to Vinton's *There! I've Said It Again*, only five non-American artists posted number-one hits. By August, 1964, that number would double. Several American artists whose careers appeared assured, suddenly disappeared from the charts. Artists such as Connie Francis, Chubby Checker, Pat Boone, and the Shirelles never again placed a single in the Top 20. These stars were not doing anything wrong. Bronson noted that there simply was a shift in tastes and attitudes in the musical world. This shift was led by an English group that made the world see rock-and-roll in a completely different light.

British Music and the American Market

For several years before the arrival of the Beatles in America, English recordings had seeped into the U.S. market. Skiffle artists, such as Bort Cort and Lonnie Donnigan, gained a modest following in 1957. Traditional pop artists, such as Laurie London, Cliff Richard, the Tornadoes, and the Chris Barber Jazz Band, had songs that appeared on the U.S. Top 40 charts. In 1958, *He's Got the Whole World in His Hands*, by Laurie London, became a bestseller, and in 1962, *Telstar*, by the Tornadoes, reached the number-one position on the charts. Despite these few successes, most of the rock music on the international level traveled from America to England and Europe. Those few English pop stars who gained popularity abroad were in actuality mere imitations of American rock personalities when they performed in the United States. British pop star Tommy Steele was often called the "Elvis of Great Britain." However, he could never manage any real American following. Then came the Beatles, who were not imitations of anything American. By the early summer of 1964, they were routinely dominating the top five positions on the charts.

Amazingly, the artist who shouldered the Beatles aside and took over number one for the week of May 9, 1964, was a 63-year-old jazz trumpet player named Louis Armstrong. More amazingly, perhaps, was the song with which he did it, the title song from *Hello, Dolly*. At 63, Satchmo became the oldest artist ever to have a number-one hit. *Hello, Dolly* is one of only two Broadway musical numbers to become number one during the rock era (the other was *Aquarius/Let the Sunshine In*).

With their phenomenal U.S. success, the Beatles drew national attention to other top-quality English artists and groups. After 1964, America suddenly "discovered" the Rolling Stones, Gerry and the Pacemakers, Herman's Hermits, the Dave Clark Five, and many others who shared a common background with the Beatles. Most of those just cited gained their first real recognition by performing routinely at Liverpool's Cavern Club, exactly as the Beatles had done. The Cavern Club's importance and influence on the American pop scene was significant and obvious. American teen newspapers such as *The Beat* featured the club's activities in weekly columns until the club closed in 1966.

For some time following the advent and enormous growth of rock, traditional American artists continued to place an occasional song in the Top 40, and even more rarely, in the number-one position. In August, 1964, Dean Martin produced one of those rare number-one hits, a romantic ballad called *Everybody Loves Somebody*. And once again, an older traditional artist, and the much older genteel tradition of American popular song, temporarily displaced the Beatles.

Dylan: Poet Laureate of Rock

B ob Dylan represents America's most important contribution to rock in the 1960s. Dylan emerged from the folk-music revival of the late '50s, making his first appearances on the national scene in 1962 and 1963. Columbia Records released his first two albums, *Bob Dylan* and *The Freewheelin' Bob Dylan*, during those years. These two records, his frequent appearances around New York, and his college and university concerts, helped establish Dylan's national reputation. Dylan's music reflected his awareness of the social issues of the day. With his songs he joined the Beatles in the fight against racism and human injustice.

For some time, Dylan's lyrics have provoked much discussion about their literary value. Many believe his lyrics are in actuality folk poetry, and Dylan has been dubbed the first poet of the mass media. In recent years, several of his lyrics have been included in elementary school literature books as prime examples of contemporary American verse. In the beginning, Dylan's style was most influenced by those from whom he learned. Woodie Guthrie served as a strong inspiration for him, and the "talking blues" became one of his most frequently used song formats.

BOB DYLAN IN A TELEVISION APPEARANCE IN 1975.

Dylan's music is a blend of folk and rock, strongly supporting the notion that in practice there is little difference between the two. Though many of his followers contend there are definite differences between his folk and rock styles, Carl Belz believed this notion was misleading because it implied that folk and rock are not the same kind of music. According to Belz, Dylan's music clearly demonstrates that rock *is* folk music.

Soul

Rock music in the 1960s, particularly that associated with protest, normally reflected cultural values and issues irrelevant to the nation's black community. During the '60s, rock grew increasingly sophisticated, and so did its general audience. Gradually, rock moved away from its beginnings as basically a folk art. On the other hand, soul, and its antecedent, black rhythm-and-blues, remained more faithful to the folk norms and issues of earlier times.

This period saw a genuine awakening in the nation's black community to social and cultural achievement. The term "soul" entered the common vocabulary of the entire black community, and became the one expression most closely identified with black culture. Blacks referred to artists as "soul brothers and sisters." Radio stations whose programming was designed specifically for the black community became known as "soul" stations, and the music they played as the "soul" sound. A newspaper, similar in format and content to *The Beat*, emerged as *Soul*. Its pages were filled with articles and comments attempting to define the term. Ultimately, most agreed that soul was more a general feeling than a particular musical style or sound.

Motown

Carl Belz believed soul was an attempt on the part of the black community to define itself culturally. Musically, one institution, probably more than any other, has come to symbolize that cultural self-definition: Motown Record Company. Berry Gordy founded Tamla Motown Records in Detroit, in 1959, with $800, borrowed from his family. The name "Tamla Motown" was concocted from two different sources: "Tamla" was a spinoff from *Tammy's in Love*, a hit by Debbie Reynolds, current at that time. "Motown" is an abbreviation of Detroit's nickname, "motor town." For the first two years of operation, Berry used the name, "Tamla," as a record label. In 1961, he switched from "Tamla" to "Motown." Though the name legally remained "Tamla Motown" until 1976, from 1961 onward the entire recording industry referred to the label simply as "Motown."

During its early days, Motown's singles had to be leased to major record companies. Consequently, its early progress was slow. Berry Gordy spent his free time writing and producing for several artists signed to other labels. Like any young businessman, he struggled with the vagaries of a new business, and spent most of his first years deeply in debt. Thirteen years later, his annual salary had grown to ten million dollars.

Motown's first permanent quarters were located in a row of run-down houses in what was once an affluent Detroit neighborhood. The accommodations were less than stunning. What had been upstairs bedrooms were turned into offices. Gordy and several of his staff members lived at the studio. Two members of the staff converted the basement into Motown's first recording studio. It quickly acquired the nickname, "the snake pit." As a sound studio, the room was barely adequate. Its soundproofed walls did little to keep noise out or music in. A toilet adjacent to the studio served as an echo chamber. At best, the room was dismal.

Gordy handpicked most of Motown's early musicians, writers, and producers. As a rule, the musicians included Detroiters with jazz backgrounds, while the writers selected were ones who knew about him and respected his ambitions, or wanted a permanent environment in which to work. Under Gordy's guiding hand, Motown quickly developed a unique, distinctive sound, a refreshing mixture of black gospel, rhythm-and-blues, and the black music community's adaptation of the new rock music. All this was combined with Motown's unique approach to the sound studio and mixing techniques. To this day, no one has been able to duplicate the exact techniques used to produce "the Motown sound," though several have tried.

Motown has produced a significant number of black artists who, over a twenty-year period, have become genuine superstars. These artists possessed an appeal that crossed all social and racial boundaries. Smokey Robinson and the Miracles were among the earliest of the Motown success stories. In fact, it was William "Smokey" Robinson who convinced Gordy to begin a record company of his own. Other stellar groups owe their monumental careers to Motown, groups such as the Four Tops, the Temptations, and America's most successful singing group, Diana Ross and the Supremes.

In 1959, four young Detroit girls got together to form a pop singing group. In the beginning, they called themselves "The Primettes." One would quit the group very soon after its formation, one would die at age 32, and eighteen years later one would still be leading the group. Mary Wilson, Florence Ballard, and Diana Ross recorded their first song for Motown, *After All,* in 1960. Two additional songs were to follow before Motown released their first single on the Tamla label, *I Want a Guy,* recorded in December, 1960. Before its release, Motown's boss, Berry Gordy, instructed the girls to find a new name. Florence

THE SUPREMES.

Ballard was the only trio member present when Gordy asked for a decision. From a list she was handed, she chose the only name that did not end in "ette," "The Supremes."

I Want a Guy and the single that followed both failed to chart. Motown began uncharitably calling them the "no-hit Supremes." For their third release, Gordy switched the girls to the Motown label. *Your Heart Belongs to Me* climbed into the Hot 100 at number 95. Over the next two years, three Supremes singles reached into the Hot 100, each attaining a successively higher position on the chart. Then came *Where Did Our Love Go* in August 1964, a song the Marvelettes turned down. The Supremes had the first of their many number-one hits.

Motown continued to produce soloists and groups who consistently appeared in the Top Five of the pop charts. In August 1963, another of the rock-era giants appeared, Little Stevie Wonder, the 12-year-old genius. August 10, 1963, marks the date on which *Fingertips* (Pt. II) appeared in the number-one position. It was the second number-one hit for Motown. It was also the first live single to become number one. Wonder had performed the piece on Motown's live show, "Motortown Reviews." The performances were so exciting that Berry Gordy, Motown producer, decided to record Wonder live. *Fingertips* was included on Wonder's first album, *The Jazz Soul of Little Stevie*. It was seven minutes in length, far too long to release as a single. However, because of the response of "Motortown Review" audiences, Gordy decided to divide it into two parts, and release it as a 45. Today, Wonder remains a driving force across the entire spectrum of popular music.

Another Motown legend, the Temptations, recorded *My Girl*, a song written for them by Smokey Robinson. The Temptations were the first male Motown vocal group to place a song in the number-one chart spot. *My Girl* rose to number one in March, 1965. The Supremes scored another number-one single in that same month with *Stop! in the Name of Love*. In June, they produced still another, *Back in My Arms Again*. In November, they posted their fourth number-one hit of the year, *I Hear a Symphony*. From early 1964 through mid-1966, the charts were dominated by British groups and Motown artists.

By the end of 1968, rock music had accumulated a huge following and enormous worldwide success. It was reveling in its international popularity and status. The Beatles had just released an album destined to become a classic, affectionately called by fans the "double white." The Rolling Stones were experiencing one of their career high points, and Bob Dylan had just returned to performing after a year's absence. From its advent in 1955 through the end of 1968, rock had grown, expanded, changed. It had matured, become more sophisticated. It possessed vital direction, provided by some of rock's most innovative artists and entrepreneurs.

However, at year's end, rock began losing direction and energy. It entered a three-year period of listlessness, during which strong leaders, such as the Beatles and Bob Dylan, failed to emerge. Rock spent much time struggling with uncertainty about its own identity. This period's problems and struggles became quite apparent during the summer of 1969 at the Woodstock Music and Art Fair.

Woodstock

On Friday morning, August 15, 1969, at approximately 7:00 a.m., Chip Monck stepped up to a microphone, welcomed the audience of over 300,000, and introduced folksinger/guitarist, Richie Havens. The Woodstock Music and Art Fair had begun. It was the largest event of its kind in this nation's history, and for three days, those in attendance exhibited all the beauty and the ugliness of a generation of youths struggling with drugs, self-discovery, and a bewildering world of technology, all of which threatened to destroy mankind.

The Founders and Their Concept. Woodstock was principally the brainchild of four young men from divergent walks of life. Their backgrounds and training did not, at first glance, reflect any commonality for a partnership in such a venture. One graduated from the University of Pennsylvania with a major in history. One was an attorney who had graduated from the Yale Law School. One had participated in the organization of the Miami Pop Festival in 1966 and was the erstwhile manager of a pop group called Diesel. The fourth member of the group was a vice president in a record company. The one characteristic they all shared was their abiding interest in the popular music of the era.

After graduating from college in the spring of 1966, John Roberts and Joel Rosenman found an apartment together in New York City. Both men were interested in writing TV sitcoms. Roberts was already a millionaire, thanks to a large inheritance, but neither of them had much experience in the business world. Looking for sitcom ideas, they placed an ad in the *Wall Street Journal*, reading, "Young men with unlimited capital looking for interesting and legitimate business ideas." Within two weeks, they received seven thousand responses!

Meanwhile Michael Lang and Artie Kornfeld were considering the idea of opening a recording studio in Woodstock, NY. The area had become home to several important rock stars: Bob Dylan, Janis Joplin, and several members of Blood, Sweat, and Tears. Because these and other pop musicians were in and out of Woodstock so often, building a recording studio there could prove a plausible and profitable business proposition. The only element lacking was funding for the project.

They approached Roberts and Rosenman with their concept: a recording studio and a retreat to be constructed at Woodstock for rock musicians who wanted all the advantages of New York without the hassles of the city itself. Kornfeld's plans also included a one-day concert to initiate the project. Rosenman became interested in the idea of the concert. He asked about anticipated attendance. Kornfeld estimated four to five thousand. Roberts suggested the concert be expanded to two days, and the proceeds be used to pay for the proposed studio and retreat. Additionally, he suggested the concert be for fifty thousand people a day, rather than five thousand. At this first meeting, the concept grew almost disproportionately. The four named their new partnership "Woodstock Ventures."

Woodstock's Original Site.

Work on the project began in earnest with a search for a suitable location in or close to Woodstock, New York. The group had agreed they needed approximately six hundred acres to lease or purchase. After an abortive attempt to lease property from Michael Lang's father, Rosenman and Roberts drove to the Woodstock area and found a real estate agent to aid in their search. The agent called Howard Mills, who owned local acreage sufficient for the project. Mills' property was zoned as industrial acreage, and was located in a small rural community called Wallkill. Rosenman and Roberts met with Mills, and secured a thirty-day, two-way option on the land. On April 18, Rosenman and Roberts met with the Wallkill zoning board and gained tentative approval of their project.

By early June, the gracious, informal relationship that had existed in the beginning between Wallkill and Woodstock Ventures had begun to deteriorate. The genteel citizens of Wallkill were not prepared for the types of individuals descending on their community. They were not accustomed to marijuana smokers and drug users. To them, everyone connected with the project appeared to wear rags for clothes and to take uncommon pride in long, unwashed hair. Wallkill began to question its decision to allow such an event to take place in its community.

On June 12, the Wallkill Zoning Board of Appeals met with representatives of Woodstock Ventures and the Wallkill community to address certain concerns voiced by citizens. Chief among those concerns was a growing apprehension about the kind of audience this festival was likely to attract. When Rosenman and Roberts had met with the zoning board two months earlier, hardly anyone beside them and board members had been present. At the June 12 meeting, the room was filled to capacity with nervous, anxious Wallkill residents, talking in agitated undertones. All the concerns expressed during that meeting centered around the question of drugs and the number expected to attend the two-day event. Woodstock Ventures and its local attorney attempted to assure the community there would be no widespread usage of drugs. They assured the board that the Woodstock organization was fully prepared to deal with any exigency that might arise. The meeting ended with some questions still unanswered, but with the community at least temporarily mollified, or so Woodstock Ventures personnel thought.

However, on July 2, Wallkill passed a new law entitled, "A Local Law Regulating the Assembly of Persons in Public Places." Made up of several sections, the new law prohibited such activities as the assembly of more than five thousand people in public places in Wallkill. It required a written permit to use any Wallkill property for the assembly of more than five thousand people, and required those making applications for such permits to furnish written statements indicating their willingness to comply with all regulations. Finally, the law gave the town board the authority to revoke such permits for even the slightest infraction of any of the regulations. Wallkill had made it clear it wanted no part of the proposed festival. The search for a suitable festival location began again.

People across the state called to commiserate with Rosenman and Roberts and offer alternate sites. Callers offered riverfronts, mountainsides, wilderness areas, ski jumps, and even airstrips. Then, on July 16, Michael Lang found a man named Max Yasgur who owned six hundred acres of dairy pasture in neighboring Sullivan County. Yasgur was willing to host the festival.

Woodstock's Final Location. Yasgur's land was located at White Lake, near the tiny town of Bethel, New York. Yasgur, a tall, slender man approximately sixty years old with thinning grey hair and tanned skin, was a successful dairy farmer, and easily the wealthiest man in the area. He was well liked and

PHOTOFEST. ©1970 WARNER BROS. INC.

WOODSTOCK, AS DEPICTED IN THE 1970 WARNER BROTHERS FILM.

highly respected in the community. On July 17, Rosenman and Roberts and their attorney drove to Yasgur's farm to meet with Yasgur and his attorney and banker. After several hours of negotiation, the group reached an agreement. August 15, opening day of the concert, was less than one month away. Construction on the site began almost immediately.

When Richie Havens took the microphone that August morning, the first words he spoke to that massive audience were "Freedom... freedom... freedom... freedom!" The hillside in front of the stage was blanketed by an estimated 300,000 people from every conceivable walk of life. For the next three days, they would hear some of the world's premiere rock artists: the Grateful Dead, Joan Baez, Sly and the Family Stone, Bob Dylan, Janis Joplin, John Sebastian, Tim Hardin, the Who, Jefferson Airplane, the Band, Canned Heat, Joe Cocker, Jimi Hendrix...

Woodstock symbolized the protest of American youth against racism, hatred, poverty, the "establishment," and most particularly, the war in Viet Nam. For three days, a population estimated at times to have exceeded 400,000, lived together in peace and harmony, and, at least in its own eyes, had thus proven to the world that war in any form was unnecessary. Woodstock became the international symbol for peace. It became a reflection of every struggle, frustration, and problem experienced by the nation's youth during the turbulent 1960s. It also signaled an end to a decade of growth and direction for rock music. Over the next few years, interest in rock apparently declined.

Rock without Elvis and the Beatles

On December 27, 1969, *Someday We'll Be Together,* by the Supremes, took its place as the year's final number-one hit. This was the last song the Supremes recorded with Diana Ross as lead singer. With Diana as lead, the Supremes had put together an impressive list of number-one hits, twelve in all, during the decade of the sixties. On January 14, 1970, Diana and the Supremes made the last of twenty appearances on "The Ed Sullivan Show." It was also their last performance together as the Supremes. Diana left the group to pursue a solo career. With Jean Terrell in Diana's spot, the new Supremes went on to record several Top 40 hits in the 1970s, though they never again had a number-one hit.

When Diana's first solo attempt was released, there was much speculation about the chances for its success. Initially, Gordy had asked outsider Bones Howe to produce the album. However, before Howe could complete the project, Gordy dropped him and assigned it to two Motown regular staff members, Nicholas Ashford and Valerie Simpson. They selected two pieces they had originally written for Marvin Gaye and Tammi Terrell, *Ain't No Mountain High Enough* and *You're All I Need to Get By*.

Ashford and Simpson completely changed the concept of *Ain't No Mountain High Enough* to fit Diana. Originally conceived as a male/female duet, the song became a long narrative with an exciting climax. Ashford and Simpson believed Diana possessed quite a sexy speaking voice and they wanted to incorporate it into the song.

Ain't No Mountain High Enough was exactly six minutes in length, when completed. It was considered too long for a single release, so it became simply one of the album cuts. When the album was released, Motown elected not to provide disc jockeys with an edited version of the song. As a result of this decision, radio stations across the nation began editing the cut on their own. Soon the song was receiving so much airplay that Motown was forced to edit the song down to three minutes, fifteen seconds, and release it as a 45. On August 8, 1970, it charted on the Hot 100 at number 70. Within six weeks, it rose to number one, displacing another Motown number one, *War*, by Edwin Starr. This was only the third time in the rock era that one Motown song had replaced another as number one.

By mid-1970, the Beatles and Elvis were well outside the current mainstream of pop music, leaving the field open to the emergence of several new talents: the Bee Gees, Cher as a solo act, Rod Stewart, Michael Jackson as a solo act, and many others. These stars were not necessarily new to the business. They simply had the misfortune of starting their careers when two names overshadowed all others, Elvis and the Beatles.

Despite his dedicated following and his concert success over the years, James Taylor has had just one number-one hit during his career, *You've Got a Friend*, written by Carole King. Taylor was born in Boston, March 12, 1948. His father served the University of North Carolina as dean of its medical school, and his mother was a lyric soprano. Taylor's brother and sister were also interested in music, and eventually both recorded albums of their own.

Taylor's Warner Brothers album, *Mudslide Slim and the Blue Horizon*, included *Fire and Rain*, a song about Taylor's drug habit and a friend who committed suicide. This song became a bestseller for Taylor. *Time* magazine featured him as its cover story for its March 1, 1971, issue, about the same time *You've Got a Friend* was released. This song climbed into the number-one position July 31, 1971. The combination of song and article helped propel Taylor into the national limelight and stardom. *You've Got a Friend* won two Grammys, one for Taylor as best male vocalist of the year, and one for Carole King for song of the year.

James Taylor's popularity is as strong in 1992 as it has ever been. He still has a large dedicated following, and he is still touring and appearing periodically on national television.

PHOTOFEST. ©DAVID VANCE 1983

THE BEE GEES.

THE BEE GEES. In the course of their career, three brothers, Robin, Maurice, and Barry Gibb—the Bee Gees—placed their first five singles in the American Top 20, but not in the Top Ten. Then they recorded *I've Gotta Get a Message to You* and *I Started a Joke,* both of which became Top Ten singles in 1968. After that came a year of excessive touring and television appearances. During this year, the brothers were racked by dissension, and in late 1969, the group split. Robin recorded a solo album, *Saved by the Bell,* steadfastly refusing to resolve the conflict with his brothers.

Finally, the three brothers reunited, and began recording again. Their first release after the reconciliation was an album, *2 Years On.* The album included their biggest hit to date, *Lonely Days,* which rose to number three. *How Can You Mend a Broken Heart,* a song Barry had written for Andy Williams, followed. On August 7, 1971, it moved into the number-one spot on the charts. The Bee Gees had the first of their nine number-one singles. Their final number-one hit, *Love You Inside Out,* appeared eight years later, in June 1979. Though in comparison with groups such as the Four Seasons, the Bee Gees' career was relatively short, it was nonetheless spectacular.

Going Solo. Artists normally associated with groups or with other single artists now began routinely appearing as soloists in their own right. In late summer, 1971, Cher, of the Sonny and Cher duo, recorded *Gypsies, Tramps,* *and Thieves.* On September 18, *Gypsies* entered the Hot 100 at number 88. On November 6, it rose to number one. Michael Jackson of the Jackson Five recorded his first solo release, *Ben,* as the theme for the movie of the same title. Released as a single, *Ben* rose to number one on October 14, 1972. George Harrison, the former Beatle, produced another of his number-one hits, *Give Me Love,* in June, 1973. Former Supremes lead Diana Ross placed *Touch Me in the Morning* in the number-one spot for the week of August 18, 1973. In October, Cher produced another number-one single, *Half-Breed.* In November, another former Beatle, Ringo Starr, saw the recording of his composition, *Photograph,* cowritten by George Harrison, rise into the number-one spot. In January 1974, Ringo repeated with another number one, *You're Sixteen.*

Disco

In the early '70s, a dance craze swept the nation. During its brief tenure, it aroused both a fiercely loyal following, and a host of others who made every conceivable attempt to rid the world of it. Almost overnight, both the dance and the music associated with it took over the pop-music world, and dance and music alike were identified by one word, "disco."

Originally, the term *discotheque* merely identified a club or nightspot where people could go and dance to recorded music. By the time it gained national recognition, disco had acquired a standard format; a dance floor, a stack of records, a disc jockey, two turntables, and a mike. In the early '60s, discos—New York's Peppermint Lounge, for example—were often identified with rock-and-roll. In October 1960, Chubby Checker had appeared on "The Ed Sullivan Show," singing and dancing his number-one hit, *The Twist.* By the end of that month, *The Twist* and its dance had invaded the Peppermint Lounge and had become the rage of the "jet set." The dance became a national pastime and set the stage for the advent of disco, which, however, was more than just a dance or music. Disco, according to Tom Smucker, was an ambience, a blend of dance, music, setting, format, drugs, and the patrons themselves.

From the beginning, disco implied dance music, and during disco's infancy, rock dominated the pop-music field. Smucker observed that the rock music heard over the radio during that period was suitable primarily for listening, not for dancing. For dance music, one looked beyond that mainstream of popular music.

Rock is rooted in blues and country. Smooth black urban pop played a major role in shaping disco. However, a recording in this vein did not necessarily guarantee a disco hit. Disco was a strange mixture of tastes. Some artists produced disco recordings that were raging hits in the world of disco, and nowhere else. Disco clubs would often begin as pure disco settings, then change to mainstream pop. Disco was at best unpredictable.

Manu Dibango, an African artist, is credited with having produced the first legitimate disco hit. His *Soul Makossa,* recorded in Paris, was released as a single in the United States sometime in 1973. During that same year, it broke into the Top 40, and disco had its first pop hit.

By 1974, disco recordings were routinely rising to number one on the charts. By 1975, disco began dictating the manner in which records were made. Some companies introduced album-sized singles, attempting to accommodate the needs of the disco movement and its DJs. These singles were remixed and extended versions of current radio singles. They became so popular, several record companies released them commercially.

Disco became a kind of plug-in formula into which almost any music could be squeezed. Disco versions of everything from Tin Pan Alley and Broadway, to Beethoven appeared. Smucker remarked, "It was as if the underground disco aesthetic was being wed to the entire spectrum of aboveground sounds." According to Smucker, the extended disco recordings began acquiring the trappings of classical form, particularly Donna Summer's disco hit, *Love to Love You Baby,* with its different movements.

Out of these developments grew disco in its purest form, Eurodisco. Rather than conventional recordings remixed and extended, Eurodisco consisted of compositions long enough to occupy an entire album side. Disco no longer depended on the past for its life. Now it had form and content appropriate to the new genre.

Disco eventually reached the masses through the movie, *Saturday Night Fever.* Before the release of this movie, the general public had little access to disco. The genre featured no recognizable, established stars, and many radio stations were boycotting disco music. *Saturday Night Fever,* released in late 1977, and its soundtrack, made disco and its setting directly available to the masses. The motion picture was shot at a real club, 2001 Odyssey, located in Brooklyn, and featured John Travolta, star of TV's "Welcome Back, Kotter," in the lead role. The soundtrack featured the Bee Gees singing the movie's hottest song, *Staying Alive.* And for everyone who saw the film, the Bee Gees were permanently wed to the disco sound. When the balance of the pop-music industry witnessed the incredible success of that wedding, old stars and new, rock and otherwise, rushed to capitalize on the new craze. By the end of the decade, disco began to fade from the pop scene. However, while it lasted, it gave popular music something it had not possessed since the beginning of the rock era, a sense of aural unification.

Mainstream Rock Continues

Despite appearances, disco did not displace all other forms of popular music. In fact, disco was a relatively brief episode in the history of pop. Even while disco was at the height of its popularity, the mainstream of rock and pop continued unabated among its dedicated disciples. In May, 1973, Stevie Wonder's *You Are the Sunshine of My Life* became his third number-one hit. It won Stevie a Grammy for best pop vocal performance by a male.

Former Beatle Paul McCartney abandoned his pursuit of a solo career after one brief year. He missed the dynamics of group participation. Sometime during 1971, McCartney called drummer Denny Seiwell and former Moody Blues member Denny Laine to ask if they would like to participate in a new group, as yet unnamed. They both agreed and traveled to Scotland to meet McCartney. There, with Paul's wife, Linda, the four cut the album, *Wild Life*. On September 3, 1971, while awaiting the birth of his daughter, McCartney came up with the name "Wings" for the group. His wife later said Paul "was thinking about the wings of an angel." *My Love*, written and produced by McCartney, was the first single released under the name "Paul McCartney and Wings." On June 2, 1973, *My Love*, a sentimental ballad written to Paul's wife, took over the number-one position for the next four weeks.

Late in 1969, guitarist Mark Farner, drummer Don Brewer, and bassist Mel Schacher got together with former Detroit disc jockey Terry Knight to form what Fred Bronson called a stereotype midwestern power trio. The trio wore their hair in the fashion of the day—long. Bronson described them as sweaty and unrestrained. They played heavy metal and proudly called themselves "an American band." Knight gave the group its name, "Grand Funk Railroad."

Grand Funk became an anomaly in the trade. They achieved monumental success without benefit of widespread acclaim from the press or the radio airplay usually associated with the kind of stardom they attained. Their Shea Stadium concert sold out in less than 24 hours. It had taken the Beatles three weeks to accomplish the same feat. Capitol Records estimated that during Grand Funk's heyday, their albums were selling at a rate of one every four seconds. In 1970 alone, the group amassed five million dollars in record sales. Critics could find no justification for Grand Funk's phenomenal popularity. However, Dave Marsh, a writer for *Creem*, declared Grand Funk to be an experience. Their concerts were events in which the audience was strongly encouraged to participate. According to Marsh, Grand Funk understood and was in touch with the youth culture of the '70s.

During the 1970s, lines between rock and country-and-western blurred, and some songs decidedly in the country-western vein became number-one hits on the pop charts. Charlie Rich, nicknamed "the Silver Fox" because of his prematurely gray hair, began his musical career as a rock-a-billy singer. Along the way, he began leaning toward country-crooner style, and late in the '60s, he completed the transition when he signed a recording contract with Epic Records, a label almost exclusively country in format and content. By the time he produced his first number-one hit, Rich had been in the business for 39 years. Epic released his recording of *The Most Beautiful Girl* in the summer of 1973. It entered the Hot 100 chart at number 83. Eleven weeks later, on December 15, it climbed into the number-one position and remained there for two weeks.

Throughout the 1970s, no single artist or small group of artists dominated the charts as in the preceding decade. Many artists claimed the number-one spot on the chart, but none very frequently: John Denver, Gladys Knight and the Pips, the Carpenters, Eric Clapton, and a host of others. Nor did any of the recordings remain number one for long periods. Most held the position for one week, some for two, and on rare occasions, a few for three weeks. Chart domination by a very few had been permanently broken.

Selected Recordings

The following recordings are listed by artist, song title, record company, and record number. (For a more detailed discography of this era, and that covered in chapter eighteen, see *The Billboard Book of Top 40 Hits,* by Joel Whitburn.)

Armstrong, Louis. *Hello, Dolly!* Kapp 573

Beatles, The. *I Want to Hold Your Hand.* Capitol 5112

——— . *A Hard Day's Night.* Capitol 5222

——— . *Can't Buy Me Love.* Capitol 5150

——— . *Yesterday.* Capitol 5498

Bee Gees. *I Started a Joke.* Atco 6639

——— . *How Can You Mend a Broken Heart.* Atco 6824

——— . *Stayin' Alive.* RSO 885

——— . *Tragedy.* RSO 918

Checker, Chubby. *The Twist.* Parkway 811

Dibango, Manu. *Soul Makossa.* Atlantic 2971

Dylan, Bob. *Like a Rolling Stone.* Columbia 43346

———. *Rainy Day Women.* Columbia 43592

Harrison, George. *My Sweet Lord.* Apple 2995

McCartney, Paul, and Wings. *My Love.* Apple 1861

———. *Live and Let Die.* Apple 1863

——— . *Silly Love Songs.* Capitol 4256

————. *Spies Like Us.* Capitol 5537

Ross, Diana. *Ain't No Mountain High Enough.* Motown 1169

————. *Missing You.* RCA 13966

Supremes, The. *Where Did Our Love Go.* Motown 1060

————. *Baby Love.* Motown 1066

————. *I Hear a Symphony.* Motown 1083

————. *Someday We'll Be Together.* Motown 1156

Vinton, Bobby. *There! I've Said It Again.* Epic 9638

Chapter 19
Rock at Maturity

The Last Days of Rock's Adolescence

As the decade of the 1970s drew to a close, disco faded into the past almost as quickly as it had risen to prominence. The '80s opened in much the same vein as the last two years of the '70s, with new names topping the charts almost every week. Several "odd couples" appeared in duo recordings: John Travolta and Olivia Newton-John, and Barbra Streisand and Neil Diamond, for example. During the second half of the '70s, the Bee Gees became the only group that kept appearing at the top of the charts. They began a series of number-one hits on February 4, 1978 with *Stayin' Alive*, from *Saturday Night Fever*. Then came *Night Fever* in March, 1978, for exactly twice as long, eight weeks, *Too Much Heaven* for two weeks in January, 1979, *Tragedy* for two weeks in March, 1979, and *Love You Inside Out* in June, 1979, for one week.

Love You Inside Out was of extraordinary significance to the Bee Gees for several excellent reasons. It was their ninth number-one hit, tying them for fourth place with Paul McCartney for this achievement. It became the sixth consecutive number-one hit for the Bee Gees, tying them with a Beatles statistic. Most significantly, *Love You Inside Out* marked an end to their Top Five chart success. It was the last of the group's number-one hits. Their first two singles of the new decade did not rise above number 30 on the Hot 100.

Between 1969 and 1971, rock began changing, at first almost imperceptibly. As the new decade progressed, rock began acquiring elements not originally considered part of the genre. This was the same phenomenon jazz had displayed in 1968 and 1969, when the jazz of Miles Davis and certain other artists was called jazz-rock, or fusion music. Elements of country, soul, rhythm-and-blues, jazz, and other streams of pop became rooted in rock. By the mid-1970s, rock had, by definition, become essentially a fusion music.

This broadened concept of rock was reflected in the music at the top of the charts, and the artists who were performing it. Olivia Newton-John's 1974 hit, *I Honestly Love You*, was a ballad infused with elements of rock, soul, and country. Billy Preston thought his hit, *Nothing from Nothing*, was a good sing-along number. It is doubtful that anyone before 1970 ever considered a pure-rock piece a good selection for a sing-along. *I Can Help*, by Billy Swan, was a mixture of blues and rock, with a touch of soul. Harry Chapin's *Cat's in the Cradle* contained some rock elements, yet fell more in the category of folk song. Rock had been transformed into a collage of every element that has ever existed in pop music.

From 1970 to 1988, new names and old continued to appear at the top of the charts with few repeaters, at least not with the regularity of the Beatles or Elvis. The Carpenters posted another of their number-one hits, *Please Mr. Postman*. (This was a recap of the Marvelettes' December, 1961 chart-topper.) Neil Sedaka began his second recording career in February, 1975, with *Laughter in the Rain*. Linda Ronstadt, who has sung every genre of music, including country, folk, rhythm-and-blues, rock-and-roll, and light opera, saw her recording, *You're No Good* rise to number one during that same month.

Fred Bronson saw what he believed to be a new type of music appear in Los Angeles in the early '70s. He called it "Southern California country rock." This music fused the sound of country and bluegrass instruments with the vocal harmonies of a music dubbed "California surfer rock." The one name most often connected with this sound was that of the Eagles. Their first number-one hit, *Best of My Love*, reached the top of the charts on March 1, 1975,

Rock's Most Enduring Album

In 1973, a group broke into the national limelight with their album, *Dark Side of the Moon*. The group was Pink Floyd, and their album was destined to remain on *Billboard*'s album chart until May 1985, longer than any other in history, 570 weeks. Before their rise to national prominence, Pink Floyd had a fanatically dedicated, but limited, following. After *Dark Side of the Moon,* their followers became legion.

In 1975, the group switched from Capitol Records to Columbia, where in 1980, they produced the double album with which they have become so identified, *The Wall.* In Roger Waters' lyrics, the metaphor of "the wall," according to a widely accepted interpretation, signifies Pink Floyd's gradual movement away from its audience as its popularity soared. The first single released from the album, *Another Brick in the Wall,* became the group's biggest hit, rising to the Hot 100 during January 1980, and to number one on March 22. It remained in the number-one position for four weeks. In 1982, Alan Parker shot a motion-picture version of *The Wall,* starring Bob Geldolf.

Milestones

New Directions from Paul McCartney. In the fall of 1979, Paul McCartney was listed in *The Guinness Book of Records* as the most successful composer of all time. Between 1962 and 1978, he wrote forty-three songs that sold over one million copies each. He accumulated forty-three gold records with the Beatles, seventeen with his new group, Wings, and one with Billy Preston. During this period, he sold an estimated one hundred million single records and one hundred million albums. For these accomplishments, he received a rhodium medallion from the British minister of art in a London ceremony on October 24, 1979.

In 1975, McCartney purchased all United States rights to the music of Buddy Holly. Holly had been one of McCartney's rock heroes when McCartney was growing up. Paul believed that those who possessed large sums of money were ethically obligated to do something constructive with it. For him, the purchase of Holly's music was both an investment and an opportunity to practice his belief. During that same year, McCartney started an annual Buddy Holly week in Great Britain. He began the event on Holly's birthday, in September. He said he knew there were kids in England and elsewhere who had never heard of Buddy Holly, and he believed they should have the opportunity to hear Holly's music and enjoy it. As of this writing, this is still an annual event in England and McCartney still participates in the celebration.

Diana Ross Leaves Motown. Momentous changes were taking place in the careers of many of rock's superstars. On September 6, 1980, *Upside Down,* by Diana Ross, climbed into the number-one spot, were it remained for the next four weeks. This was her biggest single yet. It was also her last hit single with Motown. At the beginning of the '80s, Diana entered her third decade in the music business, and she felt the time had come to sever her professional ties with Motown. She signed a new contract with RCA Victor for the United States, and EMI/Capitol for the balance of the world. Diana did not end her friendship with her mentor and long-time business associate, Berry Gordy. She merely wanted more control over her career. After leaving Motown, she never again placed a single in the number-one position. However, over the next several years, she did place several singles in the Top Ten.

Tragedy for John Lennon. On December 27, 1980, John Lennon's *(Just Like) Starting Over* rose to number one, where it remained for the next five weeks. Nineteen days earlier, Lennon was shot to death in the darkened archway just outside the courtyard of the building in which he and Yoko Ono lived. This tragedy was intensified by John and Yoko's recent completion of a new album, *Double Fantasy,* which appeared to be a new beginning for John. *(Just Like) Starting Over,* one of the album cuts, was released as a single October 24, and began to climb the charts. Fred Bronson believed that John Lennon's assassination affected millions of people almost as profoundly as John F. Kennedy's tragic death in 1963. Yoko asked that a memoriam of silence be observed for John on December 14 for ten minutes at 2:00 p.m., E.S.T. This silence was observed worldwide.

A Unique Beginning. Sheena Easton secured her first recording contract under the most strenuous conditions imaginable. In May 1980, a BBC documentary show, "The Big Time," agreed to produce a film on her search for stardom. The British network arranged an audition for Sheena with EMI Records, which they would televise nationally. If Sheena secured a recording contract from the audition, BBC would travel with her for one year, video-recording her success or failure as a pop star. If she failed, all Great Britain would be witness. Sheena agreed to the terms.

BBC arranged the audition, but offered no assurances Sheena would succeed. Should she fail, the documentary group would simply find another subject. The audition for EMI's Brian Shepherd began with cameras in place and filming. Shepherd remarked later that he actually had no intention of signing an unknown; but when he heard Easton perform, he was captivated by her talent. He surprised everyone, including himself, by offering Sheena a contract.

Sheena's first single, *Modern Girl,* produced less-than-spectacular results, climbing only to number 56 on the British charts. It was released before the summer 1980 airing of the documentary. Her next single, *9 to 5,* was released just before the televising of the documentary. The program proved the best publicity Sheena could have received. *9 to 5* shot up the British charts to peak at number three. At the same time, *Modern Girl* gained new life and rose to number twelve. Sheena had two hits in the British Top 20, the first time a female singer had accomplished this feat since Ruby Murray in 1956. Sheena was also the first British female pop singer to place her first two singles in the Top 20.

9 to 5 was retitled and released in America on February 14, 1981, as *Morning Train (9 to 5)*. Eleven weeks later, on May 2, it rose to number one on *Billboard*'s charts, and remained there for two weeks. In the mid-'80s, Sheena completed her conquest of America by landing a principal role for several episodes as Don Johnson's wife in the national TV series, "Miami Vice."

MTV Arrives

MTV made its entrance into the pop-music field on August 1, 1981. That same day, Rick Springfield's *Jessie's Girl* topped the charts for a two-week stand. It seemed appropriate that Springfield and MTV "arrived" on the same day. Springfield was a regular on ABC-TV's daytime soap, "General Hospital." Fred Bronson thought Springfield's national exposure on this show made him an excellent candidate for the new pop-music medium.

Warner Amex Satellite Entertainment Company had invested more than twenty million dollars in a new concept called "music television." Its executives believed such a 24-hour-a-day show would produce a sizable profit. By the third year of operation, MTV had earned Warner a profit of over $8.1 million and had pumped new life into the recording industry.

Superstars of the 80s

The Michael Jackson Phenomenon. On March 5, 1983, *Billie Jean*, a solo single by Michael Jackson, reached the number-one spot. It held that position for seven weeks. This was a signal accomplishment for that period. However, there were aspects of *Billie Jean* that far overshadowed its position on the charts. It came from a Michael Jackson album called *Thriller*, an album that through 1985 had sold over forty million copies. With that accomplishment, the album became the bestselling record of all time. It rose to the top of the *Billboard* album chart and held that position for thirty-seven weeks, longer than any other LP except for the cast album from *South Pacific* and the sound-

MICHAEL JACKSON.

PHOTOFEST

track of *West Side Story*. It produced a record seven Top Ten singles. Jackson became the first artist in the history of the *Billboard* charts to produce a number-one single and a number-one album simultaneously. And he did this in both the pop and black categories! Just one week after this record-shattering performance stateside, *Billie Jean* and *Thriller* simultaneously rose to the top of the British charts.

Across the decade from 1980 to 1987, Michael Jackson's name was connected with every phase and facet of popular music. From 1980 through at least 1985, Jackson received the preponderance of Grammy's awarded each year in several different categories. If there was any one force who influenced and dominated pop in the 1980s, it was Michael Jackson. With the arrival of MTV in 1981, Jackson's career took another leap upward. The video medium appeared to be tailor-made for Jackson and his sophisticated solo and ensemble dancing.

From 1985 through 1989, Jackson faded from the public eye. This did not occur as a result of a loss in popularity. He took the step deliberately to free himself to work on projects other than recording and touring. For example, he played a major role in the design and filming of video and light shows for

Disney World's Epcot Center in Orlando, Florida. In 1990, he reemerged with a multimillion-dollar deal with Sony, as an artistic consultant in the production and filming of video events.

Madonna. Madonna Louise Veronica Ciccone was born in Bay City, Michigan, on August 16, 1958. Throughout her childhood, she displayed a strong attraction for all forms of music, especially dance. She began studying ballet at age fourteen with Christopher Flynn. When she graduated from high school, she won a dance scholarship to the University of Michigan at Ann Arbor.

Madonna left college after two years, and in the late summer of 1978, moved to New York to pursue a professional dance career. She arrived in the city literally with the clothes on her back and about $37. In the beginning, work was scarce. For a time, she posed as a figure model for artists, and acted in some "underground soft-core" films. Eventually, she won a company spot with the Alvin Ailey Dancers.

After dancing with the Ailey company for a short time, a significant event occurred in her life. She met and began dating rock-and-roll musician Dan Gilroy, through whom she developed a strong interest in rock-and-roll. She left the dance company, and in 1982, formed her own rock-and-roll band with drummer/songwriter Steve Bray, a former boyfriend from her Ann Arbor days. She and Bray wrote songs strongly influenced by the new-wave rock bands of the day, such as the Pretenders and the Police.

As time passed, Madonna's music slowly changed, becoming more and more dance-oriented. Though her first album, *Madonna,* met with only limited success, her second, *Like a Virgin,* catapulted her into the international limelight, and into a pop-music icon. According to many critics, her title role in the film, *Desperately Seeking Susan,* proved to the world-at-large that Madonna was also a legitimate actress. By 1987, she was an undisputed and unqualified rock and film star.

Almost from the beginning, Madonna has been a controversial figure. And rather than seeking to quell the controversy, she has openly and deliberately exploited the more risqué aspects of the suggestive characteristics of her music, both in lyrics and in dance. For this, she has been continually castigated by some segments of the media and highly praised by others. Madonna herself has been content simply to allow the controversy to help propel herself and her music into a multi-million dollar enterprise.

Since 1987, Madonna has put together a list of impressive coups, including her highly successful 1989 album, *Like a Prayer,* her leading role as Breathless Mahoney in the film, *Dick Tracy,* and its sound-track album, her 1990 Blond Ambition Tour, and its resulting documentary film, *Truth or Dare,* and her

MADONNA.

most controversial video to date, *Justify My Love*. It is interesting to note that *Justify My Love* numbers among the very few videos ever banned by MTV during its ten-year history.

Though Madonna's albums have sold exceptionally well, her most important and most impressive contribution to the commercial-music industry has been, and continues to be, her business acumen. According to the October 1, 1990, issue of *Forbes*, since 1986 Madonna has earned at least $125 million. In 1990 alone, she brought in an estimated $39 million in pretax earnings. And, according to *Forbes*, Madonna has garnered more than a half-billion dollars in records sales for the entertainment firm of Time Warner.

Currents within the Mainstream

The late '70s and early-to-mid-'80s witnessed the rise of two new genres of rock—punk and rap. Punk was a radical development with performance practices and stage dress reminiscent of previous groups, such as Kiss and Alice Cooper. However, punk extended beyond the performing groups themselves.

Its fans reflected the influence of punk by wearing the hair and clothing styles of the groups. In this respect, punk became a cult, with a limited, but dedicated, and occasionally fanatical, following. This kind of societal influence was not new. It was merely a continuation of the trend begun by Elvis Presley and the Beatles. Like many such fads, punk has since receded into the backwaters of the pop mainstream.

Punk. Punk emerged in the mid- to late-'70s in Great Britain as a reaction against what the '60s generation would have called "the establishment." Punk was an attempt to return to a "garage-rock aesthetic" that declared rock to be a music anyone could write and perform. According to Dave Marsh, however, this assessment of punk is accurate only because those who perform it do not take into consideration the inability of everyone to do these things equally well.

Few of the original punk groups remained together long enough to produce records that sold. Most punk recordings did not even receive enough airplay on popular radio stations to become familiar to the bulk of the pop audience. After a time, punk dissipated into several small factions, each with its own particular view of the purpose punk really served. One faction featured elitist groups who advocated certain primitive rock styles. Another believed punk was a fashion statement, and for them, only the latest trends in clothing and hairstyles mattered. From its inception, punk was strictly a white rock-and-roll movement confined almost entirely to England. According to Dave Marsh, its *raison d'être* was the total destruction of rock history. And Marsh believed it was at least partially successful in this goal.

"Punk rock" as a designating term probably first appeared in a *Creem* magazine article. From 1969 to 1973, the *Creem* writers, including Dave Marsh, often expressed points of view that the rock community considered vulgar, belligerent, and quite disrespectful. For these points of view, collectively and individually, the writers were often referred to as "punks." This less-than-complimentary allusion to the *Creem* writing staff eventually led to their coining the phrase, "punk rock."

Punk-rock groups apparently took extraordinary pleasure in selecting the names of their various groups: "? and the Mysterians," "the Sex Pistols," "the Talking Heads," "Devo," "Bow Wow Wow," and "Boy George and Culture Club." This penchant for names that are, at the least, quite uncommon, reflects the punk movement's attitude of rebellion against the rock mainstream.

Rap. Rap enjoys a much larger and more current following than punk. It is an evolutionary development of sorts, springing from the marriage of Motown and MTV. From the abundant evidence provided by current music videos, it is reasonable to conclude that since the advent of MTV, there has been an increasing interest in those elements surrounding the music, rather than in the music itself. In particular, there has been strong interest in the dance aspect of music videos, thanks in large part to Michael Jackson. Dancing has become a vital element in rap performance.

By its nature, rock is a genre that makes little use of complicated or extended melodic writing. In rock, melody has never been a vital or central element. It is, by design, relegated to a position of secondary importance. Rhythm, often involved and intricate, and always dynamic, has become the one criterion by which any rock piece is measured.

Rock has never pretended to be a music to be consumed by a passive audience. Its primary attraction has always been as a dance music. Consequently, over the past twenty years, rock melodies have become increasingly fragmented, and at times, nonexistent. Rap appears to be a logical extension of this progression. Every aspect of rap music is based on its rhythmic structure.

Odd though it may appear, there is a strong parallel, though unquestionably unintentional, between rap and an ancient musical form from the early 1600s, *dramatic monody*. The *Harvard Dictionary of Music* defines dramatic monody, or *stile rappresentativo*, as "the fundamental musical novelty of the earliest opera." According to *Harvard*, this style of musical composition attempts to "imitate speech in song... To this end, its rhythmic pace is freely declamatory, following closely the accentual patterns of the text." In this early form, harmonic structure, as such, did not exist. Its most important element was "spoken song." Composing by this structural precept would produce a music based entirely on the aspect of rhythm. Rap is based entirely on rhythmic speech and possesses no discernible or deliberate harmonic structure. Even its accompaniment is based entirely on rhythm. And its "rhythmic pace is freely declamatory." It is possible rap represents, at least in primitive form, a full-circle return to the past.

Like break dancing, rap is a phenomenon of the street. It began about the same time as break dancing did, but has continued to grow in popularity, whereas "breaking" has followed the path of most fads. "Rapping" is, literally, speaking words, sometimes in rhyme, sometimes in blank-verse form, to specific rhythms. The rhythms employed appear to come from the naturally stressed and unstressed syllables of the text. Stresses are often placed on syllables not normally stressed, and vice versa, for text emphasis, in much the same manner as vocal or instrumental music employs shifting meter for musical and/or text emphasis.

Rap apparently originated as a form of one-upsmanship, primarily among the nation's black youth. Young males would compete in an exchange of putdowns, presented in the form of a chanted verse. This was done in the presence of friends, who then judged the best put-down. This was called "rapping." From this simple beginning a national movement developed.

In the beginning, rap was just a novelty in the pop-music world. It furnished excellent material for a new style of dancing. Rap performers simply moved about the stage in random patterns, using a series of arm and body movements, and chanting their words, which at first were merely vehicles for unique and arresting rhythm patterns. As demand for the new "music" grew, its performance characteristics began to acquire standardized routines and patterns. When rap first began, only the rappers themselves appeared on stage. As the format matured and developed, dancers were added to the groups for visual effect and text emphasis. At present, rap normally includes a lead rapper, a backup rapper, and a rhythm rapper, much the same as lead, backup, and rhythm guitar in a rock group, and a highly choreographed routine for anywhere from five to as many as fifteen dancers.

Rap texts have changed significantly. Now there are raps on every subject imaginable; love, sex, hate, religion, drugs (for as well as against), and in particular, social issues. Rap is no longer a random, spontaneous street activity. It has acquired the trappings of form and style. Even the annual Grammy Awards now honor the best of the year's rap and rappers.

Rap-group names are less radical than punk rockers'. However, they still are not what one would term run-of-the-mill: (M. C.) Hammer, the Fat Boys, Vanilla Ice, Run-DMC. (Vanilla Ice is a white rapper. In the beginning, rap was the undisputed domain of black groups. Now, several white groups have entered the field.)

In the opinion of many music historians, during the early stages of human development, music consisted entirely of rhythmic grunts and periodic shufflings. As man developed, his music became increasingly complex. In the Western world, we are prone to call the Romantic Era the culmination of great melodic writing. Many believe there will never again be melodists such as Schubert or Puccini or Tchaikovsky. The increasing distancing of classical music and its characteristics from the mainstream tends to strengthen these beliefs significantly.

Rock and Society

One of rock's most distinctive characteristics has always been its periodic involvement in current social issues. As a result of this involvement, one genre of rock has acquired the designation, "protest music," a term closely associated with the American folk music of the 1930s and '40s. Rock composers and performers have routinely addressed such issues as racism, injustice, sexism, poverty, war, and world hunger.

In 1985, the African nation of Ethiopia was at the height of a devastating famine. During the previous fall, Bob Geldolf, lead singer and manager of a British rock group, the Boomtown Rats, had initiated a project designed to relieve at least a portion of Ethiopia's suffering. He had solicited the participation of six prominent British rock stars in the recording of *Do They Know It's Christmas*. This song raised over ten million dollars for the relief of African hunger victims.

Encouraged by this success, Geldolf then began organizing what he considered to be a logical follow-up to the record, an international Ethiopian benefit concert. Alternately called Band Aid and/or Live Aid, this concert took place on July 13, 1985. It raised more than forty million dollars for African hunger relief, and earned Geldolf a Nobel Peace Prize nomination.

During this same period, American farmers were experiencing their own national crisis. Giant farms were going out of business at an alarming rate. Families who had been farming for generations were declaring personal and business bankruptcy in wholesale numbers. The nation's food supply was in jeopardy. Borrowing the concept of Live Aid, American pop musicians organized Farm Aid, a concert to relieve the plight of the American farmer. Farm Aid took place during the fall of 1985, in Zupke Memorial Stadium on the campus of the University of Illinois at Urbana-Champaign. Its success prompted a follow-up concert for the same cause in July 1986.

Rock video made history with its broadcast of the Live Aid concert. This concert was viewed by more people than any previous live television event in the history of the medium. Viewer estimates ran to approximately one and one-half billion. Concert participants were located in London, Philadelphia, Moscow, and several other cities throughout the world. Their live participation was made possible by simulcasting off nine satellites to one hundred different countries.

In view of MTV's recent arrival as a rock medium, these statistics become even more astounding, and the impact of music television more dramatic and apparent than ever. Little wonder that MTV has become *the* vehicle for the dissemination of popular music. Current stars from every pop music genre depend on the video industry the way former stars depended on the record industry and the LP album. In previous years, album cuts reflecting significant listener demand were the ones that became singles. As of 1991, the large-scale manufacture of LPs has been discontinued. Now, the pop audience may purchase cassette or CD singles taken from their favorite videos. Artists still record collections of songs, but the collections contain fewer songs than the older LP format, and they appear on cassette tapes and compact discs.

Censorship: The Issue Continues

Events such as Live Aid and Farm Aid were positive promotion for popular music and its proponents. However, this period also witnessed several negative events of far-reaching consequence for not only popular music, but the entire national art community. In 1971, then Vice President Spiro Agnew spearheaded a drive to "rid popular music of drug references." In 1985, a new protest against rock music arose, this time directed by an organization called the Parents Music Resource Center (PMRC). This powerful group was directed by a small number of Washington women with powerful contacts, who persuaded the U.S. Senate Commerce Committee to hold hearings on the lyrics of certain heavy-metal songs.

After a long and furious battle, the PMRC and the nation's record companies finally reached an agreement whereby records would henceforth be rated and labeled according to the lyrics they contained. As of this writing, a portion of that controversy has once again arisen. Groups such as the PMRC are now concerned that the nation's youth are purchasing record numbers of albums containing highly explicit lyrics *because* of those very labels intended to prevent such purchases.

These and similar events and circumstances have, of course, called into question vital issues such as censorship and artistic freedom. Though not specifically within the field of popular music, a recent chain of events merits mention here. Photographer Robert Mapplethorpe, who died of AIDS, left a collection of black-and-white photographs that have raised a storm of protest in the artistic community, and sharply divided the nation at large on the issue of what specifically divides fine art from pornography. In 1990, Mapplethorpe's work was displayed in some of the nation's premier museums and art galleries. Cincinnati took the collection and Dennis Barrie, director of the city's Contemporary Art Center, to court in an effort to ban the exhibit. The citizen group bringing this action saw the photographs not as fine art, but rather as pornography parading as fine art. The courts found for the collection and the curator.

Also in 1990, this same issue surfaced in popular music. 2 Live Crew, a popular rap group, employed highly explicit lyrics in its touring show. A Florida community took the group to court to block their performance in the community. The group was arrested and charged with obscenity. Again, the court found for the defendants and against censorship. This issue is of immense importance and consequence, for it directly concerns one of the basic tenets on which this nation was founded. One suspects, regardless of recent court decisions, this issue is not dead at all. It has been merely "swept under the rug."

Payola Again

In January 1988, another old issue raised its ugly head, payola. Once again, record companies, disc jockeys, and, this time, video jockeys, were accused of accepting bribes in exchange for the promotion of specific albums and tapes.

The evidence uncovered prompted a Los Angeles grand jury to hand down several indictments in April of that year for interference with free commerce by the deliberate biasing of public opinion.

During the 1980s, popular music reached a point of aimlessness, similar to the period that followed Woodstock. In fact, beginning in 1987, advertisements began appearing, reflecting a certain yearning for Woodstock days. Popular music publications printed ads labeled "Return to Woodstock," "Woodstock II," "Woodstock Remembered." Throughout this nation's history, its people have displayed a nostalgic bent, particularly during times of protracted national stress and tribulation. During the latter part of the 1980s, rock reflected this national characteristic in its yearning for a "return to Woodstock."

The Future of American Popular Music

This text is, by design, a descriptive historical survey. As such, any reference to definite cause-and-effect is entirely unintentional. However, it is impossible to construct such a tome and not feel the need at least to speculate about the meaning of all those events reported upon. With this in mind, some consideration concerning the future of popular music in America seems in order.

As all true folk music should, popular music, primarily rock, continues to record, and comment on, the everyday events in the life of this nation and the world, though at present, this genre of music appears to be in a kind of holding pattern. Recently, its prime concern has been in the area of electronic development, rather than in the composition of new materials. Since the 1960s and early '70s, no artist or group of artists has emerged to lead pop in new directions, as did Presley and the Beatles. Consequently, popular music has settled into a state of circularity, leaning heavily at times on the past for materials to record. Since 1983, a significant number of "oldies, but goldies" have been rereleased by current artists. This smacks of uncertainty in the field, uncertainty about direction and about the future. At least, so it would seem. However, in reality pop music may be functioning exactly as it should be, as pulsekeeper and mirror for the nation. At present there is much uncertainty in the world at large about every conceivable facet of life. Pop may merely be reflecting this uncertainty.

A scholar in philosophy once remarked that one could recognize the dawning of a new philosophical age by the new questions that appeared on the horizon, rather than by the hackneyed answers that kept appearing to all the old questions. Perhaps music is about to witness the dawning of a new age, be it popular or otherwise. All the "questions" in popular music in general appear to have been answered many times over. All music seems to be awaiting the arrival of either a new Bach or a new Beatle. Be it a Bach or a Beatle, one must wonder in what direction he or she will lead.

Selected Recordings

The following recordings are listed by artist, song title, record company, and record number, where appropriate. (For a more detailed discography of this era, see *The Billboard Book of Top 40 Hits,* by Joel Whitburn.)

Band Aid. *Do They Know It's Christmas?* Columbia 04749
Bee Gees. *Stayin' Alive.* RSO 885
_____. *Tragedy.* RSO 918
Culture Club. *Karma Chameleon.* Epic/Virgin 04221
Easton, Sheena. *Morning Train (Nine to Five).* EMI-America 8071
Jackson, Michael. *Beat It.* Epic 03759
_____. *Billie Jean.* Epic
Run-DMC. *Walk This Way.* Profile 5112

Bibliography

Anderson, Jervis. *This Was Harlem: A Cultural Portrait, 1900–1950.* New York: Farrar, Straus, & Giroux, 1982.

Archer, Gleason L. *Big Business and Radio.* New York: American Historical Company, 1939.

Bane, Michael. *The Outlaws: Revolution in Country Music.* New York: Country Music Magazine Press, 1978.

Barnouw, Eric. *The Golden Web: A History of Broadcasting from 1933 to 1953.* New York: Oxford University Press, 1968.

Barzun, Jaques. *Music in American Life.* Bloomingon, Ind.: Indiana University Press, 1965.

Belz, Carl. *The Story of Rock.* New York: Oxford University Press, 1972.

Bergreen, Laurence. *As Thousands Cheer: The Life Of Irving Berlin.* New York: Viking Press, 1990.

Birge, Edward Bailey. *History of Public School Music in the United States.* New York: Oliver Ditson Company, 1928.

Blesh, Rudi. *Shining Trumpets: A History of Jazz.* New York: Alfred A. Knopf, Inc., 1946 (rev. ed., 1958).

——— , and Harriett Janis. *They All Played Ragtime.* New York: Oak Publications, 1971.

Boeckman, Charles. *Cool, Hot and Blue.* Washington D.C.: Luce, 1968.

Bowers, David. *Put Another Nickel In.* New York: Bonanza Books, 1966.

Bronson, Fred. *The Billboard Book of Number One Hits.* New York: Billboard Publications, Inc., 1985.

Brown, Peter, and Steven Gaines. *The Love You Make: An Insider's Story of the Beatles.* New York: McGraw-Hill, 1983.

Burton, Jack. *Blue Book of Tin Pan Alley.* 2 vols. Watkins Glen, New York: Century House/American Life Foundation, 1962.

Carr, Patrick. *The Illustrated History of Country Music.* New York: Doubleday, 1980.

Chapple, Steve, and Reebee Garofalo. *Rock 'n Roll Is Here to Pay: The History and Politics of the Music Industry.* Chicago: Nelson-Hall, 1977.

Charters, Samuel B. *Jazz: New Orleans 1885–1957.* New York: Walter C. Allen, 1958.

———, and Leonard Kunstadt. *Jazz: A History of the New York Scene.* New York: Doubleday, 1962.

Chase, Gilbert. *America's Music.* Rev. 2nd ed. New York: McGraw-Hill Book Company, 1966.

Claghorn, Charles Eugene. *Biographical Dictionary of American Music.* Nyack, N.Y.: Parker Publishing, 1973.

Cohen, Daniel and Susan. *Rock Video Superstars II.* New York: Simon and Schuster, 1987.

Coker, Jerry. *The Jazz Idiom.* Englewood Cliffs, N.J.: Prentice-Hall, Inc., 1975.

Collier, James Lincoln. *The Making of Jazz: A Comprehensive History.* New York: Dell, 1978.

Coon, Caroline. *The New Wave Punk Rock Explosion.* London: Orbach and Chambers, 1977.

Cooper, Al, with Ben Edmonds. *Backstage Passes: Rock 'n Roll Life in the '60's.* New York: Stein & Day, 1977.

Corio, Ann, and Joseph DiNona. *This Was Burlesque.* New York: Grosset and Dunlap, 1968.

Crabb, Richard. *Radio's Beautiful Day.* Aberdeen, S.D.: North Plains Press, 1983.

Curwen, J. Spencer. *Studies in Music Worship.* First Series (2nd ed.). London: J. Curwen & Sons, 1888.

Dachs, David. *Anything Goes: The World of Popular Music.* Indianapolis: Bobbs-Merrill, 1964.

Dalton, David and Lenny Kaye. *Rock 100.* New York: Grosset & Dunlap Publishers, 1977.

Dance, Stanley. *The World of Duke Ellington.* New York: Scribner, 1970.

Dannen, Fredric. *Hit Men.* New York: Times Books, 1990.

Davies, Hunter. *The Beatles.* New York: McGraw-Hill, 1968.

Davis, Clive. *Inside the Record Business.* New York: Morrow Publishing, 1975.

Davis, Elizabeth A. *Index to the New World Recorded Anthology of American Music.* New York: W. W. Norton & Co., 1981.

Davis, Sharon. *Motown: The History.* New York: Guinness, 1988.

De Long, Thomas A. *The Mighty Music Box: The Golden Age of Musical Radio.* Los Angeles: Amber Crest Books, 1980.

Denisoff, R. Serge. *Solid Gold: The Popular Record Industry.* New Brunswick, N.J.: Transaction Books, 1975.

———. *Tarnished Gold.* New York: Transaction, 1986.

———, and Richard A. Peterson, eds. *The Sounds of Social Change: Studies in Popular Culture.* Chicago: Rand McNally, 1972.

DeTurk, David A., and A. Poulin, Jr., eds. *The Folk Scene: Dimensions of the Folksong Revival*. New York: Dell, 1967.

Dichter, Harry and Elliott Shapiro. *Handbook of Early American Sheet Music 1768–1889*. New York: Dover Publications, Inc., 1977.

Douglas, George H. *The Early Days of Radio Broadcasting*. McFarland & Company, 1987.

Dunleavy, Steven. *Elvis. What Happened?* New York: Ballantine, 1977.

Elson, Louis C. *The History of American Music*. New York: Lenox Hill Publishing & Distributing Co. (Burt Franklin). Originally Published: 1925. Reprinted: 1971.

——— . *The National Music of America*. New rev. ed. Boston: L. C. Page & Company, 1924.

Evans, Tom and Mary. *From the Renaissance to Rock: Music, History, Construction and Players*. New York: Paddington Press, 1977.

Ewen, David. *All The Years of American Popular Music: A Comprehensive History*. Englewood Cliffs, N.J.: Prentice-Hall, 1978.

——— . *Great Men of American Popular Song*. Englewood Cliffs, N.J.: Prentice-Hall, 1970.

——— . *The Life and Death of Tin Pan Alley: The Golden Age of American Popular Music*. New York: Funk and Wagnalls, 1964.

Fisher, William Arms. *One Hundred and Fifty Years of Music Publishing in the United States*. Boston: Oliver Ditson Company, Inc., 1933.

Galliard, Frye. *Watermelon Wine: The Spirit of Country Music*. New York: St Martin's, 1978.

Gelatt, Roland. *The Fabulous Phonograph, 1877–1977*. 2nd rev. ed. New York: Macmillan, 1977.

Gillett, Charlie. *The Sound of the City: The Rise of Rock and Roll*. Rev. ed. New York: Pantheon Books, 1984.

Goldberg, Issac. *Tin Pan Alley: A Chronicle of American Popular Music*. New York: Frederick Ungar, 1931; paper, 1970.

Goldberg, Joe. *Jazz Masters of the Fifties*. New York: The Macmillan Company, 1965.

Green, Douglas B. *Country Roots: The Origins of Country Music*. New York: Hawthorne Books, 1976.

Green, Stanley. *The Rodgers and Hammerstein Story*. New York: The John Day Company, 1963.

Grissom, John. *Country Music: White Man's Blues*. New York: Coronet, 1970.

Groia, Philip. *They All Sang on the Corner: New York City's Rhythm & Blues Vocal Groups of the 1950's*. New York: Edmond, 1973.

Hadlock, Richard. *Jazz Masters of the Twenties*. New York: The Macmillan Company, 1965.

Handy, William Christopher. *Father of the Blues: An Autobiography*. New York: The Macmillan Company, 1941.

Hatch, David, and Stephen Millward. *From Blues to Rock: An Analytical History of Pop Music*. New York: St. Martin's Press, 1987.

Hearn, Lafcadio. *American Miscellany; Articles and Stories Now First Collected by Albert Mordell*. 2 vols. New York: Dodd, Mead & Company Inc., 1924.

————. *A History of Radio to 1926.* New York: American Historical Company, 1938.

Heintze, James R. *American Music before 1865 in Print and on Records: A Biblio-discography.* New York: Institute for Studies in American Music, 1990.

Hitchcock, H. Wiley. *Music in the United States: A Historical Introduction.* 2nd ed. Englewood Cliffs, N.J.: Prentice-Hall, Inc., 1974.

Hopkins, Jerry. *Elvis: A Biography.* New York: Macmillan, 1971.

————. *Elvis: The Final Years.* New York: St. Martin's, 1980.

Howard, John Tasker. *Our American Music.* Rev. ed. New York: Thomas Y. Crowell Company, 1939.

Hurst, Jack. *Nashville's Grand Ole Opry.* New York: Abrams, 1975.

Irvine, John. *Jukebox Saturday Night.* Secaucus, N.J.: Chartwell Books, 1977.

Jackson, Michael. *Moonwalk.* New York: Doubleday, 1988.

Johnson, R. Fenimore. *His Master's Voice Was Eldridge R. Johnson.* Ardmore, Pa.: Gold Star Publishing Co., 1974.

Jones, LeRoi. *Blues People: Negro Music in White America.* New York: William Morrow Company, 1963.

————. *Black Music.* New York: William Morrow Company, 1968.

Keith, Michael. *The Radio Station.* 2nd. ed. Boston: Focal Press, 1989.

Lang, Paul Henry, ed. *One Hundred Years of Music in America.* New York: G. Schirmer, Inc./Macmillan Publishing (originally published by G. Schirmer, Inc., 1961).

Larkin, Rochelle. *Soul Music.* New York: Lancer Books, 1970.

Laurie, Joe Jr. *Vaudeville, from the Honky Tonks to the Palace.* New York: Henry Holt, 1953.

Lichter, Paul. *The Boy Who Dared to Rock: The Definitive Elvis.* Garden City, New York: Doubleday & Company, 1978.

Lowens, Irving. *Music and Musicians in Early America.* New York: W. W. Norton & Company, Inc., 1964.

Makower, Joel. *Woodstock: The Oral History.* New York: Tilden Press, 1989.

Manilow, Barry. *Sweet Life: Adventures on the Way to Paradise.* New York: McGraw-Hill Book Company, 1987.

Marcuse, Maxwell F. *Tin Pan Alley in Gaslight.* American Life Foundation. Watkins Glenn, N.Y.: Century House, 1959.

Marks, J. *Rock and Other Four Letter Words.* New York: Bantam, 1968.

Marsh, Dave. *Fortunate Son.* New York: Random House, 1985.

————. *The First Rock & Roll Confidential Report.* New York: Pantheon Books, 1985.

Marsh, J. B. T. *The Story of the Jubilee Singers.* Rev. ed. New York: Negro Universities Press, 1969.

Mason, Daniel Gregory. *The Dilemma of American Music.* New York: The Macmillan Company, 1928.

McCabe, Peter, and Robert D. Schonfeld. *Apple to the Core: The Unmaking of the Beatles.* New York: Pocket Books, 1972.

McCarthy, Albert J. *The Dance Band Era: The Dancing Decades from Ragtime to Swing.* London: Spring Books, 1971.

McFarland, David T. *Development of the Top Forty Radio Format.* New York: Ayer Company Publishers, 1979.

McKnight, Gerald. *Andrew Lloyd Webber.* New York: St. Martin's Press, 1984.

Miller, J. *The Rolling Stone Illustrated History of Rock and Roll.* New York: Rolling Stone Press, 1980.

Morgan, Alun, and Raymond Horricks. *Modern Jazz: A Survey of Developments Since 1939.* London: V. Golancz, 1957.

Nanry, Charles, ed. *American Music: From Storyville to Woodstock.* New Brunswick, N.J.: Transaction Books, 1972.

Nye, Russell Blaine. *The Unembarrassed Muse: The Popular Arts in America.* New York: Dial, 1970.

Palmer, Robert. *The Rolling Stones.* New York: The Rolling Stone Press, 1983.

Palmer, Tony. *All You Need Is Love: The Story of Popular Music.* New York: Grossman/Viking, 1976.

Pattison, Robert. *The Triumph of Vulgarity: Rock Music in the Mirror of Romanticism.* New York: Oxford University Press, 1987.

Pleasants, Henry. *The Great American Popular Singers.* New York: Simon and Schuster, 1974.

Ritter, Frederic Louis. *Music In America.* New York: Charles Scribner's Sons, 1884.

Robinette, Richard. *Historical Perspectives in Popular Music: A Historical Outline.* Dubuque, IA: Kendall/Hunt, 1984.

Rosenman, Joel, John Roberts, and Robert Pilpel. *Young Men with Unlimited Capital.* New York: Harcourt, Brace and Jovanovich, 1974.

Sanjek, Russell. *American Popular Music and Its Business.* Vols. 1–3. New York: Oxford University Press, 1988.

Schafer, William J. *Brass Bands and New Orleans Jazz.* Baton Rouge: Louisiana State University Press, 1977.

Schuller, Gunther. *Early Jazz: Its Roots and Musical Development.* Vol. 1. New York: Oxford University Press, 1968.

Shapiro, Nat, and Nat Hentoff, eds. *Hear Me Talkin' to Ya; The Story of Jazz by the Men Who Made It.* New York: Rinehart, 1955.

Shaw, Arnold. *The Rockin' '50's.* New York: Hawthorn Books, 1974.

Shepherd, John. *Tin Pan Alley.* Routledge, Chapman & Hall, 1982.

Simon, George. *Simon Says: The Sights and Sounds of the Swing Era.* Arlington House, 1955.

———. *The Big Bands.* New York: Simon & Schuster, 1971.

Sklar, Rick. *Rocking America: How the All-Hit Radio Stations Took Over: An Insider's Story.* New York: St. Martin's Press, 1985.

Smith, Joe. *Off the Record: An Oral History of Popular Music.* New York: Warner Books, 1988.

Sonneck, Oscar George Theodore. *A Bibliography of Early Secular American Music (18th Century)*. Revised and enlarged by William Trent Upton. Washington: The Library of Congress, Music Divison, 1945.

Southern, Eileen. *The Music of Black Americans, A History*. New York: W. W. Norton & Company, 1971.

Spaeth, Sigmund. *A History of Popular Music in America*. New York: Random House, 1948.

Stanley, Robert H. *The Broadcast Industry*. New York: Hastings House, 1975.

Stearns, Marshall. *The Story of Jazz*. New York: Oxford, 1956.

Stein, Charles W., ed. *American Vaudeville As Seen by Its Contemporaries*. New York: Knopf, 1984.

Stevenson, Robert. *Protestant Church Music in America*. New York: W. W. Norton & Company, 1966.

Taylor, Derek. *It Was Twenty Years Ago Today*. New York: Simon and Schuster, 1987.

Tobler, John, and Stuart Grundy. *The Record Producers*. New York: St. Martin's Press, 1982.

van der Merwe, Peter. *Origins of the Popular Style*. New York: Clarendon Press-Oxford, 1989.

Walker, Leo. *The Wonderful World of the Great Dance Bands*. New York: Doubleday, 1972.

Waller, Don. *The Motown Story*. New York: Scribner, 1985.

Whitburn, Joel. *The Billboard Book of Top 40 Hits*. New York: Billboard Publications, Inc., 1987.

Williams, Martin. *Jazz Masters in Transition, 1957–69*. New York: The Macmillan Company, 1970.

Yorke, Ritchie. *The History of Rock 'n Roll*. Toronto: Methuen/Two Continents, 1976.

Zadan, Craig. *Sondheim & Co*. 2nd ed. New York: Perennial Library, 1989.

Index